Equality on Trial

POLITICS AND CULTURE IN MODERN AMERICA

Series Editors: Margot Canaday, Glenda Gilmore, Michael Kazin, Stephen Pitti, Thomas J. Sugrue

Volumes in the series narrate and analyze political and social change in the broadest dimensions from 1865 to the present, including ideas about the ways people have sought and wielded power in the public sphere and the language and institutions of politics at all levels—local, national, and transnational. The series is motivated by a desire to reverse the fragmentation of modern U.S. history and to encourage synthetic perspectives on social movements and the state, on gender, race, and labor, and on intellectual history and popular culture.

Equality on Trial

Gender and Rights in the Modern American Workplace

Katherine Turk

PENN

UNIVERSITY OF PENNSYLVANIA PRESS

PHILADELPHIA

Published by
University of Pennsylvania Press
Philadelphia, Pennsylvania 19104-4112
www.upenn.edu/pennpress

Printed in the United States of America
on acid-free paper

10 9 8 7 6 5 4 3 2 1

A catalogue record for this book is available from the Library of Congress.
ISBN 978-0-8122-4820-3

For Erik

Contents

Introduction: Notions of Sex Equality

In 1964, as part of its landmark Civil Rights Act, Congress outlawed workplace discrimination on the basis of personal attributes like sex, race, and religion. The provision, known as Title VII for the portion of the act in which it appears, laid a new legal foundation for women's rights at work. Lobbying for the bill in the final months of his life, President John F. Kennedy described equality before the law as "a moral issue" that was "as old as the scriptures" and "as clear as the American Constitution. The heart of the question," he contended, "is whether all Americans are afforded equal rights and equal opportunities, whether we are going to treat our fellow Americans as we want to be treated."[1] While Kennedy and other lawmakers expressed similar high hopes for Title VII, early attempts to police the provision were thin and inconsistent. But in the absence of a consensus definition of sex equality in the law or society, those efforts were also malleable.

Two years after Title VII's passage, a factory worker from suburban Boston wrote to government officials to express her personal expectations for her new right to sex equality. In her letter to the nascent Equal Employment Opportunity Commission (EEOC), the agency tasked with interpreting Title VII, Thelma Pilch set out her many grievances. Her boss frequently called her "out of [her] sick bed" to go to work, and as a result, she had contracted bronchial pneumonia. Her requests for her preferred morning shift and for less physically demanding work were denied, and she had been passed over for promotions because managers did not tell her about job openings. Pilch also objected to the unsanitary conditions in the plant itself, explaining, "the ladies room is so rotten dirty I wouldn't let dogs go in there." In sum, she claimed, her employer was "doing everything to hurt or discriminate against me." Pilch conveyed her hope that the new EEOC would grant substantive protections akin to those organized labor could provide when she asked, "We have no union but we do have some rights don't we[?]"[2]

As one of the thousands of letters that overwhelmed the EEOC in its first few years, Pilch's claim was rooted in an expansive understanding of sex equality that is no longer conceivable in those terms. But in her time, the absence of a concrete legal definition or an effective mechanism for combatting sex discrimination created space for Pilch and many others to imagine Title VII as a counterweight to conditions they perceived as unfair. A half-century later, formal sex equality before the law has been all but achieved. Title VII is a well-established area of employment law, our government dedicates millions of dollars annually to combatting workplace sex discrimination, and even the possibility of a future Title VII lawsuit cows employers into investing in costly worker trainings and human resources departments. Yet we live in an era marked by dramatic inequalities that deepened in the same years that saw sex equality law become more accepted and efficient. What can explain the strengthening of laws that guarantee equality and the concurrent growth of social inequality that have shaped our recent past?

This book answers that question by examining what happened when workers like Pilch engaged Title VII to express their expectations and test the boundaries of its promise. It explains how these workers dispatched broad notions of sex equality in their lives, their workplaces, and the law as they navigated an era of grassroots mobilization, economic reconfiguration, and conservative constraint.

*   *   *

As women streamed into the paid labor force at ever-higher rates over the course of the twentieth century, they transformed its demographics more easily than its culture. Particularly in the years after World War II, when men returned stateside and rolled back women's wartime employment gains, women encountered a labor force marked by dramatic sex segregation.[3] Men monopolized positions with significant authority, higher pay, and autonomy, and they used their power to relegate women to supportive roles. This division of labor was buttressed by an elaborate system of sex-specific state "protective" laws that framed breadwinning as a masculine enterprise and construed women's wage labor as inherently less valuable than men's. It was also reinforced in popular culture through archetypes like the "girl Friday," the dedicated office assistant who was indispensable to her boss, but whose accumulated wisdom would never embolden her to make a play for his job. Such labor force segmentation gave weight to a workplace "gendered imagination": a naturalized order that framed men as best suited to be in charge and women as appropriately ensconced as their helpmeets.[4]

Sex equality laws established in the mid-1960s offered workers and activists a new language and set of tools to use in their efforts to chip away at this gendered regime and remake the world of work. In particular, Title VII of the Civil Rights Act of 1964 sparked a grassroots social movement that ignited a revolution to define and create equality between men and women.[5] Prior to Title VII, most workplaces were sites where sex differences were upheld and legitimated. In the age of Title VII, these same workplaces became experimental sites where the viability of different visions of sex equality could be tested.

Title VII positioned race and sex discrimination as twinned legal harms, but these problems emerged from distinct histories. Racism at work was a legacy of coerced forms of labor and Jim Crow segregation. By the 1960s, decades of civil rights activism had forged a mainstream definition of workplace race discrimination as a problem of stigma and subordination that stymied minorities' access to good jobs. Accordingly, many activists sought to use the law to destabilize race as a relevant employment characteristic, dismantle barriers to upward mobility, and buttress campaigns for race-conscious affirmative action to counter the effects of past exclusion.[6] As this conception of race discrimination gained momentum, some feminist attorneys analogized sex and race in their fight against women's long-standing legal marginalization.[7] But, far from a foregone conclusion, the meaning of Title VII's sex provision spawned decades of debate over the essence of workplace sex equality. Did Title VII require employers to extend sex-specific state protections to men, or should they be wiped out for everyone? Could the law accommodate women where their life patterns and domestic responsibilities differed from men's? Did it apply where workers experienced intersectional forms of discrimination, infusing their sex-based claims with references to their race, class, age, or sexuality? Could it help workers in female-dominated jobs that lacked a male corollary, and were men entitled to protections when they sought to enter the same "pink-collar" sphere some women fought to leave? One bedrock question underscored all the rest: did Title VII require employers to do more than equalize women's treatment to men's?

Workplace sex equality thus had to be invented. But workers and activists did not wait for lawmakers to breathe life into Title VII on their own. Instead, the law's initial ambiguity inspired many to confront government officials with their own understandings of its potential. Unions, state agencies, and interest groups had long been sites of working women's activism. Title VII transformed and amplified these labor feminist efforts, inspiring workers to reframe a range of decades-old demands as matters of sex equality and feed them into the legal system.[8] In such disparate workplaces as factories, hospitals, hotels, and offices, workers sought to leverage Title VII by applying for jobs typically held by workers of the opposite sex, filing grievances, retaining attorneys, and sometimes fighting their employers in court. Burgeoning feminist organizations built multivalent campaigns that emphasized the law's potential to deliver economic justice. Men pursued protected access to some of the same feminized jobs women sought to transform, and gay workers demanded the right to reveal their sexuality free from negative consequence. These campaigns took aim at the long-standing gendered division of labor. But they also pushed Title VII's interpretive boundaries in many directions at once, framing appeals for control and autonomy on the job—in the form of safer workplaces, flexible schedules, higher wages, and freer gender and sexual identity expression—as issues of sex equality.[9] Their efforts tapped into a deep American tradition of workers, activists, and government officials who have located robust labor rights at the heart of civil rights and defined state-enforced equality to encompass dignified work and economic self-sufficiency.[10]

This history of efforts to define and create workplace sex equality bolsters and contests a vibrant literature on labor, social movements, and civil rights. In existing accounts of Title VII's origins, scholars have debated whether the sex clause's eleventh-hour addition to a provision designed to alleviate race discrimination represented an earnest attempt to boost women's status or a more sinister plot to undermine the Civil Rights Act altogether.[11] Those taking a longer view have evaluated Title VII's legacy from opposite perspectives. Some have praised Title VII for significantly democratizing the workplace, attributing the inequities it left untouched to developments that unfolded outside of the law: the erosion of the labor movement, the decline of mass activist groups, and the rise of conservative opponents who perfected strategies that neutralized it.[12] Others have attributed these changes in part to Title VII itself. This perspective holds that the law marked a conservative turn, encouraging workers to replace collective labor rights claims with identity-based alternatives, bureaucratizing the processes for achieving workplace fairness, and sacrificing militant critiques of the economy in favor of expanding demographic diversity.[13] Both of these accounts emphasize that Title VII expanded in reach and legitimacy during its first several decades. But foregrounding sex-based workplace rights campaigns reveals how the law opened up interpretive possibilities. This book considers what happened to the broad visions of sex equality Title VII fostered as they reverberated through workplaces, state agencies and courts, and labor and feminist groups, transforming each along the way.

*   *   *

Equality on Trial begins in Title VII's turbulent first few years. In its wake, the nascent EEOC was faced with claims from women like Thelma Pilch, who conceived of their new right to workplace sex equality in terms that were at once expansive and specific. Lacking instruction or definitive precedent, some EEOC officials experimented with time-intensive efforts to customize workplace justice for women. But within a few years, the agency gravitated toward a narrower definition of sex equality. Trading flexibility for efficiency and organizational and conceptual disarray for structure, the EEOC came to treat sex and race discrimination as mirrored offenses less as a response to laboring women's own demands than as a way to systematically address the mounting backlog of claims and bend to feminist pressure. But by streamlining the processes for handling sex discrimination claims, officials also helped to cement their legal meaning, defining state-policed sex discrimination more as a problem of statistics than of women's varied understandings of harms and their remedies.[14] By the early 1970s, the EEOC had become the powerful and efficient muscle early claimants envisioned, but officials' perspectives on what might constitute violations of their rights had diminished considerably.

Title VII proved a tantalizing weapon for the feminist and labor activists who reframed long-standing grievances as legal matters in their efforts to channel its power. Throughout the 1970s, diverse groups of women and men projected their claims onto this new federal mechanism, testing its boundaries through workplace caucuses and feminist activist groups. While the thousands of people who registered complaints, joined protests, and built class action lawsuits did not always see themselves as part of a women's or union movement, they helped to win some of those causes' most tangible victories in those years.[15] Title VII also reconfigured feminist politics. Women's rights activism had long seen advocates of social justice pitted against those who prized formal equality. The law's initial ambiguity, coupled with its potential to punish violators, inspired bold approaches to harnessing its muscle that initially fused these older traditions.[16]

These efforts to claim Title VII's power generated interpretive struggles whose resolutions, while far from inevitable, ultimately choked off the concerns of working-class women and women of color while reinforcing their labor force subordination. Constrained by the mechanics of class action lawsuits and pressured by powerful corporations, plaintiffs and their attorneys came to prioritize the pursuit of affirmative action for elite workers and deemphasize the more substantive workplace transformations pink-collar women demanded. For their part, burgeoning feminist organizations struggled to define and chart a consensus course toward workplace equality. After a protracted conflict, these activists jettisoned workplace rights strategies that emphasized local improvisation, pragmatic gains, and economic justice in favor of a united push for passage of the proposed Equal Rights Amendment to the U.S. Constitution. Title VII's first decade thus saw activist campaigns surrender much of their militancy and adaptability as they positioned themselves to win its benefits—ultimately helping to concretize the laws' meanings in ways that drained the lifeblood from more inclusive conceptions of rights.

Organized labor's efforts to stretch Title VII's sex provision came to fruition in the 1980s. Those years saw union leaders most fully embrace a woman-centered agenda in response to the decline of male-dominated industrial jobs and the rise in female membership—especially women of color. Public sector union-led campaigns for comparable worth represented workers' and advocates' most ambitious attempts to push the boundaries of state-enforced equality. In particular, they sought to use Title VII to expand the reach of the Equal Pay Act of 1963 in order to reverse the historic devaluation of feminized jobs. This strategy met notable success in federal courts in the early 1980s. But organized business interests and conservative politicians also gained momentum in their campaigns to discredit capacious conceptions of state-enforced sex equality. By mid-decade, when courts began to roll back early comparable worth wins, labor unions had remade their women's rights agenda to foreground legal strategies. As courts and administrative agencies continued to delimit the range of viable Title VII claims across the decade, private sector union attorneys narrowed their arguments in kind, ultimately accepting the definition of sex equality as interchangeability and forfeiting the labor force segmentation and gendered protections some working-class women favored. This conception of sex equality dovetailed with long-standing employer efforts to merge, deskill, and intensify jobs across the service sector.

These years also saw men work to expand Title VII's meaning on their behalf. Gay petitioners waged unsuccessful campaigns to convince legal officials to "reason from sex" and declare sexual orientation to be an immutable and protected identity.[17] Instead, courts drove a powerful wedge between women's rights and gay rights before the law, a development that shifted the emphasis of gay rights efforts to local struggles and voluntary employer efforts. Men's efforts to use Title VII to buttress their campaigns to enter female-dominated jobs also fell short. While men pried their way into some feminized work, their efforts to win jobs that involved providing intimate care to women, children, and the elderly faced considerable resistance from courts, hospital administrators, and female coworkers alike. Title VII thus left male-oriented valuations of labor intact and enshrined the heterosexual male and masculine ideal while pushing many men's claims outside its scope.

By the early 1990s, sex equality's interpretive trial period was in its twilight. One by one, courts, advocates, and employers sparred over outstanding questions about Title VII's applicability to women's assumed and actual domestic burdens, employers' accountability for women's reproductive health, and sexualized interactions at work. These conflicts saw arguments that nondiscrimination could mean something beyond nondistinction founder on the shoals of divisive interest group politics, legal and administrative processes, enduring sex stereotypes, and the triumph of neoliberal work regimes. When activists sought passage of a robust Family and Medical Leave Act that could meaningfully offset workers' domestic commitments, Congress authorized only twelve weeks of unpaid leave—a benefit professional women were the least likely to need, and which working-class women could scarcely afford to use.

By century's end, the law defined sex equality primarily in terms of nondistinction among groups and individuals—whether by comparing the proportion of women job applicants to the proportion hired, by determining whether facially neutral policies treat women unequally in practice, or by punishing unwanted references to a worker's sex, sexuality, or private life. Title VII had spawned a robust field of legal practice, and the state mechanism that punished offenders was strong and efficient. But the range of violations the law might address and activists' approaches to state-enforced sex equality had sharply contracted. Along the way, the relationship between sex and class in the American labor force had been reworked. Those women who were poised to enter professional jobs wielded a narrow form of sex equality to break the glass ceiling. But employers delivered the gendered division of labor into the age of sex equality by repackaging it as a class divide, lowering the floor for everyone else as they pressed pink-collar jobs into the expanding service sector.

*   *   *

The half-century of efforts to cement Title VII's meaning should reground our conceptions of the forces that have shaped recent American social history. Scholars have long charted the history of class in the twentieth century as an arc that peaked at midcentury, when early social and economic divisions gave way to consensus and new forms of equality. Newer works extend this account by framing the last third of the century as years of declension spurred by the rupturing of the New Deal order, the collapse of unifying ideas of society and fixed notions of identity, and the ascent of the New Right. According to this narrative, the lack of consensus within and between the Left and liberals created space for conservatives to advance their vision of a neoliberal world of declining solidarities and a revitalized patriarchal order. This social and intellectual fragmentation was allegedly demobilizing for women, as they endured identity-based struggles that warped and delimited feminism's political agenda.[18]

But from working-class women's perspective, the last decades of the twentieth century were years of transformative potential and missed opportunity rather than steady decline.[19] While some female workers made significant gains within their labor unions at midcentury, broader social coalescence was predicated on women's exclusion from full citizenship. Postwar fracture broke apart these centuries-old forms of dependency, opening new conceptual space and fostering struggles over the meaning of sex equality that were most robust—especially among feminist activists—when the term was not defined. One prominent historian has argued that postwar liberalism was stymied in these years because it "lacked an economic blueprint to match its social agenda."[20] But Title VII emboldened women to craft just such an agenda, imagining new solidarities, building a robust class politics, and ultimately engaging the law to generate a pivotal battle over the terms of democracy, fairness, and the role of the state in labor relationships for all Americans. Beyond opening full economic citizenship to laboring women, they sought to use Title VII to reset the terms of economic citizenship from laboring women's perspective.

But these efforts met obstacles they could not overcome. Activists struggled to maintain cross-class and interracial unity in their efforts to stretch Title VII's sex provision to encompass the full spectrum of women's rights claims. Women's workplace groups initially viewed such coalition as essential to their Title VII campaigns, but the practical challenges involved in legal proceedings and the preexistence of race-based conceptions of workplace equality ultimately convinced them to emphasize the sexes' interchangeability and downplay working-class women's more complex claims. Feminist efforts to channel Title VII's potential forced activists to reckon with the relationship between sex equality and workplace justice, bringing class politics into high relief. Some feminists conceived of sex equality from working-class women's perspective, subjecting to scrutiny and potentially transforming all aspects of work in the name of fairness. Others gave priority to eroding the gendered division of labor and expanding opportunities. Initial attempts to engage Title VII to bridge these perspectives collapsed under the weight of clashing feminist visions and mounting conservative opposition. Although these efforts ultimately fell apart, uncovering their history reframes gendered fracture less as a spark for decline than as a productive opening of ideological space that gave rise to robust and experimental conceptions of equality and related activism that necessarily transcended New Deal masculine conceptions of democracy.

Further, working-class men did not join their female counterparts' efforts until conservative forces were firmly ensconced in positions of political and economic power. Other accounts of this era have pointed to the shrunken industrial labor force, permissive business climate, and solidification of economic conservatism at the grassroots and in more elite channels in order to characterize the 1970s as a "pivotal decade" when the nation "traded factories for finance," generating a "psychic meltdown" among white men that weakened class as a meaningful identity for all Americans.[21] These accounts tend to locate women as one group among many of neoliberalism's passive victims. But they also overlook how working-class white men closed themselves off to the more inclusive conceptions of class power women offered in those years, instead retreating into what we might consider the "psychological wages of gender." Their efforts to find refuge in gendered privilege largely failed, as most working-class white men have since joined women and men of color in the same dead-end service jobs women sought to transform.[22]

Finally, conservative interests undermined campaigns to infuse economic justice into workplace sex equality law in its formative years. Title VII was not necessarily the antidote to the New Right, but in transforming the landscape of feminist and labor politics, the law provided an opening through which conservatives could shrink and bend the legacy of the rights revolution to their benefit. Employers discovered, through their efforts to retain control and profitability amid new federal interference in their labor practices, that sex equality defined as nondistinction between men and women could allow them to comply with Title VII without more substantively restructuring to workers' advantage. Akin to the conservative intellectuals who disparaged affirmative action as an affront to equality of opportunity, conservative political leaders appointed allied judges and bureaucrats who acceded to sex equality law by interpreting it narrowly, extinguishing the potential for more substantive rights officials had located in the same provisions just years earlier.[23] As these efforts gained momentum, they collapsed the conceptual terrain of sex equality struggles as they played out in the law and broader culture—helping to deliver, and ultimately to legitimate, neoliberal transformation.[24]

*   *   *

The chapters that follow spotlight sites where we can perceive the changes, incremental and sometimes dramatic, through which workplace sex equality assumed its current meaning. The narrative moves from the offices of the nascent EEOC to the meeting rooms where the New York Times Women's Caucus constructed a class action lawsuit against the flagship publisher. From there, it examines the street protests and feminist gatherings that saw the National Organization for Women build a campaign that sought to transform the employment practices of Sears, Roebuck and Company, then the nation's largest retailer. The lens next turns to labor union efforts to harness Title VII, examining one campaign waged by the American Federation of

State, County and Municipal Employees and another by the New York Hotel Trades Council. The two concluding chapters excavate men's attempts to claim sex-based protections and the narrow form of sex equality, firmly enshrined by the early 1990s, that was manifest in workplaces, public policy, and culture. As sex-based workplace rights took shape in the law and American life, these chapters reveal, their reach expanded as their potential scope diminished.

The expansive approaches to citizenship rights profiled in these pages advanced an interpretation of the law—rooted in dignity and personal autonomy—that sought to transform institutions while remaining accommodating and flexible. Their story suggests that workers and activists of both sexes who are frustrated by recent rollbacks to labor rights need not look too far back in time to recover a vision of industrial democracy rooted in workers' own conceptions of fairness. If notions of sex equality are malleable, we might change them again.

Chapter 1

Defining Sex Discrimination

Months prior to taking effect, Title VII of the Civil Rights Act of 1964 was already forcing government officials to reckon with the law's ambiguous ban on workplace sex discrimination. In March 1965, Senator Robert F. Kennedy, a former U.S. attorney general, received a letter from Mrs. Leo Howdeshell, an employee of the Morrell Packing Plant in Ottumwa, a small town in southwest Iowa. Howdeshell described her working conditions and asked whether her employer was in violation of Title VII. Over the past few years, plant managers at Morrell had begun to merge and eliminate jobs held primarily by women, while hiring only men to fill open positions. In her efforts to convince Kennedy, a former labor lawyer and avowed civil rights advocate, to intervene on her behalf, Howdeshell expressed her fear that Title VII would affirm employment policies that were on the surface sex-blind but that disadvantaged women in fact. Because "a lot of the women cannot do all of the jobs and in fact all of the women cannot do some of them," she wrote, complying with Title VII should require employers to shield women from poor treatment and make substantive improvements to their working lives. In her plant this might mean designating a separate set of women's jobs to be kept safe from male encroachment. Howdeshell asked Senator Kennedy to weigh in on her suggestion in light of Title VII.[1]

In the foggy first few years of federal equal employment laws, Senator Kennedy had no ready answer to Mrs. Howdeshell's letter. Instead, his office forwarded it to the Women's Bureau of the Department of Labor. Frank Cantwell, the bureau's legislative liaison, investigated the matter and found no resolution. Existing state law provided no guidance, for Iowa's state fair employment practices law banned race discrimination but did not include sex. Further, Mrs. Howdeshell did not suggest that Title VII mandated the elimination of provisions that recognized sex difference—the widely held interpretation of existing race discrimination laws. To the contrary, she claimed that creating workplace equality for women should require attention to their unique desires and physiology. Cantwell conceded that this first federal provision to ban sex discrimination in employment not only lacked instructive precedent, but also butted up against hundreds of state laws that required employers to treat men and women differently. He advised Kennedy's office to respond to Howdeshell by urging her to be patient until July, when the Equal Employment Opportunity Commission (EEOC), the agency created to investigate and interpret Title VII, would be up and running. He demurred, "It will be the responsibility of the commission which is to be appointed shortly to resolve such questions as those raised by Mrs. Howdeshell."[2] Officials like Cantwell hoped that the EEOC would soon begin to intervene in such disputes, giving much-needed shape to Title VII's sex equality provision.

Three months after Mrs. Howdeshell put pen to paper, the EEOC first opened its doors to face a backlog of more than one thousand complaints, inquiries, and demands regarding the new rules governing sex in employment. But their claims were not received by the efficient and powerful entity many imagined. Instead, the small agency was overwhelmed by the volume and complexity of workers' claims. Commissioners lacked processes for investigating accusations of discrimination and had no power to enforce their findings. Neither did the agency have an ample or adequately trained staff. Two of the five original EEOC commissioners left within the first year, and those who remained decried their shortage of capable coworkers.[3] All of these concerns were compounded by the expanding pile of unresolved complaints, which grew to more than eighty thousand by late 1966.[4] The EEOC's meager budget, smaller than that of the Office of Coal Research, prevented the agency from expanding to keep pace.[5] These problems convinced many onlookers, chief among them feminists and civil rights activists, that neither President Lyndon Johnson nor the Congress intended the EEOC to be an effective agency in the fight against workplace discrimination. Summarizing this political neglect, one government official told the *New York Times*, "For the last two years Title VII has been the unwanted child of the Civil Rights Act of 1964."[6]

The EEOC also struggled to interpret the law it was charged with enforcing. Title VII had been designed to attack racism in the workplace—a problem the mainstream civil rights movement typically defined, and the legislators who passed the Civil Rights Act understood, as exclusion and segregation due to stigma and stereotype.[7] Yet Title VII also contained a last-minute ban on sex discrimination—thus juxtaposing race and sex discrimination as twinned offenses. But unlike the race provision, Title VII's ban on sex discrimination was not the result of united advocacy or public consensus that women lacked freedoms at work. To the contrary, at Title VII's passage every state had a unique combination of laws that required employers to differentiate between the sexes. These laws manifested the widespread assumption that men and women should play distinct roles in the workforce—roles that seemed to reflect their natural preferences and abilities. Women's advocates were also divided on the issue, with the activists and officials on President Kennedy's Commission on the Status of Women (PCSW) studying and debating the problem, but ultimately advocating equal pay and rejecting a blanket workplace equality provision in its 1963 report.[8] Neither the legislators who passed Title VII nor the president who signed it into law offered any guidance to the EEOC as it struggled to define sex equality in light of state laws, advocates' lack of consensus, and the long-standing gendered division of labor. Title VII blasted apart the foundations of women's state-enforced workplace rights, but the EEOC had no clear mandate to guide efforts to rebuild them.

EEOC staffers labored to give form to the fluid concept of sex equality, but working women were not similarly perplexed. Rather, they rushed into the breach to offer their own interpretations of their rights—filing four thousand complaints in the agency's first two years alone.[9] In free-form letters to the EEOC and other government officials fashioned to evoke sympathy and action, many rearticulated long-standing workplace concerns as issues of sex equality.[10] They imagined that Title VII addressed them personally as they attempted to stretch the nascent category of state-enforced sex equality to fit their many concerns. Complainants framed sex equality claims in terms of their personal circumstances—including poor treatment because of their health problems, unfair bosses, and breadwinner status—as well as women's poor economic status and other broad social inequalities. They argued that at the heart of state-enforced sex equality were such positive rights as decent wages, bodily autonomy, reasonable hours, and a measure of control over their labor relationships. The available archived letters of the women who wrote directly to the EEOC indicate that they were less likely to be professionals or aspiring professionals than pink-collar and industrial workers. Most expected Title VII to guarantee them their own notions of fair treatment and offset the worst elements of feminized service work, not simply grant them access to what men already had.

Confronted with such complex claims and lacking a fully formed sex discrimination policy, the EEOC did not make much perceptible progress in its first few years. Previous studies have looked primarily to feminist interest group records and collective memory to explain this lag. From this perspective, the EEOC appears to have been deliberately unresponsive to women until a burgeoning feminist movement came to power in the late 1960s and compelled the commissioners to address women's demands for freedom from stigma and access to male-dominated jobs.[11] But in addition to some officials' sexist attitudes, the agency's records also reveal their uncertainty of their obligations to women. In the absence of precedent or clear instructions, some in the EEOC began an earnest effort to breathe life into the legal category of sex equality by responding to the personal and nuanced claims women sent to them. Customizing workplace equality was a slow and tedious process. Over time it become untenable, as internal conflicts and the mounting backlog of complaints strained the fragile agency at its seams. These initial struggles were compounded by the mounting pressures applied by feminists who saw the agency's lack of progress as foot-dragging and other government officials who were reluctant to expand the EEOC's budget and authority absent measurable accomplishments.

In pursuit of respect and efficiency, the EEOC came to approach sex discrimination as a statistically quantifiable problem of sex segregation. Research displaced investigation as the EEOC's focus by the early 1970s. Many in the burgeoning feminist movement supported this shift, as did the mounting body of rulings by federal courts that analogized sex and race as categories protected under the Fourteenth Amendment.[12] But this new approach also extinguished more flexible conceptions of women's workplace rights, driving a wedge between many women and federal officials as the legal category of sex equality took shape. Sex discrimination became a phenomenon the government identified by studying the language of employer policies and the numbers of women who applied for and gained work in different employment categories. The agency no longer considered the range of elements bound up in a worker's own sense of fairness as relevant to Title VII. Thus, within a decade of Title VII's passage, it became possible for a worker to be a victim of sex discrimination without assenting to that classification and for violations of her self-identified rights to be denied legal legitimacy.

*   *   *

Title VII marked a dramatic turning point in the decades-long struggle to define women's rights in the workplace and to identify the government's role in policing them. While American women had always performed waged and unwaged labor, the consolidation of industrial capital in the late nineteenth century transformed women's employment patterns and opportunities and inspired a generation of advocates who sought to limit the dangers they faced at work. At the turn of the century, thousands of women left relatively informal and intimate work relationships in agriculture or domestic service for sex-segregated positions in retail establishments, factories, and offices. Labor reformers argued that the speed, monotony, and long hours of these new occupations posed grave health threats to workers, male and female.[13] But the U.S. Supreme Court quashed their campaign for sex-neutral state labor laws in the 1905 case *Lochner v. New York*. These activists retooled with a gendered strategy, framing the state as a powerful guardian of women's physical and moral well-being. By this route, they won federal support for sex-specific state labor laws in the U.S. Supreme Court. In the 1908 case *Muller v. Oregon*, the Court ruled that the state of Oregon could limit the number of weekly hours worked by women in laundries in order to protect their health and reproductive potential. Sex-specific labor laws generated significant controversy among women's activists, with groups such as the National Consumers' League and the Women's Trade Union League supporting the efforts of the Women's Bureau of the Department of Labor to strengthen the provisions, and other groups, especially the National Woman's Party, viewing them as an obstacle to the formal legal sex equality that an Equal Rights Amendment to the U.S. Constitution would provide.[14]

These sex-specific protective laws held firm into the mid-twentieth century even as government officials and labor movement activists began to articulate an "equality with protection" model of women's workplace rights. As women made dramatic inroads into male-dominated enclaves of the workforce during World War II, male and female war workers alike demanded equal pay for equal work, and the norms of public morality that had justified bans on night work for women seemed less pressing in wartime. Further, mid-century proponents of racial equality had issued powerful arguments linking state-enforced workplace opportunity with democracy—culminating in the creation of the first federal agency charged with investigating race discrimination in the workplace, the Fair Employment Practices Commission (FEPC). While the FEPC did not investigate claims that solely alleged sex discrimination, women were included where they were also members of racial minority groups.[15] The Women's Bureau of the U.S. Department of Labor responded to these changes by launching new campaigns for equal pay extending some sex-based protections to men. Yet the bureau balanced its new emphasis on nondistinction between the sexes with continued demands for accommodations for women that recognized their special status as potential mothers. Officials argued in 1960 that disability insurance programs should include maternity benefits, maternity leave, and reemployment rights and "provide for the establishment of day care programs at the state and community level through federal grants-in-aid to states on a matching fund basis."[16] At the same time, the women who rose to prominence in labor unions began to argue for substantive fairness—a practical balance of opportunities and protections. The Cold War constrained this nascent but strong labor feminist movement, but some of its aims became union policy and federal law. For example, several unions pushed for the inclusion of sex in state FEP laws and the Equal Pay Act became law in 1963, albeit with the weaker provision of equal pay for "equal" rather than "comparable" work.[17]

In 1964, the EEOC assumed the burden of interpreting the new federal law of sex equality amid a patchwork of sex-specific state provisions.[18] While the Civil Rights Act had itself generated controversy throughout the nation, legislators and most activists shared a mainstream conception of the law's promise to racial minorities, forged by decades of struggle by African Americans for federally protected rights at work. Starting in World War II, government agencies had begun to promote equal opportunity for African Americans as the antidote to labor force segregation and stigma.[19] President John F. Kennedy implemented race-based affirmative action programs in government employment and among private companies holding government contracts. Kennedy also tapped Vice President Lyndon Johnson to chair his Committee on Equal Employment Opportunity, which secured pledges from corporations and labor unions to work to "eliminate any differential treatment of employees or applicants for employment" and to level the playing field for meritorious minorities.[20] Once the Civil Rights Act was proposed in Congress, legislators recounted their vision for the new EEOC as a bulwark against workplace segregation. By 1964, the federal government and civil rights agencies had defined racial equality as workplace integration, the removal of barriers to upward mobility, and decentering race as a relevant employment characteristic. Laws in twenty-five states prohibited race discrimination in employment on the eve of Title VII's passage, and momentum for these provisions was growing. In these same years, women's workplace rights policy stirred deep divisions as it grew more nuanced.[21]

The Civil Rights Act created the EEOC as a new federal agency that would be directed by a five-member bipartisan commission and empowered to interpret Title VII's ban on discrimination in workplaces with more than seventy-five employees, labor unions with more than seventy-five members, and government agencies on the basis of "race, color, religion, sex, or national origin."[22] At the helm of the new agency was Franklin Delano Roosevelt Jr., fifth-born child of America's thirty-second president and his wife, civil rights pioneer Eleanor Roosevelt. Despite his famous name, striking similarity to his father in appearance, and a voice so like his father's that it evoked "a ghostly feeling" in those who listened, FDR Jr.'s political talent fell far short of his ambition.[23] A decorated war veteran and attorney, Roosevelt served on President Truman's Committee on Civil Rights in 1947 and 1948, then won election to the House of Representatives in 1949 upon the death of a sitting member. After several terms, Roosevelt pursued the Democratic nomination for the governorship of New York, the position from which his father and distant relative Theodore Roosevelt had launched successful White House bids. Against his wishes, the state Democratic Party instead nominated Roosevelt for attorney general, a race he lost in 1954. Roosevelt spent the next half-decade enmeshed in various Democratic Party causes, and after campaigning for presidential candidate John F. Kennedy in forty-five states, he was rewarded with the position of Undersecretary of Commerce. From there, Roosevelt seized the opportunity to head the new EEOC, and many onlookers speculated that he saw the chairmanship as a springboard into another bid for executive office in New York. Compounding that allegation, Roosevelt requested a two-year term rather than a five-year term, because, as he said, "I can't look that far down the road."[24] As EEOC chairman, recalled fellow commissioner Richard Graham, Roosevelt "just wanted to keep things quiet," presumably to minimize the risk of tarnishing his political reputation as he continued to climb.[25] Indeed, Roosevelt left the EEOC after just one year to run once again for governor in New York.

Roosevelt's four fellow commissioners, appointed to staggered five-year terms, approached their mandate to interpret and implement Title VII from a range of perspectives. Luther Holcomb, appointed as EEOC vice chairman, was a white Baptist minister and had served as executive director of the Greater Dallas Council of Churches and chairman of the Texas Advisory Committee to the U.S. Civil Rights Commission. Reflecting his religious background, Holcomb described workplace equality as an ethical issue. According to an EEOC press release, "His main theme is that Title VII is right, it is fair, and it meets the moral command of a concerned society."[26] Commissioner Samuel Jackson was an attorney from Topeka, Kansas, and former president of the Topeka branch of the NAACP. A Republican and an African American, Jackson's fellow commissioners came to see him as "the most political person on the Commission."[27] Richard Graham, a white Republican, had been an engineer and civil rights activist in Milwaukee before he was tapped to direct the U.S. Peace Corps mission to Tunisia in the early 1960s. Graham became the commission's most vocal advocate for strong enforcement of the sex discrimination provision. He described women's workplace rights as a "gut issue"—a matter of simple fairness—and referenced his respect for his wife, a "very bright and energetic and effective person" who had headed the Milwaukee chapter of Planned Parenthood.[28] The fifth commissioner, Aileen Hernandez, was an African American and the group's only woman. Hernandez had been a teacher and a labor organizer before assuming a position as assistant chief of the California FEPC.[29] Hernandez told the *Washington Post* that she hoped her appointment to the EEOC would challenge stereotypes such as "woman's place is in the home," and "women who work lose their femininity."[30] Yet, she did not wish to become pigeonholed as the commission's expert on women. She claimed, "I would be pleased to let my personal experience be a guide, but I would like to see all the commissioners get their share of cases involving sex discrimination and begin to think about the problems."[31]

The EEOC encountered obstacles as soon as it opened in July 1965. President Lyndon Johnson had nominated the commissioners less than two months earlier, and the U.S. Senate confirmed them only weeks before the commission began its operations.[32] This left the agency with little time to hire staff, and commissioners scrambled to piece together a group of investigators and support personnel. By its opening day, the EEOC had culled sixty-five employees from twenty-three other federal and state agencies, from the President's Commission on Equal Employment Opportunity to the

Atomic Energy Commission, to help investigate complaints of discrimination.[33] Commissioners set up a four-day seminar on Title VII to orient the new staff.[34] One staffer recalled the hectic first months at the agency. "Before we could even think of trying to conciliate charges of discrimination, we had to devise a filing system, determine which complaints appeared to be valid charges," and decide "which charges should be investigated, by whom and in what manner."[35] Among her coworkers, recalled staff assistant Susie Foshee, some were "people who had worked in civil rights," while others were "specialists of some type, like sociologists, lawyers, teachers, etc."[36] Yet, in attempting to hire current government workers who could bring much-needed expertise in public policy, the EEOC assembled an overwhelmingly white staff. Civil rights groups came to criticize the commission for operating what one journalist called a "plantation hiring system."[37] All these issues threatened to derail the nascent agency as it rushed to get up and running.

Further, from the start, onlookers and commissioners worried that the EEOC did not have sufficient authority to carry out its mandate.[38] It was limited to mediating voluntary compromises between workers and employers. Where the agency could not broker an agreement, Title VII directed the EEOC to refer evidence of "patterns or practices" of discrimination to the Department of Justice, encourage individuals to file private lawsuits, and write amicus curiae briefs. This lack of enforcement powers limited the agency to the tactics of persuasion and negotiation—educating employers about how to comply with Title VII voluntarily.[39] In one early campaign, the EEOC held public hearings on race discrimination in the textile industry in 1967 but relied on the muscle of the Office of Federal Contract Compliance to apply direct pressure and consequences for employers who resisted.[40] From the beginning, the agency pursued more might. FDR Jr. testified before the General Subcommittee on Labor of the House of Representatives in the EEOC's first month of operation to request enforcement powers. "To divorce the conciliation function from the enforcement function, as Title VII has done, seems to be a questionable decision," he claimed. "Conciliation is most successful when the parties know that effective machinery for enforcement is readily at hand." Roosevelt explained that the commission needed stronger enforcement powers in order "to achieve the progress toward equal employment opportunity which the Congress expects and which the nation demands."[41] This lack of authority shaped commissioners' actions. Richard Graham recalled that his colleague Luther Holcomb secretly sought the counsel of the U.S. Supreme Court justice Abe Fortas regarding the court's interpretation

of Title VII so that the agency's fragile authority would not be further diminished if the court publicly diverged from the agency.[42]

The commissioners were also challenged by Title VII's ambiguities with
regard to sex. The EEOC looked to legal and administrative precedent in interpreting the race provision of Title VII, yet all agreed that measuring and
remedying sex discrimination would be difficult.[43] EEOC attorney Richard
Berg wrote in 1969, concerning the legislators who passed Title VII with no
discussion of how to apply the sex provision, "It is fair to say that the peculiar
problems of administering a general prohibition against sex discrimination
in employment were perceived dimly, if at all."[44] Hesitant to transpose the
doctrine of race discrimination onto sex, Roosevelt consulted Congress,
the Department of Labor, and the president for guidance. In his appearance
before the House of Representatives Subcommittee on Labor, Roosevelt asked
for assistance in interpreting the sex provision.[45] Commissioners addressed
similar questions to the Department of Labor. In particular, they asked how
the commission should respond to "inquiries as to sex in employment applications; employment agencies servicing men only or women only; help wanted
ads for males or females; seniority lines organized by sex; [and] separate facili-
ties for men and women."[46]

They did not receive the guidance they sought. Roosevelt expressed his
frustration at this ambiguity in a speech to the National Conference of
Women in 1965. He explained that Title VII's sex provision "was tacked on
rather suddenly without the usual committee hearings, to a law concerned
primarily with racial discrimination." Thus, the EEOC was required to "un-
dertake its enforcement without the benefit of the guidelines, the legislative
history and the court decisions that we can rely upon in pursuing some of
our other responsibilities under Title VII."[47] Further, lawmakers saddled Title VII with a clause that allowed employers to discriminate on the basis of
sex, religion, and national origin where having a particular attribute was a
bona fide occupational qualification (BFOQ) for the job—thus forcing the
EEOC to determine which elements of the gendered division of labor could
pass muster under Title VII.[48] Sex discrimination was "a much more difficult problem" than race discrimination, claimed EEOC staff attorney Sonia
Pressman Fuentes, and thus, it came to absorb a great deal of the EEOC legal
staff's time and effort.[49] Other EEOC staffers were more critical. Commissioner Aileen Hernandez reflected, "The actions taken by the EEOC in its
first year of enforcement of the provisions against sex discrimination might
be best described as 'confused.' "[50]

The most difficult question facing the EEOC in its struggles to interpret Title VII was whether the doctrine of sex equality could coexist with state protective laws.[51] Some policy makers supported sex-based protections for the important benefits they provided to working women, while others argued that the new federal mandate for sex equality should supersede them.[52] The PCSW's 1963 report revealed the committee's particular concern that states continue to guard against forced overwork and hazardous working conditions.[53] PCSW member and Women's Bureau director Esther Peterson recommended that the EEOC evaluate protective laws one at a time, asking whether each was a pretext for discrimination or an important safeguard of workers' health and safety. "The key, I believe, is to move firmly in effectuating the new law and protecting women's rights guaranteed by that law but not to do so in a manner that would destroy protections already won."[54] But just how to balance protections against freedoms was unclear to the commissioners, who proceeded cautiously.[55] Aileen Hernandez suggested to her fellow commissioners that sex-based protections that granted rest periods and adequate seating for women might be extended to men.[56] Chairman Roosevelt explained, "We are making a careful study of all of these points of view and are building our policy case by case."[57] Feminists were dismayed by the guidelines on sex discrimination the EEOC issued in its first year, which they perceived as vague and toothless. In particular, they criticized the agency's unwillingness to condemn sex-segregated classified job advertisements.[58]

Lacking guidance from executive, legislative, or judicial authorities regarding sex-specific protections, the EEOC waited for courts to weigh in. In the meantime, where state laws and Title VII seemed to conflict, the EEOC promised to seek "practical solutions which would enable employers to comply with both Title VII and state laws." In one such effort, the EEOC helped the Scott Paper Company to adhere to both Title VII's promise of equal treatment and a Michigan state law that restricted women from jobs requiring them to lift more than thirty-five pounds. The EEOC investigation revealed that while the job the female claimant pursued involved lifting fifty-pound boxes of staples, the staples were stored in ten-pound rolls that a male worker could unpack. The company awarded the job to the complainant and overturned its ban on women in carton-stitching jobs. Where such compromises were out of reach, the commission encouraged women to take their claims to court.[59]

The commissioners pursued a similar compromise in the meatpacking industry. Meatpacking plants employed both men and women, but the jobs

Figure 1. Many of the women who wrote to the Equal Employment Opportunity Commission in its first few years, like the bacon slicer pictured here, worked in the industrial and service sectors. Their understandings of Title VII's promise to them were at once broad and specific. Photograph by Les Orear. Courtesy of the Illinois Labor History Society.

inside were highly sex-segregated (Figure 1). Male and female production lines typically corresponded to contemporary notions of men as physically stronger and women as more dexterous. Prior to Title VII, the agreement between the Amalgamated Meatcutter's Union and plant management provided that an employee who was laid off in his or her own department could displace the most junior employee in the plant, on the male line, if a man, or on the female line, if a woman, if he or she could perform the job or learn it within a reasonable time. In anticipation of Title VII, most plants merged the seniority lines in early 1965, allowing women to displace men and men to displace women.[60] Under the merged seniority system, women quickly received EEOC relief when they were denied access to formerly male-typed jobs. In the case of Jenny Fry, who was laid off from the J. J. Morrell plant in Arkansas City, Kansas, EEOC investigators found that her seniority should have allowed her to pursue a position as a sausage stuffer—a newly integrated job. The EEOC asked Morrell "to permit the charging party to exercise her right of seniority with regard to the next vacancy, or promotion, to the sausage stuffing department."[61]

Yet most women who wrote to the EEOC objected to the merged system, arguing that the new law of sex equality should provide both opportunity and protection. Margaret Brooks wrote that because so many women in her Iowa plant had seniority, when a senior woman was laid off, her only option was to take the job of an unskilled man. She criticized this option, for among those jobs, "there are some jobs a woman can handle but in the majority the jobs are physically impossible for a woman to do. Either too heavy, too high or running tractors, pushing trees, etc. Some jobs a tall good sized woman might do but a short hundred pound woman could not," and most of these senior women "are in their upper forties to close to sixty age bracket." Brooks acknowledged the intractability of the problem. "I do not know the answer to this but I do not believe that equal rights means women must either be able to compete physically with men or get out. In a packing plant women cannot lug beef, push heavy loads etc. No mere bill can make women something they just aren't."[62] Josephine Flores told a similar story of her St. Paul, Minnesota, plant, where most of the jobs for senior, displaced women were "on the hog, beef and sheep kills, and even operating huge electric saws which are very dangerous. These type of operations have never been done by female employees in the Swift and Co. Plant in the last 46 years." Flores wondered about legislators' motives. "What does this administration think? Do they no longer have any respect for the American female who carried the production load during World War II? I want you to know that I feel I still am a lady and all of us wish to be treated as so."[63] To these women, sex equality should not upend common-sense sex differences.

Weighing these and other concerns, the agency crafted a compromise "ABC" job classification system. Each position in a plant would be assigned a letter, with "A" jobs defined as "jobs which are primarily of interest to males," and "B" jobs defined as the female corollary. The third category included jobs consisting of "physical and/or environmental demands such that the normal male or female would be qualified to perform the jobs or learn them within a reasonable time."[64] EEOC attorney Richard Berg described this scheme as a pragmatic compromise. "Title VII does not permit the establishment of sex-oriented categories, but would permit the establishment of *functional categories* based on matters such as heavy physical labor, dexterity, etc., even if such categories would in practice be composed predominantly of members of one sex."[65] EEOC attorney Sonia Pressman Fuentes

concurred with Berg that the ABC system represented the best possible outcome for women. She explained that "the merger of all jobs" would have remade meatpacking as a male-only trade, for "pilot projects in the industry
revealed that this would ultimately have the effect of removing women from
the industry."[66] In a 1967 speech to the United Auto Workers Women's Department, Pressman Fuentes explained that the struggles to implement Title
VII in meatpacking convinced her to abandon her "rigid, simplistic approach." She had initially argued that "all male and female job distinctions
had to be abolished." Yet, she observed, "this approach resulted in complaints
of new difficulties from all sides—the women, the men, the companies, and
the unions," and "it became necessary to work out some more complicated
adjustments than the simple merger of jobs in one category."[67] Addie Wyatt,
a leader in the United Packinghouse Workers' Association, urged the EEOC
to continue to address sex discrimination in meatpacking "realistically," protecting women's jobs while providing routes to advancement.[68]

In early 1967, EEOC officials traveled to Iowa to broker an industry-wide
agreement among the Dubuque Packing Company, Local 150 of the Amalgamated Meat Cutters and Butcher Workmen, and seventeen individual
women who had filed complaints with the EEOC. To classify jobs within
the ABC system, the EEOC established a ten-person committee consisting of
representatives of labor, management, and male and female employees. The
group analyzed and categorized two thousand jobs.[69] The agreement ratified
the ABC classification system; neither men nor women would be required to
take jobs primarily of interest to the other sex, but could do so voluntarily. The
women agreed to drop their charges. EEOC chairman Stephen Shulman
lauded the meatpacking compromise as a great success. "The opportunity
for cross over between groups lies at the heart of our approval of the agreement," Shulman said. "Other methods may well be developed, but this one
constitutes a great step forward at this time."[70] This time-intensive, industry-
specific approach embodied early EEOC attempts to accommodate women's
desires for protections under Title VII's promise of sex equality.

*   *   *

The EEOC's meatpacking compromise reset the industry standard, at once
addressing hundreds of its pending complaints. In the EEOC's first year,

around one-quarter of the nearly nine thousand complaints the agency received alleged sex discrimination.[71] From across the nation and all sectors of the labor force, complainants sent free-form letters to the agency that projected their own aspirations onto the nascent law of sex equality. Sidestepping the issue of upholding or dismantling protective labor laws that compared women to men, many claimants framed their rights claims in terms of fairness and economic security. Referencing their personal situations and sacrifices, they expressed their hopes that the new law of sex equality could address the long-standing problems of inflexibility, low wages and physical danger while accounting for a worker's personal status—whether she was the head of household, widowed, elderly, or disabled. Many early EEOC claims shared the presumptions that a woman's sex should not handicap her at work, but that creating equality also required employers to account for women's personal circumstances and broader sex differences.[72]

Some women wrote to the EEOC about protective legislation, already a main concern of the agency. Objecting to sexist protections were skilled women workers like Mildred Fischer, a certified welder, who labored alongside of men at her Marion, Ohio, workplace. She wrote, "It seems very unfair to me when we work 9 hours a day and 4 1/2 hours on Saturday that I must go home in 3 hours after I drive 50 miles a round trip to get to work as the law was 48 hours [per week] for a woman."[73] Yet other women, like the meatpackers, feared that the elimination of protective legislation would leave them at a disadvantage. Mildred French hoped to ensure that state or federal law would continue to "prohibit management from placing women on heavy machines, having always been classified as men's heavy machines. . . . No woman should be forced to operate a heavy machine and if unable to do so be terminated."[74] Similarly, Mrs. E. L. Greathouse proclaimed that women in Texas lacked adequate state protections, and thus were "worked like horses and paid like slaves." Mrs. Greathouse considered this lack of government intervention to be "discrimination against women" which was "every bit as bad as the discrimination against any race of people."[75] Working women offered arguments on both sides of the protective legislation debate. Some viewed protective labor laws as oppressive and intrusive, while others saw them as a necessary safeguard against the particular dangers and challenges wage labor posed for women.

Yet other working women who wrote to the EEOC in its first few years sidestepped the issue of state legislation. Instead, they argued that Title VII should accommodate individuals' personal and family needs. Their detailed letters offered specific suggestions. Frances Huber suggested that workers with dependents, regardless of their sex, should receive preferential treatment in hiring and wages that enabled them to fulfill their caregiving responsibilities. "There needs to be provision included that would instantly give priority to the individual head of household although the individual can only afford one rented room and is in need of employment and has the experience and qualifications!"[76] Working conditions at the A. E. Staley Company in Decatur, Illinois, explained Evelyn Clesson, were intolerable because "several of we women are widows with our only means of support being our job at Staley's."[77] Frances Glade asked, "We have to work, having sick husbands and children to raise. . . . How are we going to live? Most factory help are people with little or no education and after years of working are too old to go and learn anything, and who will hire us?"[78] Grace Ivey thought the government should ensure her employment because of an outstanding debt: "I owe $5,000 and I need to get it paid."[79] To these complainants, realizing Title VII's promise entailed reckoning with and accounting for women's personal circumstances.

Other correspondents argued that their low salaries violated Title VII—not in comparison to men's salaries, but based on their financial need. These women argued that Title VII should provide equity, beyond equal pay to men's. Marguerite Losicki, a janitor in South Bend, Indiana, claimed that her pay did not support her and her three children. In order to make ends meet, she estimated, "I need a job 8 hrs a day, 5 days a week, and at least $1.75 per hour or $65 dollars a week take home pay. Please help me to get a job a steady job. I am not afraid to work. I have the experience. Please answer my letter soon. I am sending you the list of jobs or work I have done. Please help me get this job as a mail sorter or mail delivery or some kind of factory work."[80] Mrs. Clarence Brigham complained that Kendall Mills paid poverty wages. Her coworker was paid so little "she makes aprons and totes on handkerchiefs to run [an] old car she had to have to go to church and to do her shopping. Ask Kendall Mills how much they pay her today. I could almost say 'I dare you!' "[81] Imogene Philp objected to employers' control over workers' economic security. "A job is a life-line to a worker. These huge companies are allowed to cut our life-line."[82] To these women, low wages were immoral, not in comparison with men's wages, but because they left workers in poverty.

Aggrieved women also argued that Title VII should protect workers from ill-meaning supervisors and misunderstandings, relying on their personal notions of appropriate employment policies. Mrs. Antoinette Mascia decried the favoritism supervisors displayed at the Detroit Frito-Lay Plant. "You must belong to the 'clique' in order to get ahead or to be recognized, otherwise you're one of the peons." Mascia explained that discrimination affected both men and women there, as management had replaced workers of both sexes with members of the favored group.[83] Mrs. Evelyn Fennell, a grade school teacher, wrote to describe the "insulting and offensive" school psychiatrist of the New York City Board of Education who had deemed her "too ill to be serving as a teacher."[84] Ruth Page lodged a complaint against Hecht Department Store, alleging, "fair treatment as well as equal employment is not practiced in the Hecht Company. The short period I was there as many as two persons a week were fired or had to resign because of being treated rude and talked to as if they were not human." Page recounted interactions with a "ferocious" supervisor who harbored a grudge against her.[85] Mrs. Meridian Miller protested that her employer did not grant her three weeks of personal leave in which to care for her ailing father. Miller attributed this denial of leave to her immediate supervisor, "who seems to have a personal resentment and dislike for me"; "he never ceases to make remarks about the luxury car I drive, my appearance, etc." Miller requested that the EEOC complete its investigation soon, so that she might tend to her father without losing her job.[86] These workers argued that sex equality law should accommodate women's personal needs—guaranteeing satisfactory jobs to dedicated employees.

Other women's letters blended race and sex discrimination claims. Ella B. Payton, a card punch operator and an African American woman in the Norfolk Naval Shipyard, described the specific details of her "corrupt and antagonizing" working conditions in a May 1966 letter to FDR Jr. Payton listed her supervisors' and coworkers' first and last names, as well as their races. She described the ordeal she had endured in great detail in the hopes that federal authorities would intervene on her behalf. In her year of employment at the shipyard, Ms. Payton explained, her supervisor "refused, in her own way, to devote time enough to sit down intelligently and teach me the various jobs in this section. She has thrown work at me, snatched work from me, and the tone in which she talks to me is almost inconceivable." Further, supervisors gave the easiest work to the white women and left her with the most complex work. Payton acknowledged that, by working for a government contractor, her work was bound up with her citizenship. "I am willing to give the U.S. government eight hours a day and try to do my very best at it," she reasoned, but laboring under such a nasty overseer made it "almost impossible to produce and give the government that which I am capable of doing."[87] EEOC staff forwarded Ms. Payton's complaint to the Pentagon, where the Department of Defense received employment-related claims, without comment.[88]

Other women offered claims that far exceeded matters EEOC staff expected to handle. Adah Payne wrote to ask whether employers refusing to hire former prisoners violated Title VII; Helen McCauley attempted to file a grievance on behalf of an unknowing, long-suffering coworker; and Jean Horton requested an unlabeled letter be sent to her, which she could give to her discriminatory employer, but which would not risk her supervisor getting into trouble with his boss.[89] The agency also fielded letters addressing discrimination in other types of institutions, such as one describing the paucity of women admitted to Cornell University Veterinary College.[90] In her letter, Wilma Asbury seemed to view the EEOC as a job placement service. "Believe me, this much difficulty in securing employment, to me, and regardless of age, is not natural. No one person could possibly be that undesirable or inefficient," she claimed. "I do not believe I am the worse looking person, however, I am no beauty; most generally, I will bend over backwards to get along, but only to a point." She asked, "can you help me, and can you please advise."[91]

Women offered various justifications when asking for EEOC assistance. Some linked their personal circumstances to their patriotism and partisan loyalty. Virgie Spradling enumerated her family's military sacrifices—"Two of my brothers served in World War I and twelve nephews and my son and brother in law served in World War II; my step son was killed in the Korean War, and I have a nephew in Vietnam and one in Germany now besides cousins fighting"—in her request for a job in a munitions factory. "I would like to be of some benefit toward this war other than just needing the money myself too—so a plant might benefit both ways."[92] In her letter, Grace Ivey described herself as "a single self-supporting adult Caucasian woman OVER 40 years of age that was a WAC during WWII during the administration of the wonderful late FDR Sr. and also a lifelong Democrat" who was currently enduring "very serious experiences and employment problems."[93] Complainant Jane Martin observed that providing jobs to the unemployed, "as a matter of dollars and cents," would be "better than forcing these people to be supported in large part by taxes[.] Is there not a way to let these honest, decent, worthwhile citizens be respected as such?"[94]

Another common line of argument asked the government to ensure employment for workers whose age handicapped their job searches, a form of discrimination that especially harmed women workers. In their letters, older women described self-sustaining employment as an entitlement and a right of citizenship unfairly denied to seniors who "have worked, paid taxes, raised families, served in the country's armed forces and generally been good and worthwhile citizens. Now they are being punished and made into second class citizens through no fault of their own, but, because they have passed their fortieth birthday."[95] Complainant Antonia Groitia protested age discrimination in more specific terms. "I am able and capable to work. What are we supposed to do, when we are between the ages of 50 and 65 years? When we need to work? We are too old to work, but too young receive our pension." Groitia offered both her age and partisan loyalty to justify her claims. She explained, "I was always a good democrat. When your father ran for a third term, I voted for him. I was devoted to him! He was a good man. I have been working since the Social Security Act started and I believe I have the right to work. I have education, experience and ability to work and learn. In the United States, no one is old."[96] While age was not a protected category under Title VII, the EEOC received about three hundred complaints alleging age discrimination within its first six months.[97]

In their letters to government officials in the wake of Title VII, many working women imagined the new law to encompass affirmative protections, respecting women's positions as family members, citizens and individuals who also bore personal and domestic responsibilities. Such claims shared the presumption that a woman's sex should not penalize her in the workplace. But these correspondents also pursued a strain of workplace sex equality that accounted for women's own circumstances, boosted their economic security, and granted them more autonomy and flexibility at work.

*   *   *

In its first several years, the EEOC assumed the time-intensive process of addressing complaints one by one. The agency also fielded hundreds of requests for information on policies from employers and local government officials. Staff read and responded to letters, deployed investigators, made phone calls, conducted interviews, and reviewed personnel files for complaints that seemed to fit the agency's protean definition of sex discrimination. At other times, the commission pursued sex discrimination charges when evidence suggested it—even if the worker had filed a race discrimination claim.[98] Some EEOC staff members went to considerable lengths to help complainants. Elvera Martin filed race and sex discrimination charges against the Maison Blanche Department Store in New Orleans when she was denied employment there in 1965. When the EEOC contacted her for more information, Martin stated that her husband had convinced her to drop the matter, but the agency continued the investigation. The EEOC staffer contacted the management trainee who had interviewed her, who described Martin as a poor fit for the position. She was "too shy, withdrawn, [and] too reluctant to answer questions to be favorably considered as a sales person." In search of more objective criteria, the investigators checked the records of several hundred other applicants. Interviewer evaluations of Mrs. Martin showed that she was rated three out of a possible five in personality, three out of four in attitude, four out of four in appearance, and two out of four in speech. Successful applicants typically scored at least four out of a possible four or five in these categories. The investigation was only fatally impaired by Hurricane Betsy. When Mrs. Martin moved out of her residence and the investigator lost track of her, the EEOC dismissed her charge.[99]

Such a time-intensive process could not keep pace with the deluge of claims the EEOC received. When the commission opened its doors in July 1965, it had an immediate backlog of one thousand claims; by December 1965, there were ten thousand. Eighteen months after the EEOC began its work, the agency had 81,500 unresolved claims—one-third of which alleged sex discrimination.[100] Fighting to chip away at the backlog represented a kind of Catch-22, wrote acting director of compliance Kenneth Holbert. The agency had to grow to keep up with the volume of complaints. But the stopgap solution, hiring law student interns, created a new glut of employees. Training them took investigators away from their work.[101] The backlog of claims also contributed to tensions among commissioners, who sparred over how to prioritize cases to investigate. In October 1966, Commissioner Jackson wrote that many of the approximately two hundred cases involving the U.S. Steel Company and the Steelworkers' Union had been on the agency's desk for more than one year. "We ought to complete our processing of these cases at once," he claimed, warning his fellow commissioners, "I know of no single issue that is likely to become more embarrassing to the commission than the continued indecisiveness in the disposition of these charges."[102]

The backlog of cases also shaped commissioners' willingness to pursue clear-cut violations of Title VII. In a letter to his fellow commissioners, Graham described the discriminatory practices of the Carolina Telephone and Telegraph Company, which had a formal policy that only women between the ages of eighteen and twenty-five were eligible to be hired. No such age restrictions affected male applicants. Yet, Graham reasoned, "the Commission is so swamped now" that filing such a charge "only prevents our ability to handle some other charge."[103] Compounding the backlog, the EEOC's jurisdiction was expanded in July 1967 beyond those companies with seventy-five or more employees to those with fifty or more—adding 44,500 more employers to Title VII coverage.[104]

In an October 1966 letter to their fellow commissioners, Commissioners Hernandez and Jackson attributed the agency's backlog to a confluence of factors: too few staffers, the need to train borrowed personnel and to retrain full-time staff, and time-consuming compliance procedures.[105] Attorney Sonia Pressman Fuentes wrote to Aileen Hernandez in June 1967, "[I] keep wondering how long we can all keep up that kind of pace—we just don't have enough attys on the staff, nor enough clericals."[106] Commissioners did not always tell each other about their findings, and staffers responded to questions or complaints about Title VII without consulting or informing each other. Further, by 1967, the agency had eleven field offices. These regional EEOC offices were set up to receive, investigate, and mediate charges occurring within their jurisdiction. Regional offices would then communicate with Washington, where commissioners would review evidence and issue rulings when local attempts at conciliation failed. This setup freed the Washington office from the practical burdens of investigations, but the satellite offices created the new problems of keeping policy consistent and staff informed. Washington EEOC staff visited eight regional offices in May 1967. Officials found as many processes as there were outposts. Similarly, deferring complaints to state and local human rights agencies lightened the EEOC's burden, but they worked from different definitions of discrimination.[107]

High staff turnover compounded these problems. One year into his term, commission chairman Roosevelt left to enter New York state politics. Roosevelt "never intended to stay on the job," Hernandez reflected.[108] Richard Graham, who held only a one-year appointment, left in July of 1966, and Aileen Hernandez resigned soon thereafter. Her stated concern was that the commission was inefficient and had "not been working as a coordinated team."[109] Graham recalled, "Aileen was a wonderful woman, but I don't think she really liked fights," and in its first year, "the commission was very con-frontational."[110] By spring 1967, the highest staff job at the EEOC had been held by three different people in twenty-one months.[111] Sonia Pressman Fuentes wrote to civil rights activist Pauli Murray in October 1967 of the high staff turnover. "Every new administration has been interested not so much in keeping people of merit and dedication and in getting the job done, but in furthering their own political and other careers and getting rid of everyone and replacing them with their own people."[112] Pressman Fuentes thus echoed civil rights groups' claims that the EEOC should reach beyond the patronage system for workers who were committed to the EEOC's mis-sion. "Morale is low, and evidence indicates that it is declining," stated an internal EEOC report in early 1967.[113]

Paralyzed by internal conflict, the EEOC was unable to set, let alone pur-sue, an agenda. By April 1967, the EEOC had referred fifteen cases to the Justice Department, yet Justice had selected only one case for action: a suit against a small North Carolina supply company.[114] The *Wall Street Journal* quoted an EEOC employee who said the agency deliberately backed away from the nation's most powerful employers. "There's a feeling on the staff level that if a complaint involve[s] General Motors, US Steel or a company of that stature, with access to the White House, then Justice will back off." An-other EEOC official concurred that the agency was unlikely to recommend a suit against a holder of a government contract in order to avoid conflict with the Department of Labor's Office of Federal Contract Compliance.[115] In a confidential memo to his fellow commissioners, Graham explained, "We are not highly regarded by the civil rights organizations, we are not highly regarded by the other agencies of our government responsible for civil rights, we have so far maintained rather precarious confidence on the part of the state organizations, and we're not considered by the President in the front rank of those that he can call upon for expert advice on civil rights."[116] EEOC staffer Timothy Jenkins expressed similar concerns in a memo to the newly inaugurated chairman Stephen Shulman. "EEOC at present has the image of a listless, confused and conservative government agency" that "has been considered a nonentity by most of the business and labor community."[117]

While the EEOC grappled with these challenges, feminists came to see the agency's lack of action as deliberate neglect. On issues such as protective legislation, help-wanted advertising, and interpreting the BFOQ exception, recalled Hernandez, "the Commission was divided and specific guidelines were slow in coming, leaving many women with the impression that they could expect little from the Commission when it came to bold policy on job discrimination against women."[118] Congresswoman Martha W. Griffiths charged the EEOC commissioners with holding "a wholly negative attitude" toward Title VII's sex provision.[119] In the hopes of pressuring the EEOC to take action, a small but influential group convened in 1966 to form what members hoped would be "an NAACP for women": the National Organization for Women (NOW). Some of NOW's founders were veterans of the PCSW, although many of the most prominent PCSW members did not support the new group. The founders and early leaders of NOW included high-profile women in the academic, private, and public sectors. NOW's founding statement proposed "to take action to bring women into full participation in the mainstream of American society now, assuming all the privileges and responsibilities thereof in truly equal partnership with men."[120] Once NOW got up and running in mid-1966, it set out to expose and end what members perceived as the EEOC's intentional disregard of Title VII's sex discrimination provision.

NOW lobbied the EEOC and other government agencies to improve women's access to higher-paying jobs, equalize wages across the gendered divide, and desexualize feminized jobs. From within the EEOC, Sonia Pressman Fuentes and Aileen Hernandez accused their fellow staffers of downplaying the sex provision, and they both, along with Richard Graham, became founders of NOW.[121] Pressman Fuentes became a "double agent," attending nighttime meetings with other NOW founders and helping them frame their approach to the agency.[122] NOW's earliest victories included convincing President Lyndon Johnson to include women in an executive order requiring businesses holding public contracts to refrain from workplace discrimination and pressuring the EEOC to ban sex-segregated columns in newspaper advertisements. NOW also held public hearings that eventually compelled the EEOC to reject airline policies that restricted flight attendant work to young women.[123] As chapter 3 of this book reveals, internal feminist debates over the nature of workplace equality for women lasted into the mid-1970s, with some in NOW arguing that Title VII should encompass the kinds of local, substantive claims advanced by the early EEOC correspondents, and others seeking to advance women's status at work by redoubling feminist efforts to ratify the Equal Rights Amendment. But NOW's early campaigns to publicize the EEOC's relative inaction on sex discrimination undoubtedly bent the agency toward a more systemic approach to women's workplace issues.

As external pressures mounted, FDR Jr.'s successor began to make internal changes to the EEOC. As chairman, Stephen Shulman gave priority to rebranding the agency as a competent and productive authority on equal employment matters. Shulman himself was an energetic career bureaucrat and reformer. Prior to assuming the EEOC chairmanship, thirty-four-year-old Shulman had held six government jobs in seven years—most recently as an attorney in the Pentagon. "Mr. Shulman has characteristics that make him look something like a Robert McNamara for the civil rights field. Like the defense secretary, Mr. Shulman puts high priority on efficiency," explained a profile of Shulman in the *Wall Street Journal*. Shulman vowed to refocus the agency on "mak[ing] the EEOC felt by the nation's employers," the *Journal* reported.[124]

The key to boosting the EEOC's profile, according to Shulman, was to assume broad, industry-wide efforts—what he labeled a "wholesale approach"—rather than fielding individual claims. Without such a shift in priorities, Shuman estimated that the agency would need to hire one hundred more investigators, doubling its then-current number.[125] The EEOC lacked the resources for any staff increase at all. Shulman claimed, "With a budget our size, we've got to be a catalyst" to force antidiscrimination activism by other government agencies such as punitive action by the Department of Labor and the cancellation of Department of Defense contracts.[126] General Counsel Duncan agreed that eliminating the backlog required a systematic approach. Rather than processing cases in the order in which the EEOC received them, Duncan suggested, the agency should triage claims, giving preferential treatment to cases "which the commission has consciously determined to be the most significant." Thus, the EEOC could make targeted investigations that accounted for "the number of employees affected, the dollar volume of the employer's business, particular kinds of cases, such as seniority systems, patterns and practices of refusal to hire or promote, etc., charges filed against employers in particular industries, or any other categories deemed appropriate by the commission." This plan's drawback, he acknowledged, was that it "consign[ed] to limbo those cases which are given a low priority. The only answer to this is that at some point, hopefully, we will have a staff adequate to process all cases."[127]

EEOC chief of conciliations Alfred Blumrosen offered more specific suggestions for how the agency might narrow its efforts to become more efficient. Blumrosen proposed that the agency focus solely on three programs that were "tailored to the sociology and economics of the problems of discrimination": investigation, working with new plants, and gathering statistics. While investigating individual complaints remained worthwhile, he claimed, statistical studies of employers' workforce data had the potential to both ameliorate the discrimination facing many more individuals and to reduce the EEOC workload. "Sociological studies indicate that most victims of discrimination do not complain at all, and of those who do, only a handful go to the law or administrative agencies." Thus, statistical measurements could stand in for individual complaints in spurring the EEOC to action. In streamlining its approach, Blumrosen explained, the EEOC would resist "the temptation to proliferate programs to meet all aspects of the problems of discrimination. The problems of discrimination are so extensive and varied, and the possible approaches to these problems are so diverse, that there is a constant pull to dilute the energies of the commission."[128]

Shulman similarly viewed statistical analysis as a more productive approach. The EEOC already collected demographic information about workers and applicants from businesses subject to Title VII on an annual form, the EEO-1. Section 709 of Title VII authorized the agency to collect information from employers that was "reasonable, necessary and appropriate to enforcement of the Title." Introduced in the fall of 1965, the EEO-1 had two sections. The form first asked the reporting business to describe "the major activity of this reporting unit," such as "manufactures steel casings, retail grocer, wholesale plumbing supplies, title insurance, etc." The second section consisted of a table that listed occupations on one axis and race and sex on the other. The rows named nine occupational categories: officials and managers, professionals, technicians, sales workers, office and clerical, craftsmen, operatives, laborers, and service workers. The form had separate vertically divided tables for males and females, and within each sex category, across the top it listed the racial groups "Negro, Oriental, American Indian, Spanish American," as well as "total all employees," "total male employees," and "total female employees."[129] Making heavier use of this EEO-1 data would allow the EEOC to compare employers and entire industries and create categories by which to codify job differences, skill level, and attributes. A data-driven approach to Title VII also squared with Shulman's definition of discrimination, which he described as "the result of a system, not the result of any one specific act."[130] He explained, "It is not rash to estimate that EEO-1 will turn up many thousands of problem plants in all parts of the country with deficiencies running into many hundreds of thousands of minority employees," Shulman wrote. "This, then, is where the pay dirt is."[131]

Shulman's emphasis on unearthing Title VII's "pay dirt" reflected the pressure from above to streamline EEOC procedures and quantify its progress. While President Lyndon Johnson did not give the EEOC much guidance or many resources, he was eager to trumpet its achievements. An April 1967 memo to EEOC commissioner Shulman from the White House staff requested "short, succinct statements of accomplishments of the Administration" that Johnson could claim. For example, in December 1963, "2.5 million older people received hospital treatment under Medicare; the number of unemployed dropped by over a million people; more than 8 million disadvantaged children in 17,500 school districts were aided; more than 600,000 people received training in schools or on the job through Manpower Development and Training Act projects; net farm income rose more than 30 percent; more than 1.4 million people moved into new or existing low rent public housing." Johnson also requested that the statements be accompanied by "relevant statistical material showing areas of progress from December 1963 to the present, with net change and percentage change."[132] The Johnson administration sought powerful yet concise figures that could indicate the EEOC's strength.

To build such impressive figures, the EEOC began to take action on the statistics collected by the EEO-1 form using commissioner's charges. Rather than awaiting a complainant to accuse an employer of discrimination, commissioners could review EEO-1 data and serve as the plaintiffs on claims. The agency would then investigate the claim as though it had been launched by an aggrieved individual. Staff attorney Alfred Blumrosen described commissioner's charges as "fundamental to the successful use of the EEO-1 data."[133] In one such charge, Commissioner Samuel Jackson alleged simultaneous race and sex discrimination against the Graniteville Company of Graniteville, South Carolina. Jackson's justification for the charge began with the EEO-1 data: out of 1,052 female employees, only 3 percent were African American. Yet upon preliminary investigation, he discovered "that Negro women are generally hired for maid and other clean up jobs and denied production jobs or assigned production jobs on undesirable shifts" and "that the employer refuses to hire Negro women who are employed as domestics by employees of the employer without the consent of such employees." In addition, "the employer's EEO-1 report indicates that it employs 46 males and 94 females in office and clerical jobs, none of whom is Negro," and "out of 647 employees classified as craftsmen, only six, or one percent, were women."[134] The commissioner's charge allowed the EEOC to act on the data revealed by the EEO-1 form without a claim of discrimination from an aggrieved employee.

In order to root out entrenched patterns of segregation and unequal pay, the commission began to use the EEO-1 data and commissioners' charges to craft a systematic approach that could target specific industries or geographical areas. In 1967, EEOC researchers examined data from nine major American cities where women comprised between one-third and nearly one-half of the total white-collar workforce. When clerical jobs were excluded from the analysis, women's share of white-collar jobs dropped in half, and when the retail grade-general merchandise category of businesses was also excluded, women's proportion of white-collar jobs fell much further. Commission chairman Clifford Alexander argued that the data represented a smoking gun. "This study indicates that women are seriously underutilized in many top management and professional jobs."[135] The phrase "underutilization" reflected the new EEOC practice of comparing the proportion of female applications for a position with their representation among those hired. In this new scheme, sex equality and sex discrimination were detected by measuring women's representation in particular job categories.

As EEOC officials came to rely on statistics, they turned to computers. Shulman wrote to President Lyndon Johnson in April 1967, "The present manual system is patently inadequate to provide needed information. We are streamlining the process to reduce the backlog, and introducing computerization to satisfy information needs and increase cost effectiveness."[136] In a letter to U.S. representative Charles C. Diggs Jr., Shulman explained that new technologies would render the EEO-1 data easier to use. "We are preparing to computerize control over this process so that we can monitor it instantly and, for planning purposes, retrieve all cases in Commission history by geography, by industry, by type of complaint, and by such other breakdowns as may be indicated." Computers would help the commission to cut down on labor time. "We have contracted with the University of Pittsburgh to store every commission decision, every general counsel opinion, and every conciliation agreement in its computers at the health law center, for instant retrieval. This will enable us to print out subject matter books on the various facets of discrimination so that all precedents will be readily available."[137] With computers, Shulman stated, "the whole legal research job can be done in five minutes."[138] A January 1968 EEOC press release stated that computer analysis of the EEO-1 provided "the total employment picture for minority groups and women in companies with 100 or more employees."[139]

As the EEOC became increasingly adept at using computers to analyze EEO-1 forms, then filing commissioners' charges based on the data, the agency gained the attention and authority it had long sought. Officials began to aggressively pursue individual women's complaints only where they pointed to entrenched patterns of discrimination by major corporations. In 1972, EEOC introduced a "tracking system," which ranked companies for investigation according to their size, industry significance, and willingness to correct discriminatory policies. One track consisted of large businesses with national or large regional presence. Smaller employers would constitute the other track and would be more likely referred to private litigation.[140] Following from both the high number of women's complaints and EEO-1 data, the EEOC released a report calling American Telephone and Telegraph "without doubt the largest oppressor of women workers in the United States." The 290-page report analyzed the company's employment practices in thirty large urban areas across America. The EEOC alleged that AT&T's recruitment, hiring, and promotion practices had created a sex-segregated workplace. EEOC statisticians estimated that sex discrimination cost women at AT&T $950 million in wages each year. In 1972, AT&T buckled to EEOC pressure, agreeing to a settlement worth more than $50 million in back pay and promotions.[141]

Congress soon boosted the EEOC's enforcement power and budget. The Equal Employment Opportunity Act of 1972 gave the EEOC the authority to sue employers, unions, and employment agencies. Thus the EEOC itself could act as a plaintiff rather than convincing aggrieved plaintiffs or the Department of Justice to file suit. The law also expanded Title VII to include federal, state, and local governments, as well as educational institutions, and rendered employers with fifteen or more employees newly subject to Title VII.[142] The EEOC's annual budget more than tripled from $12 million to $42 million, and its staff grew from 250 to more than twenty-five hundred workers.[143]

Armed with computer-sorted EEO-1 data, investigations, and commissioner's charges, the EEOC continued to win major concessions from some of America's largest corporations. Building on the AT&T settlement, the EEOC established task forces to investigate four more of the nation's largest employers: General Electric; General Motors; Ford; and Sears, Roebuck. These investigations also targeted entire industries. In 1974, the EEOC filed suit against the nation's nine largest steel producers. Less than six months later, the parties promised to provide up to $20 million in back pay, desegregate seniority lines, and promote women and minorities to trade, craft, and supervisory jobs.[144] A 1978 settlement against General Electric provided nearly $30 million to minority and women workers. The EEOC repudiated the ABC classification system in meatpacking and rejected the old sex-specific state protective laws. Its new guidelines for Title VII's interpretation stated, "The principle of nondiscrimination requires that individuals be considered on the basis of individual capacities and not on the basis of any characteristics generally attributed to the group."[145] By the mid-1970s, the EEOC had become a powerful federal agency that understood sex discrimination in the same terms by which it had always conceived of race discrimination: unequal treatment and labor force segmentation for members of minority groups.

*   *   *

When the EEOC began its work in 1965, it was weak, underfunded, and overwhelmed. Confusion over the meaning of state-enforced sex equality contributed to the chaos of the EEOC's first few years as the agency struggled to gain legitimacy, articulate its purpose, and establish processes for investigating complaints. In the absence of a consensus definition of Title VII's sex provision, complainants offered a range of interpretations of its promise, and some within the EEOC began to customize sex equality on complainants' own terms. Yet there was an immediate and widening disjuncture between many women's experiences and understandings of discrimination—whose contours and remedies they defined for themselves—and the EEOC's statutory mandate to investigate discrimination occurring within certain demographic categories.

Within a decade, the EEOC gained conceptual mastery over sex discrimination, but this sharpness also limited its meaning. Working women's claims that were tailored to their circumstances and justified by their personal notions of fairness lost traction as the EEOC struggled to build its reputation as an effective agency. Faced with an enormous backlog of complaints, bureaucratic hurdles, and pressure from other government officials and increasingly powerful feminist groups, EEOC staff came to believe that defining sex discrimination as structural was the only way to systematically identify, categorize, and address it. This shift rendered the EEOC simultaneously more capable and less responsive. By narrowing and standardizing its definition of sex discrimination, the EEOC positioned itself to affect women's workplace conditions on a massive scale. But by defining sex equality as a statistically verifiable problem of access to and representation within job categories, the EEOC shaped the meaning of discrimination in ways that left many women's perceptions of their rights outside the new legal definition.

Court decisions also supported the EEOC's new treatment of sex discrimination as a quantifiable phenomenon characterized by language and patterns bureaucrats could observe, rather than experiences and expectations women relayed. The U.S. Supreme Court decision *Frontiero v. Richardson* held that institutions seeking to discriminate based on sex were subject to heightened scrutiny, making it more difficult for any distinctions between the sexes to retain legal legitimacy.[146] Three other federal court cases—*Bowe v. Colgate Palmolive, Diaz v. Pan Am*, and *Weeks v. Southern Bell*—overturned sex-based distinctions attached to job categories.[147] Further, in 1971, the U.S. Supreme Court ruled in *Griggs v. Duke Power Company* that employment policies that are neutral on the surface can be discriminatory if they adversely affect members of protected classes.[148] The disparate impact theory further bolstered the EEOC's use of statistics—comparing the race and gender composition of potential employees against the demographics of those chosen for employment or promotion—to identify discrimination. The U.S. Supreme Court framed statistical analysis as critical to employment discrimination law in the 1977 case *Teamsters v. United States*. The court agreed with the plaintiff union that quantitative data "showing racial or ethnic (or sexual) imbalance" often represented "telltale sign[s] of purposeful discrimination." The opinion noted that courts increasingly relied upon statistics as "the only available avenue of proof . . . to uncover clandestine and covert discrimination by the employer of union involved."[149]

In the decades that followed, women brought claims of discrimination to the EEOC—through workplace caucuses, feminist organizations, and labor unions, and as individuals. In those same years, activists fought to push such new theories as comparable worth, sexual harassment, and sexual orientation discrimination under Title VII's umbrella. Yet the fundamental EEOC definition of sex discrimination as a problem of inadequate representation and unequal treatment and effects assumed its permanent form in the early 1970s. And as women fought to marshal EEOC resources against their employers, they found that claiming Title VII's muscle required them to engage with legal and bureaucratic processes that were less and less inclined to address claims that invoked fairness rather than sameness. As the EEOC put the law of sex equality into action, defining and systematizing its approach, the commissioners bypassed many of those who best understood the nature of sex discrimination at work.

Chapter 2

Class and Class Action

Armed with Title VII and buoyed by a burgeoning grassroots movement, women in the late 1960s began to reframe long-standing workplace griev- ances as instances of sex discrimination. Across the American workforce, they bridged race and class divisions to identify common concerns, pressure their employers, and file class action lawsuits that challenged some of America's most prominent corporations—including Ford Motor Company, General Electric Corporation, American Telephone and Telegraph, and many more.[1]

Women offered particularly strong criticisms of their working conditions in journalism. In that field, men monopolized jobs with high pay, status, and responsibility while women provided supportive labor or were relegated to working on the women's section of the paper. Susan, one of two dozen re- searchers at *Reader's Digest* in 1972, explained that her job was crucial to her employers but disrespected and poorly paid because women typically per- formed it. Of her female coworkers, she explained, "only a handful have graduated into higher jobs and hope of escape is limited. . . . Men move on to be senior editors, but like the furniture, the women remain."[2] By contrast, while Betsy Wade was named the first woman copy editor at the *New York Times* in the mid-1960s, she came to realize that her sex delimited her wages and future prospects. She recalled, "Despite the fact that I was clearly doing a man's work, I wasn't going to get a man's pay or a man's job."[3] In Title VII's wake, such indignities convinced many women in journalism to define their interests against their employers', to describe their experiences as sex discrim- ination, and to feed their claims into the legal system. The *Times* was one of several significant early sites where these Title VII campaigns emerged.[4]

Newspapers encompassed a range of professional, blue-collar, and pink-collar jobs, and nearly all were sex-typed and sex-segregated. Most women at the *Times* were clustered in low-paid but critical supportive positions as researchers and secretaries. Other women who performed nominally sex-neutral jobs such as selling classified advertisements were tethered to their headsets, working long and inflexible shifts. By contrast, salesmen were encouraged to form personal relationships with the *Times'* high-profile clients—a mission that gave them more autonomy and required them to leave the office for social outings. Those women who became reporters or editors were typically confined to the women's pages, where they followed a parallel series of assignments in a section of the paper that allegedly reflected the distinct interests and capabilities of their sex. The few women who obtained male-dominated jobs faced pressure to downplay their sex coupled with extra scrutiny of their work and outright harassment. To address all of these problems, women began to organize against their employer, forming the New York Times Women's Caucus in the late 1960s. After a decade of consciousness-raising, strategizing, and building a class action lawsuit, the caucus convinced the *Times* to accept a $300,000 settlement and adopt plans to aggressively promote women to editorial and managerial positions in 1978.[5]

Through campaigns like the Timeswomen's, women who organized against their employers contributed to broader feminist efforts. In the 1960s and 1970s, individual workplaces were key sites where women challenged the sexist logic that framed men and women as distinct and unequal, although scholars have looked primarily to feminist and labor movement organizations to find women's workplace rights consciousness.[6] But labor unions waging a class-oriented struggle on behalf of a wide swath of workers and feminist groups pursuing a broad agenda could be out of sync with workers' own demands. Wade said of feminist challenges to the *Times'* employment and editorial policies in 1974, "The pickets and the NOW women, all of them energetic and well-meaning, sometimes run at cross purposes to the women who are trying to move the *Times* from the only possible point of effectiveness—within."[7] As Wade suggested, women's internal workplace organizing was by definition targeted and local. They drew from a personal and immediate rights consciousness, issuing tailored claims and leveraging preexisting relationships with supervisors and corporate leaders. Their workplace caucuses lacked the legal status of labor unions, but such informal groups commanded employers' attention as they became increasingly adept at leveraging Title VII. These women won some of the era's highest-profile feminist victories even if they did not always believe they were acting as emissaries of that movement.

Despite these advantages, the Timeswomen's campaign shifted and narrowed over time, leaving behind some early aspirations and the expansive notions of sex equality that underpinned them. Caucus leaders initially built a campaign designed to draw strength from its numbers. They emphasized gender solidarity and downplayed class differences in order to build a legal class of as many of the *Times*' women workers as possible. Stretching their agenda to fit their many grievances, the caucus accused the *Times* of a wide range of violations against white-, pink-, and blue-collar workers. Yet the caucus changed course when faced with significant obstacles. Its leaders struggled to build their campaign amid a parallel movement by minority workers that seemed to sap *Times*' executives' attention and potential members from their ranks. They also met resistance from a labor union reluctant to give priority to their concerns and company officials who dug in their heels. The range of claims aggrieved women offered also posed a challenge. Reasoning from their own experiences, Times women expressed divergent understandings of sex equality. Some argued that Title VII's benefits would radiate outward from a diverse and flexible campaign that was attuned to a wide range of women's grievances. They interpreted Title VII's promise as both putting the sexes on an equal footing and making all jobs better. Others emphasized the first half of this agenda. They claimed that the fruits of new sex equality laws would trickle down through efforts to weaken sexist stigmas and erode barriers to women's upward mobility. Appealing to their common sex allowed women to claim Title VII's protections, but their varied notions of workplace justice threatened to divide them.

The caucus resolved these tensions through its efforts to harness Title VII's potential, as the women navigated a legal system that was already more attuned to Title VII claims based on interchangeability rather than accommodation. The group's leaders came to believe that both their best legal strategy and the challenges the plaintiffs would face at trial required them to emphasize the claims of the professionals among them—those women whose impeccable skills and reputations made the strongest case that their sex was their only disadvantage. In the end, the Timeswomen declared their settlement a total victory, but its substance fell far short of their initial demands. While the token annuities and affirmative action targets at the settlement's core would enable middle-class women to make significant gains, the agreement did not force the *Times* to restructure its business practices or to improve the conditions of work for women beyond the professional sphere. Far from a vindication of women's initial grievances, then, the settlement reflected the actions and agendas of the specific workers, activists, and attorneys who pursued a win amid formidable challenges.

As perfecting affirmative action and equal pay practices became cemented as the route to sex equality, working-class women's remaining concerns—sex segregation, inflexibility, low pink-collar pay, intersectional race and sex discrimination, and more—came to be overshadowed by the struggles and successes of women who entered male-dominated spheres of work. Thus, while lawsuits like the Timeswomen's provided the new workplace rights feminism with some of its most significant victories, those lawsuits also yielded the greatest benefit to more elite women while sacrificing more complex sex discrimination claims that were inflected with class- and race-based concerns. As some women capitalized on Title VII settlements by moving up into jobs that had once been reserved for men, those who stayed behind to perform feminized work were vulnerable once again to the presumption that they belonged there.

*   *   *

Women made their first significant inroads into journalism in the late nineteenth century, when newspapers across the country began to create women's pages designed to draw an audience for advertisers marketing to female consumers. The women's section was distinct. It contained different content, such as social events, fashion, home economy, and advice columns; it was written in a sentimental style that was unlike the objective, austere prose in the rest of the newspaper; and it represented women's first meaningful opportunities for employment in journalism.[8] To newspaper editors, readers of the women's section sought content of their own—and might not even glance at the rest of the paper. Marie Burke, editor of the women's department of the *New York Daily News*, explained that the female reader "prefers a happy blend of features that keep her apace with the times, and articles about love, etiquette, and other subjects that have withstood the test of time."[9] In the 1880s, 288 of more than twelve thousand journalists nationwide were women; twenty years later, that number had risen to 2,193 women out of thirty thousand journalists. This trend reflected the dramatic growth in newspaper readership, to which women were substantial contributors in the early twentieth century.[10] In those same years, the clerical labor force expanded throughout the American economy, and women were increasingly tapped to fill supportive office jobs.[11] While women's representation on newspaper staffs increased steadily until the mid-twentieth century, their relegation to clerical roles and the women's pages was constant, albeit with a temporary softening of these rigid gender norms during World War II.[12]

At the *New York Times*, considered by many to be the standard-bearer for the nation's newspaper industry, most women found it impossible to obtain a job that was not sex-typed for them.[13] The *Times* cultivated a reputation for deference to tradition and thorough coverage of serious news. A 1961 article in *Time* described the newspaper as "play[ing] ball in a journalistic major league all its own."[14] Yet the *Times*' women workers did not share the view that their employer deserved full-throated praise. Grace Glueck was a graduate of New York University and had edited that university's literary magazine before she obtained a secretarial job at the *Times* in 1951. After a few years she secured a position as a picture researcher in the book review section—a female-dominated job. For a decade, her efforts to move out of that position into one where she could write were met with suggestions that she placate herself by getting married instead, or that she do "something special" to ingratiate herself to the men who might promote her.[15] Nancy Davis was in her mid-twenties when she first gained employment at the *Times* in 1972. A native of small-town Ohio, Davis married a jazz musician and moved to New York City to pursue a career in acting. After a few years, she changed plans, and she held a variety of temporary office jobs before securing what she considered to be her "first real job" in the *Times*' classified advertising sales department. Davis's initial elation quickly dissipated as she discovered the sex hierarchy that structured her department. In an open room of tables and telephones, closely supervised women made call after call to solicit classified advertisers. Davis noticed that the few men who entered classified sales in that "inside," female-dominated role were promoted to "outside" sales in a matter of months. There, they had more flexibility, higher-profile clients, meal allowances, and the opportunity to earn commissions.[16] Davis recalled that many of her older coworkers had held their positions for decades, having abandoned efforts for outside sales jobs or to lessen the oppressive elements of their jobs. "Some of them were so discouraged they stopped trying."[17] Pink-collar women at the *Times* struggled to improve the terms of their labor and to cross into male-dominated jobs.

A few women managed to breach the wall dividing men's and women's work at the *Times*, and they found that they were treated as outsiders on the other side. Betsy Wade, who became one of the three highest-ranking women at the *Times* and one of the organizers of the Women's Caucus and the lawsuit, had distinguished herself as an undergraduate at Barnard College and earned a graduate degree in journalism from Columbia University in 1952. Yet she learned that her abilities in the classroom did not translate into professional opportunities. Her instructors treated her more as a curiosity than a serious pupil. "I was their most able student," she recalled. "But this was clearly of no use because it was like, you know, a dog that stood on its back legs and talked. It was an interesting exercise but of what practical use can this thing be?"[18] Wade found a temporary job at the *New York Herald Tribune*, but she was fired when she became pregnant. Several years later, she was hired by the *New York Times* as one of seventy-five copywriters and the first woman in the position.[19] In an effort to blend in, she downplayed her sex as much as possible. She cut her hair and purchased new, less feminine clothing, which surprised department store sales staff. Wade recalled wondering, "how does one ask the lady at Saks: 'Please, a suit in which I can sit in the middle of an ocean of men and not be noticed?'" To mark her arrival, Wade's coworkers removed the cuspidors and fastened a lace petticoat to her paste pot.[20] Wade coped with these indignities, hoping that the quality of her work would deflect attention from her sex.

Another Women's Caucus member and *Times* lawsuit plaintiff, Eileen Shanahan, was a similarly accomplished journalist who attempted to advance her career by blending in with men. Shanahan was an editor of the student newspaper as an undergraduate at George Washington University. She got an entry-level job at United Press, where she was mentored by Walter Cronkite, and she became interested in writing about economics when she covered price controls during the Korean War. In 1962, Shanahan left a job as the highest-ranking woman at the U.S. Treasury Department in order to work as an economics reporter for the Washington Bureau of the *New York Times*.[21] Like Wade, Shanahan hoped that the *Times* would operate as a meritocracy; while her gender would not afford her special favors, neither would it hold her back. She recalled, "I always had a sense of myself as a smart person—and not a smart girl or a smart woman, a smart person."[22] Shanahan distinguished herself at the *Times*, writing dozens of front-page stories on topics related to complex matters of economic policy. Yet she was never promoted to an editorial position, and she suspected that her sex was to blame.[23]

None of these women initially advocated a broad feminist agenda, but each came to realize that her sex marked her as different and that the feminist objective of dismantling fixed sex roles at work could also benefit her. Professional and pink-collar women diverged in their ability to advocate for themselves, however. Shanahan and Wade knew that expressing too much interest in women's issues threatened their tenuous positions as women in male-typed jobs. Shanahan struck a careful balance between her coverage of the women's movement and her economics writing. She explained, "I was respected and valued in my regular role in economics. And what I feared, to the point of never suggesting it, was that if I had become full-time the national status-of-women beat reporter that within six months I would have lost all that respect because I was no longer covering stuff the power structure cared about."[24] Wade recalled, "You practically had to go in and take an oath that you didn't believe in the women's movement in order to cover the women's movement."[25] While Wade and Shanahan attempted to downplay their sex and their interest in women's issues in order to protect their professional credentials, workers in female-typed jobs like Glueck and Davis did not have the option to try to blend in with men. After a decade of deflection and harassment, Glueck's repeated efforts to become a reporter were rewarded in 1963, when she was offered a weekly art column. By contrast, Davis applied nine times for an outside classified sales job within her first two years at the *Times*. All that her efforts gained her was a reputation as "a pushy, uppity young woman."[26]

In response to these struggles, professional and pink-collar women alike came to challenge the *Times*' employment practices. They began by voicing their individual concerns about women's plight directly to their superiors and meeting in small groups. In July 1969, Glueck wrote a memo to the publisher, Arthur Ochs Sulzberger, to document the company's failure to place women in powerful positions. He promised to discuss her concerns with "key management executives" but never responded further. Glueck and Wade began to informally solicit complaints from the women in their departments, and they convened a gathering of like-minded female coworkers. In February 1972, a group of nine professional women from editorial departments went out to lunch at an out-of-the-way restaurant above Times Square. "It was just us chicks from the newsroom," Glueck recalled, and they compared experiences and shared stories. They also vowed to talk to other women and began "to poke around, sort of, three or four of us in unison, to lift up the corners and see what dust was under the rug. And we found incredible situations."[27] Wade asked one of her supervisors why she had never been promoted. He replied, "When I was looking for an assistant foreign editor I looked right through you; I didn't even see you."[28] In the sports department, they found a single female employee: a secretary who wrote articles on women's sports for the *Times* on her days off but was never paid or addressed as a reporter.[29] The women combed Newspaper Guild data and found sex discrepancies in hiring practices and recruitment, as well as differences between maternity and sick leave policies. Analysis of salary data revealed that the average wage of the eighty-eight men in one area of the paper was $59 a week higher than the average pay of the twenty-six women who worked alongside them.[30]

Armed with this statistical and anecdotal information, the nine women who had met for lunch wrote a letter to their approximately six hundred female coworkers in February 1972. In it, they called for "a company-wide movement" to "improve things in all departments." They laid out their predicament and their options. "The situation is basically unfair to us and federal law gives us a right to complain and have the situation changed." But they also reasoned that women's increased presence would improve the paper, for example, "if more news events were described from a women's perspective as well as a man's, . . . if more news of women of importance to women were included, and if more women were involved in management decisions." They cited unequal pay and the lack of promotion, recruitment, and training opportunities.[31] Small group discussions and meetings yielded a larger gathering the next month. About sixty women from all job levels and various departments attended. They labeled themselves the New York Times Women's Caucus, and they rented a locked office in the *Times* building where they could store documents and receive mail. Attendees were asked to indicate their concerns and priorities, to provide lists of women in their departments, and to contribute $3 in dues toward the office rent.[32]

As they built their campaign, caucus leaders sought to recruit as many women from as many departments as possible. They advertised widely, published a newsletter, and held frequent meetings in order to field grievances and strategize. The caucus took advantage of its members' common sex by posting notices on the backs of the doors in the toilet stalls and on the mirrors in the women's restroom. Wade and reporter Joan Cook divided the names on the list of women at the *Times*, calling several at a time during their breaks. They also became close friends, talking about their families and sharing tips for balancing workplace and domestic pressures. To keep track of members and recruits, Wade created a method of tracking every woman employed at the *Times* using index cards. Cards were color-coded based on the woman's level of participation in the caucus. "If a woman came to any meeting at all, she got another color card. If a woman sent any money, she got another color card. If a woman could be relied upon to turn out at nine o'clock at night to stuff a batch of envelopes, she got another color card." Wade recalled changing and occasionally forgetting the code, but she preferred to be secretive than to be infiltrated by management.[33] For recruitment, leaders relied on the free time and perseverance of caucus members. Members divided lists of dozens of names of women, parceled them into groups of five, and distributed them out to members to make cold calls. The meeting attendance varied from more than one hundred to fewer than ten participants. Wade recalled, "We had a very amorphous group, constantly changing people."[34]

The caucus leaders were primarily women with professional skills and aspirations. Most of them shared the grievances reporter Edith Evans Asbury described in a 1973 caucus meeting, where she decried "the penalties she has paid simply for being a woman."[35] Yet the group also attracted more working-class women, including "classified saleswomen, data processors and clerks," recalled Glueck.[36] These women brought to the caucus a different set of concerns. Elizabeth Moody, an administrative secretary in the editorial department, encouraged the caucus to pressure the *Times* to differentiate among secretaries. Moody had worked for the *Times* for more than a decade. She objected to the fact that the title of secretary had become "a catch-all— for the girl just out of high school to the extremely valuable and experienced woman who handles so much for her boss." Moody suggested one potential caucus goal: "if a secretary works for a top man in the company and proves her ability in the post, she should automatically become a 'staff asst.,'" differentiating among workers in feminized jobs and allowing some to escape the stigma associated with the title of secretary.[37] Laurie Johnston, who worked in the news department, urged the caucus to advocate for more than the equalization of the sexes. She urged caucus leaders to "keep an eye toward a more flexible and imaginative use of women AND men, according to their individual strengths, specialties, contacts, life-styles and other disparate contributions"—including finding ways to accommodate the fact that women more often than men required flexible work arrangements and assistance in balancing their domestic and professional commitments.[38]

Other women in feminized jobs asked the caucus to help stem the tide of unwanted changes in their working conditions. Office administrator Louise McKellip explained that her manager had intensified the pace and content of her job without her consent, as workers she formerly supervised were dismissed or promoted and not replaced. "I now do much of the work myself which I had formerly been able to delegate—now there is no one to delegate it to," she claimed.[39] McKellip also described how her boss changed her work assignments arbitrarily and with no warning, replacing more enjoyable work with less interesting tasks. In addition, her work environment had deteriorated. "I had formerly shared an office (and work load) with one other secretary. Now I have been put in a 'general office' where there is constant noise and distraction, and where I have become a receptionist, office clerk, telephone answerer and a general depositary for various odds and ends which no one knows what to do with."[40] McKellip did not look to exit supportive office work; rather, she wanted to improve the terms of her job. Many pink-collar women who sought the caucus's assistance hoped that the group would advocate for gains that went beyond helping professional women to work alongside of men.

Some caucus leaders envisioned the group as an advocate for all the women at the *Times*. They believed that cross-class activism and high numbers of members would lend legitimacy to their cause. Wade's status as a union steward convinced her that the women who were furthest from the levers of power needed the most help and would have strong rights claims that would bolster those of more elite women. She also believed that the caucus's power would be proportional to its size. In a presentation at a 1972 caucus meeting, Glueck encouraged members to work on behalf of all their female coworkers, "from copy girls and stenographers to those who hold managerial jobs. Because, make no mistake about it, we're all discriminated against."[41] In a March 1973 meeting, caucus leaders were pleased that women "from all job levels . . . representing a large number of departments" were in attendance. They vowed to examine their own departments for "patterns of discrimination—salary, job classification, promotion, hiring—with an eye toward remedy."[42] Wade argued that building the caucus's class and racial diversity would be key to meeting their goals. The caucus made numerous attempts to contact women of the building services staff, but they found only a few moderately willing participants.[43] And when African American caucus member Barbara Campbell offered to assume a leadership role, at least two white women offered to give up their own seats on her behalf.[44] Wade believed that including women from outside the professional class would demonstrate the scope of the *Times'* objectionable practices and would improve working conditions for all women there—even the most elite.

Caucus leaders like Wade and Glueck envisioned the group as a flexible advocate for all Timeswomen. They used the newsletter to spotlight the different forms of sexism that plagued the company. A 1975 newsletter described advertising sales at the *Times* to be "a glaring example of a sex-segregated department." The article claimed that a caucus count revealed that women made up 15 percent of outside sales and 85 percent of telephone solicitors, and women were rarely given the chance to break out of telephone sales work. The wage difference between the positions was at least $111 per week. The article also described the roadblocks faced by women who did not want to be promoted to outside sales, but sought higher pay for inside sales. One woman who asked for a merit raise was denied because "everyone would want one."[45] Wade described eroding the "historic confinement of women in the classified ad department" as "hard work every inch of the way."[46] Wade and the caucus also intervened on behalf of women who lost their jobs, even when the Newspaper Guild avoided becoming involved.[47] The caucus monitored individual women's promotions and successes.[48] Caucus leaders also devised creative solutions to working women's problems. For example, a 1973 caucus newsletter suggested that perhaps some male-dominated jobs could be "broken into two part-time jobs" to make them more plausible for women.[49] Reasoning that "strength reposes in the whole group," they sought to build their campaign by addressing the diverse needs of all Timeswomen.[50]

Yet women's shared status could seem a weak binding agent in light of the differences among the *Times'* six hundred female employees. At the first lunch meeting, one attendee attempted to build group unity by discussing their mutual concerns as reporters. When Wade identified herself as an editor, "it was as if I had come in and said, 'No, actually I'm a plumber.' They didn't want to be reminded of that. And a lot of reporters . . . found editors to be oppressive, awful, obnoxious, stupid, [and] uncreative."[51] Wade also found that many professional women rejected her assertion that their fate was bound up with their working-class sisters'. She recalled "a lot of elitism": "I think there was a great deal of hostility to women who had come in as secretaries and who had not gotten out of it, almost as if this was a choice that they made that they couldn't get out of it." Wade explained that many professional women feared that they would cast doubt on their own abilities by emphasizing their similarities with less accomplished women. Wade summarized their attitude: "We've made it. Why are we going to damage ourselves by affiliating with these people who can't make it?"[52] Wade explained that many of these women saw the caucus as a vehicle to help them improve their lot as individuals. She often felt that she was "pushing people who would defect if given one good assignment for one day."[53] These tensions reflected their divergent perspectives of the caucus's purpose: to change the system, or to help the most talented women to advance within it.

Despite Wade's efforts to recruit women from throughout the *Times* and to advocate a broad conception of the harms women workers experienced there, most caucus members were white and held professional aspirations. Wade labored to convince them to broadly define their own interests. A 1975 *Times* editorial on the United Nations World Conference on Women chided the women in privileged nations who waged high-pitched battles for higher pay and better job opportunities. By contrast, the editorial lectured, women in poor nations "have no hope even for equal food, medical care or education. The issue is not status but survival." The editorial acknowledged that single mothers in America faced similar economic challenges; they "struggl[ed] with the breakdown of social institutions and the need to raise a family on unequal pay and under covert discrimination." The piece declared those problems to be legitimate by contrast to the demands of "the over-privileged few who worry about specialized forms of sexual liberation and exalted executive expectations."[54] The caucus fielded the angry responses of Timeswomen and printed them in the caucus newsletter. One woman asked, "If men, or minorities, were under discussion, would the *Times* use such language? No. The *Times* would undoubtedly refer to 'legitimate aspirations' and imply a necessity to bow before the momentum of upward mobility."[55] The caucus leaders' focus on creating opportunities for women's upward mobility increasingly shaped the group's agenda.

While caucus members did not participate in formal feminist organizing, they benefited from the nationwide pressure feminists exerted on the media from the outside. In 1970, the radical feminist periodical *off our backs* declared that "'sexism' in the newspaper industry" permeated newsrooms and was reflected in news coverage. The story spotlighted the *New York Times* for being "well known for its male chauvinism."[56] Feminists sought media coverage for women's issues that critically analyzed women's subordinate status in the law and society, as well as accurate coverage of their movement.[57] Gloria Steinem told a gathering of the American Newspaper Publishers Association (ANPA) in 1973, "If I believed what I read about the women's movement in the press, I'd have nothing to do with it. If I believed what I read about myself in the press, I'd have little to do with me."[58] Steinem launched *Ms.*, which became a crucial platform for feminist writing and activism, in 1972. Feminists also lobbied the EEOC to desegregate classified employment advertisements, a goal they achieved over the objections of the ANPA. In 1974, NOW issued a nationwide call to feminists to comb their local newspapers for evidence of sexism and to confront their publishers; to replace references to women's marital status with "Ms."; and to stop referring to adult women as "girls."[59] Feminists sought to reform the media both in terms of women's employment opportunities and the media's portrayals of women.

The caucus did not reach out to feminist groups. Instead, members sought support from within the *Times*. Many saw their union, the Newspaper Guild of New York (NGNY), as a potential ally. From its founding in 1933, the guild had espoused equal pay for equal work and the elimination of sex and race discrimination in hiring and promotion.[60] In 1946, NGNY required that all new contracts contain guarantees against race and sex discrimination.[61] At a 1970 women's rights conference sponsored by the American Newspaper Guild, rhetoric and objectives were inflected with feminist terminology. Attendees linked women's exploitation as workers and as females. They proposed two years of partially paid maternity leave, better health insurance and coverage for abortion, childcare centers, and workers' right to collaborate with management in crafting their job descriptions.[62] At the *Times*, however, NGNY resisted Wade's attempts to compel it to advocate for women more strenuously.[63] Wade encountered "yawns and outright rudeness" from NGNY men when she sought their support for improved maternity leave policies at the *Times*. Wade mused, "Men seem to think that women have babies by themselves and for themselves, mainly to irritate their fellow workers."[64] Guild leaders proved unwilling to assist the Women's Caucus, viewing the problems facing minority workers as a higher priority.[65] She recalled getting "the runaround" each time she asked an NGNY representative to come to a caucus meeting. Wade suspected this was because leaders "want to lump together women and minorities—which is just the argument the *Times* keeps giving us: we must stand in line and take our turn."[66] The guild provided personnel data and office support, but no formal support to the women.[67]

As the caucus began to organize, racial minorities' simultaneous activism at the *Times* proved a double-edged sword for women. While it provided an obvious example to follow, it also seemed to monopolize the guild's resources and attract women of color who might have joined the Women's Caucus instead. African American, Latino, and Asian American workers at the *Times* shared women's experiences of segregation and unequal treatment. Many white-owned newspapers limited news about African Americans to a separate area of the paper and restricted what few African Americans they hired to covering news about their own community. A 1961 survey found that the *Times'* news department had one black copy editor and two black reporters.[68] Asian Americans were similarly marginalized. Morgan Jin was a Chinese American World War II veteran who began working as an administrative supervisor at the *Times* in 1967. For five years, he applied for promotions and eventually lost his job when his department was restructured. At the *Times'* 1973 stockholder meeting, Jin accused the company of hypocrisy for claiming to be an equal opportunity employer "when it has on its staff hundreds of blacks and other minority groups pushing mops and brooms, and proclaim[ing] to the world that its responsibility is being fulfilled."[69] Jin filed discrimination charges with the New York State Human Rights Division, then began to recruit other Asian, black, and Latino workers to form the Minority Caucus.[70] The guild gave financial assistance to the suit and eventually became a named plaintiff itself—support it denied to the Women's Caucus. Further, two of the four named plaintiffs in the minority lawsuit were women in pink-collar jobs, a group the Women's Caucus struggled to recruit as their suit approached trial.[71] While these campaigns shared a common target and used similar tactics, they progressed on parallel tracks. Thus, while the wider feminist movement and internal minority rights activism reinforced the Timeswomen's convictions, their lack of strong allies at the *Times* convinced them to focus their energy inward.

*   *   *

Several months after the Women's Caucus formed, the group began to bring its concerns to *Times'* management. The evidence they put forth and the tactics they deployed demonstrate that women's upward mobility was the centerpiece of their agenda. In a May 1972 letter to *Times* executives, the women expressed concern that while "the voices of women are being heard in greater number today in this country, [a]t the *Times*, we note little change in the basic situation of women." In particular, explained the letter, women at the *Times* did not "reach positions in the vital decision-making areas of the paper." They used visual evidence to support their contention. "We call your attention to the 21 names on the masthead—both editorial and business executives. Not one is a woman."[72] The women also suggested that sex equality would require more opportunities for women to work in male-dominated areas of employment. Their letter pointed out the inequity in the sex ratio of reporters—forty women to 385 men—especially taking into account that eleven of the forty women were in the female-dominated family and style department. The women urged their employer to adopt a strong affirmative action program that would make "full use of the talents and training of the women already employed in the news, Sunday and editorial departments." In a nod to the caucus's pink-collar members, the letter also drew the attention of *Times*' management to the gendered pay discrepancy across all employment categories. The caucus asked for specific goals and timetables, as well as a face-to-face meeting with management.[73] To lend credibility to their cause, the caucus recruited the signatures of fifty-two of the most respected women reporters, editors, and critics at the paper.

The caucus's initial approach of pointing out inequities and asking that they be remedied seemed to make an impact. Sulzberger met with representatives of the group later that month and acknowledged the grievances expressed in the women's letter, but he also explained that delivering solutions would be difficult. "Our problem is not in finding qualified women—we have no shortage of qualified women—our problem is finding the openings for qualified women, or qualified men for that matter." He also explained, "We've got to make a deliberate effort to find blacks to fill the openings. So it's going to be a balancing act."[74] Yet Sulzberger seemed concerned, and he promised to inform the Women's Caucus of job openings in male-dominated positions.[75] Economics reporter Eileen Shanahan left the meeting optimistic. "I came out of it just bubbling over, 'Oh, they're going to fix it, they're going to fix it, everything's going to be wonderful.' And I really felt that way."[76] Caucus members hoped that they would be able to persuade their employer to take action before they were forced to resort to more confrontational tactics. "In the beginning, even as a group, we had on our white gloves and party manners," recalled Glueck.[77]

Within several months, the caucus members' initial hopes of avoiding more adversarial measures faded when they saw little change occur. In a

November 1972 meeting, caucus members assumed a more militant stance. "Unless something positive comes out of this meeting, we shall no longer consider our actions a private matter between us and the *Times*," they reasoned.[78] They observed that in the six months since the initial meeting, progress had been slow or nonexistent. Pay equalizations had lagged; the $59 wage differential between men's and women's salaries in the newsroom had only been reduced to $54. Women had received no new job opportunities in male-dominated departments, and management had not kept its promise to apprise the Women's Caucus of new job openings.[79] Following the meeting, Sulzberger circulated a memo that seemed to indicate his intention to meet the caucus's demands. He claimed, "We must have equal pay for equal work, full use of the talents and training of women employed at the *Times*, initiatives in hiring greater proportions of women, especially in positions where women are now excluded, and training opportunities that will allow women to attain jobs of greater responsibility, including the most responsible."[80] Yet the memo did not outline specific steps, and caucus members did not notice any changes in its wake. By early 1973, they began investigating how to take legal action against the *Times*.

The caucus joined a nationwide movement of women journalists challenging their employers under Title VII. Some such women took action as individuals. For example, in 1969, sports reporter Elinor Kaine sued Yale University for entrance to the press box in order to cover an exhibition game between the New York Jets and the New York Giants for her syndicated column, "Football and the Single Girl." Yale appealed to tradition and the unenclosed rest rooms of the press box in denying her entrance.[81] Other women filed class action lawsuits on behalf of all similarly situated women in their workplaces—a tactic made more accessible by recent changes to the federal guidelines for civil class actions.[82] These newswomen filed class action lawsuits against some of the most high-profile media outlets in the country. Women at *Reader's Digest* filed such charges in 1972. They protested being restricted to sex-segregated menial jobs. They also described being forced to work overtime, having to ask a male supervisor for bathroom privileges, and not being allowed to wear pants where men could wear blue jeans. One plaintiff said of her position as researcher, "You would think the job would be held in high regard and such things as equal pay for equal work would be natural . . . but nothing is farther from the truth." Invoking racial segregation and exploitation, she described *Reader's Digest* as "the northern-most plantation in America."[83] Similarly, in 1974, forty female employees of *Newsday* filed EEOC charges for promotion into professional jobs, back pay, equal story assignments, and equal benefits. Management responded that nearly one-quarter of its staff members were women, but the women claimed they had never seen evidence supporting this statistic.[84] The suit was settled in 1981 with both sides declaring victory. The settlement resulted in $130,300 being paid to women, strengthened goals for women's hiring and promotion, and *Newsday*'s assumption of the women's legal fees.[85] In the late 1970s and early 1980s, women reached similar settlements with NBC, Reuters, the *Washington Post*, and the Associated Press.[86]

Media women also used extralegal strategies to gain power and authority in their field. In 1974, women journalists protested their exclusion from Washington D.C.'s Gridiron Club and its annual dinner by staging a "counter-gridiron" in the gymnasium of a nearby women's college the same night. While 450 attendees were expected at the white-tie gridiron dinner, the counter-gridiron attracted 800 guests, featured free beer and carnival booths, and raised thousands of dollars to benefit a legal defense fund for reporters who were jailed for refusing to reveal their sources.[87] At a 1974 luncheon of women journalists in Boston, Pat Carbine, the publisher of *Ms.* magazine, encouraged attendees to be more like men by enacting "that wonderful 'male' trait called aggression. We must come together in an organized way and assert our human and professional rights. We must use the tool of journalism to influence our culture and contribute to our culture right now."[88] Further, even events that had initially emerged to celebrate women's uniqueness evolved to become sites to strategize women's integration. Starting in 1960, the department store J. C. Penney and the University of Missouri sponsored an annual award and conference celebrating newspaperwomen in women's pages and fashion reporting.[89] At the 1970 gathering, attendees suggested reorienting the women's pages as a tool of feminist movement building. Marie Anderson of the *Miami Herald* described the fluffy content of women's news as "what we have been giving women for years," and therefore, it was "all they think they are entitled to." She explained that the women's news section could also broadcast a feminist message. "I have exposed women in my community to the woman problem and they are aware of it. This, too, is your responsibility."[90] By the early 1970s, women journalists had taken up a range of strategies to pressure their employers for more pay, respect, and promotions.

Women at the *New York Times* joined this wave of activism. They abandoned the tactics of informal persuasion in favor of state-enforced pressure when they began meeting with attorney and law professor Harriet Rabb in

January 1973.[91] Rabb had an impressive résumé. Although she was only thirty-one years old, Rabb had won victories for women at *Newsweek*, New York Telephone, and other major New York City employers.[92] Rabb was also the director of the Columbia Law School Employment Rights Project. She thus had access to federal funding and eager law students who could assist caucus leaders in gathering information. To prepare women workers' challenge to the *Times*, Rabb and her team analyzed the data about pay and sex segregation the caucus had collected from the guild, prepared reports to present to state and federal employment rights agencies, and helped workers to file individual charges with the EEOC.[93] Using her battle-tested methods, Rabb began to help the Timeswomen to lay the groundwork for a class action lawsuit.

The Timeswomen found that the movement-building tactics they had already developed—in particular, discussing, collecting and registering their concerns, and designating women in different areas of the paper to persuade and recruit coworkers they already knew—were easily adapted to the early stages of developing a class action. Caucus leaders designated one woman in each department to counsel her female coworkers about the benefits and procedures of filing formal sex discrimination complaints with enforcement agencies.[94] For women who did not feel comfortable discussing the lawsuit at work, these organizers also mailed EEOC complaint forms and prepaid, preaddressed envelopes to the New York City EEOC field office. Rabb instructed the organizers to distribute the complaint forms widely; Wade relayed her advice that "the more forms from the more departments, the better." This reflected Rabb's conviction that a high volume of complaints would bolster their allegations that systemic sex discrimination defined the *New York Times*' employment practices.[95]

The Timeswomen responded to the caucus's call. Secretary Eileen Butler described her inability to escape pink-collar work. She wrote, "To my knowledge, the *New York Times* has no affirmative action programs or development system in which women could move from, say, traditional secretarial jobs to professional jobs. There are no training programs and little encouragement in this area." Classified sales representative Elizabeth Flynn wrote that less qualified men were promoted over her. "In my some twenty years of employment here I have watched this practice of discrimination proliferate with the steady procession of men entering the classified advertising dept. working briefly as telephone solicitors and proceeding to advertising salesmen with some succeeding to positions to management." Janitor Catherine

Stevens objected to unequal pay practices. "We as cleaning women, for instance, do the same work as many of the porters. But the porters get paid more money than we do for what they do."[96] Betsy Wade recalled her elation when Stevens submitted her complaint. "My heart just leaped up because then I knew that any judge or arbitrator or anybody who looked at that could not say, 'this is a bunch of elitist women. What are they complaining about?'"[97] Wade believed that this diversity would strengthen the women's suit.

While Wade solicited complaints from a range of Timeswomen, other professionals had not anticipated that women in supportive office jobs would want to join. The caucus mailed an envelope of sex discrimination survey forms to the caucus members in the Washington, D.C., bureau. Shanahan distributed them and was surprised when the secretary to the bureau chief emeritus requested a form. "Laura Walz was one of the most thoroughly courteous and proper people I've ever known," recalled Shanahan, but her complaint form "came back filled out in first-class, eloquent English about what kind of work she did and what her researcher duties were and how she was paid as a secretary and accorded no standing, no respect, and in particular, no money." Shanahan reflected that women like Walz "probably suffered more than the professional women did."[98] Building the suit exposed some Timeswomen to the unexpected range of grievances their coworkers harbored. Within six months, eighty-four women had filed complaints. This group included the dance critic, fashion editor, antiques columnist, and the secretaries of the news editor and the managing editor.[99]

Yet the caucus came to identify recruiting high-profile complainants as the best way to convince the corporation to buckle. Leaders gave priority to gathering their claims and projecting their concerns. Wade recalled that recruiting Shanahan to the case was itself a victory. She "had credentials that were going to survive any amount of bloodshed in this lawsuit. She was the kind of person where they said, 'Eileen, we can't answer that question. What is the answer?' The sort of person who really was pre-eminent in her field."[100] Wade recalled anticipating that the *Times* would reference her relatively high salary as evidence that she did not face discrimination. She claimed, "For that kind of work, you should be paid lots of money. And if I was paid lots of money—and I don't think it was lots of money—it wasn't because Sydney Gruson thought that I was cute. It was because I was holding down a very big job."[101] Shanahan had been unhappy at the *Times* for several years and had been considering whether she "could leave the great mother ship." She worried about retaliation and harm to her career, but she also told her husband that she "didn't think I could ever look my daughters in the eye again if I ran away from this just because I was afraid of the consequences to myself." He responded that if she felt that way, she should join the suit.[102]

In September 1973, as Timeswomen submitted their individual EEOC claims, Rabb and Rubin met with *Times* management to discuss specific charges and to attempt to conciliate their grievances.[103] *Times* officials boasted a new affirmative action plan, but Rabb deemed it vague and impossible to monitor. Rabb's law students began gathering evidence by interviewing plaintiffs one by one. "The students want specific information on conditions: which are the prestigious jobs, and who gets them; how are selections made; how did we get our jobs; which are jobs with titles but no power; did we get shunted out of the area we wanted and then get stuck; were we required to meet standards that men were not required to meet."[104] The caucus and Rabb met with *Times* management throughout the next year to discuss improving the affirmative action plan, but negotiations made little headway.[105]

By mid-1974, Rabb and the caucus members had waited far longer than the six months the EEOC required in order to initiate a lawsuit. They felt confident that the *Times* had no serious plan to improve women's status there. Rabb found *Times* management to be friendly, but ultimately uncooperative, with, for example, *Times* lawyers responding to her requests for information with illegible or incorrect documents. A caucus publication fumed that despite two years of organizing, women there still lacked "a real voice in the management of the paper," earned lower salaries than the male average, and had "little hope of progressing toward policy-making jobs, and with no women in the higher ranks to whom we could take our case."[106] In September 1974, the Women's Caucus voted overwhelmingly to proceed with legal action against the *Times*.[107]

Rabb and the caucus took more formal steps toward filing a class action lawsuit. Rabb asked Wade to find twelve potential named plaintiffs, of whom they would select eight. Wade suggested "us old war horses," herself and the other caucus leaders. Rabb indicated "that a variety of experience would be good, such as one secretary and one telephone operator etc." Yet Wade observed that "our 80 complainants are not very widespread—we had one cleaning woman, who has retired, and no phone operators and no one from the classified ad dept., for example, and we cannot go recruiting new ones at this moment without tipping our hand."[108] Wade also wanted to ensure at least one African American named plaintiff, but she could not conceive of a caucus member who would fit their specifications short of recruiting someone new, a move that might offend existing caucus members.[109] The Times-women had trouble recruiting women of color to their cause both because they were more often clustered in secretarial, clerical, and maintenance jobs, and on account of the simultaneous minority class action suit. They eventually found an African American plaintiff in Andrea Skinner, a news clerk. Skinner made a strong case that she was overqualified and underpaid in her job. Although she ran her department, she was paid at the secretarial level.[110]

The inherent risks of serving as a plaintiff in a grueling lawsuit, Rabb's case strategy, and caucus members' priorities convinced them to foreground well-established, professional women as the standard-bearers of the suit. Such plaintiffs needed to be prepared to seek employment elsewhere, for they would likely be "on the shit list for the rest of [their] time at the *Times*."[111] Wade recalled, "It was not that easy to get people who were going to stand up in front and get shot at."[112] Rabb sought plaintiffs who would not be finan-cially or professionally devastated by their character being smeared, and who could demonstrate that they earned unequal pay and had been denied up-ward mobility. Well-respected, high-profile plaintiffs would be most likely to preserve their reputations and land on their feet in another job. Of the seven named plaintiffs, three were married, and their husbands were supportive of the suit.[113] Six of the seven plaintiffs—all but the classified advertisement solicitor Nancy Davis—had worked at the *Times* for more than fifteen years. They could presumably leverage that experience into a similar job at a dif-ferent newspaper if necessary. Thus, serving as a named plaintiff in a class action suit posed challenges that made women with professional credentials and financial resources more plausible candidates.

As two of the *Times'* most accomplished women, Wade and Shanahan could make a strong case that their sex had stunted their careers there. Both "arrived with honed skills, we both demonstrated ourselves thereafter, we progressed and unfolded, we improved upon our performance, we kept on going. And if they couldn't give us the jobs that we wanted, then there had to be an explanation, and there was really only one explanation": illegal sex dis-crimination.[114] Wade was confident that her sterling credentials would hold up at trial. "I knew they didn't want to pick me off because whether or not I was going to succeed or get a better job or become managing editor, I was very valuable. I did a lot of revolting work" that required patience, attention to detail, and administrative skill.[115] Shanahan's credentials also set her apart as someone who was preeminent in her field. Shanahan recalled, "They couldn't say I was lousy in my job. They just couldn't, given all my internal awards."[116]

In selecting named plaintiffs, Rabb also sought women who would be able to withstand grueling experiences of character attacks and hostile depositions. Rabb spoke with potential plaintiffs to determine what kind of witnesses they would be. She warned Shanahan, "Don't think this is going to be fun. They will retaliate against you in every way just short of anything I can prove in court is illegal retaliation." Rabb also anticipated that the *Times* attorneys would attempt to intimidate her. Shanahan responded, "Hey, Harriet, I've covered those hot-shot lawyers in Washington for years and I've been in Wilmer, Cutler and Pickering's conference room, which is one of the most prestigious law firms in D.C., where they had these genuine antique maps of the era of Columbus on the walls and so forth," she said. "So that isn't going to scare me. I've been in places like that before." Rabb sought plaintiffs who would not be easily cowed.[117] Grace Glueck observed that the process of the lawsuit required "much painful digging . . . not only for the hard facts to prove discrimination, but in our own psyches, to examine the relationship between ourselves and the great institution to which—for better or for worse—many of us had committed our working lives."[118] While the caucus attempted to show a pattern of discrimination against women, of which the named plaintiffs were representative, the *Times*' attorneys would seek to discredit each plaintiff's claims one by one.

Yet the impeccable credentials that made women hardy plaintiffs also left them vulnerable to accusations of greed. The *Times* lawyers argued, "This is a case where . . . highly paid women, who have been well treated by the *Times*, now assert for some reason undeterminable from their papers herein that they have suffered discrimination because of their sex." Rabb responded, "It's as if they believe that once a woman makes more than $17,000 a year, she loses her constitutional rights." When the judge learned Wade's salary, he suggested that Rabb find more suitable "victims." Rabb told a group of feminists, "Don't think of this company as the liberal *New York Times*, think of it as the Georgia Power Company. They don't treat their women any differently."[119] Rabb's cocounsel, Howard Rubin, commented, "You do not think of a person earning $30,000 a year as being a victim compared to a person earning $7,500 per year working in a tobacco field. One does not catch your sympathy as much as the other. But the question is, would that person be earning more if she were not being discriminated against?"[120]

When the caucus attorneys accessed the *Times* personnel files, they uncovered confidential notes that revealed supervisors' sexist attitudes toward the most successful Timeswomen. Editorial personnel manager Dick Buritt had written in Shanahan's file, "Great legs. Face only fair."[121] They also found male supervisors' comments about other women such as "gorgeous chest and not above dressing it to advantage," and "I think her real ambition is to get married."[122] Of Wade, a supervisor had written she was "able to do a man's work with a woman's delicacy."[123] Caucus members believed that such descriptions of professional women would serve as strong evidence of a culture of sexism at such a prestigious news outlet as the *Times*. Betsy Wade reflected that much of their struggle had consisted of convincing others to give credence to their experiences. "The idea that it would be grotesque and ghastly at the *New York Times* filled our colleagues in the industry with amazement and distress. I think most of them figured they'd swap places with us in a minute."[124]

Although they focused more and more on recruiting and distilling the complaints of professional women, the caucus did not abandon efforts to involve the women clustered in female-dominated areas of the paper. The standard complaint language Rabb had written for the women to copy into their individual forms accused the *Times* of discrimination in "recruiting, hiring, placement, promotion and conditions of employment."[125] While the first four allegations applied most directly to women who held or sought equity with men, the reference to "conditions of employment" referred to the forms of discrimination pink-collar women described. While about two hundred of the six hundred women at the *Times* worked in classified advertisement sales, organizing them and channeling their concerns proved difficult. Many were part-time, and Wade reasoned that "this created an ambivalence about whether their fate was with the *Times* or whether their fate was with their spouse's job." For example, when the union bargained over health care, classified department women tended not to fight over the terms of their plans. "They were being carried on their spouses' plans, which were probably better plans, anyway. So it was hard to get them. And sometimes when the bargaining agent would go in to get a show of hands, there wouldn't be a big show of hands and they would sell out. They would sell out for an extra three dollars a week, in lieu of. The famous lulu's."[126] Despite their ambivalence, Wade recalled that the women in classified sales "worked in this vast sea of headsets on the telephone all day long and under really oppressive conditions."[127] By contrast, the men working outside sales had higher wages and more autonomy. Rabb convinced Nancy Davis, a classified salesperson in her late twenties, to be a named plaintiff. Davis saw taking action against the *Times* as a matter of simple justice. She related, "I entered the suit because it was so obviously right," adding, "I didn't think I was particularly gutsy. It was the one time in my life—the only time there will ever be—for me to participate in history."[128]

Rabb and the class filed suit in the Southern District of New York in November 1974. While the named plaintiffs personally alleged discrimination in wages and promotions, the suit offered a range of accusations. The women alleged that the *Times* maintained sex-segregated departments and placed men in the most responsible, highest-paid jobs, paid unequal wages, did not post jobs fairly to give women a chance to apply, paid women fewer bonuses and merit raises, used irrelevant factors—including women's appearance and familial status—for hiring, and did not give women the kinds of "jobs necessary to the acquisition of professional contacts and recognition, thus limiting females' promotion prospects, outside job offers, and free-lance and independent job potential."[129] The plaintiffs asserted that the *Times*' personnel records revealed discrepancies in women's pay and placement. "Women either are not hired at all for jobs in some departments or, if hired, are disproportionately placed in traditionally 'women's' jobs (e.g. secretary, picture researcher, classified ad taker, telephone operator, indexer) or in jobs in the lower groups within the department."[130] The court certified the class in April 1977. It consisted of 545 women who were covered by the guild contract and had worked for the *Times* between 1974 and 1977.[131]

With the exception of Davis, the seven named plaintiffs represented the interests of professionals and aspiring professionals (Figure 2). Six of the seven named plaintiffs had had long careers there and could demonstrate that they were not promoted as men were. In the complaint, Wade claimed that she had been bypassed by at least ten men.[132] Louise Carini, a benefits administration clerk in the accounting department, argued that she had been surpassed by seven men and was paid less than men who did equivalent work. Joan Cook, a reporter in the metropolitan news department, was also paid less than male reporters doing similar work. Despite receiving praise for her articles, she had not received a merit raise in twelve years. Grace Glueck alleged that she was paid less than men who were also arts reporters. Shanahan claimed that she was paid less than other male domestic correspondents in the Washington bureau who had equivalent or less ex-

Figure 2. The named plaintiffs in *Boylan v. New York Times* were the standard-bearers of a major Title VII class action lawsuit against the newspaper. *Front row, left to right*: Nancy Davis, classified advertisement sales; Andrea Skinner, editor of children's fashion section; Grace Glueck, art editor. *Back row, left to right*: Betsy Wade, national desk; Eileen Shanahan, Washington correspondent; Louise Carini, accounting; Joan Cook, metro desk. Photograph by John Sotomayor. Courtesy of Betsy Wade.

perience. Andrea Skinner alleged that she was not given promotions or appropriate pay for her skill level.[133] With the exception of Davis, these women required primarily the ability to distinguish themselves based on their pedigree and abilities. The *Times'* attorneys sought to leverage the plaintiffs' professional status in their efforts to debunk the women's claims. While the caucus presented the named plaintiffs as representative of other women at the paper, the *Times* countered that they were "highly-paid women" whose complaints "could hardly be typical of claims of any purported class."[134]

As the attorneys sparred in the pretrial deposition process, the *Times* lawyers quickly zeroed in on Davis as the weak link in the caucus's case. Rabb's case strategy of emphasizing the denial of pay and promotions to well-qualified women proved sound in the cases of Wade and Shanahan, yet the *Times'* expert witnesses strongly refuted Davis's claims. Davis had begun working at the *Times* in 1972 and referred to the job as her "first job of any account since school."[135] Davis had applied for nine promotions in two years, but she found that job openings were filled by men who spent several weeks in sales, then leapfrogged the women. Mabel Phelan, assistant personnel director, testified that Davis was passed over because she was grossly unqualified. "Of the four jobs where a man was promoted rather than Ms. Davis, one was a minority male, and one had an MBA from Columbia University, a scholastic achievement well beyond that of Ms. Davis. One was a job Ms. Davis applied for after less than five months at the *Times* which was given to a man who had a journalism major with editing experience and had far more seniority than Ms. Davis."[136] By contrast, the other named plaintiffs were able to cite their professional credentials, external validation, and blatant inequities in pay with men who did substantially similar or identical work. The *Times'* claim that salary differentials reflected "qualifications and experience" could be most effectively levied against Davis.[137]

In September 1978, the caucus and the *Times* reached a settlement several days before their trial was scheduled to begin. Although both sides declared total victory, the terms of the settlement reveal how, through building the suit, the caucus's claims had become circumscribed. The *Times* agreed to pay a modest annuity to all members of the class and to pay the plaintiffs' attorneys fees.[138] The *Times* also promised to implement an aggressive affirmative action plan, complete with specific percentage goals and timetables. The plan would require each *Times* unit to keep records of the number of men and women in each job group, the number of available positions in each group, and the date, sex, and title of the worker for each position filled. In addition the *Times* pledged to post job openings and to list them for the Women's Caucus. If a woman did not receive a job and asked for advice, a supervisor would inform her of specific steps that would improve her qualifications.[139] The settlement also required that a woman fill one of every eight openings in the highest corporate levels and one of four openings at the levels of managers and editors for the next four years. Jobs included in the one-in-eight category included president, publisher, vice presidents, secretary and assistant secretary, treasurer and assistant treasurer, and department directors. Jobs included in the one-in-four category included editors of every major section of the paper.[140] The *Times* offered no promise to equalize wages among men and women, or between male-dominated and female-dominated jobs requiring equal skill—thus overlooking earlier campaigns aimed at broad reforms on behalf of women across the office hierarchy. Instead, it framed sex equality in terms of women's access to upward mobility and dismantling prejudices that kept women from advancing on par with their training and ability.

Both sides praised the settlement, which inspired similar campaigns by other women and presaged the minority workers' settlement with the *Times* in 1981.[141] Grace Glueck emphasized the relative progress it reflected, declaring, "Considering where we were in 1972 this is the sun and the moon and the stars."[142] Rabb explained that reaching a consensus with the *Times* directly was preferable to taking a gamble in the courts.[143] She also indicated the significance of the affirmative action plan the *Times* proposed. "There has never been an affirmative action plan in the media, and I believe there has never been one in any other industry, which sets goals for filling the top corporate offices."[144] Attorney Howard Rubin framed the agreement as an important victory for professional women. "I hope this settlement will lay to rest forever the ignorant, bigoted notion, asserted by one of the *New York Times*' experts, that women, particularly those with families, are not really interested in attaining responsible, demanding jobs and are, therefore, less valuable employees."[145] Wade expected the settlement's benefits to reach further. She anticipated that opening "the top management levels of the paper" to women would "affect what goes into the *Times*, and over the long run . . . the attitudes of our society."[146] Shanahan framed the settlement as a victory over an industry leader, stating that it "made many thinking people across the country aware that even our most prestigious institutions do engage in sex discrimination."[147] *Times* officials celebrated as well. Executive vice president James C. Goodale declared the settlement "a total vindication" that generously "spare[d] the women involved a painful public evaluation of their performance."[148] In the end, both sides focused on what they had gained. But the caucus also overlooked what it had sacrificed: continued advocacy on behalf of those women for whom treating the sexes interchangeably would not yield equity.

＊　＊　＊

In a statement to women in other media outlets in the wake of their settlement, caucus members described the mighty obstacles their campaign had faced and explained that collective action had been their salvation. In efforts like theirs, they wrote, women have had to resist the urge to advance their rights as individuals, instead seeing themselves as members of an aggrieved class. "The system has taught them that they are in competition for a small quota of good jobs with good pay and the safest thing you can do, baby, is cast your lot in with a man or management." Yet, only by coming together could they perceive that their personal experiences were produced by a larger system. "The times we thought we were suffering some individual indignity, we were just suffering what every other woman was suffering, in another way. Being apart, we could not share our woes or seek a solution."[149] Caucus members reflected that their commitment to collective action had shaped their understanding of workplace discrimination and guided their campaign.

This message expressed leaders' initial vision, but it failed to capture how their efforts evolved. As they steered their campaign, the caucus members also shifted its underlying logic. Faced with a powerful and resistant foe, they came to emphasize those women whose experiences of sex discrimination could be addressed by dismantling barriers to upward mobility. This decision paid off in forcing the *Times* to the bargaining table; it may have been their only way to win any concessions.[150] In these same years, feminists undertook similarly ambitious efforts to leverage Title VII, pressuring some of the nation's largest corporations to root out sex discrimination in its many forms. Like the Timeswomen, these activists found that efforts to build a campaign that had the size and stamina to succeed also strained preexisting fault lines of identity and ideology. As they worked to articulate their movement's relationship to sex equality in the labor force, business interests developed new ways to undermine their efforts.

Through early efforts to harness Title VII such as the Timeswomen's, the consensus definition of state-enforced sex equality narrowed as it took shape, placing professional women and managers in agreement while closing off the concerns of women whose racial minority and pink-collar status produced more expansive rights claims. Settlements like the *Times*' gave professional women a notable boost in their quest for equity. By the early 1990s, one-third of copy editors at the *Times* were women, along with 23 percent of reporters, correspondents, and critics. Women held one of six vice president positions and four of fifteen seats on the paper's editorial board.[151] But such accords also permitted employers to weather the rights revolution by reinforcing a strain of sex equality that privileged the male standard—a standard that women with professional credentials were most likely to be able to meet. These partial victories did not change women's fundamental relationship to the corporation. Instead, they helped to individualize workplace equality, deepen divisions among women in the same workplaces, and obscure the bonds that remained.

Chapter 3

Feminism and Workplace Fairness

Title VII reset the foundation of feminist campaigns to expand women's rights at work. Activists had long pushed to improve women's working conditions through their labor unions and promoted a web of state-level laws designed to shield women from exploitation on the job—reform efforts that highlighted women's distinctiveness.[1] In Title VII's wake, some feminists sought to preserve sex-specific protections until they could be extended to men. But others seized on new antidiscrimination laws as they built what they termed "a civil rights movement to speak for women." Frustrated by the EEOC's seeming lack of interest in policing Title VII's sex provision, a group of mostly middle-class women and men came together in 1966 to form the National Organization for Women (NOW). NOW's founding document declared the group's intention to engage new sex equality laws to put the sexes on equal footing in the workplace by "isolat[ing] and remov[ing] patterns of sex discrimination" in order "to ensure equality of opportunity in employment."[2] In NOW's first two years, the group pressured the EEOC to evaluate sex-segregated job advertisements and airlines' restriction of flight attendant jobs to select women. NOW also filed an amicus curiae brief in the federal court case *Mengelkoch v. Industrial Welfare Commission* to challenge a California law that limited women's working hours to eight per day. NOW's national leaders sought to use Title VII to discredit sex-specific laws and destabilize sex as a relevant employment characteristic.[3]

As NOW grew, some of its members developed more expansive understandings of sex equality, arguing that labor feminists' long-standing goals related to workplace fairness were bound up in Title VII's new protections. In line with the self-fashioned rights claims women sent to the EEOC in its first several years, for example, members of NOW's Chicago chapter conceived of Title VII as a broad and flexible counterweight to workplace problems as diverse women experienced and defined them. To advance this vision, Chicago NOW worked both to move women into male-dominated jobs and to adjust the balance of power between women and their employers. In addition to highlighting the essential similarities between the sexes in pursuit of sex equality, they sought to flatten gender and class hierarchies at work. As Chicago NOW grew and gained power within the national organization, its members broadened NOW's national employment rights agenda from below. NOW expanded its initial efforts to dismantle the gendered division of labor, fostered campaigns to improve working conditions in the pink-collar jobs where women were clustered, and combated employers' attempts to widen the divide between full-time and contingent labor. By the early 1970s, NOW targeted the range of injustices that women faced at work through its efforts to enforce and expand Title VII's sex discrimination provision.[4]

NOW put this employment rights strategy to the test in its campaign against the retailer Sears, Roebuck and Company. This effort was born in the Chicago chapter after the EEOC announced its plan to channel its resources toward a handful of industry leaders. Chicago NOW set out to demonstrate that the problems faced by women in sales and clerical positions at Sears, the nation's largest retailer and second-largest employer of women, drove nationwide trends: a stark gendered division of labor that shunted women into either pink-collar and part-time work that offered little pay or flexibility or positions that were virtually identical to male-dominated jobs yet offered low pay and no benefits, and the mutually reinforcing problems of age discrimination, racism, and sexism. NOW framed Title VII as a potential antidote to all these problems, arguing that creating workplace sex equality required employers to both open top jobs and make systematic improvements for women throughout Sears's labor force. NOW activists could be more aggressive and confrontational in their attack on Sears than the women organizing from within the *New York Times* because their own jobs were not at stake.

In its Sears campaign, NOW developed new legal strategies and served as both a local direct service and a national activist organization. As the historian Serena Mayeri has shown, feminist attorneys pioneered legal arguments in these years that analogized race and sex.[5] Yet some grassroots feminists took a different tack, reasoning outward from pink-collar workers' own claims and conceiving of equality in terms of substantive fairness rather than as a measure of the similarities between disfranchised groups. In these efforts to stretch and strengthen sex equality law, NOW members acted as legal agents, educating workers about their new rights, encouraging them to file official grievances, and pressuring government agencies to uphold their mandates on behalf of working women. They were also legal activists who pressured the EEOC to adopt and police their broad interpretation of Title VII. By 1975, several years of Chicago-based activism against Sears had produced a highly organized and rapidly expanding national antidiscrimination campaign that had captured EEOC officials' attention. NOW was poised to chisel Title VII into a formidable weapon against the range of problems women faced at work. They believed that this broad definition of equality tailored to working-class women's claims would benefit more elite women as well.

But as the Sears campaign grew, it gave rise to tensions that ultimately reshaped NOW's relationship to sex equality and class politics. Then the nation's largest and most prominent feminist organization, NOW was primarily white, moderate, and middle-class. But this demographic homogeneity did not protect the group from ideological tensions. By the mid-1970s, some members felt that NOW's grassroots-driven, federated structure had rendered their growing organization politically ineffective. Their vision of a more streamlined, centralized NOW was, they reasoned, better suited to the pursuit of their main goal: the proposed Equal Rights Amendment (ERA) to the U.S. Constitution. These members argued that the ERA would eradicate all sex-based distinctions in American law and chip away at sexism throughout American society, including in the workplace. While the ERA's passage had seemed assured several years earlier, its progress had stalled as grassroots conservatives built an anti-ERA campaign that raised provocative questions about the practical implications of strict sex equality in the law.[6] The Chicagoans did not oppose the ERA, but they were concerned that remaking NOW into a top-down advocate for formal legal equality would limit their ability to meet the practical needs of working-class women, for whom equalizing opportunity could not deliver equity. These opposing feminist visions produced bitter conflicts, and eventually a dramatic rupture, within NOW.

NOW's internal struggles over how best to define and pursue sex equality reveal that the "new feminism" of the 1960s and 1970s, like the EEOC, became more efficient but less expansive as it matured. Once the ERA advocates took control of NOW in 1975, they centralized power in the hands of a few national leaders, remade NOW into a political advocacy group, and discontinued the Sears campaign. These changes strengthened NOW's internal unity and political effectiveness. But they also forfeited NOW's militant stance toward the government and employers and ceded NOW's critique of the unchecked market as generating mutually reinforcing sex and class inequalities. This makeover left workplace advocates within NOW to use the tactics of a lobby group, to follow the terms set by government actors, and to advocate for conceptions of discrimination as an interpersonal problem faced by individual women.[7] At the height of its power, the flagship American feminist organization pushed direct challenges to women's collective economic subordination beyond the scope of its own agenda.

*   *   *

NOW was established in 1966 with a federated structure whose local and national components worked in tandem to advance a broad feminist vision. The national organization helped chapters to germinate and loosely monitored their progress. Once incorporated, a chapter could take any steps its members believed would help to "bring women into the full participation in the mainstream of American society." Initially, the national organization did not maintain chapter membership lists, collect dues, or issue a publication. Instead it expected local chapters to set their own priorities and grow their membership, taking action "on any subject which is directly related to the purpose of NOW." According to the standard chapter bylaws, such activism might include "equal rights and responsibilities in all aspects of citizenship, public service, employment, education and family life, and it includes freedom from discrimination because of marital status or motherhood." NOW's third president, Wilma Scott Heide, proclaimed the organization to be "interested and active in just about everything that affects and/or would substantially improve the status of women."[8]

While NOW had over forty thousand members and six hundred local chapters by 1973, it remained a national organization in name and reach only.[9] Most of NOW's early activism took place at the grassroots because recruitment and chapter building were key organizational goals. An issue of *Do It NOW*, the organization's member magazine, noted that attracting new members required reaching women in their homes, communities, and places of business and drawing them into the movement by appealing to their own lives. As a widespread concern for women, employment discrimination activism seemed to many in NOW as a sure way to attract new members. One internal NOW brochure asked, "Can you assist women who may need or wish to file complaints against employers? Let the community know that you will assist women and persons with problems in discriminatory practices by their employers and they will come to you."[10] As late as 1974, 70 percent of NOW members identified a local chapter as their primary connection to the organization.[11] In NOW's first few years, attracting members to vibrant and visible local chapters was a more pressing priority than articulating a coherent and concise feminist agenda.

In the five years between the founding of the Chicago chapter of NOW in 1967 and its first action against Sears, it grew to become one of the strongest chapters in the nation. Catherine Conroy, a union organizer and the founder of Chicago NOW, was amazed at the organization's early growth there. "NOW grew by itself," she recalled. "We just have to knock people on the heads to join unions, but NOW—you can't keep them away. They bother you to death, call you up, call you back. I couldn't believe it."[12] Some women joined NOW out of a desire to affect national policy; in Chicago, however, most joined the movement to ameliorate material grievances within their own lives or local communities. This was a reflection of the particular brand of grassroots feminism already well established in Chicago by 1970. As the industrial center of the Midwest, Chicago was a major urban area; yet members of Chicago NOW were farther from the seats of national political or economic power than were feminists in New York or Washington, D.C. Additionally, many Chicagoans were transplants from smaller midwestern cities and towns. Four of the earliest leaders of Chicago NOW, for example, hailed from Wisconsin. For most of the Chicago members, politics was local. For them, a social revolution had to start with the immediate and the material, and they focused on addressing practical needs rather than building ideological unity.[13]

In the years leading up to the Sears action, Chicago feminists took on a variety of pressing issues in their community. Health-oriented organizations such as Jane, an underground abortion service, offered assistance to all, allowing members (many of whom learned to perform abortions) to exercise their politics through local, direct initiatives. According to one participant, "We in Jane were fortunate that we were able to create a project that met an immediate, critical need and, at the same time, put into practice our vision of how the world ought to be." Other groups such as the Midwest Academy and the West Side Group were run by trained community organizers who worked to empower individuals to solve local problems and build enduring institutions.[14] Chicago feminists also found ample opportunities to spread the word about their movement through academic routes. By 1970, approximately a dozen Chicago colleges and universities offered courses in women's studies, many of which were overenrolled. Members of the feminist community spoke out against sex discrimination in academia when women at the University of Chicago held a daylong conference addressing issues facing university women. In addition, the Chicago Women's Liberation Union opened one of two major "liberation schools" nationwide in 1971 to "correct women's mis-education." To counter the patriarchal notion that certain types of knowledge were off-limits to women, the school taught courses ranging from automotive mechanics and health to economics and family planning—eventually enrolling more than one thousand women citywide.[15]

Another influential organization that set the tone for Chicago feminist activism was the Young Women's Christian Association (YWCA). The YWCA had always provided institutional support for local organizations, and in the early 1970s it was the seat of the grassroots feminist movement in Chicago. Serving more than 163,000 local women and children, the Loop YWCA accommodated a striking variety of women's causes. Middle-class women's organizations such as Chicago Women for Flexible Careers, the Illinois Women's Political Caucus, and the American Association of University Women held meetings there, and working-class women received free legal advice and welfare and daycare assistance. In 1970 the Chicago YWCA hired its first African American executive director, Doris V. Wilson, who recommitted the organization to serving women of all backgrounds. "We want every professional woman or ADC [Aid for Dependent Children] mother to believe that the YWCA should exist. We are a women's movement and we want to serve the needs of women. We are not about to get hung up in status and social strata. We will articulate the stance of women; we will advocate social change, and we will work for new institutional arrangements that deal with urgent problems." As the venue for many of Chicago NOW's formative meetings, the YWCA epitomized the direct-action, participatory vision of feminism that the members of Chicago NOW brought to their chapter.[16]

In its first few years, Chicago NOW was small but vibrant. The group had approximately two dozen members in 1968, most of whom were in their twenties and thirties. Early members included Catherine Conroy, the theologian Betty Farians, the physicist Nan Wood, and a handful of undergraduate students from the University of Chicago. Mary Jean Collins, Chicago NOW president from 1968 to 1970, remembered this early group as "a little ragtag army." Mary-Ann Lupa, who led Chicago NOW from 1971 to 1973, recalled that the "NOW address was my home address," its office "my dining room complete with answering machine." Even so, the chapter had little success in recruiting African Americans and labor movement members. Collins hired an African American freelance photographer "just to make sure we had one black person in the room," and Chicago NOW distributed its newsletter to African American community organizations through the Chicago Urban League. Attracting African American members remained an unmet objective of Chicago NOW through the 1970s.[17]

New members arrived in Chicago NOW by various routes, including involvement with the New Left.[18] Both Collins and Lupa took part in the civil rights movement as undergraduates at Alverno, a small Milwaukee liberal arts college, in the 1960s. They determined that social injustices that had kept African Americans from full citizenship plagued women as well, and each joined Chicago NOW upon moving south from Wisconsin. Other women followed a more direct route to feminist activism. Anne Ladky, who served as president of Chicago NOW between 1973 and 1975, found that her academic success at Northwestern University did not translate into career opportunities. Women whose grades paralleled or exceeded men's in business or finance courses could find jobs only as bank tellers or secretaries. Ladky eventually found a position in the publishing world that seemed to promise upward mobility. One of the women in her office carpool, equally disgusted by women's lack of employment opportunity, was a member of Chicago NOW. In such an environment, Ladky began attending meetings and joined the group soon thereafter.[19]

Chicago NOW grew in the late 1960s and early 1970s by encouraging women to examine their own lives and bring their own concerns and priorities to the group. "There were so many wonderful things going on in the early 70s in NOW," said Ladky. "We wondered, if we take a feminist view of x—be it education, religion, economics—what would that look like?" The Chicago chapter sought to involve as many people as possible, toward as many goals as could be squeezed under the umbrella of feminism. "We tried to do everything," recalled Collins.[20] By 1973, Chicago NOW had become a thriving organization of more than 220 members, some of whom commuted to meetings from the north and west suburbs. More than half of Chicago NOW members were between ages of twenty-two and thirty, and about one-quarter were between the ages of thirty-one and forty. Approximately half of the members were married, and about one-quarter had children. Three-quarters had attended college, and 40 percent had or were working toward an advanced degree. Most had full-time employment, but their occupations varied widely. The highest proportion of members classified themselves as clerical or secretarial workers; the second and third most common occupations were writer and educator, and there were a handful of middle-class professionals. These demographics seem to have been relatively constant through the 1970s. Chicago NOW "was one of the biggest and most effective chapters," recalled Ladky. "We wanted to be a serious organization with serious local presence." Chicago NOW was the first chapter to retain its own full-time staff person, surpassing even the national organization in this respect. To Lupa, "that was like having arrived."[21]

Advancing women's rights at work was one of NOW's founding priorities. Some of the local chapters similarly emphasized workplace activism, and owing in large part to Catherine Conroy's own background as a union leader, employment rights were of singular importance to the Chicagoans from the outset. "We were much more involved in the employment issues than anyone else in the country," explained Collins. "We just felt employment and economic issues were extremely important, both in terms of what would advance women in society and what would get the most people" to participate in the women's movement. By contrast, Chicago NOW's abortion committee chair, Madeline Schwenk, saw that chapter members were less interested in lobbying for legislative changes on reproductive rights. Schwenk recalled, "no one cared to beat their heads against the wall in Springfield" because Illinois legislators were so opposed to abortion. By contrast, employment efforts provided concrete tasks that "made you feel like you were changing reality." Chicago NOW remained focused on workplace rights activism on account of both members' priorities and the local political climate.[22]

Members of Chicago NOW quickly discovered that women across the city shared their commitment to boosting women's rights at work. In August of 1970, on the fiftieth anniversary of the passage of the Nineteenth Amendment, NOW held a national women's strike for equality, the largest demonstration for women's equality to date. Chicago NOW attracted more than fifteen thousand women to the city's civic plaza for the protest. "Don't iron while the strike is hot," urged the event slogan. Women from across the city left their workplaces to attend the protest, responding to NOW's proposal that working women withhold their waged and unwaged labor.[23] At the rally, speakers presented women's entrance into male-dominated jobs and improving pink-collar jobs as equally significant objectives. One of the strike leaders expressed Chicago NOW's intention to include all women in their movement and to encourage them to demand fair treatment in paid and unpaid work. "I propose that the women who are doing the menial chores as secretaries put covers on their typewriters and stop! I propose that the telephone operators unplug their switch boards, the waitresses stop waiting, the cleaning women stop cleaning, the teachers stop teaching, and the nurses and aides in the hospitals stop! Stop! In every office, every factory, every laboratory, every school. And we will spend the day discussing the conditions which keep us from being all we might be, that keep women from breaking through to executive positions and our full capacity."[24] Through employment-focused campaigns, Chicago NOW members both pressured the government to enforce existing nondiscrimination law and advanced particular interpretations of its meaning. Chicago NOW envisioned workplace sexism as a collective problem affecting all women. The group began to initiate employment rights campaigns that sought both to expand women's access to male-dominated jobs and to foment substantive changes for pink-collar and part-time women workers, working mothers, older women, and women of color.

Chicago NOW found that while new nondiscrimination laws gave women new leverage in their negotiations with employers, feminists would need to both encourage and pressure the responsible state agencies to police the provisions. Providing preassembled evidence of discrimination to enforcement agencies increased the chances that women's complaints would be addressed. Thus, members learned how to collect and present evidence that could convince government officials to act. In preparing a class action lawsuit against the City of Chicago, Chicago NOW members interviewed every complainant to assemble their own numerical and narrative data. Members asked every interviewee about her salary, her work history, her relationships with supervisors, and whether any other witnesses could confirm her experiences. The composite information made a strong case that sex discrimination plagued city jobs: NOW found that "in ten departments in city government, eighty-one percent of all women are paid under $800 and ninety-one percent of all employees paid over $14,000 are men. Only three of the forty-one city departments are headed by women—supervising less than one-half of one percent of the city's 35,000 employees. Women exclusively hold the jobs 'maid, janitress, and scrubwoman,' and are paid lower wages than equivalent job titles for men."[25] Chicago NOW positioned itself at the nexus of workers, employers, and government agencies. "We filed all these charges," recalled Collins. "We said to the government, 'you have to enforce the law,' but then we went and picketed them. . . . We tried to use the skills we had to fight the establishment on their own terms, but we also then tried to recruit public support by our more public activities."[26] To make new sex equality laws work for women, feminists took a confrontational stance toward employers and state enforcement agencies alike.

In 1972, Chicago NOW members began to set their sights on larger corporations when the EEOC announced its plan to channel its resources toward a handful of industry standard-bearers. The agency vowed to dedicate up to half of its annual budget and forty-five full-time staff members to investigating four or five major corporations at a time.[27] In contemplating how to command such an influx of EEOC attention for a NOW target, the Chicagoans saw NOW's recent national campaign against the American Telephone and Telegraph Company (AT&T) as an obvious model to replicate. AT&T was an industry giant: one out of every fifty-six American women in the labor force worked for AT&T in 1970, and one year's new hires at the company equaled the total number of employees in the nation's next eight largest utilities combined. Further, both AT&T and NOW had federated structures, enabling simultaneous local and national pressure on the company. In 1970 NOW members nationwide held demonstrations to publicize AT&T's practices and amassed evidence of systemic sex discrimination at the corporation's local subsidiaries. NOW provided the legwork, but the EEOC provided the muscle. AT&T spent more than $60 million in defending itself against feminists' charges, according to NOW estimates, but by convincing the EEOC to investigate and punish AT&T, NOW helped to catalyze a $50 million payout that was then the largest-ever employment discrimination settlement for women and minorities.[28] Some in NOW criticized the settlement for undermining union-won seniority benefits. Yet the AT&T campaign showed that pressure from NOW could bring substantive change to working women, as AT&T met more than 90 percent of its affirmative action goals in 1974. In the AT&T effort, NOW's dual-front strategy—pressuring both the government and the employer—exposed the discrimination, convinced the EEOC to investigate, and forced the company to the negotiating table.[29]

In the wake of the successful AT&T campaign, Chicago NOW began to mobilize against Sears, Roebuck and Company in 1972. The Sears action became NOW's most expansive employment rights campaign, following the model of previous grassroots efforts. NOW undertook a difficult task in attempting to transform Sears's reputation from benign retail giant to sexist exploiter. Sears began as a humble mail order company and expanded steadily throughout the twentieth century. In 1974, Sears employed more than four hundred thousand people, which amounted to twice the labor force of its nearest competitor.[30] Because Sears was the world's largest general merchandise retailer in 1970, most Americans had some form of regular contact with Sears, whether as employee, stockholder, credit holder, or consumer. In 1977 one out of every 204 employed Americans worked for Sears in some capacity, and one-third of American adults carried a Sears credit card. Sears "was so mainstream," explained Mary-Ann Lupa. "Everybody bought their children's clothes from Sears," which were "good quality and reasonably priced."[31] For many women, contact with Sears extended beyond their roles as consumers; the retailer was the country's second-largest employer of women. During the 1970s, Sears was firmly entrenched in the public mind as a symbol of the American ideals of thrift, quality, and value.

Yet Sears was an attractive target for feminists. Sears was a staunchly antiunion private business that was managed via an "old-boy's" network. Although Sears was enormous, as a retailer it was sensitive to its customers' behaviors. Unlike the telephone company—essentially a protected monopoly—Sears's customers could spend their money elsewhere. Chicago NOW reasoned that even a local action could pressure Sears to change if enough shoppers became angered by the company's practices. Further, Chicago NOW believed that Sears's national presence could facilitate simultaneous local and national action because "everywhere there was a NOW chapter there was also a Sears Roebuck."[32] Thus Sears's size provided both a challenge and an opportunity. Such a large company was unlikely to bargain willingly with what began as a handful of women activists, but if the local Chicago campaign could be adopted by national NOW, and a national NOW campaign succeeded, one of the nation's largest corporations would be forced to admit wrongdoing, permanently restructure its employment policies, and make public amends to current and former workers. Further, a feminist campaign against Sears could help build the movement's ranks. Collins believed that the campaign had "the potential to involve many different constituencies: older women, minorities, and women earning the lowest wages. They can be recruited on the issues of employment, credit, or consumer practices that discriminate against women."[33]

In their Sears campaign, Chicago NOW devised a flexible, multiple-front strategy that attacked Sears at its corporate headquarters, at Chicago-area stores, in the media, and before the EEOC all at once. Members began by gathering available information on Sears's employment practices. As a federal contract holder, Sears was legally obligated to have an affirmative action program and to publicize information about the jobs held by women and minorities. Sears refused to release such data. "The competition will try to hire them away if we tell of outstanding female and minority employees," demurred Sears vice president for personnel Charles F. Bacon. "[Montgomery] Ward would be after them. We've been known to do the same occasionally." Sears held firm despite significant prolonged pressure from Chicago NOW. "Sears has set itself up as a leader in preventing access to public information," the women concluded.[34] Sears fought well into the 1980s in and out of court to withhold its affirmative action plan and store-by-store breakdown of employee sex and race.

Chicago NOW members resorted to the more informal types of research they had used in past campaigns, eventually building a strong case that sex discrimination was endemic at Sears. Members entered the stores, counted the number of women in each department, and noted their tasks. They found that in commission sales, "the women were selling the low tech and the men were selling the high tech" merchandise. Men sold high-commission items such as tires and large appliances while women earned low hourly wages selling buttons and children's clothing. NOW also contacted current and former Sears employees, including those who had already filed complaints, to ask questions such as, "Are women told about promotions?"; "Have you ever asked for a transfer or promotion to a different department, especially one which is particularly male-dominated, and been refused?"; and "How does your salary compare to those of men who do comparable work?"[35] Their research revealed that the company was practicing the same type of systemic discrimination women had experienced at AT&T. A handful of different jobs were available for women at Sears, but most of them offered poor compensation and little opportunity for advancement even when they paralleled identical male-typed jobs. Sears also forced women into part-time positions with no benefits that required full-time hours or fired them when they married. To foster men's expectations that even low-level sales jobs held management potential, managers openly hazed women who sought male-dominated positions. The tagline of the Sears management training program was "Sears Jobs for Sears Men."[36] The historian Bethany Moreton identified Wal-Mart Corporation's similar tactics in these years, creating a gendered "family in the store" among its retail workers that ensconced men in positions of authority even as those positions increasingly assumed the trappings of traditional women's work. When NOW got ahold of Sears's own annual report, the group learned that five of every six women at the corporate headquarters were clericals. As Collins recalled, "it was rough data, but it was real."[37]

Chicago NOW members hoped that their participatory research methods would draw Sears's women workers into the feminist movement through their experiences as employees. Members of Chicago NOW recalled standing outside the local corporate headquarters of Chicago businesses, handing flyers to women as they left work (Figure 3). The brochure for the Sears campaign was a one-page newsletter called *The Tower Tattler*, which provided a few paragraphs about the campaign and a perforated membership application that could be completed and sent to Chicago NOW. The chapter received numerous letters and financial donations from female Sears employees. One Sears woman wrote to Chicago NOW that the longer a woman stayed in a clerical job, the less willing her supervisor was to let her ascend the office hierarchy. "Although executives value our support they will not make it known where it counts for fear of losing us by promotion." Her coworker similarly described the typical Sears clerical who had the "knowledge and experience [that] qualify her for promotion to a checklist position—but instead she finds that she is training MBA's for the position she has worked to obtain."[38] Women at Sears also sent NOW evidence of age and race discrimination, as well as the difficulties women faced in attempting to open a Sears credit card.[39] The Sears campaign was a largely middle-class movement that put working-class women at its center. While evidence suggests that the campaign did not draw many Sears women into NOW's ranks, some workers risked their jobs by giving information and support to the feminist effort.[40]

In August 1974, the U.S. Commission on Civil Rights held hearings on women and poverty in Chicago. Before representatives of the federal agency, feminists presented their evidence against Sears, and women workers and company officials responded.[41] Darlene Stille of the Chicago-based clerical advocacy group Women Employed accused Sears of assigning women and men who performed essentially identical work to different job titles and wage scales. Stille explained that men at Sears earned 202 percent higher wages

Figure 3. Members of Chicago NOW demonstrate in front of Sears, Roebuck's headquarters on Women's Equality Day, a national feminist day of activism in support the proposed Equal Rights Amendment in 1974. As their protest signs reveal, equal rights and economic justice went hand in hand for Chicago feminists. *From left to right*: Kathy Rand, Nancy Burton, Kim Kemmerer, Sharon Ronjue, and Agnes Giocanda (behind "NOW for Jobs and Justice" sign, in sunglasses). Photograph by Howard D. Simmons. Courtesy of the *Chicago Sun-Times*.

than their female counterparts, largely on account of this sex segregation.[42] In each of Sears's buying departments, a buyer was supported by an assistant buyer, a buyer's assistant, or both. "The job assistant buyer and buyer's assistant are different titles for the same job," Stille claimed. The only meaningful difference was in pay and benefits. "Buyer and assistant buyer are checklist or salaried positions, accompanied by many fringe benefits," and 88 percent of the assistant buyers in a NOW study of six buying departments were men. By contrast, buyer's assistants were "paid weekly, and are known as timecard and earn much less and they are denied these additional fringe benefits." Ninety-one percent of the buyer's assistants identified in the NOW study were women. And although the jobs were similar, women found that exiting a buyer's assistant job for an assistant buyer's position was nearly impossible.[43] Stille accused Sears of maintaining a concrete sex-caste system in its buying departments.

Anne Ladky buttressed Stille's testimony with evidence that Sears was pioneering new techniques to keep women workers contingent and impoverished. Chief among these was reclassifying full-time positions as part-time. Sears had recently announced a new initiative to render 60 percent of its sales staff part-time. Ladky explained that a part-time job at Sears could be identical to a full-time position in all but pay, benefits, and flexibility. She asked, "What does it mean to be classified a part-time employee at Sears? It means no commission on sales. It means no substantial benefits, no promotability, no participation in Sears's famous profit-sharing plan. It also means being paid less than a living wage. And it means you can be required to work 40 hours a week and still be classified as part time." She reasoned, "Clearly, this policy is not intended as a service to provide the convenience of part-time work for women. It is intended to keep Sears' labor costs down."[44] Such practices were of vital public concern, Ladky claimed, because all Americans were harmed by Sears's efforts to reclassify workers and depress their wages. She asked, "If part-time employment involves doing work that is substantially equal to work done by full-time employees, should benefits be denied to part-timers? . . . How many Sears workers are subsidized under public assistance and the food stamp program? Is the public subsidizing Sears' low wages?"[45] Ladky argued that economic security was a civil right, and that state-enforced sex equality should prevent employers from cashing in on assumptions that framed women and their labors as inherently less valuable than men's. Feminists argued that Sears, like AT&T, practiced dramatic sex discrimination, inventing new ways to subordinate women in its stores and offices while claiming to be a model employer.[46]

At the hearings, testimony by Sears's women workers reinforced the feminists' claims. Judy Krusinger, a buyer's assistant in the furniture department, explained that while she held a bachelor's degree in business administration from a local college, she was automatically funneled into a clerical job when she arrived at Sears eight years earlier. She explained that there was little difference in the job responsibilities of buyer's assistants and assistant buyers, yet in her department, nine of the ten assistant buyers were male, and all twelve of the buyer's assistants were female.[47] Krusinger described the women's low morale. "The feeling among clerical women in our department is that we have reached the point, this is it, this is as high as we are going to go, and everyone is very frustrated by that feeling."[48] Geraldine Holder, a clerical assistant who had worked in the hardware department for seven years, described the climate for women in her unit as "very negative . . . hardware, it seems that the management feels, is not a field for women."[49] Toby Atherton, a clerical assistant in the buying department of men's sportswear, explained that the men in her department joked that "the women are the ones that are really doing the work," and she and her female coworkers resented training new male recruits who were soon promoted above them. Only eight of the sixty-five women in her department held checklist positions.[50] Sears's women's claims supported feminists' contentions that the company segregated women in jobs that offered little pay, respect, or mobility.

African American women testified that the sexism in Sears's employment practices was marbled with racism. Deborah Easley had completed some college coursework when she applied to work at Sears three years earlier. Yet personnel managers told her that the only job available for her was a clerical position in the heavily African American and female customer relations department.[51] Easley quickly identified a generational divide among the black women in her department. The older women seemed content, but "the younger women, the black women, they were trying to get out; but it seemed so every time they try and receive promotion or try and apply for a better job, they would be called into the office and told that their attendance was not good, or they have been late too much, or they weren't doing their work, they were talking on the phone; there was always some stall to keep them from obtaining a promotion." Tired of seeing her own and her friends' requests for better work rebuffed, she confronted a black male personnel manager. "I was complaining a lot to him because I wanted something better, I was tired of the job I had, I felt that I was qualified for more." He told her that he could not offer her any assistance. Easley recalled his comments: "Well, the thing of it is, you know how whitey plays this game, and I'm trying to get ahead myself and I'm not going to rock the boat." She took his response as a cue to seek employment elsewhere. "I figured an organization like Sears where they don't like to promote black people, or shall I say they haven't promoted black people, I felt I wasn't going to get ahead with the attitude I had."[52] Easley accused Sears of limiting black women to the least-desirable clerical jobs regardless of their credentials or ambitions, and as an ultimate sign of her frustrated ambitions there, she quit her job with the company three weeks prior to the hearing.

In response to the women's claims, Sears's representatives insisted that the company was a sterling employer. Charles F. Bacon, Sears's vice president for personnel, described their testimony as "extremely misleading and false."[53] He explained that Sears's increasing reliance on part-time workers resulted from shoppers' preferences. "Part timers are used because our stores are open from 72 to 75 hours a week, 7 days, nights, and the only way we can provide coverage for our customers is to resort to part-timers. We couldn't conceivably afford to have that many full-time people on payroll and remain competitive and be an organization providing good value to our customers."[54] Bacon also refuted feminists' allegation that assistant buyer and buyer's assistant were substantially similar jobs.[55] And to the extent that Sears's women experienced poor treatment, Bacon attributed this to a few unreliable outliers rather than an endemic culture of sexism. "Like the rest of America's society, we have our male and female chauvinists," he explained. Yet, the women who testified "cannot be considered to be representative of over 200,000 female employees at Sears."[56] Feminists had anticipated this response in light of Sears's long history of replacing workers rather than addressing their grievances. Ladky recalled that Sears had been "a very tough company when it came to the civil rights movement."[57] Sears' robust campaign to beat back unionism within its labor force dated to the 1920s.[58] Throughout the 1970s and early 1980s, Sears sought to burnish its reputation and proclaimed its innocence of feminists' charges.

NOW channeled the momentum the hearings generated and expanded its Sears campaign. At its 1974 convention, NOW adopted the Sears campaign as a national priority. The Chicagoans Mary Jean Collins (Figure 4) and Anne Ladky assumed the mantle of national Sears Task Force cochairpersons and worked to nationalize the anti-Sears tactics they had honed in Chicago. As Collins and Ladky explained, the Sears campaign could "function in different ways: educational, legal, legislative, and in negotiation and direct action. It can have national, regional, and local forms and still be based in the heart of the organization—chapter actions. This strategy can help us solidify NOW's past gains, take credit for our victories, and build NOW with a major win." Ladky and Collins encouraged chapters to use local resources and to improvise based on their members' interests and expertise. The national Sears campaign adopted the philosophy, developed in Chicago, that "local pressure has a tremendous impact on top management and will enable us to obtain concessions in areas of corporate policy." As of October 1974, more than one hundred NOW chapters took local action as part of the

Figure 4. Mary Jean Collins was president of Chicago NOW and co-coordinator of NOW's national Sears campaign. She and other Chicago feminists fought to place working-class women's issues at the forefront of NOW's agenda. Photograph by Klepitsch. Courtesy of the *Chicago Sun-Times*.

nationally coordinated Sears campaign.[59] "Sears can be beaten, but it must not be underestimated," Collins and Ladky wrote.[60] Title VII and the EEOC would provide critical leverage in a campaign that could force, rather than attempt to persuade, Sears to remake its employment practices.

As they orchestrated NOW's national Sears effort, Ladky and Collins encouraged chapters to be flexible and creative. They wrote to chapter leaders, "Corporations like Sears are inventing new ways to maintain the status quo of cheap female labor, and NOW will have to begin to develop strategies to meet this challenge."[61] They instructed local chapters to both gather information and protest at their local Sears stores. "We need extensive first-hand information of the sort needed for charges to determine the extent of discrimination at Sears," they wrote. "Direct contact [with women workers] is essential both for developing our strategy in line with the issues of greatest importance to women employees, for impact on the EEOC, and because real change at Sears is more likely if the women there act on their own behalf and gain confidence as they work with NOW."[62] Further, gathering such information about Sears's specific employment practices would allow NOW to levy accurate demands for pay and promotion once the case reached a settlement. The EEOC was not collecting such specific data, Ladky and Collins warned, and "if we leave the settlement entirely to EEOC, we may be faced with one as totally inadequate as that reached recently by EEOC and the steel industry."[63] Ladky and Collins instructed chapter members to count the number of men and women in different jobs on the sales floor, as well as to talk to women employees. One suggested approach was to "mention how tiring it must be to be on your feet all day—'I suppose when you become a department manager, you won't have to do that anymore.' Wait for a response. If you don't get one, prod the person by saying, 'How many years would you have to wait for a job like that?'" Another of Ladky and Collins's suggestions to local chapters joining the national Sears campaign was to send members to store entrances to distribute leaflets about the campaign to employees.[64] Local chapters' data would bolster NOW's fight to pry open the details of Sears's presumably inadequate affirmative action plan and employment practices.

NOW members became experts in the emerging law of sex discrimination as they built their case against Sears based on women's own experiences of harms. NOW's research uncovered stark patterns of unequal treatment for women. "All the women interviewed stated that when they applied for openings at Sears, they were only offered one job. In each case, the job offered was a low-paying, traditionally female one."[65] The timecard employees were "doing the work of assistant buyers, and . . . do not receive compensatory salary or benefits."[66] Atlanta NOW found that female sales clerks at Sears were most concerned with "the plight of the part-timers," who "do the same work as the full-timers, and in some cases work a full day (one worked 40 hours per week) but have neither the security nor the benefits that the full timers do."[67] Ladky and Collins sent chapters specific instructions for helping disgruntled employees to prepare EEOC charges. "Allow yourself about two weeks to write the charges. It usually takes this long because of last-minute problems and questions. During this time, get the affidavit signed by the women from Sears, fill out the EEOC charge form, and have it notarized. The forms are available from any EEOC office."[68] NOW chapters acted as intermediaries between Sears women and the EEOC, filing third-party EEOC charges against Sears that allowed the women workers themselves to remain anonymous.[69]

Ladky and Collins sought to balance the need for a cohesive and unitary Sears campaign with encouraging local chapters to target the corporation in creative ways. The national task force required chapters to provide extensive details about the potential for local action. Participating chapters had to designate a Sears coordinator, convene a Sears action committee, and research the number of local Sears stores and the compliance agencies that could field employment discrimination complaints.[70] Further, the Sears task force published monthly bulletins offering tips, suggestions, sample press releases, and updates on national events.[71] To "exert pressure on Sears on as many different fronts as we can with as many different tactics as we can," Ladky and Collins suggested picketing local stores, writing press releases, making contacts with Sears workers and shoppers, and encouraging employees to file discrimination charges. They asked chapter leaders to send them "clippings, leaflets, releases, and photographs" documenting successful actions that others could replicate. The more than fifty chapters that took part in the countrywide National Sears Action Day in December 1974 used both humorous and serious approaches. Some wrote press releases and complaint letters and picketed stores; others wrote and sang songs, distributed candy, and dressed in costume. One Wisconsin chapter member dressed as Mrs. Santa Claus and asked shoppers not to buy from Sears, while the Chicago chapter held an in-store ceremony in which Ebenezer Scrooge accepted a Sears "discredit card" from the chapter president.[72]

By the mid-1970s, NOW pressure began to yield results in the forms of an expanded campaign, government attention, and Sears's defensiveness.

Sears proved a strong and determined foe, yet NOW's efforts bore fruit as the EEOC began its own investigation and named Sears one of a handful of its high-priority cases. NOW was confident that victory was near. In August of 1975, Chicago NOW claimed to have "received word that there will be a settlement late in the fall. In total dollars it will be the largest in history." Comparing Sears's size with AT&T's, NOW expected that the amount would top $100 million in back pay and reparations.[73] The campaign reached its apex in February 1975, when members of NOW met with EEOC Chairman John H. Powell Jr. Powell agreed to fulfill NOW's request to review the consent decree in the Sears settlement—which all agreed was inevitable and forthcoming soon—before it was finalized.[74] A NOW-affirmed settlement could require Sears to permanently bend its employment policies toward NOW's objectives, boosting women's access to male-dominated jobs while improving the pay, benefits, and working conditions of the clerical and sales jobs that were overwhelmingly held by women.

Members of Chicago NOW built a national grassroots employment rights campaign that embodied their vision of feminist activism and reflected NOW's structure and philosophy. Locally devised and loosely coordinated at the national level, the campaign sought creative interpretation of basic goals based on Sears's workers' own claims and inclusion of as many participants and organizational allies as possible. NOW's efforts gained traction in local establishments and the national policy arena alike. By mid-1975, NOW had crafted its own brand of grassroots legal feminism that positioned feminists at the nexus of workers, employers, and government agencies and rendered Title VII a potential counterweight to the full spectrum of problems women encountered at work.

*   *   *

But the Sears campaign did not survive the mid-1970s. The feminist ideology that sprouted and sustained it was subsumed by changes in NOW's leadership and strategy. Earlier in the decade, the Chicagoans' priorities and favored tactics had aligned with national leaders'. In 1973, NOW had announced its "Action Year Against Poverty," encouraging members to work to "effect meaningful changes in the economic status of all women."[75] NOW vowed to pressure states to raise the minimum wage and extend benefits coverage to domestic workers, to push employers and government to provide free child care and job training to low-income parents, and to pass "legislation to provide for a full employment program for the United States in which private industry and the public sector expand opportunities for work for all so that each person can have a realistic chance for meaningful employment at a decent rate of pay."[76] The Chicagoans had also been able to enact their brand of feminism because NOW's power structure was diffuse and gave chapters significant latitude. Any member or chapter could identify an issue, devise a strategy, and pursue the support and visibility of the national organization.

Yet NOW's grassroots popularity only amplified its internal political divisions, as competing factions began to develop mutually exclusive feminist visions. NOW's membership quadrupled between 1971 and 1973, as members flooded into more than four hundred local chapters. As NOW grew, healthy diversity and relative harmony within the national organization gave way to deepening divisions at the 1974 and 1975 conventions. In 1972, convention campaign literature for presidential candidates could include only "a standard single-sheet statement of qualifications and a standard (approx. 5 × 7) picture for use in the display which the conference will assemble and exhibit." Three years later, these rules were gone. In newly heated elections, candidates distributed limitless professionally produced materials: studio headshots, colorful brochures and booklets, buttons, and stickers.[77] These new campaign materials reflect the increased time and money candidates spent on their presidential bids. A new emphasis on self-branding and promotion replaced the assumption that a candidate's list of accomplishments would speak for itself and exemplified the newly heated national debate over NOW's future direction. Lupa recalled the infighting that increasingly paralyzed NOW meetings. At national conferences, "so many issues were so divisive—abortion issues, gay and lesbian issues." Policy disagreements could become character attacks, and there were few formal rules of order in the meetings to help keep peace. Catherine Conroy described these "housekeeping problems" as a "depressing" distraction that reflected poorly on the entire group; "it's no way for adults to act."[78]

In the 1974 election for NOW's national presidency—the group's first contested election—two demographically similar candidates offered distinct visions for NOW's future. In NOW's first half-decade, the national board had chosen candidates, and members ratified the board's selections at the convention. In those years, recalled Lupa, "there were elections, but one person was groomed and sort of assumed . . . [to be] President-Elect." In 1974 the board supported Mary Jean Collins for the national presidency. Her opponent was Karen DeCrow, a lawyer from Syracuse, New York. That year, the East Coast and Midwest were by far the strongest regions of NOW representation, with approximately 33 percent of members hailing from both areas. Both Collins and DeCrow came from strong local chapters and had held regional leadership roles. Both were white and had been involved in civil rights activism before discovering feminism, and both had held full-time professional employment. Like Collins, DeCrow was an early president of her local chapter, and each encouraged her chapter to gather local data through surveys and to take protest action. DeCrow's Syracuse chapter sustained the same multitude of task forces as Chicago's, and DeCrow, like Collins, believed that workplace rights and equal pay were crucial components of the feminist agenda.[79]

Yet their divergent strategies pulled Collins and DeCrow in different directions. Collins argued that action-oriented task forces focused on "the bread-and-butter issues such as employment, education and health" should remain the foundation of NOW's structure. Collins supported the ERA—she had advocated its passage in a front-page editorial in *Do It NOW* in 1972—but primarily as a means to boost women's employment rights. To Collins and her Chicago chapter, grassroots employment activism was the ideal NOW priority. Such actions had already reached many women and had the potential to include millions more; they could yield incremental results; and they were less dependent on one single victory than was purely political activism. Collins claimed, "we need programs that address the significant problems that women face to win concrete results. We must indicate in our strategies as well as our words that this movement is about improving women's lives."[80] Collins and her allies argued that employment-focused action simultaneously struck at the heart of women's exclusion from full citizenship and attracted feminists of all stripes to their movement. To Collins, ensuring feminists' ideological unity and organizational discipline was much less significant than NOW strategy's demonstration to women "that their victories are the result of their action. Through action on their own behalf, women learn their own power and potential to reshape the country."[81]

Unlike Collins, DeCrow became interested in issues of doctrinal equality and eroding sexist stigmas in law and culture that allowed women to be treated differently than men. DeCrow argued that "the 'hydraulic pressure' at work in virtually all litigation involving women is the misogyny present in legal institutions, and in the men who create and run them." Her chapter, Syracuse NOW, initially organized around the issue of equal pay, but De-Crow herself became more interested in issues of public accommodation. She explained, "it was really good that we got off employment; there was no way we were going to change the employment patterns in Syracuse." Further, the members of Syracuse NOW "did not want to change the society; they wanted equal opportunity. . . . We were white, middle class, professional, urban, academic people." DeCrow and her fellow members filed legal motions and demanded to be seated at all-male lunch counters and bars. When DeCrow was elected to NOW's national board, she encouraged other NOW leaders to give priority to actions that dramatized the formal barriers to women's full participation in public life. To DeCrow, public accommodation was "a dramatic issue" that attracted "'the right kind' of members."[82]

At the 1974 national convention, these feminist visions faced off.[83] De-Crow and thirty-six of her allies dubbed themselves the Majority Caucus, suggesting that while they were a minority within NOW's leadership, they spoke for the majority of NOW's members.[84] Hailing from western and eastern states, caucus members advocated a more tightly organized NOW in which local chapters acted as the arms of a more focused national organization. While she did not eschew grassroots tactics, DeCrow wanted to consolidate NOW's leadership in a single Washington, D.C., headquarters and abandon the various campaigns and task forces that she believed had pulled NOW in too many directions and diluted its message. "It is time for NOW to approach the substantive areas of feminist concern in a less haphazard and more organized fashion," she argued.[85] DeCrow and her supporters disagreed with the Chicagoans' view that NOW's strength could be increased through sheer numbers of members working toward diverse objectives. By streamlining NOW's membership and message, DeCrow sought to foster ideological and operational unity through concerted work toward fewer goals. The ERA was the quintessential Majority Caucus priority. Their slogan, "out of the mainstream, into the revolution," distilled their belief that mainstream political tactics could yield radical change.[86]

Deep philosophical differences underscored this divergence in tactical priorities. The Majority Caucus conceived of women's rights as belonging to, and best fought for using the rhetoric of, the individual. They argued that strong stances on political issues as well as "personal liberation, sexist justice, cultural changes (such as de-sexing the language, books, movies)" could alienate some people, but political change would secure the types of material advances the Chicagoans tried to foment through employment action alone. Further, the Majority Caucus sought to create NOW chapters based on common status rather than geographical location. They wanted to organize "women on the basis of the work they do and where they do it until we have Nurses NOW, Teachers NOW, Welfare Rights NOW, Office Workers NOW, Homemakers NOW, and so on."[87] The Chicagoans preferred collective action that openly acknowledged and celebrated diversity. Their experience in economic justice struggles at the grassroots level showed them the simultaneous difficulty and importance of bringing working-class and minority women into the fold. They argued that encouraging members within a single chapter to adopt efforts on each other's behalf was preferable to dividing women by profession and encouraging them to advocate explicitly for themselves.

The Majority Caucus's interest in doubling down on the ERA fight was also a response to a brewing grassroots anti-ERA campaign that threatened its recent momentum. A feminist goal for half a century, the ERA finally seemed poised to be written into law when it sailed through both houses of Congress in 1972.[88] But as ERA advocates pursued its ratification by the necessary thirty-eight states, opponents of the provision began to build political capital by framing the ERA as harmful to women. Phyllis Schlafly, a Catholic mother of six and hard-line anti-Communist author and activist, became the figurehead of the anti-ERA movement. She formed the grassroots group STOP ERA (with "STOP" as an acronym for Stop Taking Our Privileges) in 1972. Schlafly and her advocates argued that the ERA would destroy domesticity and named the specific threats to gendered order that state-mandated sex equality would create: same-sex bathrooms, same-sex marriage, reduced legal benefits for wives and mothers and expanded access to abortion, and, especially inflammatory as the Vietnam War raged on, a sex-neutral military draft. But the ERA's "biggest defect," Schlafly wrote several years after its defeat, "was that it had nothing to offer American women."[89] As Schlafly and her allies began to find success in rebranding the ERA from a commonsense protection of equal rights to a radical infringement on cherished protections, members of the Majority Caucus rightly sensed that without more feminist activism in support of the ERA, the grave threats the provision faced would prove mortal.

In pursuit of their respective politics, the Majority Caucus and the Chicagoans brought their own slates of candidates to the 1974 and 1975 conventions—a previously unimaginable tactic. Thus, for the first time, rather than voting for individual candidates for national office based on their personal achievements, members of NOW chose between opposing groups. Collins explained that while she hoped to be elected president, NOW's contested leadership was "a sign of growth." Collins reasoned: "we're now big enough to absorb a variety of different approaches. That's a healthy point to be at too." Evidence does not suggest that DeCrow and Collins were personally antagonistic, but tensions plagued the conventions. In both 1974 and 1975, NOW hired the American Arbitration Association to conduct the election because the conflict spawned deep mutual distrust.[90] DeCrow won the presidential election in 1974 over the board-selected Collins, though the national board remained dominated by the Chicagoans and their allies. The 1975 convention was even more conflict-ridden. The Majority Caucus pejoratively dubbed their opponents "the Chicago machine," and the Chicagoans accused their opponents of bussing local high school students to the convention and registering them on-site to artificially inflate Majority Caucus support. One Wisconsin NOW member recalled lining up for an evening vote to find the voting machine temporarily broken. Refusing to retreat from the line, "members were literally crawling to the voting booths. Some didn't get to vote until 6 or 7 am."[91] By the mid-1970s, NOW's united fight for diverse priorities had given way to mistrust, acrimony, and factionalism.

The Majority Caucus takeover was completed in 1975, as DeCrow and her allies secured the presidency and most of the national board seats. As they began to remake NOW in line with their vision, the Chicagoans disappeared from national NOW leadership. The Sears campaign was a casualty of this transition. As Collins recalled, Sears activism had become "an incredible football within the administration," and as a hallmark of the Chicago chapter, it was swiftly sidelined once the Majority Caucus came into power. Ladky recalled her frustration that NOW would change course so dramatically. The new leadership "did not see it as we did, as potentially embarrassing for the organization to have started this whole campaign and not continue to be responsible to it. You don't put your organization's credibility on the line and then walk away from the fight."[92] Many former chapter leaders withdrew from Chicago NOW. Collins became a union organizer, Ladky began to work for the Chicago-based advocacy group Women Employed, and Lupa refocused

Figure 5. Karen DeCrow (fourth from Gerald Ford's right with other feminist leaders at a White House meeting) led a faction within NOW that gave priority to winning formal equality and sought to concentrate the group's power in the hands of national leaders. After defeating Mary Jean Collins in the 1974 contest for NOW's presidency, DeCrow and her allies made NOW more effective in the political realm. But this transformation also sacrificed much of the militancy that had powered NOW's employment rights campaigns. National Organization for Women, Chicago Chapter Records, NOWC_0121_0005_002, Special Collections, University of Illinois at Chicago Library.

her energies on her career as a graphic designer. On what seemed to be the brink of the settlement NOW had pursued for years, feminists left the Sears action and its female workforce in the hands of the EEOC.

The DeCrow administration set about making NOW nimbler and more focused (Figure 5). The Majority Caucus member and future president of NOW Eleanor Smeal declared NOW to be "saddled with an outdated structure." She explained that "NOW needs streamlining and reorganizing. NOW by-laws were adopted originally when the organization had few members, few chapters, and no state organizations. NOW has grown to the extent where the present by-laws are no longer adequate to manage the affairs of the organization." Indeed, NOW had ballooned to fifty-five thousand members in seven hundred chapters. At a 1976 bylaws conference, NOW voted to decrease the executive committee from thirteen volunteers to five salaried officers.[93] NOW leaders also began to dismantle the task force structure, which divided members based on their area of interest, in favor of skill-oriented subgroups. Members would contribute to NOW's more limited agenda based on their abilities in lobbying, communications, and more.

This more streamlined NOW was especially suited to fighting for the ERA. Because the ERA could help NOW to solve many of women's societal problems, DeCrow argued, building a united campaign for its passage was preferable to sustaining multiple smaller fights. The ERA would also carry tremendous symbolic value for women, she claimed, for "not to be constitutionally equal in one's own country is humiliating."[94] NOW had always supported the ERA, and members were optimistic in the early 1970s that it would soon become law. Many states already had such provisions in their constitutions, and both Houses of Congress approved the federal amendment in 1972. By mid-decade, however, the ERA drive began to lose momentum. In response, NOW leaders redoubled their ERA efforts. President DeCrow urged local chapters to focus on the ERA above all other issues and to channel their creativity into ERA activism. "Each chapter must and should do what it believes best to pass the equal rights amendment," DeCrow urged. In a memo to NOW's national board, she wrote, "Each task force ought to publicize how the area of its particular concern will suffer if the ERA is not ratified, and how it will benefit with ratification."[95] DeCrow's successor, Eleanor Smeal, intensified NOW's commitment to the provision. In her 1977 presidential victory speech, Smeal encouraged NOW members to adopt an "integrated, national [ERA] campaign directed by a national strike force, to be chaired by the president of the organization in order to demonstrate to ourselves and to the country that we are totally unified for the ERA." In 1978, NOW declared an ERA "state of emergency," intensifying critics' fears that NOW had become a one-issue organization.[96]

Years of NOW's dedicated advocacy did not avert the ERA's 1982 expiration. But the organization's strengthened top-down structure and focus on the national policy arena outlasted the ERA fight. NOW's mid-1970s transformation also permanently reset the group's approach to the problem of institutional sexism at work. NOW stopped pressuring employers and government to broadly interpret laboring women's rights, instead accepting equality of access—to employment as well as education, political participation, healthcare, and more—as feminism's bedrock goal. NOW's retreat emboldened Sears. The corporation sparred with the EEOC for another decade, refusing to accept a settlement or admit wrongdoing. The case NOW had built a decade earlier went to trial in 1986. Absent interest group support or much effort from the then far more conservative EEOC, Sears handily won in federal district court.[97]

*   *   *

NOW's Sears campaign brought feminists' competing notions of sex equality into high relief. To some in NOW, exemplified by the Chicagoans, sex equality was best defined in terms of fairness rather than sameness. They argued that the benefits of using Title VII to boost working-class women's status would emanate upward to help more privileged women. Other feminists gave priority to formal equality, arguing that the benefits of eliminating sex-based distinctions among workers would trickle down to the pink-collar sphere. These divergent understandings of sex equality created different visions for NOW's structure. Critics of the streamlined ERA strategy held that the shift stripped NOW of healthy democracy and local variation. Exemplified by the Chicagoans, they proclaimed that Title VII's guarantee of nondiscrimination required flexible and multivalent advocacy for substantive fairness, and they saw the ERA as one weapon in the broader fight for women's economic security. This vision was derailed in the factional fight at the national level, as ascendant proponents of the ERA-first strategy countered that NOW's original structure bred disunity and could not sustain either the swelling membership or the targeted campaigns that could bring national policy change. After 1975, NOW's newly centralized structure strengthened its capabilities in the legislative arena but foreclosed its ability to use Title VII to target economic inequality.

The feminism of the 1960s and 1970s deeded a mixed legacy to working women. Since then, feminists have engaged Title VII to delegitimize gender distinctions in the workplace and pry open new paths to career advancement for professional women. But in adopting this narrow strain of sex equality, NOW also ceded its critique of market capitalism as an engine of systemic disadvantage for all working women—particularly those whose objective was not to enter all-male enclaves of the workforce. The mainstream feminist discourse that once linked the issues of sex equality and class justice has since separated them. And if the primary distinction between salaried, well-paying "checklist" jobs and hourly, low-paying "timecard" jobs at Sears in the 1970s was the sex of the person performing them, since then employers have widened the gap between these forms of work and increasingly subjected white men to the low-wage service sector.

Efforts to create workplace rights by reasoning from working-class women's needs did not die in the mid-1970s when NOW shifted course. In the same years that saw women's workplace caucuses confront their employers and feminists pressure corporations and government officials while struggling to articulate their movement's relationship to Title VII, public sector unions pushed to expand the reach of sex equality laws as part of their efforts to deliver economic justice to their members. But for labor activists, as for the others, clashing visions stoked internal tensions that threatened to constrain or derail these efforts. And when labor advocates' efforts to enshrine sex and class justice in employment rights law crested in the mid-1980s, they also faced a newly empowered phalanx of conservative interests determined to discredit them.

Reevaluating Women's Work

In 1980, Minnesota worker Sharon Isker left a position as a switchboard operator and receptionist in the Washington County welfare department to become a janitor at the county courthouse. Isker's union, the American Federation of State, County and Municipal Employees (AFSCME), spotlighted her job change in its national newsletter to introduce the new centerpiece of its fight for women's rights. The story juxtaposed two photographs of Isker at work (Figure 6). In the first image, she wore a neutral expression while seated at a desk, dressed in a blouse and holding a phone. The accompanying text explained that as a pink-collar office worker, Isker had answered up to eight hundred calls per day while greeting and assisting everyone who entered the massive building. She reflected, "It got so I'd go home just mentally exhausted, sleep only one or two hours and wake up worrying about the job." Her replacement began asking for a transfer after just three days in her shoes, she noted. The second image showed Isker posed with a broom, her broad smile reflecting her satisfaction in her new role. Isker's transfer had delivered an immediate raise from $3.89 to $5.45 per hour although the new job was considerably less taxing. Summarizing her situation, she explained, "I'm a perfect example of a worker who got paid less just because I was in a traditional woman's job." Jobs like Isker's office position were "grossly undervalued" precisely because women typically performed them, explained AFSCME staffer Andrea DiLorenzo.[1] As such, AFSCME officials had come to believe that attacking women's secondary labor force position called for different strategies, beyond helping a fortunate few break into male-typed work.

As in workplace caucuses and feminist groups, Title VII forced labor unions to reckon with the meaning of sex equality. In the early 1970s, a

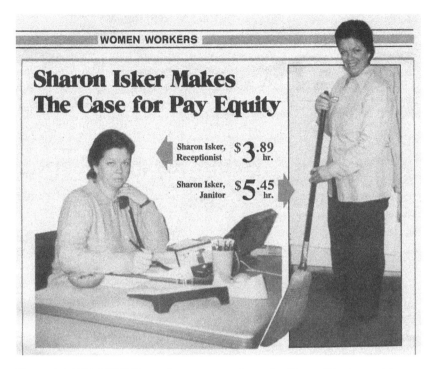

Figure 6. A 1980 AFSCME newsletter portrayed member Sharon Isker's transition from pink- to blue-collar worker. Isker pointed out that her work as a janitor was considerably less difficult but paid higher wages than her secretarial job. Workers like Isker became the focal point of AFSCME's campaign to enshrine comparable worth into sex equality law. Courtesy of Walter P. Reuther Library, Wayne State University.

coalition of labor and feminist groups led by AFSCME began to argue that Title VII should apply to pay practices across the gendered division of labor. Women's wages were artificially depressed because they remained clustered in a handful of low-pay occupations, advocates argued, and creating meaningful equality required more than boosting women's access to work typically performed by men. Instead, they demanded an expanded interpretation of sex equality law: equal pay for work of *comparable worth* to the employer, or what they also termed pay equity. Comparable worth advocates claimed that the statistical difference between women's and men's average wages, which for decades had hovered around 40 percent, was a vestige of the family wage ideology: the notion that a worker's pay should reflect his or her presumed status as a male provider or female dependent. In the era of state-enforced sex equality, they argued, the wage structures workers had inherited from earlier times reflected the systematic devaluation of feminized work rather than the value-neutral output of an impartial labor market.[2] As labor lawyer Winn Newman explained, "There was historical discrimination against women going back to the 1930s, when it was legal, and even though the pay scales were relabeled after sex discrimination became illegal, in many cases, the same basic pay structure was kept." As a result, he claimed, "every day, with every paycheck, there is continuing discrimination."[3] To root out this long-standing injustice, pay equity proponents like Newman argued that the sex equality promised by Title VII required employers to recalculate wages using methods that were unfettered by sexist values—according to the value a worker's labors created.[4]

Comparable worth represented a radical threat to the long-naturalized gendered division of labor and the logic of late twentieth-century capitalism. It rooted women's social advancement in systemic economic reconfiguration. Government officials first introduced comparable worth during World War II as a way to safeguard high wages in industrial positions temporarily held by women. Labor feminists fought to push comparable worth into state and federal laws in the 1940s and 1950s, and in the early 1960s, the theory had powerful advocates in government and feminist circles.[5] When a renewed grassroots feminist movement became strong and savvy enough to leverage sex equality laws in the 1970s, it largely ignored the comparable worth issue. Yet feminist priorities gained renewed momentum within the labor movement in those same years. Public sector unions identified comparable worth as a key goal as they became more attuned to the concerns of the growing number of women in their ranks. As the sociologists Linda M. Blum and Michael W. McCann have shown, while pink-collar women were mostly disappointed by the state-mandated affirmative action policies some won in the 1970s—such as the Timeswomen's profiled in Chapter 2—those campaigns had elevated their expectations and centered their gaze on litigation. Many such women saw state-oriented comparable worth activism as the logical next step on the route to workplace justice.[6]

Emboldened by federal court decisions in the late 1970s and early 1980s that tentatively affirmed comparable worth under Title VII, AFSCME built the largest litigation department of any labor union in the country. The flagship public sector union began to win major comparable worth victories in federal courts and state and local governments. Civil rights activist and former EEOC chair Eleanor Holmes Norton declared in 1983, "What affirmative action was in the 1970s, comparable worth is in the 1980s," proclaiming her belief that this expansive interpretation of sex equality law, while divisive, would become ensconced in national labor policy.[7] The next year, Democratic presidential contenders Walter Mondale and Jesse Jackson thought the theory significant enough to deploy their wives to testify to their husbands' support of pay equity before Congress.[8] Its advocates hoped to leverage public sector victories to make gains in the private sector, and they observed that many Americans viewed comparable worth as a common-sense step in the struggle for sex equality. This issue bore particular significance for African American women, who were less likely than whites to have the professional training that could boost them out of pink-collar jobs, and who worked in public sector jobs in large numbers.

Through the lens of the comparable worth movement, the 1980s appears not as a decade of steady backsliding for the Left, but as a testing ground for activists' most dramatic effort to use Title VII to remake American labor practices.[9] A bright spot in years the historian Nelson Lichtenstein has characterized as "a downward spiral" for organized labor, pay equity's demise at the end of the decade was not the result of a consistent mainstream consensus that it was too radical, but of poor timing.[10] Its advocates in the government and labor and feminist movements never synced up their power when they were at full strength. When feminists and some federal officials advocated the policy in the 1960s, comparable worth was not among union leaders' top priorities. In the 1970s, comparable worth was peripheral to feminist social movement groups' agenda even as its advocates in the labor movement and the federal bureaucracy slowly built the groundwork for its adoption in equal employment law through careful study and supportive legal precedents. This deliberateness gave probusiness opponents time to muster a powerful countermovement as part of their broader attacks on organized labor. Antagonism to comparable worth also found a prominent foothold in government circles, as President Ronald Reagan replaced formerly sympathetic bureaucrats with hardcore social conservatives who denounced the theory as beyond the scope of sex equality law at mid-decade.

Competing definitions of the nature of sex discrimination lay at the heart of the debate over comparable worth. Was it a systemic phenomenon produced by biased structures of work or an interpersonal problem of biased individuals? Pressured by powerful corporations and buttressed by increasingly mainstream conservative ideologies, courts and federal officials ultimately chose the latter. The push for comparable worth outlived its legal potential, as the unionists' legal strategy was rendered ineffective by the same courts and agencies that had once been receptive.[11] In the end, the lack of a comparable worth moment of convergence permitted the low wages that were once justified by sex-based arguments to span the service sector under the banner of sex equality. And while the wage gap between working men and women has narrowed, it has stubbornly persisted, compounded by race.

*   *   *

The theory of comparable worth rests on the notion that the pay gap between working men and women stems from discriminatory wage-setting practices—even if the disparity is unintentional or matches prevailing market rates. Prior to the mid-twentieth century, employers routinely paid different wages to men and women for identical work. A 1940s-era Westinghouse Electric Corporation Wage Administration manual explained the sex-based wage differential by reference to women's distinct characteristics. "The gradient of the women's wage curve is not the same for women as for men because of the more transient character of the service of the former, the relative shortness of their activity in industry, the differences in environment required, the extra services that must be provided, overtime limitations, extra help needed for the occasional heavy work, and the general sociological factors not requiring discussion herein."[12] Those "general sociological factors not requiring discussion" reflected contemporary commonsense knowledge about the distinct attitudes, work choices, and family responsibilities that seemed to fit women and men for separate workplace roles. Collective bargaining agreements often listed different wages for the sexes even when they worked side by side and in the same jobs.[13]

Midcentury economic crisis forced some employers to revisit this logic and emboldened working women's advocates to amplify their calls for equal pay legislation. But the precise standard of this equality—whether identical pay for *equal* or for *comparable* work—remained in question. During World War II, the lower pay rates women commanded in the industrial jobs men had departed threatened to permanently depress the wages for returning veterans at war's end. Led by the International Union of Electrical Workers (IUE), some unionists began to argue that pay rates should reflect labor's worth, not the laborer's sex. Many government officials agreed. To counter business owners' claims that women's lower wages matched prevailing industry standards, the War Labor Board issued a unanimous 1943 opinion that endorsed setting women's wages based on the value created by their work. Only two states had established equal pay laws prior to World War II, but states began to pass such laws with greater frequency during the war and in its aftermath. At war's end, the Women's Bureau of the Department of Labor took up the comparable worth cause, drafting a model state equal pay law that would ban "payment of a lesser rate to women than men for work of a comparable character," would require employers to "re-evaluat[e]" women's work, and would contain strong enforcement measures.

Officials' and advocates' demands for an equal pay law that included comparable worth grew through the late 1940s and 1950s. In 1945 and in each year prior to the passage of the 1963 Equal Pay Act, one or both Houses of Congress considered but ultimately rejected equal pay legislation that contained a comparable worth provision.[14] Comparable worth also gained momentum among labor advocates overseas, as the International Labor Organization's Convention No. 100, which addressed sex and equal pay, included a comparability standard starting in 1951.[15] By the end of the 1950s, equal pay had considerable momentum. Twenty states had established such laws, and invested parties debated the proper standard for "equal": sameness or some more comprehensive measure.[16] The President's Commission on the Status of Women, an advisory group convened in 1961 that consisted of government officials and national figures from the fields of education, from civic groups, and from organized labor endorsed a broad interpretation of equal pay. Noting that women earned substantially less than men as bank tellers, office workers, X-ray technicians, and physical therapists, the commission declared in its final report that "remuneration in all types of employment should be based on skill and not on the sex of the employee" and endorsed "the principle of equal pay for comparable work."[17]

In 1961, even before the commission published its official endorsement of comparable worth, President John F. Kennedy proposed national pay equity legislation that included it. In June 1962, members of Congress debated an Equal Pay bill mandating that "work of 'comparable character on jobs the performance of which requires comparable skills' must be paid for on an equal non-discriminatory basis."[18] Several lawmakers expressed reservations that the comparability standard was too vague. Representative Phillip Landrum, a moderate Georgia Democrat, was concerned that the bill granted the Department of Labor the power to erase meaningful skill-based distinctions. If the department declared all jobs in a plant to be comparable, it could wipe out blue-collar women's narrow foothold in industry. Representative Katharine St. George, a moderate New York Republican, shared Landrum's concern that the comparability standard "gave tremendous latitude to whoever is the arbitrator in these disputes." She proposed replacing the phrase "for work of comparable character" with "for equal work," a suggestion incorporated into the bill's final version. Representative Charles Goodell, a New York Democrat and the bill's sponsor, explained as it neared passage in both houses, "We went from 'comparable' to 'equal' meaning that the jobs involved should be virtually identical."[19] Passed in this narrowed form as an amendment to the Fair Labor Standards Act of 1938, the Equal Pay Act of 1963 mandated equal pay for jobs of "equal skill, effort, and responsibility, and which are performed under similar working conditions."[20] Comparable worth did not become federal law in the 1960s, but many in government and women's and labor rights networks backed it as a commonsense protection for working women.[21]

Even as policy makers declined to write comparable worth into law, some in the labor movement continued to endorse it as a critical issue. Starting in 1963, AFSCME, the nation's largest public sector union and an AFL-CIO affiliate, became the nation's most forceful advocate for comparable worth as the union entered a period of dramatic growth and feminization. AFSCME's history runs counter to the general narrative of U.S. labor history. Public workers faced formidable challenges in the 1930s and 1940s, years that saw private sector unions flourish.[22] Public sector unions like AFSCME lacked many of the protections private unions enjoyed, but they also evaded some of their constraints. The restrictions of the Taft-Hartley Act of 1947—which dramatically curtailed unions' freedom to recruit new members and enact strikes—did not apply to public employees.[23] Further, in 1962, President John F. Kennedy issued Executive Order 10988, a provision that granted federal employees the right to collectivize and bargain. In addition, the Kennedy and Johnson administrations built new agencies that swelled the federal workforce. In 1971, thirteen million American civilians worked for the government—an increase of four million in a decade.[24] The next year, Congress extended Title VII protections to public sector employees.[25] Public workers' rights also expanded at the state level in the 1960s and 1970s, as thirty-seven states legalized collective bargaining for their workers. While the overall unionized labor force was shrinking, workers flocked to public sector unions.[26] AFSCME had approximately one hundred thousand members in 1955. A decade later, AFSCME was growing by one thousand per week—reaching one million members in 1978.[27] In the 1960s and 1970s, as industrial unions faced mounting obstacles, AFSCME bargained from a position of increasing strength, building its size and clout and winning new contracts in schools, libraries, hospitals, and offices.[28]

As the industrial workforce stagnated, female-dominated sectors of the workforce expanded, and this rise in clerical and health industry jobs largely propelled AFSCME's dramatic growth.[29] Women's representation in public employment rose from nearly 44 percent in 1973 to more than 48 percent in 1981. On the whole, organized labor was slow to adapt to the swelling of the pink-collar workforce. Sociologist Linda M. Blum notes that between the mid-1950s and late 1970s, unions dedicated 75 percent of their resources to manufacturing and industry, while 90 percent of new jobs were in feminized service occupations.[30] But AFSCME began a targeted campaign in the early 1970s to better incorporate its growing ranks of women members.

At the union's 1972 convention in Houston, attendees adopted a sweeping resolution on sex discrimination that leaned heavily on legal remedies and blended sex and class concerns in its broad definition of sex discrimination. The resolution urged the extension and strong enforcement of the Equal Pay Act and noted that state legislatures should refuse to ratify the ERA until remaining protective labor laws then specific to women were extended to men. It also vowed to push for legislation to strengthen the EEOC and "laws which protect both men and women against exploitive working conditions" and "provide adequate working condition standards for all employees regardless of sex." The resolution also pledged to pursue maternity leave in contracts and legislation, as well as child care centers and tax credits. Finally, the resolution looked inward, vowing to increase women's presence as AFSCME officers and staffers and creating an Interim Committee on Sex Discrimination to channel members' interests and offer more specific policy recommendations.[31]

Over the next several years, AFSCME built a robust women's rights program. The Interim Committee on Sex Discrimination was chaired by Mozell McNorriell, a fifty-year-old African American Detroit woman who worked at the county juvenile court and was the union's only female international vice president.[32] From the start, the twenty-four-member committee sought to boost women's leadership and pursued legal approaches to the problem of sex discrimination. Noting that only 13 percent of presidents and 37 percent of secretaries of AFSCME locals nationwide were women, the committee recommended that AFSCME subsidiaries work for affirmative action on behalf of women; that locals be apprised of their responsibilities to follow EEOC guidelines and be given new tools to fight sex discrimination, including model contract language; and that AFSCME publish a bulletin on the ERA and on "future legislation concerning women." In late 1973, AFSCME offered a strong endorsement in support of ERA ratification. A 1974 AFSCME newsletter emphasized pay discrimination, urging members to check their workplaces to see whether men and women earned the same wage for equal or "substantially the same work," and whether "most females [are] hired in at a lower rate of pay than most males."[33] Throughout the 1970s, AFSCME locals formed women's rights committees to address the specific concerns female members identified, including pay equity, sexual harassment, job training, child care, and job safety.[34] As AFSCME officials devised new strategies on behalf of women, envisioning the law as key to this struggle, the union also propelled women into leadership roles.[35] By 1982, one-third of AFSCME local presidents and nearly half of local union officers were women.[36] In 1985, AFSCME president Gerald McEntee could boast that the union had more women leaders than any other in the nation (Figure 7).[37]

As AFSCME officials worked to distill and advocate for women members' demands, an innovative grassroots campaign reshaped the union's sex equality agenda from the bottom up. In 1973, the Washington State branch of AFSCME publicly accused Washington governor Daniel Evans of perpetuating wage discrimination in state employment. Regardless of officials' intent, AFSCME officials argued, the state violated women's rights by paying unequal wages to male- and female-dominated jobs that yielded equal value.[38] As scholar Joan Acker notes, the public sector was especially ripe for comparable worth campaigns because local governments tended to have preexisting merit-based pay systems.[39] To investigate AFSCME's accusations, Evans ordered state officials to analyze the state personnel system, to compile sex-based wage statistics, and to estimate how much it might cost to correct any discrimination discovered.[40] Noting a study of this nature and scale was unprecedented in the public sector, staffers nonetheless devised a rough system by which to compare substantively different jobs according to their required training, expertise, and skill. They concluded that male-dominated jobs were paid approximately $100 more per week, or 20 percent more, than equivalent female-dominated jobs.[41] Their calculations indicated that remedying this imbalance would cost between $27 million and $34 million. "Justice

Figure 7. Gerald McEntee addresses the tenth anniversary conference of the Coalition of Labor Union Women in 1984. When McEntee became AFSCME president several years earlier, the union had already made internal changes to become more responsive to its growing ranks of female members. Courtesy of the Walter P. Reuther Library, Wayne State University.

is not cheap," retorted a 1974 AFSCME publication.[42] Evans acknowledged this finding, but his administration was slow to attack the disparity, and his successor as governor wrote the project out of the state's budget for 1977.[43] Even as the comparable worth theory made quick headway in Washington, it threatened to be quashed with equal speed.

AFSCME took Washington State officials to court when they declined to implement comparable worth voluntarily. AFSCME officials believed federal courts had already laid the necessary groundwork for the sea change in national sex discrimination policy which a victory in Washington could generate. Two federal laws could address issues of sex equality and pay: the Equal Pay Act or Title VII. While the final version of the Equal Pay Act contained the narrow language of substantial similarity rather than comparability, Title VII's general ban on sex discrimination held more promise.[44] For example, a pink-collar worker might be able to prove that her wages were lower than a blue-collar worker's "on account of" her sex. The lawmakers who debated Title VII foresaw this possibility and attempted to foreclose it. Before approving the bill, the Senate added the "Bennett amendment" to Title VII. By declaring it lawful for employers to "differentiate upon the basis of sex in determining the amount of the wages or compensation paid . . . if such differentiation is authorized by . . . the Fair Labor Standards Act," the Bennett amendment sought to ensure that Title VII's sex equality provision would not supersede the Equal Pay Act's stricter standard.[45]

Yet federal courts began to narrowly interpret the Bennett amendment in the late 1970s, paving the way for more expansive arguments under both the Equal Pay Act and Title VII.[46] The U.S. Supreme Court offered comparable worth advocates a substantial, albeit partial, victory in the 1981 Title VII case *Gunther v. County of Washington*. The case involved a prison that systematically paid female guards at a lower rate than males. The prison justified the disparity by pointing out that the male guards' jobs required more physical strength, while the female guards performed more clerical and administrative work that officials believed to be less difficult. In a 5–4 decision, the court held that the female guards could pursue equal wages to their male peers even if the substance of their work was not identical.[47] Workers' victory in *Gunther* seemed to open the door to a broad reinterpretation of sex-based pay schemes that privileged male-typed work and devalued feminized skills—even where the differences between the jobs were not at issue. Further, Congress had recently granted the EEOC jurisdiction over both the Equal Pay Act and Title VII, accelerating their convergence in federal officials' and activists' minds. By the early 1980s, federal court rulings had encouraged AFSCME to build a legal strategy to test comparable worth's viability under Title VII's sex equality provision.[48]

In *Gunther*'s aftermath, comparable worth advocates coalesced around litigation as their key strategy. Widely known as the "grandfather" of the comparable worth movement, AFSCME attorney Winn Newman believed comparable worth would have to be instituted through the courts. He had taken up employment at AFSCME in 1980, leaving a similar position at the IUE because the larger union was willing to expend significant resources on comparable worth litigation. According to Newman, "It is time to move comparable worth from the conference room to the court room" because "it will not happen voluntarily nor will it happen as a result of collective bargaining alone, despite the best efforts of unions." Calling on "labor unions, women's rights groups and individual female workers" to "step up the pace of filing discrimination charges and litigating these cases," Newman predicted, "a number of dramatic court victories will do more to inspire 'voluntary' compliance, effective collective bargaining and belated government enforcement than further hearings, reports and studies. The teaching of the enforcement of civil rights laws is that a lawsuit or the threat of a lawsuit is often the best way to educate."[49] Invoking the role of the NAACP's early courtroom wins in helping to spark a mass civil rights movement, Newman believed that successful comparable worth litigation could invigorate and expand American feminism. IUE general counsel Carole Wilson hoped that such legal victories would create a new standard. "There was a huge storm of protest to the Equal Pay Act," she explained, but "today employers comply with it." Wilson predicted, "It will be the same with the *Gunther* ruling."[50]

Newman believed that race-based civil rights litigation had outpaced its sex-based corollary, and he viewed comparable worth as a necessary antidote to wage discrimination against women. He described the notion that the unfettered market set wages fairly as "a smokescreen for bigotry and discrimination." He stated, "The Supreme Court's holding that segregation is 'inherently unequal' applies with equal force to race or sex segregation in the workplace, i.e., a racially or sexually separate job structure inherently results in inferior wages because such structure 'denotes the inferiority of the [female] group.' Job segregation and wage discrimination go hand in glove. When an employer has segregated the workforce, wage discrimination invariably follows." To employers who claimed that they did not discriminate but just "pa[id] the going rate," Newman responded that "the market itself is distorted by discrimination." He explained, "Our society has advanced to the point where only a bigot would publicly state that because of the 'market' blacks and Hispanics should be hired for less money, or that because of the tragic unemployment rate of black workers they should be hired for less money."[51]

Alleging that systemic sex discrimination infused the state's pay structures, AFSCME filed federal suit in the Western District of Washington against the state in 1980. In building its case against the State of Washington, AFSCME's attorneys secured class certification for the more than ten thousand female state employees in occupations that were more than 70 percent female.[52] Each plaintiff formally alleged that the state "discriminates against me on the basis of sex in compensation by intentionally paying my job less than predominantly male jobs of equal or lesser value to the employer and equal or lesser levels of skill, effort and responsibility." One class member, Peggy Holmes, detailed her experiences as a secretary at the University of Washington. Holmes claimed that many of the tasks she performed required "the same skill, effort and responsibility as predominately male jobs which are paid at a higher salary." Holmes also claimed that she had been barred from scaling the career ladder despite her qualifications and that she was often required to perform higher-grade duties that were outside her job description.[53] Other plaintiffs, carefully selected for racial and occupational diversity, included Helen Castrilli, a shorthand secretary; Exa T. Emerson, a counselor at a school for disabled children; Lauren McNiece, a library technician; Louise Peterson, a licensed practical nurse; and Willie Mae Willis, a food service worker.[54]

At trial, Newman argued that the State of Washington had known for years that its pay policies were discriminatory and had chosen not to remedy the disparities.[55] Among AFSCME's expert witnesses were Ray Marshall, secretary of labor under President Jimmy Carter, who testified that his own analysis of Washington clericals' pay—which examined the data in terms of knowledge and skills, mental demands, accountability, and working conditions—found significant disparities in male- and female-dominated jobs that the State of Washington should have corrected. Former EEOC chairperson Eleanor Holmes Norton also testified on behalf of AFSCME. She explained that sex-biased wage disparities kept skilled women in poverty. "For example, a maintenance man with no skills will make more than a skilled typist."[56]

The State of Washington fought AFSCME's allegations, refuting the union's suggestion that complying with sex equality law required dramatically refiguring wages. In her opening statement, Assistant Attorney General (and future Washington State governor) Christine Gregoire claimed, "The question before this Court, your honor, is whether you should ratify an individual's subjective evaluation of the worth of a job with no reference whatsoever to the marketplace and the marketplace determination as to the value of that job insofar as pay is concerned."[57] Attorneys for the state marshaled the testimony of elite experts and state employees to demonstrate both the absence of sex discrimination and the unfeasibility of comparable worth. Roger Sanford, General Personnel Services unit manager in the state Department of Personnel, testified, "To my knowledge we have never recruited for employment with the state for what is termed 'male' or 'female' employment," and "neither I nor any other person with whom I work in state government to my knowledge has ever intentionally discriminated against women in state employment."[58] Economist June O'Neill argued that comparable worth was both unfeasible and contradictory to basic market principles. "The idea that the price of things should be based on an idea of intrinsic worth was long ago dispensed with. Arguments over the 'just price' were in vogue in the days of St. Thomas Aquinas. Nowadays, most people would agree that it would be inefficient, if not downright foolish, to set a schedule of consumer prices based on an independent evaluation of what their prices ought to be."[59]

In 1983, Judge Jack Tanner ruled in favor of AFSCME. The State of Washington was ordered to immediately begin giving comparable worth raises. Lead attorney Winn Newman declared that the victory "put meat on the Gunther skeleton" by demonstrating the kind of evidence that could convince courts to implement comparable worth.[60] Newman compared the win to landmark civil rights decisions and predicted that more victories would follow: "This ruling will break the back of sex-based wage discrimination in this country. . . . The case takes recognition of the fact that employers have deliberately segregated workers according to sex, paying one group at an inferior rate. It's really an extension of the Supreme Court's school desegregation decision, which said that separation of the races denoted the inferiority of one race."[61] Nancy Reder, NCPE executive director, described the 1983 ruling in *AFSCME v. Washington* as "the proverbial crack in the wall in the dam."[62]

Judge Tanner also indicated that he expected the wage disparities to be speedily addressed. He rejected as too weak the state legislature's 1982 vote to commit $1.5 million to a ten-year effort to implement comparable worth in state salaries. He commented, "I can't find any cases where, once discrimination is found, you can take ten years to correct it."[63] State officials estimated that complying with the ruling would cost between $839 million and $978 million over eighteen months. They projected that generating these funds would require raising taxes or cutting services by at least 20 percent. To these figures, Newman responded: "Congress, long ago, decided that you don't put a price tag on discrimination. The state deliberately cheated these women and has been financing itself off their backs."[64] Emboldened by their victory, AFSCME officials launched a nationwide effort to use Title VII to turn comparable worth into reality, filing local, state, and federal charges with government agencies and in court.

AFSCME's high-profile comparable worth campaign amplified a nationwide conversation about the value of work and the nature of sex discrimination. Clerical workers in AFSCME Local 101 in San Jose, California, struck for nine days, winning pay equity adjustments ranging from 5 percent to 15 percent. California governor Jerry Brown signed into effect section 19827.2 of the state labor code, establishing a "state policy of setting salaries for female-dominated jobs on the basis of comparability of the value of the work."[65] In Los Angeles, AFSCME brokered comparable worth raises for nearly four thousand city clerical workers in 1980. Gloria Larrigan, AFSCME local 3090's chief negotiator, commented, "We've been paid far less than our work is worth for years and years," and described the new contract as "a genuine breakthrough." The contract allowed for monthly salary raises of $100 or 10 percent, whichever was greater. Local 3090 member Jan White commented, "City clericals are fed up with not being recognized. We're not just coffeemakers anymore—we're the backbone of this city."[66] Between 1980 and 1983, AFSCME filed comparable worth wage discrimination charges against more than ten jurisdictions, including Philadelphia, Los Angeles, New York, Chicago, and the states of Connecticut, Hawaii, and Wisconsin.[67] In addition, AFSCME's research department conducted pay equity studies that revealed that female-dominated public sector jobs were typically paid between 15 and 35 percent below comparable male-typed positions.[68]

In filing these charges, AFSCME sought to force states to study and then publish figures to illustrate the wage disparity among men and women in various public sector occupations. Across the country, AFSCME locals surveyed state employees about their wages. Upon gathering this data, a group consisting typically of selected workers and representatives from management and the union came together and assigned points to each occupation based on the job's responsibility level.[69] Perhaps concerned that AFSCME's Washington victory would be replicated nationwide, many states produced their own pay equity studies in the early 1980s. For a fee, private consultants offered to "analyze state and counties' current compensation plan to determine whether a pay inequity exists among specified classes which are dominated by one gender." If consultants discovered an inequity, they would develop a personnel payment system that was easily adaptable across the state and considered such diverse job elements as "expertise—education and training; decision-making—impact of decision, independence of decision-making; supervisory responsibility—number of staff supervised, nature of groups supervised, type of supervision exercised; contacts with others required by the job—types of contacts, purpose of contacts; working conditions—physical effort required by the job, hazards and exposure incurred in the course of work."[70] By the early 1980s, the comparable worth struggle bore fruit through successful state and local public sector campaigns to expand the meaning of Title VII beyond equal pay for equal work.

As of 1982, AFSCME had the most active litigation program of any union in the country, and this effort was squarely focused on the fight for pay equity.[71] In explaining why litigation was the centerpiece of the comparable worth struggle, AFSCME officials emphasized past instances where legal mandates produced dramatic victories for workers without disrupting the economy. Many of these labor laws had been initially controversial but had become widely accepted. Testifying before the House Committee on Civil Rights in 1982, AFSCME president Gerald McEntee described comparable worth as settled law. "It is not debatable whether equal pay for jobs of comparable value is required by law. . . . Title VII clearly prohibits discrimination in compensation. It is not debatable whether pay equity is economically feasible. Every time employers are forced to provide more fairness and justice in their employment practices, the corporate Chicken Littles predict economic collapse. But there wasn't any such collapse when the Fair Labor Standards Act was passed, when the National Labor Relations Act was passed, or when the Equal Pay Act was passed, and there won't be when employers start paying their female employees a full salary."[72]

AFSCME's comparable worth strategy also included building partnerships. AFSCME was a founder of NCPE, "the first national panel dedicated to the pay equity struggle." The NCPE was formed in 1979 to "serve as a clearinghouse and action center for activists fighting to upgrade the jobs and wages of women workers." At its founding, 130 delegates came to Washington. Linda Lampkin, AFSCME associate research director, gave a speech describing the union's pay equity activism. "In hearings and negotiations all over the country," Lampkin stated, "AFSCME locals and councils are now arguing that equal pay for jobs of comparable worth should be established to address pay inequities. And we've achieved pay adjustments for underpaid workers, both women and men."[73] NCPE's statement of founding principles framed pay equity as the next frontier in workplace sex equality while committing itself to legal strategies. Only pay equity could foment "a reversal of a historical pattern of devaluing work done by women," as well as a critical "solution to the problems of women workers in female-dominated occupations." The document also framed comparable worth as "an intrinsic part of the goal of Title VII of the Civil Rights Act of 1964."[74] NCPE's litigation task force held two meetings in the aftermath of the *Gunther* decision. The first was limited to Title VII lawyers, and the other, open to all comparable worth activists.[75] By 1984, NCPE consisted of more than one hundred groups and individuals ranging from unions, government agencies, professional groups, and women's rights and civil rights groups.[76]

Women's labor advocates joined the comparable worth struggle as well. The Coalition of Labor Union Women (CLUW) was founded in Chicago in 1974 to address members' "special concerns as unionists and women in the labor force . . . in an inter-union framework."[77] Like AFSCME's Interim Committee on Sex Discrimination, CLUW saw sex equality law as key to advancing the interests of women unionists. CLUW's statement of purpose asserted that strong labor laws for women could ensure "full employment and job opportunities and shorter work weeks without loss of pay, child care legislation, a livable minimum wage for all workers, improved maternity and pension benefits, improved health and safety coverage, expanded educational opportunities, mass action for final ratification of the Equal Rights Amendment, guaranteed collective bargaining rights for all workers, the right to strike, and an extension of truly protective legislation for all workers."[78] By 1979, the seven-thousand-member CLUW was at the forefront of advocating for federal protections for comparable worth.[79] There was considerable cross-pollination among these groups, as AFSCME Interim Sex Discrimination Committee leader Mozell McNorriell served on CLUW's national coordinating committee.[80]

Feminist social movement groups publicly committed to the comparable worth struggle as well. NOW action vice president and former Sears campaign leader Mary Jean Collins urged the group to put its full support behind pay equity in 1984. "Most women know there is something wrong with their paychecks and if we frame the issue properly, we have unlimited possibilities for state and local actions involving public and private employers, and for legislative and public information activities." She reminded her fellow officials about the recent ERA campaign. "The more the ERA became a pocketbook issue, e.g. 59 cents and insurance discrimination, the stronger the support became both for the issue and for NOW."[81] That year, NOW's national convention passed a unanimous resolution in support of comparable worth.[82]

Chicago-based Women Employed pursued "a litigation strategy that will get the best wage-gap cases to the Supreme Court for decision," according to Nancy B. Kreiter, the group's research director. Women Employed worked to pressure federal and state civil rights officials to view the wage gap as the problem of the 1980s, just as boosting women and minorities into nontraditional jobs was the issue of the 1970s.[83] Nancy Perlman, director of the Center for Women in Government, a nonprofit group based in Albany, publicly rejected the excuse that different jobs could not be compared. "You can compare apples and oranges if you compare their nutritional qualities rather than the superficial appearance. It's the same with jobs."[84]

As courts wrestled with comparable worth and labor and feminist groups coalesced to fight for it, officials in government agencies tasked with interpreting sex equality laws came to embrace it outright. President Jimmy Carter's administration strengthened sex equality law enforcement, boosting budgets, cutting red tape, and appointing civil rights advocates to powerful positions. Key among these was Eleanor Holmes Norton, EEOC chairperson between 1977 and 1981. A civil rights activist and attorney, Norton had participated in the Student Nonviolent Coordinating Committee and the Mississippi Freedom Summer as a college student. She served as the assistant legal director of the American Civil Liberties Union until 1970, when she was tapped to lead the New York City Human Rights Commission. There, she presided over the nation's first public hearings on sex discrimination. She also represented a class of women employees of *Newsweek* magazine in their Title VII lawsuit.[85] Norton's dedication to strengthening sex discrimination law defined her tenure as the EEOC's first female chairperson. Upon assuming that role, she began a deliberate campaign to infuse comparable worth into national policy.

Norton and her staff surveyed legal options and scholarly research, coordinated hearings on the issue, and built public support.[86] She explained that a key obstacle facing comparable worth was the fact that "the average woman hasn't heard of it."[87] To convince the public that objective science made the case for comparable worth, in 1977 the EEOC hired the National Research Council of the National Academy of Sciences to conduct a national wage study and determine whether a comparable worth policy could raise women's wages nationwide.[88] The study, "Women, Work and Wages: Equal Pay for Jobs of Equal Value," identified "substantial discrimination in pay" nationwide and prescribed "job evaluation plans" as a solution to women's systemic low wages. Concluding that female-dominated jobs were paid less "at least in part *because* they are held mainly by women," the report suggested comparable worth pay adjustments as a viable solution.[89] In the spring of 1980, the EEOC held hearings on comparable worth, where representatives of business, labor, and feminist groups voiced their support or opposition. Norton opened the hearings by characterizing pay inequities across job segregation as "the largest and most difficult issue left unresolved under Title VII today," describing the hearings as "the most important hearings this commission has had in a decade."[90] She noted that job segregation and wage discrimination were traditionally addressed separately, and she intended to uncover how they worked together. She explained, "The time has come to resolve this question, systematically and carefully."[91]

The Norton-led EEOC also wrote amicus curiae briefs supporting comparable worth in several federal court cases, including *Gunther*. That brief framed pay equity as the proper next step in the history of Title VII's sex provision. Starting with the EEOC's founding, the brief stated, the commission "issued a series of decisions that clearly demonstrate that it did not deem a finding of 'equal work' necessary to establish a sex-based discrimination claim," listing specific cases between 1966 and 1971 when the EEOC found lower pay scales for women discriminatory. In short, the EEOC's brief claimed, several of its early rulings gestured toward comparable worth, and none of its previous opinions ruled it out.[92] After the *Gunther* decision, Norton and the EEOC began to enshrine comparable worth into its permanent policies, issuing new guidelines for its field offices requiring officials to investigate sex-based wage discrimination claims that went beyond equal pay for equal work. They advised that "counseling of potential charging parties should be expanded to reflect the scope of *Gunther*."[93] Comparable worth gained remarkable momentum in the late 1970s and early 1980s. Officials like Norton realized that making comparable worth a permanent part of Title VII law would require them to take patient steps toward building public support and a legal foundation. In 1983, pay equity campaigns were unfolding in more than 140 cities, states, and local areas.[94]

*   *   *

As comparable worth's advocates began to coalesce and gain momentum, so did its opponents. A number of scholars have recently written about business leaders and political conservatives' increasing influence in these years. Emboldened by an early-1970s global economic crisis that left a fog of malaise and uncertainty in its wake, these powerful men deployed the abstract metaphor of the free market as an antidote to many of the nation's specific problems. Forming associations and lobby groups that fought to defang regulations and discredit the welfare state, they also advocated individuals' "right to work" free from state or union interference.[95]

These groups took explicit aim at Title VII. A group of corporate leaders formed the Equal Employment Advisory Council (EEAC) in 1969 as a privately financed lobby group. The group began a "legal counter-attack" on the rights revolution by drafting and feeding proposed labor legislation to conservative members of Congress. In the mid-1970s, the EEAC helped to convince the U.S. Supreme Court to block workers' efforts to gain a flexible Sabbath day under Title VII's religious discrimination clause and spoke out against requirements for government contract holders to establish affirmative action plans that could render them vulnerable to countersuits by aggrieved white males. As comparable worth gained momentum, the group shifted its focus, filing amicus briefs and publishing a book, *Comparable Worth: Issues and Alternatives*, in 1980. Echoing arguments from the book, the EEAC filed a brief in *Gunther*, also supported by the National League of Cities, which framed comparable worth as a sure route to distorting the power of the judiciary. The brief claimed that comparable worth would grant judges unchecked authority to declare jobs comparable or not. It reasoned, "This is precisely the analysis Congress rejected as unworkable and an inappropriate exercise for the courts." Norton warily described the EEAC as "a force to be reckoned with."[96]

Business interests also took aim at comparable worth in smaller arenas. In Florida in 1985, the state's biggest business lobby, Associated Industries of Florida (AIF), targeted comparable worth out of their concern that public sector pay equity adjustments could be extended to the private sector. The group successfully stalled HB 63, a bill that aimed merely to create a pay equity study commission for the state. An AIF-funded report found that implementing comparable worth in state salaries would cost each Florida resident $871 in extra taxes. AIF and other Florida business interests seized on this figure, countering pay equity advocates' framing of the issue as a matter of fairness with a new narrative centered on taking from taxpayers to give to undeserving state employees. This pressure from industry also illustrates one reason why advocates found it so difficult to win any kind of redistributive model of equality. Conservatives became increasingly adept at substituting one definition of equality for another, arguing that sex equality had already been achieved. They accused pay equity advocates of violating sacred market principles and distorting sex equality provisions' inherent meaning.[97]

In 1985, conservatives amplified these pro-business arguments to break the back of pay equity advocates' Title VII strategy. That year saw the U.S.

Commission on Civil Rights (CCR), the EEOC, and federal courts issue resounding condemnations of comparable worth. After holding two days of hearings, the CCR, a bipartisan federal advisory agency, voted five-to-two to reject comparable worth as an appropriate remedy for sex discrimination.[98] The official report and commissioners' public comments represented a range of conservative arguments.[99] CCR staff director Linda Chavez expressed her fear that comparable worth would harm working-class women, "inducing" their employers to "replace them with more highly skilled workers or with automated technology."[100] Commission vice chairman Morris V. Abram similarly argued that comparable worth would harm women because they "work less hours, have less seniority and work more intermittently" than men.[101] Commissioner Esther Gonzalez-Arroyo Buckley explained that comparable worth would undermine the free market principles that had already begun to boost women's workplace status. "If you implement a comparable worth system, you eliminate the drive to compete." Further, she said, "you no longer have society saying, 'Hey, you are female. Forget it.' Now, if you are a female doctor, a female surgeon, jobs are a lot more open."[102] Commission chairman Clarence Pendleton had especially harsh condemnation of comparable worth. In one oft-cited remark, Pendleton described comparable worth as "the looniest idea since [the children's television show] Loony Tunes." Describing comparable worth as "a radical departure from the policies underlying our market economy," he accused advocates of engaging in "a disingenuous attempt to restructure our free enterprise system into a state-controlled economy under the guise of 'fairness.'"[103] Pendleton also shared his colleagues' view that comparable worth would harm working-class women. "If you're going to raise those wages, there's not going to be much left for the lowest paid," hypothesizing that "if wages of some office workers were raised then they would be replaced by coffee machines."[104]

The CCR's dramatic rejection of comparable worth drew equally impassioned rebukes. The two progressive commissioners, Mary Frances Berry and Blandina Cardenas Ramirez, issued their own statement in tandem with the majority's. The argued, "Comparable worth or pay equity, like any other concept, should be applied prudently with a full recognition of any limitations that might exist." They described pay equity as "an important tool in the arsenal for attacking employment discrimination."[105] NOW president Judy Goldsmith called the CCR report on comparable worth "an abomination, and quite simply, [it] makes a mockery of the once independent, once respected, once credible civil rights commission." Goldsmith accused the CCR of neglecting its mandate in order to cater to business interests. "In issuing a report that could have been written by the Chamber of Commerce, the National Association of Manufacturers, or any other business organization, the commission has chosen to ignore the realities facing employed women today."[106] In 1985, NCPE's chairman Eileen Stein, previously a CCR general counsel, testified before that commission, remarking on how much her former employer had changed. "I am particularly saddened that the commission has become little more than a tax-supported advocacy group—one which publicizes the Reagan administration's anti–civil rights philosophy and seeks to undermine the rights of all Americans to be free from discrimination in the workplace." As a result, Stein stated, the CCR was "out of step with the rest of the country." She continued, "Indeed, it is ironic that the commission claims job evaluation systems are inherently subjective and unreliable, while its own staff, like most of the federal sector, is paid according to just such a 'subjective' system—i.e. the G.S. rating."[107]

Several months later, the EEOC similarly condemned comparable worth. President Ronald Reagan had replaced Eleanor Holmes Norton as EEOC chair with conservative jurist and civil servant Clarence Thomas—a move Winn Newman characterized as "plac[ing] the foxes in charge of the chicken coop" by appointing to civil rights offices officials who were "uniformly hostile to the programs they are supposed to administer."[108] Thomas put a halt to the agency's preliminary endorsement of comparable worth, allegedly so that the commission could study it. After several years, Chairman Clarence Thomas announced his agency's decision that "sole reliance on a comparison of the intrinsic value of dissimilar jobs—which command different wages in the market—does not prove a violation of Title VII. We are convinced that Congress never authorized the government to take on wholesale restructuring of wages that were set by non–sex based decisions of employers—by collective bargaining—or by the marketplace."[109] In addition to declaring comparable worth beyond the scope of Title VII's intended meaning, Thomas also accused advocates of fabricating public controversy that far outstripped workers' actual interest in the theory. "Comparable worth cases represent a tiny fraction of all wage discrimination charges we receive," he claimed.[110] The EEOC stopped fielding comparable worth complaints in the wake of Thomas' pronouncement.[111]

Even earlier gains began to slip away, as federal courts also began to reject the comparable worth theory. In 1985 the Ninth Circuit Court of Appeals reversed the lower court's finding in favor of AFSCME in *AFSCME v. State of Washington*, rejecting comparable worth as the grounds for a Title VII sex discrimination complaint. The next year, the Seventh Circuit Court of Appeals threw out a similar case filed by Illinois nurses. The court's en banc ruling described comparable worth as "not a legal concept, but a shorthand expression for the movement to raise the ratio of wages in traditionally women's jobs to wages in traditionally men's jobs."[112] In 1988, the U.S. Supreme Court diminished Title VII's potential as a route to across-the-board challenges to seemingly sex-neutral employment policies that yielded divergent outcomes for groups. The court ruled in *Watson v. Fort Worth Bank and Trust* that Title VII challenges to promotion systems could be subject to only disparate treatment, rather than disparate impact, analysis.[113] As we will see in the next chapter, by the late 1980s courts and federal civil rights agencies had drained Title VII's potential as a bulwark against the intersectional sex, race, and class discrimination faced by those women who were unable to climb out of the pink-collar ghetto as individuals.

*   *   *

In the heyday of their campaign in the late 1970s and early 1980s, pay equity advocates pursued a range of strategies in high politics and at the grassroots. But throughout, Title VII remained the centerpiece of their plan; the law brought the muscle that could force employers to accept comparable worth. In their efforts to channel Title VII's power to transform workplace practices and punish violators, advocates put the bulk of their resources into comparable worth litigation. Yet unions were investing in their ability to use legal strategies just as conservative officials invested in new strategies to diminish them. In the wake of conservative victories, comparable worth activists were limited to public sector and state-level activism and the narrower language of the Equal Pay Act. By the late 1980s, litigation was no longer the cutting edge of advocates' comparable worth strategy; it had become, according to NCPE executive director Claudia Wayne, "clearly a strategy of last resort."[114]

State and local comparable worth activism yielded some benefits to public sector workers. AFSCME continued to pressure state governments at various levels to reveal wage rates and lay bare the disparities between rates of pay for specific male- and female-dominated jobs. The NCPE remained active, publicizing international and local developments and pressuring states to take action.[115] Twenty states spent over $400 million for pay equity raises between 1984 and 1988. By that year, forty-three states and D.C. had conducted at least preliminary research on pay equity; twenty-three states and D.C. had conducted pay equity studies; twenty states had adjusted salaries; and six states were in the process of completing broad implementation of comparable worth plans. Minnesota was the only state to completely implement its pay equity plan.[116] AFSCME continued to squeeze state and local governments, some of which agreed to out-of-court settlements. Women's Rights Department acting director Cathy Collette claimed, "Whatever is happening in the courts, we're doing very well at the political level and at the bargaining table." Winn Newman concurred. "The lawsuits, even if they lose, have been the conduit for change. They have raised everyone's consciousness."[117]

Measured against advocates' hopes for comparable worth, its successes appear quite limited. But comparable worth campaigns marked a critical turning point in Title VII's history because they forced all the major players involved in efforts to define and implement sex equality law—labor and feminist activists, workers and employers, and attorneys and state officials—to reckon with its essential nature. Could Title VII transform employment systems, or was its reach more limited, primarily helping deserving individual workers to be treated as interchangeable? In adopting the latter, less expansive interpretation, courts and government officials also affirmed conservative arguments that the labor market was a sex-neutral mechanism whose unequal outcomes reflected individual choices and the intrinsic value of work.

By the time of the comparable worth controversy, American workers had long encountered a bifurcated system that reserved elite and well-compensated jobs for white men and confined women and most men of color to a subordinate, low-wage job ghetto. By rebranding this two-track system as a class divide, conservative jurists and government officials shepherded it into the era of sex equality. And working-class women such as the hotel maids profiled in the next chapter found that employers could turn this narrowed strain of sex equality against them, undermining their efforts to hold onto vestiges of the gendered world of work that had granted them a measure of freedom.

Sex Equality and the Service Sector

As comparable worth advocates sought to apply expansive interpretations of sex equality to the public labor force, others tested the boundaries of the law in the private service sector. In the late 1970s, nearly half of working women were in occupations that were at least 75 percent female, and their concentration in these feminized jobs had only intensified in recent years. But sex equality provisions still held promise for these workers. Courts and federal officials had begun to apply the Equal Pay Act of 1963 (EPA) across the gendered division of labor—where workers engaged in substantially equal, but not necessarily identical, tasks.[1] In line with a recent federal court opinion, the United States Department of Labor (DOL) in 1977 directed hotels to pay equal wages to the male-dominated custodial position of houseman (also called housekeeping attendant), which typically involved the heavier and more varied aspects of housekeeping work, and the female-dominated position of maid (also called room attendant), which entailed more repetitive tasks. The EPA banned employers from reducing wages in equalizing pay rates; thus, hotels would have to raise the maids' earnings to match the housemen's in order to conform to the new DOL policy.[2]

In most cities, this adjustment was easily carried out because the wage gap between male- and female-typed housekeeping work was negligible. But in New York City the disparity was significant. Hotel managers there rejected this capacious interpretation of the EPA, instead continuing to pay the unequal rates and precipitating a bitter legal struggle that lasted from the late 1970s until the early 1990s. As the showdown between the unions and the hotels unfolded, the Hotel Trades Council (HTC), an association of hotel trade unions, was increasingly on the defensive, hamstrung by coterminous struggles and declining strength, the mounting power of the New York Hotel Association (NYHA), and comparable worth advocates' recent losses. Concerned about the unions' own Title VII and EPA liability and in pursuit of even diminished concessions, the HTC built a case to raise the maids' pay that emphasized the similarities between their jobs and the housemen's.

This strategy drove a wedge between the maids and their advocates. The maids, many of whom were immigrants and women of color, advanced sex equality claims that drew legitimacy from the gendered division of labor. Shielded from some of the most physically taxing aspects of housekeeping work, they refused to compare themselves to their male counterparts. Plaintiff maid Lucy Osorio denied that the jobs of houseman and maid were interchangeable. The job of housekeeping attendant "corresponds to a man," she explained, adding, "I don't think we can do it." Osorio had long refused to perform such tasks as filling the linen closet, moving furniture, and cleaning soiled walls, duties she viewed as "men's work."[3] In pursuing equal wages by emphasizing their work's difficulty and intrinsic value, the maids sought to shore up the sex-based protections embedded in the long-standing segmentation of hotel work. But their vision of workplace justice became irrelevant to their own campaign, as their advocates fought to build a winnable case within a shrinking legal and political landscape.[4]

The conflict over the value of hotel housekeepers' work reveals the multiple channels through which sex equality provisions were drained of their potential to deliver substantive benefits to workers. Historians have written extensively on how notions of gender difference legitimated the twentieth-century expansion of the service sector and the devaluation of service work.[5] But late twentieth-century efforts to formally de-gender these jobs degraded them further. Service sector sex equality campaigns like the maids' played out as hotels joined other employers in developing new methods of labor control. They turned federal courts' narrowing interpretations of worker protections such as the EPA and Title VII and the lengthiness of legal processes into advantages the workers' advocates could not effectively counter. While the HTC channeled its efforts into resolving the sex equality issue through legal avenues, the NYHA adjusted aspects of housekeeping work in ways that lowered the stakes of that conflict. Shifting toward a more consumer- and luxury-focused business model, the hotels merged and flattened distinctions in what had once been a highly fragmented labor force. Managers contained housekeeping costs by eliminating the houseman position, adding their heavy tasks to the maids' workload and increasing the amenities that required cleaning in each room. At the bargaining table, the embattled union conceded some of the maids' desired protections in order to gain across-the-board wage increases. This strategy freed the NYHA to make still more changes to the housekeepers' jobs that rendered sex-based arguments for equal pay largely irrelevant by the time the union won wage equalization a decade later.

By the early 1990s, the maids' concerns about equality-as-interchangeability had come to fruition. NYHA agreed to a settlement that proffered all housekeepers the same backbreaking work: equality without protection. The narrow strain of sex equality that leveled wages across the gendered divide delivered workers a pyrrhic victory amid the general degradation, merging, and outsourcing of low-wage service jobs like theirs. Workplace protections increasingly defined to equalize the rights of individuals freed employers to remake the work itself, preventing service workers from deriving substantive benefits from workplace equality provisions, affirming efforts to degrade their jobs, and delimiting related activism along the way.

*   *   *

The housekeepers' wage equalization lawsuit marked a single conflict amid decades of struggle over the terms of work in the segmented hospitality labor force. When hotel workers began to organize in the late nineteenth century, they conceived of themselves as skilled and subdivided, and they organized their labors along a craft, rather than an industrial, model. Soon after the American Federation of Labor (AFL) was established in 1886, local unions of waiters, cooks, and bartenders sought independent charters. In 1891, those fourteen unions affiliated as the Hotel and Restaurant Employees National Alliance (HRE). By 1904, the HRE had more than fifty thousand members nationwide.[6]

Yet hotels were complex work systems that remained fractured by skill, ethnicity, and sex. The food and beverage servers, electricians, building service operators, office workers, upholsterers, and painters employed in a single hotel each belonged to their own separate AFL locals and bargained independently with management.[7] Early HRE meetings were conducted in at least three languages—French, German, English, and others when needed. One HRE leader referred to the union ranks as "a regular League of Nations" on account of the many races and cultures represented.[8] Despite this diversity, the HRE exercised caution in organizing new immigrants and the unskilled. The crush of immigrant workers to New York after 1907 brought southern and eastern Europeans rather than the Germans and Scandinavians of decades past. These immigrants arrived by steerage and joined waiters' or cooks' benevolent associations led and peopled by others of their own nationalities. Many of them viewed the HRE—colloquially termed "the Irish bartenders' union"—with suspicion. Until 1938, no hotel in New York had enough union members within its ranks to be considered a union hotel.[9]

For decades, divisions of ethnicity and skill foreclosed the possibility of unionizing on an industrial model. HRE historian Matthew Josephson described the typical hotel dining room as, "in effect, a 'shop'" operated by workers with competing interests. "The waitress who marks too many of her orders for cocktails as 'rush orders' may be rebuffed by the busy service bartender—and she may be seen sometimes bursting into tears of vexation. The cooks in the kitchen line up their work in methodical fashion and sometimes resist the urgent demands of nervous waiters for speed. The bartenders, in any case, used to take pride in the fact that they dealt directly with the public" and "tended to look down upon the 'menials' who cooked and washed dishes, and upon the waiters as well."[10] Single work sites within hotels, such as kitchens, saw ethnic tensions as well. In 1902, one hotel chef described his workplace's profound divisions. He informed the president of the HRE, "you will never live to see the day when the skilled workers of American kitchens will lay aside their peculiar clannish ideas and wholeheartedly cooperate with each other."[11] One HRE employee recalled that Cardinal Spellman of the New York City Catholic Church approved the selection of managers and their assistants. Many times the employers avoided hiring entirely; a straw boss chose people who spoke his language in exchange for a kickback.[12] Ethnic differences among workers thus mapped onto labor force divisions.

But New York hotel workers began to rethink their segmentation, noting that hotel managers' cooperation reinforced their poor working conditions. The NYHA became the largest organization of hotel operators nationwide; by the 1930s, it represented 167 member hotels that varied widely by size, profitability, clientele, and price.[13] In response to New York hotels' increased collaboration, union leaders began to join forces to fight for improvements to their mutually dismal terms of work. Facing scant job security and crushing hours, hotel workers also earned wages described by a 1938 New York State Department of Labor report as "the lowest paid of any service industry."[14]

They created the HTC as an umbrella organization that could coordinate efforts while allowing each affiliated local to maintain its independence.[15] Convening craft unions of electricians, operating engineers, painters, office workers, telephone operators, upholsterers, and more, the HTC also saw individual printers, laundry workers, plumbers, and steamfitters join where their own craft unions did not belong to the council.[16] The historian Joshua Freeman has noted that such joint trades councils were unusually common in New York. There, unions representing garment workers and related trades formed such a council, and unions of painters, wallpaperers, and decorators coalesced in another. Employer associations like the NYHA were also typical. One postwar study indicated that three-quarters of unionized New York workers were covered by contracts negotiated with an employer association rather than a single employer, by contrast to a nationwide rate of one-third.[17]

In 1938, the HTC and NYHA formally recognized each other as bargaining agents and empanelled an impartial moderator to assist with contract negotiations and disputes.[18] Their inaugural agreement codified a long-standing gendered division of labor in hotel work. Sex-specific state labor laws also buttressed this divide. New York women were restricted to an eight-hour maximum workday and a forty-eight-hour workweek. State labor laws also banned them from working as bartenders and bellhops, jobs state legislators judged as morally compromising and too strenuous.[19] The 1938 agreement between the HTC and NYHA reflected this logic by sorting housekeeping tasks by sex. Maids performed "routine duties in the cleaning and servicing of guests' rooms and baths." They changed and remade bedding, cleaned fixtures, vacuumed carpets, and arranged furniture.[20] Housemen performed more strenuous and less repetitive housekeeping work including "heavy cleaning operations in hotel halls, public baths, showers, and lavatories; mov[ing] furniture and prepar[ing] rooms for periodic renovations." The 1938 job description explained that physical strength was essential. While the houseman position "is frequently a beginning job for which experience is not required," an applicant "should be strong enough to stand sustained and arduous work."[21] Thus, while maids felt the constant pressure of time, working to meet a daily quota of rooms, housemen performed heavier, but less routine, tasks. In addition, maids in larger hotels frequently had the support of a bath maid, a woman who deep-cleaned each room's bathroom and freed the maid to attend to other tasks. The sexed divide in hotel housekeeping correlated to a vast pay disparity; the

1941 HTC-NYHA contract listed housemen's weekly wage rate as $21.50 and the maids' as $14.85.[22]

As in housekeeping, nearly every hotel job was sex-segregated and hierarchically organized, with the occupations designated for men involving heavier work and commanding higher pay. According to a 1938 HTC list of hotel jobs and wages, a linen man, linen boy, or linen-room houseman would receive and dispose of dirty laundry, separate and count soiled items, and maintain the linen supply in maid closets. A linen-room woman or girl examined and sorted pieces prior to laundering, then checked and stacked laundered articles. Similarly, while a lobby porter performed "general cleaning duties such as dusting, washing and mopping mezzanines, foyers, lobbies, lavatories adjoining stairways and their equipment," for a lower wage, a mezzanine maid cleaned the public ladies rest room and replenished lobby supplies.[23] Hotel work's craft orientation contributed to this gendered specialization. For example, the 1955 collective bargaining agreement contained more than 150 job classifications, many of which were explicitly gendered—such as "vegetableman" and "vegetablewoman." Wages for each classification were distinct despite their similarities.[24]

With the exception of a brief leveling out during World War II, women's wages hovered below men's in comparable hotel jobs. Hotels suffered severe wartime labor shortages, and women assumed many waiter, cook, and dishwasher positions. A few even worked as managers and bartenders.[25] In 1938, full-time women hotel workers earned an average of twenty-eight cents an hour, but that rate rose to fifty-four cents per hour in 1945.[26] But hotel occupations in New York City were rapidly resegregated at war's end. A 1946 survey found the chambermaid and bath maid categories to be entirely female, while bellboys and the entire maintenance department were 99 percent male. A second 1946 survey found that pervasive sex segregation existed on account of jobs being designated for men "because they involve heavy lifting (porter, bellboy, fireman)." But more often, as the historian Dorothy Sue Cobble observed, jobs such as room clerk or bartender were simply "men's jobs because of tradition." The explicitly gendered division of labor intensified at war's end.[27]

Amid this sex-typing of hotel work, women advocated through their HTC unions to raise wages and improve working conditions. At the 1956 convention, maids vowed to fight to put "$2 into the pay envelope of every member of the housekeeping department."[28] Maids at the Times Square Motor Hotel won a raise in 1976 by cleaning "only as many rooms as they felt management was paying for" and staging a protest that convinced many guests to change hotels or to speak to management on their behalf.[29] Yet maids never called for the elimination of sex-based distinctions in the work of male and female housekeepers. Both before and after the mid-1960s passage of federal sex equality laws, maids frequently referred to women's limited physical capabilities in attempting to protect themselves from extreme physical exertion on the job. A 1948 HTC survey found that maids throughout the city resented being "expected to do much heavier work than formerly" including "lifting heavy furniture; cleaning Venetian blinds; carrying linen from the linen room to the floors; and working a six-day schedule, which is still done in some shops." Maids and their union representatives fought these changes through the parties' official arbiter.[30] Later that year, the arbiter found that a maid was justified in quitting a job requiring her to move furniture. The maid, whom the arbiter noted was fifty years of age and weighed approximately one hundred pounds, had been required "to perform heavy work which housemen perform in most other hotels."[31] Two years later, maids at the Hampshire House protested when such chores as "turning mattresses, lifting heavy furniture, cleaning Venetian blinds, washing walls and carrying linen" were added to their list of tasks.[32]

At the maids' own insistence, the HTC fought to spare them from the heavier aspects of housekeeping work. The HTC newsletter boasted that maids at the Marcy Hotel had been able to reverse management's direction "that fresh linen should henceforth be delivered on the floors and soiled linen picked up there for return downstairs." Instead, maids "will put their soiled linen in bags and leave it at a specified time for the elevator men to pick up. No more back breaking toil of carrying heavy bundles of linen up and down. The union has been asking for this system in a number of hotels, and it has gone into effect in some."[33] Maids at the Edison Hotel in 1948 fought the installation of new vacuum cleaners that consisted of "about 12 feet of hose, 24 feet of cable and five feet of pipe and were entirely too heavy for a woman to manage." The maids unanimously opposed the new vacuums, and the union housekeeping committee decided "that it must be considered a vacuum man's job and that maids could not accept the work."[34] Overwhelmingly, maids asked for protection from physically challenging tasks, not to share the work assigned to their male counterparts.

The HTC's sex-based strategy to improve the maids' working conditions thus diverged from its race-based efforts. While both hotel maids and the HTC framed the women's rights in terms of their physical differences from men, the HTC simultaneously fought to equalize opportunities for racial minorities in its membership. Upon Title VII's passage, the HTC called for a "realistic equal opportunity program" that would target "fuller minority representation in some hotels but primarily . . . better representation overall in certain departments."[35] In 1964, members of the HTC met with representatives of the Congress on Racial Equality, the National Association for the Advancement of Colored People, and Puerto Rican civil rights groups to discuss the need to train and upgrade minority employees.[36] The NYHA did not resist, issuing a joint statement with the HTC pledging "employment and promotion opportunities for workers from minority groups, which has been unanimously endorsed by civil rights organizations, who have agreed to designate a representative each to meet periodically with the joint industry-union committee to review progress made."[37] The 1966 contract between the HTC and NYHA banned discrimination on account of race, color, creed, and national orientation, but sidestepped sex.[38] Thus, even as invested parties agreed on the need to address racial imbalances, they affirmed sex segmentation as affording women necessary protections in housekeeping work.

*   *   *

In the mid-1960s, Title VII and the EPA invested government officials with new authority to evaluate the gendered divisions in housekeeping work. While Title VII banned sex discrimination "on account . . . of sex," the EPA established a more specific standard, outlawing sex-based wage discrimination in work requiring "equal skill, effort, and responsibility." But as the previous chapter revealed, these laws' precise language belied the challenges of articulating their relationship to each other and applying them to disparate corners of the labor force. Initially, the DOL interpreted the maids' and housemen's jobs as too dissimilar to merit equal wages under the EPA. But in the early 1970s federal courts began to favor Title VII's broader standard, deeming some sex-based pay schemes illegal even where the male- and female-typed work at issue was not identical. As the legal scholar Catharine A. MacKinnon has noted of these cases, federal courts determined that "Equal . . . meant substantially equal."[39]

The EPA's relationship to gendered janitorial work was spelled out by the U.S. District Court for the Southern District of Texas in the 1974 case

Brennan v. Houston Endowment Company. The DOL sued a Texas office building management company, alleging that the ten-cent wage differential paid to maids and janitors violated the EPA despite the jobs' gendered dissimilarities. The court agreed. While the men typically performed such tasks as operating "floor buffers, wet vacuums, or carpet pile lifters" as well as "those chores requiring the use of a step-ladder," whereas the women were tasked with "dusting, cleaning, removing trash, vacuuming, tile scrubbing, spot cleaning of walls and carpets, [and] cleaning venetian blinds," these jobs bore enough similarities to merit equal pay. The Fifth Circuit Court of Appeals upheld the decision. In the wake of this ruling, the DOL issued an opinion letter in 1977 stating that male- and female-typed hotel housekeeping work should be identically compensated.[40]

In most parts of the country, maids earned approximately $1 to $2 per week less than housemen, and the hotels bumped up the maids' pay. But the contract between the NYHA and HTC established a weekly pay gap of nearly $14.[41] Both HTC and NYHA officials expressed concern about the DOL's new position. In an executive board meeting, HTC leaders anticipated "an uproar here if the maids have to get a $14 increase and nothing goes to the housemen."[42] But they vowed to pursue equal pay, motivated by their own potential vulnerability for having fought for unequal wages in these positions since the 1930s. NYHA leaders refused to raise the maids' wages. They pointed out that DOL opinion letters were not binding and that federal courts often disregarded them.[43] Joseph Formicola, executive vice president of the NYHA, claimed that adjusting the maids' wages would disrupt the equilibrium of pay practices, threatening "the entire wage structure in the industry."[44] Yet HTC leaders were convinced that equal wages were inevitable in equivalent housekeeping jobs. President Jay Rubin warned Formicola that stalling on the equal pay issue "is endangering every individual employer who might be faced with having to pay retroactively under the Equal Pay Act of 1963 for this inequity."[45] HTC claimed that much of the work formerly shouldered by housemen had already been shifted to maids, thus demonstrating the jobs' essential interchangeability. Yet the NYHA maintained that these jobs were not equivalent and did not merit equal pay.

When the NYHA refused to eliminate the pay discrepancy, the HTC took the matter to the parties' formal arbiter, Millard Cass, in 1981.[46] After reviewing both sides' evidence and observing male and female housekeepers at work, Cass noted significant differences between the jobs. These included the "nature of the work itself, quotas for one and not for the other, physical requirements of strength for one and not the other, etc." Cass suggested one possible method for bringing sex equality to housekeeping: women who could meet preset "size and strength" standards could "be given a house-keeping attendant position when one is available," although no one could recall any situation where a male or female housekeeper worked in the opposite sex-typed position.[47] Despite the notable differences between these jobs Cass identified, the recent DOL opinion letter inspired him to mete out a compromise. Cass ordered "the equalization of the basic wage rates of room attendants and housekeeping attendants at the rate of the housekeeping attendants in all hotels." But he also granted the NYHA permission to increase the maids' workload, assigning each "up to three additional rooms in any week without extra compensation." HTC leaders condemned Cass' ruling. They believed that the extra work undermined the intent of the EPA and alleged that hotels abused the compromise by assigning the extra rooms to part-time employees and overloading some maids in order to lay others off.[48] Convinced that they had exhausted other options, HTC leaders traded formal bargaining for legal action.

But by late 1985, when the HTC and a class of fifty-eight maids filed EEOC charges accusing NYHA hotels of violating both Title VII and the EPA, the legal climate was becoming much more conservative with respect to sex and work. Federal courts had begun to block comparable worth advocates' efforts to leverage Title VII to remake pay schemes by more strongly emphasizing the Bennett amendment, a rider attached to Title VII that limited its application to pay practices to the stricter standard set by the Equal Pay Act. Thus hamstrung in the types of arguments they could make, HTC attorneys set out to prove that the disparate job descriptions of housemen and maids belied substantially similar occupations. They sought the elimination of the expanded room quota and the payment of back wages to room attendants from December 1982.[49] Because approximately thirty-five hundred women labored under the current discriminatory contract, the HTC alleged, New York City hotels "illegally took over $2.5 million per year from the women."[50] Responding to courts' increasing emphasis on workplace sex equality as interchangeability, HTC attorneys set out to demonstrate that maids' and housemen's work were essentially equivalent.

The standard job descriptions for housemen and maids in the HTC-NYHA contract indicated substantial differences between the jobs. Housemen experienced greater autonomy and a more casual work pace. According to the description, housemen wiped and cleaned mirrors and ash urns on assigned floors, moved furniture as needed, swept hallways and stairs when necessary, and did "general cleaning": giving a small number of vacant rooms a very thorough treatment that included vacuuming carpet, dusting ceilings, and cleaning wallpaper, fire extinguisher stations, and wall sconces.[51] By contrast, room attendants' work was much more detailed and repetitive. Room attendants maintained a daily room quota, and each room required a ritualized set of steps: "First, turn on all lights to check if any are out; open drapes, curtains and window to air the room; empty all ash trays and waste baskets, plus take out trays if any; strip bed, take dirty linen out, also from bathroom; bring in clean linen for bed and bathroom." Then, after cleaning the bathroom and dusting the entire room, they made each bed according to a specified order of operations: "Put bottom sheet on bed mostly to top so it can tuck in (miter the corner); put second sheet to top enough to fold over blanket; put blanket on; put 3rd sheet over blanket miter the bottom corners, go to the other side, miter corners of bottom sheet, if tuck in at bottom tuck in top the same. Now pull second sheet, blanket and third sheet over, miter corner don't tuck. Put top sheet at top under blanket, put second sheet over both, put on bedspread, put pillowcase on, but don't hold pillow under the chin. Lay pillow on bed (be sure no spots are on linen, bedspread is clean)."[52] The written job descriptions for maids and housemen conveyed the jobs as clearly distinct.

In efforts to uncover disparities between the formal job descriptions and the actual performance of male- and female-typed housekeeping jobs, the HTC hired occupational evaluator Norman Willis to examine and compare them.[53] Representatives of Willis's firm visited eleven hotels in 1985, observing room attendants and housekeeping attendants at work.[54] Willis then compared the jobs along four basic axes: knowledge and skills, which included "all the specialized or vocational or technical skill or aptitude that you have to have to perform any job satisfactorily"; mental demands; accountability; and working conditions, which referred to "the physical or mental effort that would be associated with the work or the exposure to physical harm or energy and the amount of discomfort which could be environmental discomfort, like working outdoors or being exposed to fumes, vibrations, and so forth. Or it could be emotional discomfort such as a fair job that has mental stress attached to it."[55] Willis found the jobs to be substantially equal, with only negligible differences in difficulty and responsibility. While housemen worked under more demanding conditions, he reported, the maids' close contact with guests' possessions and spaces required more accountability.[56]

Willis's findings buttressed the HTC's attorneys' efforts to prove that the labels of "houseman" and "maid" more accurately expressed the worker's sex than the job's content.[57] Labor advocates sought to re-label hotels' separate pay rates for these substantially similar jobs as vestiges of long-standing sex discrimination and a newly illegal practice.

*   *   *

As HTC attorneys and union officials built their equal pay case by emphasizing the commonalities between maids' and housemen's work, they gave rise to new tensions with the maids themselves. Advocates struggled to assemble a class of aggrieved room attendants who would claim that their work was essentially similar to housekeeping attendant's. Many of the women the HTC approached were hostile to the lawsuit. Those who were willing to participate refused to argue that their work was interchangeable with housemen's, and no plaintiff maid was willing to express her interest in the housemen's work. Instead, participant maids typically argued that their work was more valuable than their wages reflected or that their work's speed and repetition was roughly equal to the heaviness of the housemen's work. Heirs to a long-standing tradition of labor feminism that rooted rights claims in notions of fairness rather than sameness, the maids sought higher pay that would reflect the dignity of their work and allow them to keep pace with the cost of living.[58] But they also claimed that the gendered division of labor provided them with desired protections. The maids' arguments in favor of equity rather than interchangeability with housemen put them at odds with their advocates, who worked to build a winnable pay equity case in an increasingly hostile legal context.

As HTC and NYHA attorneys built their respective cases, attorneys for the NYHA interviewed the maids who were members of the class. In their testimony, many of the plaintiffs directly undermined their attorneys' claims by arguing that the maid and houseman jobs were essentially different and were properly sex-typed. Even when the room attendants argued that they might be able to perform the housemen's work, they viewed that work as male-typed. In 1986, plaintiff Marie Adamson explained that when she sought employment at the Dorset Hotel, she had not indicated that she would like any other job than room attendant. The NYHA attorney asked her, "If the unemployment or state employment office, actually, contacted you and they had said, Ms. Adamson, we do not have a chambermaid's job, we have a housemen's job, what would you have said to them?" Adamson replied, "I could do it," because, she reasoned, "what we do now is mostly move furniture. If I had to move furniture I would move it. Most of the time I do. If we do a room, and have to move a chair, I'm not going to wait for [the housemen], I have to do it."[59] Yet Adamson explained that she would not have accepted the hypothetical houseman job offer. That job was appropriately a man's, she explained, and she would prefer to be a maid supported by housemen to help with the heavier elements of her work. "I don't want it," she claimed, because "I'm satisfied with what I'm doing."[60]

Other maids echoed Adamson's insistence that they were capable of performing a houseman's work but did not want a houseman's job. Plaintiff Elise Andre claimed that she would reject the opportunity to work as a houseman, even for higher wages, because she was satisfied where she was: "I can do it, but like I tell you, I get used to my job, I like what I'm doing."[61] Similarly, room attendant Jacqueline Larry explained that she occasionally filled in for housemen on her floor. She found that work to be more difficult than her tasks as a maid, and she argued that such work was inappropriate for women. She reflected, "The rooms were like more dirty and dusty and it was like doing—It was like working like a man because we had to do like a houseman was doing." Larry stated that while she believed she was physically able to do the houseman's work, she would not want that job because it was too dirty.[62] Similarly, plaintiff Jeanine Jolibois claimed she knew that she could earn more money if she took on the housemen's heavier work, just as she would if she worked overtime or cleaned extra rooms. Yet she was satisfied with the length and content of her workday.[63] The maids' testimony reflected the value they attached to performing female-typed work and the freedom to set boundaries against tasks they found objectionable.

Yet the maids' depositions consistently revealed their interest in earning higher pay. Mildred Prince, a maid at the New York Hilton, was a widow from Barbados with five children. She had previously worked as a nurses' aide in a nursing home and constructing wheels in a bicycle factory. Prince claimed that her wages were simply too low for her to make ends meet, and she was equally troubled by the lack of fair pay even for long-time workers. She stated, "Look at my salary. I can't even go for a loan; everybody on the job 20 years, look at the salaries. It is incredible."[64] Other maids echoed Prince's concerns about their meager wages. On April 18, 1985, more than four hundred room attendants received what amounted to a pay cut because they dropped the rooms Cass had allowed NYHA to add to their quotas. Thereupon, militant room attendants complained about low pay, with one arguing, "Rent is rising, food and everything else costs more. I know no one wants a strike but everyone has to know we need a decent wage to live on and will do whatever the union asks."[65]

Other plaintiffs argued that they deserved higher pay to correspond to the difficulty of their work. Prince was asked how the hotel discriminated against women. She responded, "because I think we have a lot of work to do. And, every time they get a new approach or something new, it is really assigned to the maids. And the houseman does the same thing all the time."[66] When a NYHA attorney pressed for an example of the types of work that evidenced the discrimination, Prince responded, "Well, when I come in the room, we have furniture, two beds in each room, if not three, or one. And we clean the lamps, the shades, wash the furniture down, put bulbs in the lamp if it is out. Vacuum the floors, we have 14 tubs, 14 walls, 14 floors, 14 toilets, 14 face basins, plus the towels, sheets on the beds and sometimes I guess, the guests ask for extra, want something special, like, different things, and you have to do it." The attorney pressed, "And how is that discrimination by the hotel?" Prince responded, "Because we have a lot more work than a man. Because when it is a bad checkout we have a lot of garbage in the room. We have a lot more to do."[67] Prince argued that maids' work was more challenging and stressful than housemen's.

The attorneys for the NYHA also attempted to prove that the members of the class did not feel personally aggrieved or understand the legal proceedings. Jacqueline Larry, a room attendant at the Helmsley Hotel, admitted that she had never filed a grievance with her union delegate and didn't know anyone who had or who had complained because they were paid less than housemen.[68] Plaintiff Maria Rubinos, a native of Cuba, was asked what the EEOC was. She answered, "I think it's for the same, equalization, equal for the woman and the man, the same rights." Yet the defense attorneys cornered Rubinos into admitting that she did not recognize either the right to sue notice or the paperwork she had signed to join the lawsuit.[69] When asked whether she believed that the hotel discriminated against her, Marie Adamson said that she didn't understand the question, for "if they didn't discriminate against us, then we wouldn't be here."[70]

Other plaintiffs expressed uncertainty about their role in the lawsuit. When deposed, plaintiff Yvonne Simon, a maid at the Essex House Hotel, described joining the action. The union official had approached her and "told me to sign these papers. He said this is concerning the job. I said, will this have any effect on me on my job, I don't want the bosses to harass me or anything, otherwise I won't do no signing in anything. He said no. And this is concerning for the years that we have been working here, some kind of a back pay or something that, you know, they have for so many years that we have been working, and they are working on it to see what would work out for us. I said, oh, yes, I said all right. I said okay, I'll sign, if it's to help out everybody, I will sign. And I did sign." Simon recalled that the union official "said I was underpaid or something." She explained that the pressures of her job did not enable her to ask clarifying questions of the union official. "After I signed it I told him I can't stay, because look at the hour, and I have to try to get these rooms done. Because I was rushing. I just rushed down and rushed back up. . . . I didn't even stay ten minutes." The union official called her another time to sign some more papers. "I said, what is this all about, he said the same thing, it's not finished, it will take awhile. And then I signed them. I said I didn't have time to stay to read, but I put my trust in you, that's what I told him. And then I signed it, the front and back or whatever, and then I left."[71] A number of the plaintiff maids expressed uncertainty about the lawsuit's process and objectives.

Apart from the disparities between the plaintiff maids' arguments and the claims advanced by the lawsuit, the HTC struggled to build and maintain a coherent class of female housekeeping employees. Attorneys relied on union organizers to recruit and keep track of class members, but the information organizers gathered and managed often lacked necessary details and accuracy. In 1985, attorney Christine Owens asked organizer Raymond Hart to look into several discrepancies. For example, many of the signatures on the forms were impossible for the attorneys to decipher, as many of the plaintiffs had been educated overseas; duplicate names on forms led attorneys to wonder whether people had signed twice; the attorneys found disparities between the signed forms and the names on the formal lists; and eight men—who were obviously ineligible for class membership—had submitted consents. Owens explained that exactness was crucial, for the defense could weaken evidence by suggesting "that we're trying to pull a fast one by including individuals who are not room attendants."[72] Further, the housekeeping sector experienced frequent turnover, and many plaintiffs moved among hotels or to other service sector jobs. HTC attorneys worried that the instability of the hotel labor force would undermine their efforts to build a stable class of plaintiffs.

When the state Division of Human Rights contacted the plaintiffs to request more information about their claims, many asked their claims be thrown out.[73] State EEOC director Edward Mercado informed HTC attorneys that some of the plaintiffs he contacted "were unaware that the charges had been filed in their names. A number of these individuals stated that they were not in fact aggrieved and did not want the charges pursued on their behalf."[74] Other plaintiffs told the EEOC that they were not room attendants. In 1986, room attendant Zelidea Rivera was listed as a room attendant in the class, but when recontacted, she claimed that she was a housekeeping supervisor who wanted "absolutely nothing to do with the union or the suits." This development vexed HTC attorney Jim Hendriksen. He expressed his concern to his fellow attorneys in 1986. "If I was confident that this was an isolated occurrence, we could deal with this specific incident." Yet, in light of Mercado's letter, Hendriksen argued that the attorneys should "request that the status of each of the individuals be checked again so that we can drop all of the non room attendant plaintiffs at one time."[75]

Another problem facing the union attorneys was what was euphemistically referred to as plaintiff "manageability." HTC attorneys found two of the plaintiffs from the Essex and St. Regis Sheraton to be difficult to control. "Each was so intent on telling the other women what they should and shouldn't be doing (and criticizing those who expressed reluctance to be named plaintiffs) that we had a hard time really nailing down the facts with them. Thus, we would prefer different plaintiffs but can certainly live with these two."[76] HTC attorney Christine Owens sought different plaintiffs for several of the other hotels as long as the switch would not pose "internal political problems."[77] Further, many plaintiffs missed meetings because of heavy work assignments, domestic responsibilities, or communication difficulties. Mrs. Osorio from the Essex House did not speak English, and the attorneys wondered whether "to find an alternative named plaintiff in this case, or leave it the way it is."[78]

A final hurdle for the union in the pay equalization campaign was the lack of member solidarity behind the cause. Attorneys found housemen to be universally unsupportive of the equal pay campaign. The housemen perceived their jobs to be more valuable than the maids', and they sought to protect their craft, prestige, and wages. Housemen from the Parklane, Dorset, New

York Helmsley, and Sheraton Centre hotels concurred that there was little or no interchangeability among the assignments of individual housemen, let alone between housemen and maids. In a 1986 meeting, the housemen's spokesman Mr. Norris told attorneys that there were "defined specialties at the hotel, and that people primarily work only in their specific assignments."[79] Edward Nugba, a general houseman at the New York Helmsley, said that only the least-skilled housemen jobs were interchangeable, and that maids and housemen could never switch jobs.[80] Juan Alonzo, a floor houseman, said that by contrast to maids, who have "a lot of rooms to clean," the houseman's job was "too heavy for a woman" because housemen "have to move furniture." Midnight housemen Humberto Joseph, Alphonso Williams, and Ron Sandiford indicated that they, like the maids, adhered to the gendered logic of housekeeping work. "Ron is asked to do check outs more frequently than the other midnight housemen. They joked and said he was better at making beds, 'just like a woman.' "[81]

The HTC worried that the housemen's opposition to the case could prove harmful if they were called to testify. Hendrickson explained, "To stereotype the situation, given the population that the workers are drawn from and the attitudes about men's and women's work, I would not be surprised that even with advance preparation the equality of the work will be substantially questioned. Moreover, aside from the equality of the work, the housekeeping attendants may also talk about how much variation there is in their job."[82] Hotel housekeeping workers, male and female, denied the interchangeability of housekeeping jobs—the argument at the heart of the HTC's case. At trial, NYHA attorneys could simply call the people who performed this work to establish that the work was different, thus undermining HTC experts' claims that the jobs were essentially equal.

Even as the NYHA publicly emphasized the distinctions between these jobs, they took incremental steps to eliminate their differences. In the wake of New York's fiscal crisis, which peaked in 1977, the city's recovery was driven by growth in the service sector—especially in corporate and tourist industries.[83] In order to attract guests to the city who might otherwise seek lodging in its surrounding environs, hotels undertook major renovations that added luxury amenities. But to control labor costs, they also intensified the pace and physicality of maids' work and flattened the distinctions between maids and housemen, eventually rendering the housemen redundant. Union leaders fought unsuccessfully to roll back these changes, but they ultimately sacrificed these distinctions in pursuit of wage increases for the workers who remained.[84]

New York's hotel housekeepers noticed a dramatic intensification of their jobs in the late 1970s. Cass, the official arbiter, typically affirmed these changes. Some of these renovations made maids' long-standing responsibilities more physically demanding. In May 1979, as part of a major renovation, the Berkshire Place hotel had purchased new beds and bedspreads. They were significantly larger and heavier than those they replaced. The new spreads weighed between nine and twelve pounds, causing maids "problems in their backs and abdominal areas." Further, prior to the hotel renovation, the rooms contained mostly twin beds; after the renovation, most rooms contained king sized beds; few twin or even queen beds remained. These new beds were taller, and to change one, "the maid must lift the corners of king size mattresses, then must move a heavy stool from the bottom of the bed and put on a heavy, fitted bedspread." To evaluate the new beds, Chairman Cass observed "a demonstration of what a maid had to do in making up a king size bed in one of the newly refurbished rooms with the new spread and the stool at the foot of the bed." The chairman left the demonstration confident that the weight of the spreads was not overly cumbersome. He ruled that the beds and spreads could remain.[85]

Hotels also added new amenities to each room that compounded the maids' workload. In December 1978, maids at the Beverly Hotel protested having to "wash dishes and clean stoves and refrigerators in rooms with efficiency type units that have these kinds of items. The union asserted that this is outside of the maids' regular duties and is the same as asking maids to do dishwashers' work." The union pointed out that cards posted in rooms stated that "room maids are not required to wash dishes," yet the maids were often left with dishes and washed them as part of cleaning the room. Cass again sided with hotel management, explaining that such work customarily fell on maids if dirty dishes were left in a room. Cass claimed that "the long-established practice in this hotel has made these functions part of the duties of the job," and that transforming dirty rooms into clean rooms was the heart of maids' work.[86] Between 1973 and 1980, maids at the Essex House had vacuumed once in a while, but a 1980 renovation resulted in new carpet that required daily vacuuming. In addition to more luxurious and labor intensive beds and carpets, each room had more mirrors and furniture, as well as a table and a glass-topped desk.[87]

These renovations also transformed rooms' more permanent fixtures. Housekeeping supervisors at the Drake Hotel complained in 1982 that the new doors to guest rooms were too heavy. Housekeepers found the new doors burdensome "because they have so many doors to open." The union asked hotel managers to either replace the doors or to reduce the number of doors that housekeepers and their supervisors had to open each day. Cass easily dismissed the case, claiming that he "found no evidence that the duties required of housekeeping supervisors in this hotel are different from or more onerous than those of other employees in this industry and no proof that their work assignments are unreasonable." While Cass again visited a hotel and observed a housekeeper opening one of the new doors, and likely even pushed the door open himself, he did not experience the repetitive stress of operating the doors many times each day.[88]

Hotel managers also sought to lower labor costs by reducing specialties in workers' skills and assignments, eventually eliminating the housemen altogether in most instances. In 1982, the Plaza Hotel sought to change the work pattern of housemen to increase productivity. Managers transformed the work from task-oriented to floor-oriented production—rendering it more similar to maids' work. The HTC responded that the new system would "result in a speed-up of employees; require increased productivity; and force housemen to work harder and eliminate jobs in their classification." The hotel responded that the change was necessary "for economic reasons": "business is off, and increased efficiency is essential." Again, Cass sided with the NYHA and permitted the change.[89] Communications among hotel management personnel confirmed their desire to reduce the housemen's specializations. In 1980, Hilton executives hypothesized, "We would be able to increase productivity in the Rehab Department if . . . wall washers could double as housemen on periods when we are receiving furniture and housemen could double as wall washers other times. Also, painters could be trained to do bathroom tile grouting when not painting, etc."[90] In 1988, maids Delores Shaw, Marie Toussaint, and Edris Knight discussed the changes over their fifteen years of employment at the Essex House Hotel. The maids explained feeling increasing pressure because of their high quota and the lack of assistance from other employees. In 1973, every floor section had had a houseman who performed heavy tasks and a bath maid who intensely cleaned the bathroom attached to each guest room. By 1988, the maids rarely had any such assistance, dusting high places, fixing fallen shower curtains, moving furniture, and scrubbing bathroom tile on their own.

HTC unions attempted to offset changes in work processes and new technologies by asking for wage increases. At the Waldorf-Astoria, the union requested a $40 per week increase for telephone operators to accompany new equipment in 1981. The hotel offered only around $10, and the union protested that it had cooperated with the hotel in facilitating the installation, which was accompanied by the dismissal of twenty-two operators. As a result, the union claimed, "the work load of the remaining operators has doubled," although "the hotel asserted that it was merely updating telephone equipment." HTC leaders claimed that by installing the new equipment and laying off operators, the hotel saved more money than it passed on in wages to the remaining operators. Cass asked the parties to reattempt to negotiate the wage increase but warned the union not to expect profits to be automatically redistributed to workers: "the increase in skill or work effort or responsibility," rather than "the amount of money that the employer saves as a result of the new equipment" would determine "any wage adjustments that may be in order."[91]

Against the stated interests of the maids, who saw their work as a feminized haven from the more physically demanding male-typed work, the HTC strengthened its emphasis on raising pay as hotel managers intensified the pace and physicality of maids' jobs while bridging the divide between maids and housemen. Eventually, the maids' responsibilities were expanded to include the housemen's heavier tasks, and the men were rendered redundant. Amid declining profits and with the blessing of their mediator, NYHA hotels began to eliminate housemen and other specialty housekeeping support staff, passing their tasks on to maids—thereby adding work without reducing their daily room quota. The union fought unsuccessfully to oppose changes to technology, hotel amenities, and work processes that made housekeeping work more strenuous, instead tightening its focus on winning wage increases for the workers who remained in increasingly interchangeable housekeeping jobs.

The NYHA's efforts to flatten the distinctions among housekeeping workers and the HTC attempts to raise workers' pay dovetailed in the 1985 strike and its resolution. As the two parties sought to renegotiate their contract, their demands differed widely. The HTC asked for 9 percent raises in each of the next four years, while NYHA offered a five-year contract with 4 percent annual raises. NYHA officials noted changes in the hotel industry that squeezed profits, but HTC officials disagreed. "They are asking us to give back in an economic atmosphere that says they are doing great," HTC president

Vito Pitta remarked, noting that the city's hotels had a nearly 80 percent oc-
cupancy rate amid room rate increases the previous year.[92] But industry
analysts suggested that hotels had overspent on recent refurbishments and
expansions.[93] In the summer of 1985, HTC unions initiated a twenty-six-day
walkout at thirty-five of the city's busiest hotels—the first industry-wide strike
in HTC history.[94] Pitta expressed his intent to protect his workers' wages in
newspaper coverage of the strike, emphasizing that hotel workers were also
members of communities and families. "You can think of them and their
jobs any way you want. But pay them as you would pay anyone who has rent
to pay, families to support and other needs."[95] After twenty-six days, Pitta
and the HTC won those higher wages, with the NYHA agreeing to across-
the-board raises of between 5.5 and 6.5 percent.[96] But in exchange, the hotels
gained long-coveted leeway to eliminate job categories. Following the strike,
men's housekeeping jobs that had been distinct—stairwell cleaner, window
cleaner, wall cleaner, curtain cleaner—were folded into the general houseman
job, making the housemen more interchangeable. The hotels also won the
option to merge bath maids' responsibilities into those of maids, eliminating the specialized assistants who had once helped maids shoulder their daily
quotas.[97]

The strike and the equal pay lawsuit unfolded as the union weathered
broader challenges. Nationwide, hotel and motel worker union membership
rates fell from nearly 20 percent in 1980 to 10 percent a decade later.[98] In New
York, HTC membership dropped from 450,000 to 400,000 between 1975
and 1985.[99] This decline in union density in concert with the 1985 strike compounded the HTC's financial vulnerability. As early as 1965, Pitta admonished members "to cut our expenses to the bone and bring about many
economies."[100] Decades later, the HTC was in dire financial straits—and once
the lawsuit got underway in the mid-1980s, its costs were enormous.[101] Norman Willis, the job evaluator, charged $1,000 per day, and his two assistants
charged about $500 each per day for about one week of work each.[102] Attor-
ney Winn Newman and his associates, who had been instrumental in recent
failed efforts to enshrine comparable worth, charged between $90 and $125
per hour. Over the eight years of the lawsuit, Newman and Pitta corresponded frequently about the bills, which often topped $20,000 in a month.[103]
HTC attorneys viewed NYHA's foot-dragging as part of a wider strategy.
Newman wrote to Pitta in 1986, "The association and the hotels are ap-
proaching this litigation with an intent to bleed the union dry and thus force
the union to drop the suit."[104] Attorney Jim Hendriksen assured Pitta, "we

have been very conscious of the costs of the litigation and have taken a number of steps to keep the costs of the litigation to the absolute minimum necessary to win these suits." The last available option, Hendriksen explained, which would have "the greatest reduction in costs," was to end the conflict.[105]

In a 1986 meeting, HTC attorneys attempted to convince Pitta to abandon his stated mission "to fight them all of the way" and instead to pursue a settlement. Attorneys argued that a settlement would doubtless produce more good for workers than "two or more years of litigation, half a million dollars of expenses, followed by defeat." The attorneys pointed to the lack of a wage differential between housemen and room attendants at some of the defendant hotels and debated whether maids at those hotels should earn higher wages than men. They reasoned, "Even if we were prepared to argue that Title VII requires a higher wage for a female job than a male job in certain circumstances (which I do not think we are), we would get no support at all on this from Willis." Further, attorneys began to suspect that they could not win their equal pay claim. Willis could testify that the jobs deserved equal pay based on his evaluation, but not that the jobs were essentially equal. Willis's data could not prove the discriminatory intent required for a successful Title VII claim. In 1938, in the first contract between the parties, "there were no quotas and no compensation for extra rooms. The maids just worked 8 hours for the pay specified in the contract."[106] Other concerns related to legal strategy were also at stake. "We are in the Second Circuit and we have [David N.] Edelstein as our judge. The Second Circuit is the worst in terms of the light/heavy cleaner cases. Judge Edelstein is crazy."[107] The attorneys doubted that their work was worth the time or expense, yet Pitta and the HTC refused to consider a settlement on the issue of equal pay "other than on the basis of total victory."[108] In their equal pay campaign, advocates encountered a range of difficulties. Many did not relate to the comparability of gendered housekeeping tasks, the key issue of the case.

Facing financial disaster and no closer to a favorable resolution, HTC leaders finally began to consider a settlement of the wage equalization case. In 1989, Newman again urged HTC leaders to "reassess the likelihood of success in the courts." He noted that HTC would face an especially high burden of proof before many of the conservative judges they were likely to face. "When comparing jobs that are not virtually identical, such as AM room attendants and floor housekeeping attendants, we must demonstrate that the employer 'was motivated by impermissible gender based considerations in

Figure 8. Attorney Winn Newman fought some of the most significant sex discrimination campaigns of the 1980s. As general counsel for AFSCME, he led the union's comparable worth campaign. He was also a lead attorney representing the New York Hotel Trades Council in its pay equity suit against the New York Hotel Association. Photograph by Morton Broffman. Courtesy of the Walter P. Reuther Library, Wayne State University.

assigning wages.' In other words, plaintiffs must prove not only that there is a wage disparity between male and female jobs not justified by the work performed, but that the employer intended to discriminate on the basis of sex in the establishment of wages."[109] Newman felt there was a serious risk that a judge would not find the jobs substantially similar and the HTC would get nothing (Figure 8).

The two sides reached an agreement in 1990. The HTC and NYHA renegotiated their contract, equalizing the pay of maids and housemen while eliminating the three extra rooms in the quota Cass had affirmed in 1985. In addition, the five-year agreement doubled workers' pensions and channeled millions more dollars to health insurance funds, which then covered fifteen thousand workers.[110] The provision also included a 5.5 percent wage increase and a $200 lump sum payment for all employees. The union agreed to drop the lawsuit.[111] Each party paid its own legal fees, and the NYHA admitted no violation of the Equal Pay Act or Title VII; nor did the maids receive back pay or remuneration for their participation in the suit. None of the changes to housekeeping staffing or work processes was offset or even mentioned.[112] By then, the lawsuit and the union's other trials of the previous decade had financially devastated the union. The HTC demanded an unprecedented $100 payment from each member in 1992 to offset the more than $2 million the union had been spent to weather the strike and to finance the equal pay lawsuit.[113]

*   *   *

Prior to the passage of sex equality laws in the 1960s, distinctions between male- and female-typed work reflected the sexist logic that assigned separate and inherent abilities to men and women. Accordingly, worksites such as hotels that employed both sexes in large numbers maintained highly differentiated opportunities and pay scales. Sex equality laws squeezed union leaders in these industries, as failing to fight these suits might have rendered them liable to violating the provisions. Faced with declining labor power and judicial hostility to collective worker rights in the 1980s, hotel union officials and their attorneys sought to win even a modest victory by arguing that complying with sex equality laws meant dismantling those long-standing distinctions. Perhaps this was advocates' only option, but these efforts to craft a winnable case also circumscribed their own conceptions of workplace equality. By framing their arguments on behalf of working women in terms of their interchangeability with men and prioritizing efforts to equalize pay, the HTC and its attorneys left the maids with the freedom to compete with men for jobs that employers had already effectively degendered and were increasingly able to reorganize and deskill. The equality the maids won was bound up in a broader race to the bottom that saw workers equally degraded and physically taxed. While organized labor has retained a notable foothold in the hospitality industry, especially in tourism-driven cities like Las Vegas, New York now has both the highest union density and the highest income inequality among major American cities.[114]

The expansion of hotel work has outpaced growth in overall U.S. employment since the mid-1980s, reflecting the spread of the service sector. Forty-eight percent more people worked in hotels in 2000 than in 1984.[115] Those years also saw hotel housekeeping jobs become increasingly physically demanding and contingent.[116] Hotel housekeeper remains a nominally gender-neutral but overwhelmingly female job. Few housekeepers have the support of housekeeping attendants and bath maids, as they had in the past, as they rush to fulfill their daily room quotas. In tight competition for high-paying customers, hotels have piled on the amenities that intensify maids' workload and render it more dangerous. For example, a housekeeper who changes fifteen luxury king-size beds per day handles approximately one thousand pounds of clean and dirty linen and lifts a corner of the 113-pound mattress sixty times. At the same time, hotels have increasingly subcontracted services considered to be "non-core," including restaurants and food service, purchasing, bookkeeping, laundry, nighttime cleaning, and payroll, while seeking to employ housekeepers on an "as-needed" basis.[117] In buttressing their rights claims with appeals to gender difference, the New York maids resorted to what appeared as the best way to protect themselves in an economy increasingly bifurcated between an elite professional class and an underclass forced to render body and soul in its service. The maids won equal wages, but the lawsuit financially devastated their union, and their employers transformed their jobs.

In the service sector, as elsewhere, employers were able to turn narrow conceptions of sex equality to their advantage and circumscribe their opponents' activism in the process. By advancing a definition of equality that dismantled labor force segmentation, corporations compounded the service sector under the auspices of new worker protections. And as men discovered in their efforts to claim new rights, articulating Title VII's promise could naturalize gendered and sexual hierarchies in the name of sex equality.

Chapter 6

A Man's World, but Only for Some

In September 1975, twenty-eight-year-old Donald Strailey wore "a small gold ear loop" when he reported to Happy Times Nursery School in San Francisco, where he had worked as a teacher for the past two years. The school year had not yet begun, and no children were present, but the nursery school head fired Strailey on the spot rather than allow him to remove his earring and hold onto his job. School officials interpreted Strailey's decision to adopt a marker of effeminacy as evidence of an essential, immutable identity that was incompatible with employment there. Strailey's attorney was not sure whether Happy Times had known of or suspected Strailey's homosexuality, but he assumed that school officials objected to the earring because they "did not want parents to see or think that [they] employed gay teachers," and that they might "think that Mr. Strailey was gay because of his effeminate image, and then pull their children out."[1] Strailey was thus fired for wearing a piece of jewelry associated with women in the female-dominated workspace of a nursery school.

Whether or not school officials knew that Strailey was gay while he worked there, he chose to reveal it upon his dismissal. Before the EEOC, Strailey accused Happy Times of sexual orientation and gender discrimination, alleging that he had been fired both "because he [was] a homosexual" and because he "failed to present a proper male image." In rejecting his claim, the EEOC sidestepped Strailey's gender-based argument, referring only to the agency's lack of jurisdiction over sexual orientation discrimination.[2] In federal court, Strailey and his attorney took a different approach. This time, they opted not to reveal his homosexuality, instead framing his claim solely in terms of gender discrimination. But in considering Strailey's plight, federal judges presumed his homosexuality, comingling male effeminacy and homosexuality while emphasizing their distinctness. In so doing, the courts agreed with school officials that a man's outward signaling of effeminacy was a reliable indicator of an internal gay identity that was unprotected by Title VII. Denying relief to Strailey, the Ninth Circuit Court of Appeals reasoned that while Title VII protected workers against "discrimination because of gender," it did not extend to discrimination based on "effeminacy" or "sexual orientation or preference." Thus, even in articulating differences between gender and sexual orientation discrimination, government officials elided them—considering male gender-bending and homosexuality each as indicative of the other, and neither as worthy of the protections of sex equality law.[3]

As working women mobilized around Title VII, a small cohort of men like Donald Strailey tested the boundaries of protected gender and sexual diversity at work. In so doing, they fought for the right to be "queer workers." The labor historian and activist Allan Berube has defined work as "queer" when it is associated with gay people, but also when it is associated with one sex and performed by workers of the opposite.[4] Thus, Strailey was doubly "queer" as a man performing feminized work who also signaled a gay identity. Arguing that new sex equality laws should reshape their working lives as well, men like Strailey challenged the legal and cultural barriers, rooted in gender stereotypes, that rendered feminized work "queer work" for men and prevented them from equal participation in the same pink-collar jobs women were fighting to transform or escape. Others pursued state-enforced protections for freer sexual identity expression on the job, breaking out of the small subset of jobs openly gay workers could perform in order to "queer" the labor force on the whole. Men also proved powerful symbols of legal inequalities, as feminist attorneys fought to expand women's Fourteenth Amendment protections using male plaintiffs. Men's Title VII claims did not rival women's in their number, but they forced government officials to untangle and then refabricate the strands of male, masculine, and heterosexist privilege in the workplace.[5]

Men's pursuit of pink-collar occupations was particularly pronounced in the female-dominated field of nursing, where their access to jobs had long been varied and uneven. Twentieth-century medical practice paired the nurse and doctor as gendered opposites, with the doctor's authority, scientific knowledge, and decisiveness offset by the nurse's patience and empathy—feminine instincts that equipped her to provide intimate care. A man who sought to transcend this gendered system and enter the feminine role of nursing seemed to cast his own masculinity into doubt. But to male nurses, these jobs promised good wages and semiprofessional status, especially for immigrants and men of color. In response to the barriers they encountered, men in nursing waged a century-long campaign for full inclusion whose logic varied over time. In the early and mid-twentieth century, they advocated for parity with women by emphasizing sex differences—particularly men's presumed physical strength, understanding of men's health, and fitness for service in combat zones. Even as they did so, they chafed against overt sexism: exclusion from nursing schools, ill treatment by coworkers, and relegation to the few subfields of nursing that required physical strength and intimate care for male patients. Title VII inspired male nurses to reframe their rights claims in terms of sex equality, arguing that a nurse's sex bore no relation to his or her ability to care for patients.[6]

Yet male nurses' sex equality claims met legal and cultural roadblocks rooted in the notion that nursing was queer work for men. In denying men equal access to nursing jobs, courts relied on a legal loophole embedded within Title VII. The Bona Fide Occupational Qualification (BFOQ) provision allowed employers to discriminate on account of sex if being male or female was crucial to a job's performance. The historian Phil Tiemeyer has shown how men convinced government officials to narrowly interpret the BFOQ provision and open flight attendant jobs to them. But courts have also invoked the BFOQ to rule against men in nursing, framing protecting female patients' modesty as a more important state aim than upholding male nurses' right to sex equality.[7] Further, the obstacles facing male nurses were as much de facto as they were de jure, as female nurses offered only tacit support to their male counterparts in order to protect their monopoly over positions of leadership in the field. Even feminists who worked to integrate male-dominated spheres of labor expressed ambivalence about men's entry into feminized jobs. While scholars have identified a "glass escalator" phenomenon that has moved some men into nursing leadership, barriers to men's participation have endured. Men's struggles to fully degender nursing demonstrate how suspicions about men in feminized roles have shaped the agendas of courts, activists, and women alike.[8]

Just as men sought to broaden gender norms in their pursuit of nursing positions, gay male workers argued that Title VII's sex equality provision should encompass their right to be open and themselves at work. Much like the feminist legal theorists who "reason[ed] from race," gay activists asked the courts to *reason from sex*, analogizing sex and sexual orientation in order to extend gay rights.[9] Their fundamental claim was that a worker's sexual orientation was irrelevant to his or her ability to perform a job, but that the freedom to signal a homosexual identity was an essential aspect of workplace equality. The gay liberation movement was thus shaped by the wider context of workplace rights activism. These activists sought to remove barriers to jobs and boost their representation therein, echoing contemporary campaigns by women and racial minorities. But they also envisioned a more tolerant workplace culture in which they could safely come out—regardless of a job's "queerness," or association with gay men—as a state-protected entitlement. In California, the epicenter of the gay employment rights movement, activists built a multivalent campaign that culminated in two 1979 court cases that tested their claim that sexual identity was bound up in sex equality law: *California Law Students v. Pacific Telephone and Telegraph* and *DeSantis v. Pacific Telephone and Telegraph*.[10] Their hopes were scuttled when judges evaluated gay workplace rights claims within frameworks already defined and interpreted in terms of women, drawing a bright new line between sexuality and sex. To the courts, declaring a gay identity by coming out of the closet might constitute protected speech, but homosexuality did not share the fixed and essential elements of other identities entitled to workplace equality provisions.[11]

Title VII's sex equality mandate was layered onto long-standing and durable norms about men's essential qualities. The "gendered imagination" that the historian Alice Kessler-Harris has argued shaped 1930s public policy also guided Title VII's implementation four decades later because the same workplaces where women won sex equality gains saw the policing of rigid gender and sexual identities for men.[12] Men's efforts to obtain protection for workplace gender and sexual diversity met resistance in the form of judges' narrow interpretations of sex equality, employers who reflected cultural biases against men who defied gender roles and sexual norms, and women's own reluctance to support them. These separate but interrelated strands of activism produced an incomplete and fragile patchwork of protections for men that continued to reward the heterosexual and the masculine while punishing men who deviated from those standards. Their story reveals an unexpected consequence of Title VII: the limits of men's own prerogatives in a work-force that remained centered around them.

*   *   *

Throughout most of the twentieth century, nurses were typically women. By performing such "queer work," male nurses seemed to court skepticism of their masculinity. Women encountered significant resistance in attempting to enter male-dominated jobs, but the androcentric assumptions about the desirability of those jobs make the men attempting to cross the other way seem even more suspect. Berube noted the dual nature of queer work: while queer jobs were often "marginal to the primary labor force," and many of their participants were not gay, such jobs enabled gay workers to "mak[e] a living as openly gay and lesbian workers."[13] But more significant than queer workers' actual sexual practices was their apparent willingness to be perceived as "failed men" who seemed to have deliberately rejected their male privilege. Thus, a male nurse's proximity and deference to a male doctor marked his queerness. The boundaries of queer work were also racialized; the same work that aroused suspicion when performed by white men could be seen as acceptable for men of color, who were typically shut out of the white-dominated professions. Thus, as with flight attendant work, men's access to nursing positions varied over time, but nursing became a queer job for white men when women outnumbered them and African Americans were denied jobs as physicians.[14]

In the late nineteenth century, nursing underwent a "sex change" that transformed the profession from an all-male into a nearly all-female field.[15] The earliest nurses in recorded history were men, and the boundaries between nursing work and doctoring work were initially fairly flexible. Hospitals were not the primary sites of medical care, and anyone could accept pay for providing nursing services.[16] As nursing became a standardized and regulated profession in the late nineteenth century, some began to doubt men's role. Hospital administrators drew from the ideology of nursing innovator Florence Nightingale and created nursing schools that recruited and trained women—whom Nightingale argued were naturally suited for nursing work. They came to favor female nurses, in part because they commanded far lower wages than men. The gendered assumptions that enabled women's paid labor as nurses also contracted men's opportunities in the field. The window for men in nursing did not close entirely; certain nursing fields still seemed inappropriate or dangerous for women. These included urology, because of male patients' presumed privacy concerns, and psychiatry, where men's presumed physical strength could subdue violent patients.[17] But overall, as the sociologist Christine L. Williams notes, men's access to nursing positions sharply declined between 1870 and 1930.[18]

Hospital and U.S. government policy helped to naturalize separate spheres in nursing. This ideology framed female nurses as apt at tasks requiring caring and sensitivity, and male nurses as physically stronger and best suited to safeguard male patients' privacy. Individual doctors and hospitals exercised complete discretion in setting policies about whether and how to employ male nurses. Even where hospital administrators continued to hire male nurses for general tasks, they argued that a nurse's sex mattered to her or his ability to perform the job. An 1896 *New York Times* article cited physicians' preferences to use graduates of the all-male Mills School to treat male patients "unless a male nurse is absolutely unavailable . . . no matter how much the patient may desire" a woman's care.[19] U.S. government policies truncated men's opportunities in nursing. Thirty years after the Civil War, the Spanish-American War prompted the federal government to systematize its approach to nursing the troops. The surgeon general, hesitant to station female nurses at the front lines, attempted to train and deploy male nurses. However, few male soldiers volunteered for nursing duties, perhaps on account of the norms of strenuous masculinity embodied by figures like Theodore Roosevelt in these years. Instead, the army recruited fifteen thousand female nurses to care for military personnel in the United States and overseas.[20]

Luther Christman, a man who became vocal advocate for men in nursing and the dean of nursing at Rush University, followed a path to nursing that was typical of men in the 1930s.[21] Christman came of age during the Depression when jobs were scarce for both sexes. His sister and girlfriend were nursing students, and his parents, who were unable to help him financially, assured him that nursing was a respectable career for men and women. Christman entered the Pennsylvania Hospital School of Nursing in 1936. At twenty-one years old, he was the youngest in his class of seventy-five. His fellow students included a middle-aged engineer and other former college students who switched to nursing school on account of its lower tuition.[22] Christman's experiences in nursing school convinced him that the fields of medicine and nursing were complementary and equally respectable. He later reflected, "It is laudable to be a doctor. But I believe it is just as laudable to be a nurse."[23] Christman saw working his way through nursing school as a practical route to a good career.

When Christman graduated from nursing school in the late 1930s with a specialty in psychiatric nursing, education and assignments were thoroughly sex-segregated.[24] Male nurses emphasized men's unique qualities in justifying their presence in even the handful of nursing jobs available to them. Nurse William H. Beha argued that only the male nurse possessed the right combination of medical training and physical strength to properly care for particular male patients. For example, many patients with heart disease were obese and would require both a man's strength to lift them and the nurse's ability to monitor their healing surgical wounds and the effects of their medications.[25] The gendered division of labor within nursing coupled with the stereotypes that kept men from becoming nurses contributed to shortages in men to fill positions in psychiatric and prison nursing.[26] Underscoring the notion that male and female nurses had separate roles and concerns, the American Nurses Association established a section for men in 1940, having excluded them entirely until a decade earlier.[27] At midcentury, advocates for men in nursing framed narrow arguments for men's limited participation in terms of men's distinctness from women. The medical profession was firmly controlled by men at midcentury, but male nurses mustered limited acceptance and opportunities in feminized work by appealing to stereotypes about men's essential qualities. Armed with these unique attributes and abilities, men in nursing argued, they could contribute to a corner of the health care industry that was rightfully dominated by women.

World War II created a vast military nursing shortage and prompted men's first vocal protest of sexism in their field.[28] Upon learning of the crisis, both the American Nurses Association and the Alumni Association of the Pennsylvania School of Nursing for Men advocated for men's participation in the Army Nurse Corps.[29] Yet the Corps refused to hire male nurses even amid a nursing shortage. The agency considering implementing a nursing draft but instead relaxed the requirements for female nurses.[30] Thus, given the choice between gender integration and lower standards, the Corps chose the latter—a notable position given the need for quality care in wartime. By the end of the war, the Army Nurse Corps had more than fifty-seven thousand members—all women.[31] Most of the estimated twelve hundred trained male nurses who were drafted during World War II were given duties outside of health care.[32] A 1941 study showed that only fourteen of thirty-five surveyed military men with nursing training had received placement in any medical field. On the eve of the war, Christman enlisted as a pharmacist in the Marines. He also wrote a letter to the U.S. surgeon general volunteering to use his nursing training in a battle zone assignment as women were typically not permitted close to combat. Upon receiving what he perceived as a "snide" rebuff from the surgeon general, Christman and the six other male nurses in his unit corresponded with legislators and supporters about their plight throughout the war.[33] Chafing at government officials' staunch sexism amid wartime emergency, they brought these experiences stateside at war's end.

In the war's aftermath, male nurses tended to be older than their female counterparts, to have come from working-class backgrounds, and to have chosen nursing only after trying and rejecting another type of work.[34] Many of these men were racial minorities, which suggests that fighting the stereotypes associated with male nurses was more desirable than fighting race discrimination in blue-collar jobs. Still, African American men described the compound resistance they encountered—first, at their medical expertise, and second, at their presence in feminized jobs.[35] Some immigrant men similarly found that the benefits of nursing as a relatively high-paying and skilled job outweighed the challenges of being a relative outsider in that field. Moses Ramharose described nursing as an excellent job for a man willing to "ignore some of the social stigma still attached to male nursing." A Trinidadian immigrant and the only man in his graduating class at Chicago's Kennedy-King College, Ramharose also encountered resistance from his wife—herself a registered nurse. But Ramharose praised nursing for its high wages relative to other careers requiring similar training and the ease of scheduling that enabled his wife and him to share childcare duties of their infant son.[36] Ramharose's work as a nurse enabled him to feel masculine and allowed him to tend to both breadwinning and parenting responsibilities.[37] Despite individual men's praise for their nursing jobs, they remained members of a tiny minority; in 1960, only 1 percent of registered nurses in the United States were male.[38]

Title VII seemed to offer men a new weapon in their campaigns to expand their access to nursing—even as government officials instead pointed to them as a group whose efforts to cross gender lines at work fell beyond the law's scope. Male nurses were on legislators' minds when they debated the limits of state-enforced sex equality at work in 1964. In the floor debates over Title VII in the House of Representatives, Representative Charles Goodell, a Republican from New York, offered nursing as an area where employers should be permitted to discriminate on account of sex. "For instance, I think of an elderly woman who wants a female nurse. There are many things of this nature which are bona fide occupational qualifications, and it seems to be they would be properly considered here as an exception."[39] At least in part because of the power of the male nurse's example, the BFOQ exemption was written into Title VII.

In determining when a worker's sex was a BFOQ for a job, judges and other government officials were effectively dividing elements of the gendered division of labor that were produced by irrelevant prejudices from those that reflected essential sex differences.[40] In 1970, Celio Diaz's case dismantled airlines' ban on men in flight attendant work, with courts and the EEOC rejecting the companies' justification that customers preferred to fly in cabins staffed solely by women. Yet while government officials rejected stereotypes of women as not strong enough for certain jobs or men as not servile enough for others, they held onto what they viewed as "commonsense" ideas about differences between the sexes—particularly where nudity and intimacy were involved.[41] Early EEOC staff interpreted the BFOQ to apply to jobs requiring privacy, authenticity, and intimacy. In 1967, EEOC attorney Sonia Pressman Fuentes declared, "It is obvious, for example, that an employer can hire only women to model female bathing suits, to portray women's roles in the theater, to work as attendants in ladies restrooms, or as fitters in ladies' dress shops."[42] Thus, while men's use of Title VII to enter flight attendant work was relatively straightforward, the more intimate elements of male nurses' jobs rendered them more vulnerable to slipping through the BFOQ loophole.

The first male nurse to take a Title VII sex equality claim to court was veteran Washington, D.C. nurse Verne Wilson.[43] When he sued his employer in 1971, Wilson had worked at Sibley Memorial Hospital for thirty-five years. He had only ever treated male patients there, while his female counterparts attended to patients of both sexes. When a patient required a dedicated nurse, the hospital arranged for her or him to hire a private duty nurse through an independent agency. If the patient rejected the nurse selected by the agency, the patient was still responsible to pay the nurse's daily fee. Wilson alleged that in 1968 and 1969, supervisory nurses themselves rejected him for assignments because he was male and the patient was female. Wilson argued that this preemptive practice denied him the opportunity to be rejected by the patient but still compensated. After Wilson's first alleged rejection, he filed complaints with the District of Columbia Council on Human Relations and the EEOC. Unable to conciliate the charge, the EEOC notified Wilson of his right to sue the hospital. In *Sibley Memorial Hospital v. Wilson*, the district and appellate courts found for Wilson—ruling that the hospital violated Title VII by interfering with employment contracts between private nurses and patients—but it did not affirm the validity of male nurses' sex equality claims.[44]

The *Sibley* victory did not directly address how to balance patients' preferences with male nurses' equality claims, and male nurses continued to challenge their unequal treatment in court. There, they typically lost on sex equality grounds, as courts emphasized patients' stated or presumed preferences and the added costs of accommodating male nurses in determining where sex posed a BFOQ. Specifically, courts relied on community standards of privacy to permit hospitals to exclude men from positions with intimate contact with females even as they allow women to perform jobs that require similar contact with males—while imposing no such restrictions on male physicians.[45] In the 1979 case *Fesel v. Masonic Home of Delaware*, the plaintiff male nurse sued the small nursing home that had refused to hire him on the grounds that female patients did not want to be cared for by men— even though Fesel was otherwise qualified and the same patients had been treated by a male gynecologist. The court held that the patients' preferences could justify excluding Fesel if the nursing home could prove that it could not reassign job responsibilities and protect patients' privacy.[46] Similarly, in the 1982 case *EEOC v. Mercy Health Center*, the court relied on feedback from patient surveys and male doctors to justify the exclusion of male nurses in the labor and delivery area of a medical facility for high-risk pregnancies. That same year, a male nurse fought to work in a labor and delivery room, and the hospital responded that in order to protect patients' "privacy and personal dignity," it would have to add a female chaperone, a move that would increase costs. The judge held for the hospital, ruling that hospitals could refuse to hire men as nurses in labor and delivery. In this and other cases, courts have cited consumer preferences in allowing hospitals to discriminate against male nurses although they had prevented airlines from using the same type of evidence to exclude men from working as flight attendants. One judge pointed out that women valued the prerogative to choose a male or female obstetrician-gynecologist.[47] Even when men in nursing won a significant victory in the best-known case that involved them, the 1982 U.S. Supreme Court case *Mississippi University for Women v. Hogan*, the Court struck down the school's ban on male nursing students but did not address their barriers to equal employment.[48]

Male nurses also filed legal claims alleging their simultaneous experiences of gender and sexual orientation discrimination. Some male nurses claimed that they were accused of sexually harassing patients as a pretext for firing them.[49] In the mid-1990s, Gary Hamner was an openly gay charge nurse in the Stress Center Unit of an Indianapolis hospital. Hamner claimed that his supervisor's supervisor, the center's medical director, would "refuse to acknowledge or communicate with Hamner, screamed at him during telephone conversations, and harassed him by lisping at him, flipping his wrists, and making jokes about homosexuals." Hamner filed a written grievance at the hospital in which he alleged that he was being harassed because of both his sex and sexual orientation. In a 2000 ruling, the Seventh Circuit Court of Appeals held that the medical directors' activities were not motivated by animus toward men. The court threw out Hamner's gender- and sexual orientation-based claims because sexual orientation discrimination was not covered by Title VII.[50]

In the absence of strong legal protections, some men in nursing countered the discomfort, ostracism, and harassment they experienced with a new campaign to recruit female allies and erode gender stereotypes in the field.[51] After returning from military service, Luther Christman began a career as a nurse and advocate seeking to prove that "tenderness and sensitivity are not sex linked."[52] Yet feminists and female nurses alike struggled over whether and how to welcome men like Christman into the fold. More moderate feminists diverged on the question of whether to prioritize encouraging women to become doctors or boosting societal respect for nursing, and feminists taking a more radical approach pursued more bodily autonomy and reproductive control for patients themselves.[53] For their part, female nurses disagreed over whether incorporating men would help boost their status as a profession or would enable men to usurp their authority. Christman found female nursing leaders to be "very discriminatory against me—mostly in very subtle ways—in derogating my efforts, or making such comments as 'what do you expect from a man' or 'men don't understand nursing', or actively working to keep me from getting on certain committees or from getting other kinds of appointments." In what he privately called the "Dallas debacle," Christman lost the 1968 race for American Nurses Association (ANA) president. He attributed the loss to a smear campaign by ANA leaders who did not want a man at their helm. Their efforts convinced him that there was "just as much chauvinism in women as there is reputed to be in men." Retreating from the ANA, Christman helped to lead the National Male Nurses Association, later renamed the American Assembly for Men in Nursing (AAMN), founded 1971 to advocate on behalf of male nurses.[54]

Men's push for equity in nursing reveals how gendered assumptions about the primacy and desirability of work associated with men shaped the composition of the nursing workforce and the boundaries of state-enforced sex equality. Men in nursing encountered many of the same barriers encountered by women who sought entry into male-dominated jobs in those same decades, but absent grassroots labor or interest group support. Gender has remained salient in nursing. Some argue that nursing itself has become gender stratified, with men leapfrogging qualified women to positions of leadership. Male nurses themselves describe a "concrete ceiling," finding that their achievements were attributed to their sex. They note constant pressure to assert their masculinity to counter patients' and coworkers' suspicion of their motives for pursuing feminized work. And absent a strong legal precedent at the federal level, male nurses have filed individual lawsuits with varying success.[55] The history of men in nursing reveals how assumptions about the queerness of men in some feminized jobs gained the force of law in an era whose watchwords were equal opportunity and sex-blindness.

*   *   *

Just as some men sought to relax the gendered barriers to feminized fields like nursing, others pursued state protections for sexual diversity at work. In the 1950s, gay men and women began a multifronted struggle for the right to express a gay identity on the job beyond the limited range of queer and working-class jobs associated with gay men such as waiting tables and hairdressing.[56] Through the nascent homophile movement, they increasingly found each other and conceived of themselves as members of a proud and coherent minority group with its own distinct needs. They stressed gays' respectability and sought integration and inclusion. With opposition to employment discrimination a key tenet of homophile organizing, activists attempted to persuade businesses and public officials to end discrimination against workers whose homosexuality was discovered. Yet detecting and rooting out instances of discrimination proved difficult, for those who were found to be gay by one employer typically avoided publicity that might disqualify them from another job. Exposed gay workers thus faced a difficult decision: they could fight back against discrimination and potentially reveal their homosexuality to their future employers, or they could hide that identity in the hopes of finding a more favorable job elsewhere.[57]

Workers who took great pains to conceal their homosexuality from employers were not being overly paranoid. At midcentury, employers widely regarded open or suspected homosexuality to be a relevant factor when evaluating current or potential workers. Many employers, including the military and civilian government agencies, perceived all gays to be unsuitable for any employment. A 1950 Special Senate Subcommittee declared homosexuality among federal employees to be "immoral and scandalous," arguing that gay workers would discredit the government.[58] Government officials similarly justified their postwar purges of suspected gays from federal employment by deeming them morally corrupt and easily blackmailed risks to national security.[59] Similarly, private employers claimed that gays' willingness to violate sodomy laws indicated their general immorality, which might harm their business and offend customers. Employers often went to great lengths to determine an employee's sexual proclivities, checking military records, observing workers' behavior, and obtaining statements from other employees. As one American Civil Liberties Union (ACLU) publication warned, "Any of the various forms that applicants and employees are required to fill out may disclose information that leads to evidence of homosexual conduct."[60] Many job applications learned about this method of employment screening the hard way. One man who was denied a job in 1964 was told, "You are 30 years old, unmarried, and live in San Francisco. Don't you get the point? We don't want your kind."[61] Far from imagining a firm barrier between employees' private and work lives, many employers saw a worker's homosexuality as evidence of his or her unfitness for a job.[62] Thus, gay men were trapped between concealing their identity in the hopes of holding onto a white- or blue-collar job, or entering queer work where they could be more open, but where upward mobility and wages were typically more limited.[63]

Yet even as employers articulated sweeping condemnations of homosexual employees, the changing legal and social climate opened new possibilities. A string of U.S. Supreme Court decisions asserted individuals' right to privacy—particularly when matters of sexuality and reproduction were at stake. Advocates followed suit, as the ACLU broadened its conception of the relationship between civil liberties and sexual freedom in the mid-1960s.[64]

A 1967 ACLU position paper on homosexuality called for "the end of criminal sanctions for homosexual practices conducted in private between consenting adults" because sexual orientation involved sacred entities that should be protected from state encroachment—"a person's inner most feelings and desires." The same position paper also urged government officials to ignore employees' sexual preferences. "There have been, and undoubtedly are today, in the vast stretches of government service, men and women who perform their duties competently, and in their private hours engage in different kinds of sexual activity—without any harmful impact on the agency that employs them," the ACLU concluded. Therefore, "the burden of proof should be placed on the government to show that a homosexual is not suited for a particular job because of the nature of that job."[65] The ACLU also joined advocates in Washington, D.C., where gay federal employees used such arguments to win job protections in court. In 1965 and 1969, respectively, the U.S. Court of Appeals for the District of Columbia Circuit ruled that workers could not be disqualified or dismissed from federal employment solely on account of their homosexuality. Further, in 1975, the U.S. Civil Service Regulations were amended to state that employees could not be fired because of their homosexuality alone, other workers' real or anticipated reactions, or the fear that gay employees would "bring public service into contempt." This regulation modified the existing ban on openly gay federal employees for their "infamous, immoral, or notoriously disgraceful conduct." Yet these gains did not represent blanket protection for gay workers. In 1972, John Singer, an EEOC employee, was fired for "flaunting and broadcasting" his homosexuality at work.[66]

In tandem with these developments in the law, the late 1960s and 1970s saw an expanded movement for gay workplace rights that was embedded within an explicitly radical gay politics. Gay liberation, which mirrored the more militant style of protest adopted by contemporary social movements, demanded cultural expression and freedom from shame. While gay liberationists were deeply suspicious of many of the institutions that ordered heteronormative society, coalescing around opposition to the military draft and rallying around such phrases as "Smash the church! Smash the state!" they did not universally eschew capitalism or participation in the workforce; rather, many sought inclusion on their own terms.[67] Thus, gay liberationists rejected arguments for workplace rights that were rooted in homophile concerns about sexual privacy, which assumed that one could—or should—leave his or her sexual identity behind at the office door. They proclaimed that a worker's sexual orientation was irrelevant to his or her ability to perform a job, but that sexuality was an essential element of personhood that should not be forcibly concealed. The liberationist impulse energized and sharpened the focus of gay workplace rights campaigns on workers' freedom to come out at work rather than guarding the door to the workplace closet. From grassroots organizing to advancing claims on corporations, legislators, and courts, gay workplace rights advocates used formal and informal channels of protest to advocate for reforms in the law and employment practices that would free gay workers from the pressures to remain in queer jobs or attempt to conceal their homosexuality in other workforce sectors.

Gay men and lesbians alike experienced the pressures to muffle their sexual identities, and both groups opposed discrimination against homosexuals.[68] But the fight against sexual orientation discrimination at work was largely a male-led effort because of gay men and lesbians' divergent relationships to power in the workplace. Lesbians' opposition to sexual orientation discrimination was bound up with their exploitation as working women. The family wage ideology that justified the low pay and dead-end nature of most feminized jobs on account of women's attachment to men seemed especially egregious to those who did not seek male partners. Further, by the early 1970s, radical feminist ideology began to color much of lesbians' activism. In some areas, gay men and women formed fruitful coalitions, but in others, their goals diverged and their politics unfolded separately.[69] In particular, lesbian feminists were increasingly suspicious of hierarchy in all forms—including that between workers and employers—and they doubted that integration alone could ever create meaningful equality among men and woman, gays and straights.[70] While lesbians critiqued both the power and structures of capitalist institutions and sexist assumptions about family composition and women's dependency, gay men offered a more single-minded push for the freedom to be out at work.[71]

California, home to some of the nation's earliest and most vibrant gay populations, saw fervent and sustained gay workplace rights organizing at the local, city, and state levels.[72] In Los Angeles, gay employment activism was driven by local political, direct-service, and religious groups. The ACLU of Southern California, later renamed the ACLU of Southern California Gay Rights Chapter (GRC), helped workers file test cases with city job rights agencies and initiated a decade-long fight to add nondiscrimination provisions to city employment codes. The Los Angeles Gay and Lesbian Center provided job counseling and training for the underemployed—even matching

gay inmates with job opportunities and securing them clothing and trans-
portation to work to help expedite their release from prison.[73] Hundreds of miles
to the northwest, the San Francisco fight for gay rights at work was equally
tenacious, yet more confrontational. San Francisco was home to a strong
culture of dissent and, like Los Angeles, a vibrant gay community.[74] There,
gay employment rights advocates organized through preexisting homophile
organizations and formed new liberationist groups that pressured local employers and politicians and built alliances with labor movement leaders.
Well-established homophile and liberationist activists also collaborated and
cross-pollinated. Homophile groups like the Society for Individual Rights
(SIR) adopted some of the tactics of more vanguard groups while new
liberationist organizations like the Committee for Homosexual Freedom
embodied a more muscular style, directing their attention-grabbing methods
toward the long-standing homophile goal of workplace integration. Liberationist, homophile, and civil rights groups also fought for workplace rights
at the state and local levels. Their campaigns found success in San Francisco
and Los Angeles by the late 1970s, but a statewide ban on sexual orientation
discrimination remained elusive.[75]

If the gay employment rights movement in California represented the
leading edge of antidiscrimination struggles, one of their main targets for
activism, Pacific Telephone and Telegraph (PT&T), was at the vanguard of
explicit homophobia. As the California subsidiary of AT&T, PT&T was a
protected monopoly regulated by the California Public Utilities Commission
(PUC). As such, PT&T was one of the state's largest employers, operating
80 percent of California's telephones and employing ninety-three thousand
people statewide.[76] Advocate groups like SIR and city employment agencies
in Los Angeles and San Francisco received numerous complaints about
PT&T's treatment of homosexual employees and applicants in the 1960s
and 1970s. SIR sparred with PT&T in 1968 when the company rejected as offensive a proposed telephone book advertisement that read, "Homosexuals,
know and protect your rights. If over twenty-one write or visit the Society
for Individual Rights." SIR appealed before the PUC and lost in early 1971,
but when SIR vowed to appeal to the state supreme court, PT&T agreed to
print the advertisement several months later.[77]

PT&T made no similar concessions to gay employees. Although AT&T
agreed to a $38 million settlement for female and minority employees in
1973, and some local subsidiaries were more welcoming to gay employees,
PT&T drew a firm line against them.[78] Company officials declared their re-

fusal to employ workers "whose reputation, performance, or behavior would impose a risk to our customers, other employees, or the reputation of the company." Citing the objections of a fictional homophobic customer, they explained that telephone companies held significant "responsibilities to the community at large" and required "tremendous amounts of public contact." Thus, PT&T was "not in a position to ignore commonly accepted standards of conduct, morality or lifestyles."[79] Company hiring officials routinely probed applicants' personal and military records for signs of homosexuality, and interviewers were trained to spot gay applicants by asking questions about marital status, living arrangements, and military discharges. PT&T flagged the applications of admitted or suspected gay applicants with "Code 48–Homosexual." While company officials assumed that PT&T already employed many homosexuals who successfully hid their sexual orientation, they summarized PT&T's policy thus: "If you're known to be gay, please stay away."[80]

Gay workplace rights activists found some initial success against PT&T at the local level in San Francisco. In 1972, a new clause in the San Francisco city code prohibited employment discrimination based on sexual orientation, and at first, PT&T refused to comply.[81] PT&T held contracts with the San Francisco Department of Public Works to install and maintain telephone booths on city sidewalks. In 1973, the city's Human Rights Commission claimed that the sidewalk telephones served an "essential public need," and that PT&T was thus exempt from the nondiscrimination provision.[82] Gay rights advocates, led by the Pride Foundation, demonstrated that the pay phones produced an annual revenue of $250,000 for PT&T.[83] After five years of continued activism in city agencies and street protests, gay rights advocates triumphed, forcing PT&T's San Francisco operation to cease sexual orientation discrimination in employment (Figure 9). Yet the ruling was unenforceable beyond that city, and PT&T had proved to be a stubborn foe.[84]

Emboldened, gay rights advocates kept up the pressure for a statewide ban. But after filing unsuccessful complaints against PT&T before the state Fair Employment Practices Commission (FEPC) and the PUC, activists began to contemplate a court-centered strategy.[85] In state and federal lawsuits against PT&T, gay workers and activists sought to draw a powerful new analogy. Because sexual orientation discrimination was a kind of sex discrimination, they argued, it was already outlawed by state and federal law. Activists set up test cases against PT&T to force judges to evaluate sex discrimination provisions that excluded sexual orientation.[86] This move was inherently

Figure 9. The California subsidiary of AT&T, Pacific Telephone and Telegraph, was one of the state's largest and most openly homophobic employers in the 1970s. In street protests and formal political channels, PT&T workers and their allies fought for the state-protected right to be openly gay at work. Courtesy of Howard Wallace, Howard Wallace Papers, Gay and Lesbian Center, San Francisco History Center, San Francisco Public Library.

risky. Activists acknowledged that "the phone company will undoubtedly resist more than someone else." But defeating such a powerful company would yield unprecedented rewards. One activist reasoned, "They are the largest business in the state. If we defeat them and their high priced lawyers, it will have an important psychological impact." By slaying the giant, they would force smaller firms to yield; thus, it seemed "better to go after the big one and settle the issue once and for all."[87]

The plaintiffs in the federal suit, *DeSantis v. PT&T*, included unsuccessful applicants and former employees of PT&T. The lead plaintiff was Robert DeSantis, a clerical worker and pastor. DeSantis had held a variety of low-level office jobs by the time he sought a position at PT&T in 1974.[88] His stint as a seminarian at the Metropolitan Community Church (MCC) in Los Angeles, an institution dedicated to serving and empowering gays and lesbians, seems to have galvanized his sense of social justice. In a church newsletter, DeSantis wrote that religious faith could "build up the egos of each individual gay person by showing each person that they are worth something to themselves, others, and God."[89] DeSantis sought employment at PT&T while he worked as a part-time minister, but his application was tossed out when the interviewer told him she knew "what the MCC is." A second plaintiff had been harassed, then fired from PT&T and refused assistance from the state FEPC; a third plaintiff had faced sexual orientation–based harassment at PT&T and quit under duress, then learned that notes in his personnel file marked him as ineligible for rehire. The *DeSantis* plaintiffs argued that they were victims of sex discrimination and entitled to relief under Title VII.[90]

Gays' attempts to analogize sexual orientation discrimination to sex discrimination borrowed some of feminists' most innovative legal strategies.[91] The plaintiffs offered three arguments to support their right to enact a gay identity at work: that Congress had intended the sex discrimination provision of Title VII to include sexual orientation; that PT&T engaged in sex discrimination by penalizing men, but not women, who preferred male sexual partners; and that sexual orientation discrimination disproportionately affected men because there were more gay men than gay women in society. Both the District Court and the Ninth Circuit Court of Appeals rejected all three arguments, but the Ninth Circuit consolidated two other cases under *DeSantis* and offered a lengthier opinion. To answer the question of congressional intent, the court referenced a 1977 opinion addressing the rights of transsexuals that declared that Title VII was only intended to refer to "traditional notions of sex."[92] The court also cited two 1976 EEOC opinions stating that Congress used the word "sex" to refer to "a person's gender, an immutable characteristic with which a person is born." By contrast, the EEOC framed sexuality as "a condition which relates to a person's sexual proclivities or practices, not his or her gender; these two concepts are in no way synonymous."[93] To the allegation of sex discrimination based on the sex of one's partner, the court responded that such a practice treated gay men and women identically.[94] Finally, the court rejected the disparate impact argument because unlike women, gay men were not a protected group. The Ninth Circuit thus drew a bright new line between sex and sexual orientation in employment law, framing one as immutable and the other as enacted.[95]

The plaintiffs in the state-level PT&T won a partial victory, but as in the federal case, the court differentiated sex from sexual orientation. The plaintiffs in *Gay Law Students v. PT&T* were a handful of law students from the University of California at Hastings and Boalt Hall who claimed that they were gay and that they had sought or would seek employment at PT&T. One of the student-attorneys, Dick Gayer, had been refused a government security clearance several years earlier because he was gay. That failed clearance would have automatically disqualified him from employment at PT&T. The Gay Law Students Association represented more than one group and one campus; it was one of an estimated 200 to 250 gay student groups on university campuses in 1974, and members sought collaboration on their lawsuit.[96] Assisted by attorneys from the Neighborhood Legal Assistance Foundation and SIR, the students filed suit against PT&T, accusing the company of committing illegal sex discrimination by refusing to hire gay people. They also sued the state FEPC for dismissing their previous claims against PT&T.

The state Supreme Court weighed in on the students' appeals in 1979. As in the federal cases, the Court refused to analogize sex and sexual orientation. Yet, in explicitly differentiating sexual orientation from sex, the majority opinion offered a concession to gay rights advocates by framing "coming out of the closet" as a protected activity.[97] Judge Matthew Tobriner wrote, "A principal barrier to homosexual equality is the common feeling that homosexuality is an affliction which the homosexual worker must conceal from his employer and his fellow workers. Consequently one important aspect of the struggle for equal rights is to induce homosexual individuals to 'come out of the closet,' acknowledge their sexual preferences, and to associate with others in working for equal rights."[98] Thus, the California Supreme Court outlined protections for sexual orientation in terms of free speech rather than a fixed, essential status. By contrast, gay workplace rights advocates had framed their claims in terms of their inherent identities—in whatever form they were enacted—rather than choices they made about how to express them. Through the language of the "manifest homosexual," the court implied that homosexual *status* was unprotected; what was protected was the act of making it known.[99] Following that decision, members of the Gay Law Students Association turned the case over to the newly founded National Gay Rights Advocates—a public interest law firm dedicated to assisting gays and lesbians—to challenge PT&T under the free speech provisions of state labor and utility codes. In the parties' 1987 settlement, PT&T established a $3 million fund for gay employees but maintained its innocence.[100]

In refusing to define sexual orientation discrimination as a form of sex discrimination prohibited by Title VII, the judges who ruled in *DeSantis* were in line with contemporary federal court opinions that denied Title VII applicability to gender nonconformity and transsexuality.[101] Law professor Rhonda R. Rivera wrote in 1985 that attempting to use Title VII to pursue remedies for sexual orientation discrimination against private employers was a "dead end route."[102] By contrast, advocates hailed the decision in *Gay Law Student Association* as "groundbreaking," if narrow; the decision marked the first time any court held sexual orientation discrimination unconstitutional when practiced by an employer apart from the federal or state government. Advocates hoped it would spur similar suits against "any discriminating employer who enjoys substantial market power or who can be characterized as a 'public service enterprise,'" including newspapers, labor unions, and universities.[103] Yet other state courts did not follow suit, and lower California state courts and agencies reached conflicting interpretations of the decision. In the early 1980s, while the Civil Service Commission of Contra Costa County found in favor of a lesbian whose application for a deputy sheriff position was rejected solely because of her homosexuality, relief was denied to a Disneyland employee who was fired in part because he wore a button identifying himself as gay when he interacted with customers.[104] Gay rights activists made a sensible move in asking courts to compare sexual orientation discrimination with sex and race discrimination, as Title VII had begun to yield tangible victories for working women and minorities. But for gay people, the courts were an unreliable route to workplace justice.

The outcome of the gay workplace rights campaigns of the 1970s was a piecemeal set of provisions that substituted voluntary corporate action, interest group pressure, and scattered local laws and court decisions in place of strong, uniform protections from discrimination. In California and nationwide, activists' battles for state-enforced gay workplace rights produced heated struggles at the local level—unlike those of women and racial minorities, whose discrimination claims could be fielded by the EEOC and adjudicated by federal courts. Although city governments began to amend employment discrimination provisions to include gays and lesbians, judges' unwillingness to analogize sex and sexual orientation left gays vulnerable to the conservative arguments, already gaining steam, that homosexuality was an immoral expression that could and should be contained or even eradicated. Gay rights provisions often generated fierce debate, helping to mobilize New Right activists who accused openly gay people of threatening the nation's moral fabric.[105] A central image in their crusade was the alleged perversion and corruption embodied by a gay teacher. In 1978, gay activists defeated Proposition 6, a California ballot measure designed to restrict teachers from "advocating, imposing, encouraging or promoting homosexual activity."[106] Amid local battles for gay civil rights, gay and lesbian workers found some success courting corporate favor, lobbying their employers for such benefits as bereavement leave and spousal medical benefits, and publicizing corporations' good or poor treatment of gay workers and consumers.[107] The 1990s saw Congress come close to passing the Employment Non-Discrimination Act (ENDA), a federal law that would ban sexual orientation discrimination at work. President Bill Clinton in 1998 also signed an executive order prohibiting such discrimination in federal employment.[108] ENDA has since neared passage several times, and a substantial minority of U.S. states now protect sexual minorities at work. But gay and lesbian Americans are only beginning to win some of the gains Title VII has delivered to other groups.

*   *   *

Through their gender and sexuality-based claims, male nurses and gay male workplace rights activists sought to redraw the boundaries around queer work. The nurses worked to discredit the gendered logic that delegitimized their pursuit of feminized labor, and thus, to "de-queer" nursing for men. The California activists sought to expand the boundaries of a second type of queer work—that is, work associated with gay people—with the hopes that state protections against sexual orientation discrimination would render any job potentially queer and thus fit for an openly gay person. Both groups' efforts were largely unsuccessful. Courts interpreted Title VII and similar provisions narrowly, blocking their challenges to the sexual division of labor and the pressures of workplace conformity. These men's experiences call into question accounts of the rights revolution that have emphasized the spread of workplace equality and the relaxation of gendered boundaries in the workplace.[109] Cultural biases also proved resistant to change. For many workers, suspicions of men in feminized work and the need to downplay or conceal a gay identity have endured.

Men's efforts to use workplace equality provisions to make space for more gender and sexual diversity in their workplaces could have lent powerful ballast to women's Title VII campaigns.[110] Unlike gay rights activists, workplace-focused feminists did not have the choice to conceal what made them different, but they could downplay and deemphasize their sex. As they fought both to open male-dominated jobs to women and to enable women to perform a less restrictive gender identity at work, their campaigns increasingly emphasized boosting women's access to all-male enclaves of the workforce, reinforcing the androcentric assumption that male-typed work was superior to its female-typed corollary. By the end of the twentieth century, working-class and professional women were equally constrained by the narrow, and by then rigid, conception of sex equality that emphasized the superiority of traditionally male-typed work. Men's sex equality campaigns reveal that as the nascent legal category of sex equality took shape, traditional masculine standards proved more powerful than the men who sought to change them.

Chapter 7

Opting Out or Buying In

In the heat of the 1992 presidential primary election season, Hillary Rodham Clinton, the distinguished attorney and wife of Democratic candidate Bill Clinton, in responding to a campaign-trail attack on her professional dealings, set off a controversy about baking cookies. In a Democratic primary debate, California governor Edmund G. Brown Jr. suggested that Mrs. Clinton had acted unethically to protect her husband's political interests in her capacity as an attorney in private practice. At a press conference, Clinton denied the allegation and attempted to frame such potential conflicts as a common risk facing two-career couples. Yet she denigrated an alternative arrangement that would have put her in a purely supportive role in her husband's affairs. "I suppose I could have stayed home and baked cookies and had teas," she said. "But what I decided to do was pursue my profession, which I entered before my husband was in public life."[1] Many women on the Left admired Hillary's ambition and accomplishments, but Clinton's opponents seized on her perceived swipe at domesticity to paint her as an unsupportive wife unfit to serve as First Lady. Bill's advisors similarly came to view a career-oriented Hillary as a liability. Over the next few months, Hillary underwent a dramatic makeover, softening her image and limiting her political message to her interest in children's rights. She also began boasting of her prowess in the kitchen, entering a "cookie bake-off" against First Lady Barbara Bush sponsored by *Family Circle* magazine.[2] Trapped by the cultural bind that pitted women's career ambitions against their private lives, Hillary ultimately emphasized her commitments to home and family and downplayed her own interests and professional achievements.

The cookie controversy spotlighted at once some of the dramatic gains Title VII had delivered to women and the tenuousness of their new foothold. In the early 1990s, women seemed finally to be gaining access to the nation's public and political life on their own terms. Delaying marriage and childbirth, women pursued higher education at record rates. In 1990, 57 percent of American women held full-time employment outside the home—compared with 50 percent a decade earlier—and women earned 53 percent of bachelor's degrees awarded nationwide that year.[3] In 1993, thousands of parents nationwide participated in the Ms. Foundation–sponsored "Take Our Daughters to Work Day," plucking girls from their classrooms and prompting them to set their career compasses toward the pinnacles of higher education and industry.[4] In popular culture, television character Murphy Brown loomed large as a career woman and single mother who had shattered journalism's glass ceiling and stood up to powerful men.[5] These cultural advances were accompanied by new legislation such as the Civil Rights Act of 1991, which enabled victims of workplace sex discrimination to pursue jury trials and financial damages for emotional distress.[6] Further, the 1991 showdown between attorney Anita Hill and jurist Clarence Thomas over her allegation of his unwanted sexualized attention in the workplace demonstrated that a woman's experiences of abuse could detour a man's career and reputation.[7] Women doubled their percentage of seats in Congress in 1992, prompting the press to declare it the "Year of the Woman."[8] By many measures, parity for working women seemed close at hand.

But beneath those ripples of progress surged a powerful undertow—manifested in the law, culture, and private life—that suggested that less had improved for working women than the optimists claimed. Some offered evidence that women's newfound equality was an illusion projected onto new iterations of persistent male privilege. In her best-selling 1991 book *Backlash*, Susan Faludi identified a society-wide and insidious movement against women's rights that made women feel "enslaved by their own liberation."[9] Faludi and other critics pointed to the persistent wage gap and sex segregation of the labor force, arguing that deep and long-standing inequalities continued to shape women's lives.[10] Sociologists added a class dimension to this analysis, identifying a phenomenon they named the "feminization of poverty." Their research revealed that the proportion of American children who lived in families headed by single mothers had risen from 8 percent in 1960 to 25 percent in 1992. That year, 46 percent of female-headed households lived below the poverty line, by contrast to 9 percent of two-parent families.[11] Some of professional women's advocates declared workplace equity to be an unrealistic goal; instead, they admonished women to focus on choosing carefully between competing with men on existing terms or "opting out" of stressful careers in pursuit of more flexibility.[12] Women of all classes identified with the findings of economist Juliet Schor in her 1992 book *The Overworked American*. Schor wrote that Americans surrendered time and energy to wage labor at unprecedented rates while women continued to shoulder the lion's share of domestic labor in their families—a phenomenon the sociologist Arlie Hochschild termed "the second shift."[13] Further, conservatives' increasingly powerful conception of freedom as unfettered choice for individuals enshrined the market as an appropriate arbiter of workplace fairness. By framing child rearing as a private matter, they sought to free the state and employers from accounting for workers' reproductive lives.

As the twentieth century drew to a close, notions of sex equality as interchangeability were deeply embedded in the law and shaped government officials', women's, and advocates' approaches to these problems. Working-class women were forced into narrow legal arguments that pitted safety against equality, as courts considered whether employers must extend to men protections that treated all women as potential mothers or dismantle female-only protections to expose the sexes to workplace hazards on equal terms. Professional women also fought to cement their new foothold in male-dominated jobs, balancing their commitments to full-time careers and their roles as primary caregivers. However, the fragility of their new position caused most to reject the creation of a corporate "mommy track" that would grant them access to separate and less stressful career paths—thereby making domestic responsibilities more manageable but threatening to stigmatize all women. Lawmakers debated the definition and legal remedies for sexual harassment in terms far removed from the creative and personal approaches to sexist workplace culture some women offered. Advocates and government officials also debated a provision to provide employees with time away from work in the event of their own or a family member's serious illness. Each of these questions was resolved in ways that located unmediated opportunity as the centerpiece of the women's workplace rights agenda, shoring up strong protections against sexist workplace culture while pushing workers' reproductive lives further into the private sphere.

The strain of sex equality that survived into the twenty-first century distilled women's rights at work into a choice between opting out of or buying into systems that had long been designed around men. For the few women who could afford to make this choice, both options came at great cost. For everyone else, it was a fiction.

*   *   *

The 1990s saw workers, employers, and courts wrestle with the nature of sex equality at work in light of the hazards some blue-collar jobs posed to women's fertility. As states began to roll back protective labor laws in the late 1960s, employers in industries that exposed workers to dangerous chemicals opened formerly all-male positions to women, trading sex-specific limits for sex-blind opportunities. Yet when blood tests indicated that women in these jobs risked bearing children with health problems, many companies enacted "fetal protection policies" that banned all fertile women from positions that would expose them to chemicals that posed a danger to pregnant women. In 1984, a class of workers and their union sued Johnson Controls, Inc., a battery manufacturer, claiming that fetal protection policies represented illegal sex discrimination. Company officials viewed the issue in terms of ethics and risk management, reluctant to expose unborn children to the dangers of lead poisoning or subject their business to costly legal claims. The U.S. Supreme Court entered the debate in the 1991 case *United Auto Workers v. Johnson Controls*. The controversy over fetal protection policies unfolded on tenuous conceptual terrain; feminists realized that conceding sex differences would mark women as incapable of making their own choices at work. But sex equality defined as nondistinction, even in hazardous jobs, left working-class women with bad choices: pitting fertility against economic self-sufficiency and equal treatment against equity.

Johnson Controls, a business at the center of the fetal protection policy controversy, was founded in the late nineteenth century as a building temperature controls company. Its factories manufactured thermostats and related equipment.[14] In 1978, Johnson Controls acquired Globe-Union, a battery manufacturer based in Wisconsin. Several of the battery plants were located in major metropolitan areas, such as Atlanta and Louisville, but most were located in small cities such as Fullerton, California, and Garland, Texas, and small towns such as Middletown, Delaware, Texarkana, Arkansas, and Holland, Ohio.[15] In these places, battery factory jobs paid unusually high wages for dangerous work. Lead, the key active ingredient in the batteries, was known to cause adverse health effects—nausea, vomiting, insomnia, and muscle aches, as well as chronic damage to the nervous, reproductive, and urinary systems.[16] While adults could reduce these symptoms by staying away from lead for brief periods to let their systems flush it out, the chemical could severely and permanently harm children and fetuses.

To limit the damage of fetal lead exposure, Globe-Union established a highly sex-segregated workforce, but this practice eventually butted up against sex equality laws. Prior to Title VII, the only women in Globe-Union battery plants worked in low-paying administrative or clerical occupations with minimal lead exposure. Yet women increasingly applied for the dangerous jobs in the decades after Title VII. In 1977, Robert W. Schildner, Globe-Union's corporate health and safety officer, sent a memo to battery plant and personnel managers outlining the challenges sex equality laws posed to the company. "Globe-Union shares a dilemma along with others who employ women in lead exposures." He explained, "We are faced with EEO and Title VII on the one hand with the risk of charges of sex discrimination if we exclude women as a class from lead, on the other hand, with the liability risk of being charged by an affected employee with injury to fetus or lead induced abortion if we allow them to work in lead exposure."[17] Globe-Union thus established a policy of counseling women about the dangers lead posed for fetal development and urging them not to become pregnant while they held lead exposure jobs.[18] The new guidelines required women who sought these jobs to first sign a release form that outlined lead's dangers for fetuses but assigned the choice to the mother herself. "Only you can make the decision to run that risk. We would have to say that it is, medically speaking, just good sense not to run that risk if you want children and do not wish to expose the unborn child to risk, however small."[19] Globe-Union officials framed pregnancy as a private, protected choice in their effort to offset the company's liability.

Like Globe-Union, other companies attempted to balance women's rights to employment opportunity against their potential liability for the future claims of the yet unborn. The historian Sara Dubow has linked the mid-1970s proliferation of fetal protection policies to the contemporary development of fetal medicine and the backlash to *Roe v. Wade*.[20] Such policies were also spurred by the growth of the regulatory state. In the mid-1970s, the nascent Occupational Safety and Health Administration (OSHA) began systematically regulating substances workers encountered on the job and gave employers significant discretion in controlling hazards. By the end of the decade, numerous businesses had established outright bans on women's work in jobs that could imperil a fetus. Olin, Allied Chemical, B. F. Goodrich, Monsanto, Gulf Oil, General Motors, and others excluded fertile women from jobs entailing exposure to lead, benzene, mercury, and a handful of other toxic chemicals.[21] Experts estimated that company policies restricting fertile or pregnant women from industrial employment in the late 1970s excluded women from at least one hundred thousand jobs nationwide.[22]

Once Johnson Controls assumed control of the Globe-Union factories in 1978, the company reevaluated the voluntary approach to lead exposure for fertile women as part of its overall efforts to improve plant safety. Johnson Controls spent an estimated $15 million to upgrade worker protections from lead, but because it was the main active ingredient it could not be eliminated from the manufacturing process.[23] Johnson Controls industrial safety officer Jean Beaudoin explained, "There really is . . . no other battery system that is as effective in doing what the lead acid battery does."[24] In order to protect workers from lead, Beaudoin explained, Johnson Controls used education and training coupled with special equipment and rigorous cleaning processes. Johnson Controls provided workers with respirators and uniforms and allowed them to shower on company time. A vacuuming system changed plant air up to one hundred times per hour.[25] Yet because the contaminant was also the key ingredient, the risks accompanying lead exposure would never be eliminated.

Johnson Controls initially left intact Globe-Union's approach of issuing stern warnings about lead to fertile women but offering them the choice to work in lead-exposure jobs. Over the course of four years, eight women in these positions become pregnant, and company doctors and attorneys deemed the voluntary approach to be "too great a risk medically."[26] In 1982, Johnson Controls introduced a new ban on fertile women in jobs that would raise their blood lead level above thirty micrograms per deciliter—the blood level OSHA deemed unsafe for pregnant women. By contrast, the allowable lead level for nonpregnant adult workers was fifty micrograms per deciliter.[27] All women were assumed to be fertile unless medical documentation proved they were sterile. The policy required fertile women to transfer out of such jobs, but the company paid them the same wage they had earned in their lead-exposure jobs. Under the Pregnancy Discrimination Act (PDA), a 1978 amendment to Title VII, a pregnant worker must be treated no worse than other employees unless she differs from others in her ability or inability to work. Johnson Controls justified its policy under the PDA because it was designed to protect a third party—the unborn fetus—as opposed to the pregnant woman. By the early 1990s, fetal protection policies were widespread in chemical, petrochemical, battery, paint, rubber, tire, plastics, and computer chip processing industries. Twenty years after Title VII's passage, fetal protection policies defined reproductive capacity against employment opportunity, framed motherhood as a handicap to employment, and thereby endangered women's tenuous foothold in many blue-collar jobs.[28]

Company officials described the new fetal protection policy as an essential safeguard for women's and stockholders' interests, but the women who held these jobs thought otherwise. A Johnson Controls spokesperson explained, "We can't be responsible if the child gets hit by a car in front of their house, but we feel obligated to take the responsibility for what occurs in our plants."[29] Women at Johnson Controls universally condemned the policy, referencing their right to bodily autonomy and their personal financial need. In Bennington, Vermont, a town of ten thousand, Johnson Controls was by far the largest employer, and Virginia Green had been happy to obtain work there after earning far less at a nearby furniture factory. After Johnson Controls implemented the fetal protection policy, Green was transferred from a job handling lead oxide to a position in the company laundry. She was fifty years old but could not document that she was sterile. Plant managers continued to pay her previous high wages, but the laundry afforded diminished opportunities for promotion and fewer shifts to choose from. Green considered surgical sterilization as a way to regain her former job, but her doctor advised her against it.[30] Similarly, Elsie Nason's supervisor demanded that she choose between proving that she was sterile or losing her job. Refusing to have surgery, Nason was transferred from her position as a site terminal welder. Like Green, she was fifty years old but could not prove that she was infertile. Workers noted that the policy affected all women in the plant by bringing renewed attention to their reproductive status. Joanne Leard explained, "It was like we were wearing a sign. Everyone knew who was fertile and who was not. The guys had a ball with it . . . they'd come on to you, naturally, if they figured they could have some safe sex."[31] As in the past, efforts to protect women also stigmatized them.

Some women at Johnson Controls chose to be sterilized. Cheryl Chalifoux, a thirty-one-year-old single mother of two, underwent surgery in order to guarantee her high wages: $15 per hour, compared to the $6.34 she had earned in a previous job. Chalifoux objected to the policy, claiming, "It's your body," and she was skeptical of plant officials' insistence that "they're doing it for your own good." Yet Chalifoux stood behind her choice because it seemed to pave the way for unlimited potential for upward mobility, reasoning, "It doesn't matter what I do in there" because "I can't have children." Cheryl Cook similarly preferred that the choice and reproductive control be left up to workers. "[You] should choose for yourself," she reasoned. "Myself, I wouldn't go in there if I could get pregnant. But they don't trust you." Cook's sterilization surgery allowed her to remain in charge of the ball mill, a tumbling machine two stories tall that produced lead oxide.[32]

In 1984, a group of eight Johnson Controls employees and their union, the United Auto Workers of America, challenged the fetal protection policy in federal court. They claimed that the policy violated Title VII by treating women of childbearing age differently than infertile women and men.[33] The named plaintiffs included Shirley Jean Mackey, of Atlanta, Georgia, who had been downgraded against her will from the position of loader to that of container punch operator.[34] Mary Craig, of Middletown, Delaware, described having been "coerc[ed] into submitting to sterilization in order to be assured of her job . . . where men in the same jobs were not subjected to sterilization."[35] Three women at the Bennington, Vermont, plant issued a joint complaint alleging that the fetal protection policy circumvented existing collective bargaining agreements and discriminated against both men and women—women, by requiring them to transfer out of certain jobs and thus denying them "employment opportunities, including promotion, transfer, hiring and placement on the basis of sex." The policy discriminated against men by "providing involuntary health hazard protection to women but not to men." Mary Estelle Schmitt was barred from a job in quality control because of lead exposure, and the position was given to a man with less seniority. Linda Burdick was denied the opportunity to transfer into a job in a lead-exposure area that would have meant a significant promotion.[36] The last two named plaintiffs were a married couple, Anna May and Donald Penney, who worked in the Middletown plant. Anna May alleged that the policy discriminated by requiring women to wear respirator masks at a lower blood lead level than for men. Donald Penney, the only male plaintiff, accused Johnson Controls of denying men the protections afforded by the fetal protection policy—namely work that was "equally clean, safe and free from hazard, [and] terms and conditions of employment compared to women."[37]

Workplace health advocates hoped that *Johnson Controls* would raise the standards for all workers in lead-exposure jobs. "The discrimination side of the issue needs to be resolved," said Joseph A. Kinney, executive director of the National Safe Workplace Institute. "But the ideal thing is to regulate lead out of the workplace and any other toxin that poses fetal damage."[38] Perhaps OSHA might revise its lead exposure guidelines to strengthen protections for workers of both sexes, suggested Environmental Protection Agency scientist Joel Schwartz. "The OSHA standard was set in 1978, and it is woefully inadequate today. We see blood pressure effects at levels much lower than the OSHA standards."[39] Lead researcher Herbert Needleman similarly advocated for stronger and sex-neutral protections, accusing businesses of banning women from jobs in order "to avoid paying money to clean up the plants."[40] By framing the work as unsafe for some women, company officials seemed to imply that it was safe for everyone else. Women at Johnson Controls explained they had observed men becoming sickened by lead. In one plant, a man who had spent twenty-five years there was placed on a five-month leave in order to lower his blood lead level. "He came back to work when it was down, but it's back up again even though he works in a low-lead area," recalled one worker. "They're so concerned about protecting the female. They should protect the men as well."[41] Some workers and safety advocates hoped that the case would force businesses to lessen workplace dangers.

Feminists similarly accused companies of focusing on the fetal protection issue in order to avoid improving health and safety for all workers.[42] But some placed special emphasis on how the policies violated the principle of sex equality, stigmatizing women on account of their reproductive lives in order to limit employment opportunity. Kim Gandy, secretary and treasurer of NOW, accused companies of "protect[ing] women right out of the good jobs."[43] Attorney Marsha Berzon, who eventually argued on behalf of the Johnson Controls plaintiffs before the U.S. Supreme Court, wrote, "The willingness to exclude women . . . is really a declaration that we can get along without the women."[44] Others pointed out that fetal protection policies were adopted in male-dominated industries only where women were deemed "marginal" workers; women continued to work with dangerous substances as laundry workers, dental hygienists, and nurses, and no one suggested that they should be excluded from such employment.[45] Others described the policies as a paternalistic effort to control women. Isabelle Katz Pinzler of the ACLU Women's Rights Project claimed, "Since time immemorial, the excuse for keeping women in their place has been because of their role in producing the next generation. The attitude of Johnson Controls is: 'We know better than you. We can't allow women to make this decision. We have to make it for them.'"[46] Journalist Ellen Goodman pointed out how these policies stigmatized working women and denied them autonomy to chart their own paths. She asked, "Is a woman's life from 12 to 50 to be governed by the possibility of pregnancy?"[47]

The Johnson Controls plaintiffs lost in district and appellate courts, whose rulings defined fetal health and businesses' prerogatives against women's autonomy, and opportunity and choice against safety. After hearing testimony from a range of medical experts debating the effects of lead on fetuses, pregnant women, and nonpregnant adults, the U.S. District Court for the Eastern District of Wisconsin dismissed the lawsuit prior to trial, ruling that Johnson Controls was justified in excluding women from lead-exposure jobs. The workers had not met their burden of proving that the company could have adopted alternative policies to protect potential fetuses, the court ruled. Johnson Controls had the right to shield itself from foreseeable liabilities, and society had a general interest in protecting fetal health.[48] The workers appealed the decision to the Seventh Circuit Court of Appeals, which similarly dismissed the case. The court found that the fetal protection policy was reasonably necessary for industrial safety—an imperative for a battery manufacturer—and that the plaintiffs did not present a reasonable, less discriminatory alternative.

In the U.S. Supreme Court, the Johnson Controls plaintiffs and their allies framed the fetal protection policy squarely as an illegal infringement on women's autonomy at work. While they had long intertwined their concerns about the lead-exposure jobs' dangers and their lack of access to them, they separated these claims in pursuit of a victory along the latter line of argument. An amicus brief filed by the ACLU, labor unions, and feminist organizations reasoned that defining fetal rights against mothers would have broad implications. "Since virtually no activity is risk-free, deference to an employer's analysis of fetal risk could limit women's participation in nearly every area of economic life."[49] The women's attorney Marsha Berzon wrote that policies like those of Johnson Controls undermined Title VII's mandate to nullify provisions that stigmatized and hampered women's workplace progress in the name of protection. "The fetal risk policies of this kind . . . if upheld, would keep women from . . . a broad range of jobs that present potential fetal risks due to toxins but also due to disease, stress, noise, radiation and also to ordinary physical accidents, like car accidents, falls, etc."[50] Berzon predicted that fetal protection policies would relegate women to the few occupations they had dominated prior to Title VII's passage: "child care centers, hospital nurses, teachers—not because there are fewer fetal risks in those jobs but because those are the jobs in which [women] are indispensable."[51] The plaintiffs framed fetal protection as an infringement on women's autonomy rather than their right to a healthful workplace, arguing that limiting women's right to weigh risks and make decisions about work and motherhood would threaten three decades of progress toward workplace parity.

The Johnson Controls plaintiffs articulated their interests in terms of safeguarding workplace choice even as feminists had begun to lose faith in the choice framework as a means to shore up abortion rights. In the 1980 case *Harris v. McRae*, the U.S. Supreme Court rejected a challenge to the Hyde Amendment, a provision that limited federal funds' availability for abortion by permitting states that took part in the Medicaid program to avoid paying for medically necessary abortions where they would be denied federal reimbursement.[52] In a 1983 essay, the legal scholar and philosopher Catharine MacKinnon critiqued the choice framework as relegating women's sexuality to the private sphere, thereby denying gender inequalities and women's greater potential for sexual coercion.[53] MacKinnon further developed this critique in her 1988 book *Feminism Unmodified: Discourses on Life and Law.* She wrote that protecting women's right to end a pregnancy legitimates what may have been the nonconsensual sex that produced it, leaving underlying power imbalances unchecked.[54]

The *Johnson Controls* plaintiffs' attorneys' emphasis on painting the fetal protection policies as a limit to workplace choice paid off; the Supreme Court invalidated the policies. But the court also dramatically limited employers' liability for fertility-related health risks at work. Justice Harry Blackmun wrote for the majority, condemning Johnson Controls' policy as "explicitly discriminat[ory] against women on the basis of their sex." Johnson Controls' policies reflected moral and ethical concerns, Blackmun conceded, but the company had not met the high standard of proving that female sterility was a bona fide occupational qualification for lead-exposure jobs. Blackmun's opinion echoed the logic of Globe-Union's voluntary protection policies of fifteen years earlier in affirming that decisions about fetal welfare must be left to parents. Blackmun also dismissed Johnson Controls' concerns about liability for the offspring of lead-exposed women. If the company adhered to OSHA standards, unborn children would not face high health risks, and if the company informed women of occupational risks, it would not be on the hook.[55] Immediately after the Supreme Court decision, Johnson Controls suspended the fetal protection policy. In 1993, the company entered into a consent decree with the charging workers, who received job transfers and back wages with interest based on estimates of their prior positions and potential transfers. For the named plaintiffs, these amounts ranged from just under $100 to $70,000. Johnson Controls also paid their approximately $475,000 in legal fees.[56] In *Johnson Controls*, the court protected a negative strain of reproductive liberty—the freedom to risk one's health and that of a potential fetus—rather than shoring up all workers' positive right to strict safety standards.

Johnson Controls bookended midcentury debates over how to dispense with sex-specific labor protections in the age of sex equality. Rather than reasoning from the needs of the most vulnerable workers by extending protections to men, as some advocates initially suggested, the archetypical worker in the age of sex equality was the breadwinning male whose main objective was unfettered job access. After the Johnson Controls decision, OSHA split the difference between the thirty microgram standard it had previously held for fertile women and the fifty microgram standard for others. Employers were required to treat both categories of workers identically: testing the blood of lead-exposed workers at least every six months, and taking action to lower the blood lead levels of any worker with test results of forty or higher.[57] OSHA required employers to "make available medical examinations and consultations" to any employee who "desires medical advice concerning the effects of current or past exposure to lead on the employee's ability to procreate a healthy child." Plant officials had to provide employees with basic health tests, but they could not interfere with workers' desire to remain on a job regardless of health risks to a real or potential fetus.[58] In splitting the difference between women's desire for full access to safe jobs and employers' interest in limiting their liability, the court held that employers could not distinguish between men and women in hazardous employment, but employers were forced to adopt a mildly higher standard of safety for male and female workers.

The questions raised and answered in *Johnson Controls* reveals how sharply the terms of sex equality struggles before the law had contracted by the 1990s, with advocates emphasizing opportunity and choice in order to protect women's newfound access to dangerous blue-collar work. Although Johnson Controls lost the battle, they won the war by successfully arguing, as Sara Dubow has pointed out, that "the trait that creates the safety problem . . . is the reproductive capacity of women workers, not the lead itself."[59] The campaigns for equal access that won the day by highlighting the sexes' interchangeability foreclosed a conversation about reducing health risks for everyone, affirming a less safe standard through efforts to safeguard opportunity.

*   *   *

Professional women were similarly insecure in the elite male world of work. Forced into narrow arguments that equated sex equality with freedom of access, those who sought to combine commitments to family and career felt the pressure to downplay the former in order to prove their fitness for the latter. Women thus largely rejected a proposed solution to the work/family paradox that would have offered an option to ease some of the stresses of professional jobs, concerned that even the availability of such a choice invited a sexist stigma. This cultural rigidity was also reflected in congressional debates over employers' relationship to workers' domestic commitments. Legislators ultimately refused to authorize a workplace leave provision that would have enabled workers to square their need to care for themselves and their families with their need for a paycheck.

In the early 1990s, women received mixed messages about pursuing careers even as their wages provided critical family income and equal participation in the workforce seemed to be a sacred right. A spate of optimistic self-help tomes suggested that for young professional women, the era of "having it all" was close at hand. In inspirational books with such titles as 1991's *Making It Work: Finding the Time and Energy for your Career, Marriage, Children, and Self*, authors promised women that with flexibility, careful planning, and good humor they could hold full-time careers without sacrificing a full home life.[60] Other publications, exemplified by 1990's *The Female Advantage: Women's Ways of Leadership*, framed women's unique qualities as essential assets in the modern business world.[61] Many were hopeful that the gates to the male-dominated sphere of elite work were finally opening to women.

Yet others cautioned that relaxing the barriers to male-dominated careers would harm families while falling short of creating parity if jobs remained structured around a breadwinning male assumed to have a supportive wife. After all, women still shouldered 70 percent of domestic responsibilities that required significant time and flexibility. "For many women, profession and family are pitted against one another on a high-stakes collision course," warned sociologists Deborah J. Swiss and Judith P. Walker. "Women's values are stacked against the traditions of their professions."[62] Studies probed at women's decisions to seek full-time employment at such high rates—often downplaying the fact that for working-class and many middle-class women, working for wages was less a choice than an imperative. Other commentators weighed the effect of mothers' time spent outside the home on their family lives and children's development as full-time jobs became increasingly time-intensive. A 1990 article in *Time* blamed working mothers for depriving their families. "Home has been left an impoverished place, little more than a dormitory, a spot for a shower and a change of clothes."[63]

These pressures were especially acute for the women who began to pour into the legal profession in the 1970s and 1980s. In 1970 women were 3 percent of lawyers and 4 percent of law students nationwide. Two decades later, they were 20 percent of lawyers and 40 percent of graduating law students.[64] To attract top female talent, many firms developed part-time options. Yet women lawyers observed that balancing roles at home and at work remained difficult—as did striking an acceptable balance between masculine and feminine behaviors. Men were considered weak if they did not devote everything to their careers, while women who did the same were perceived as poor wives and mothers. Yet those women who sought to trade fewer hours for more family time were perceived to be less serious. The part-time track morphed into a female ghetto. "We are beginning to have two-tier law firms," Fern Sussman, executive director of the Association of the Bar in New York, explained in 1988. "The top tier is the full time partnership track lawyer, who has all the perks and prestige, and the bottom tier is the part time track, made up largely of women."[65] Despite attorney Carol M. Finke's long workdays and weekends spent at the office away from her young children, Finke saw "no chance" to make partner at her firm. "I don't see how a woman with kids can compete," she told the *New York Times* in 1988, but "you accept it because your kids are worth it."[66] In 1988, the American Bar Association condemned "overt and subtle barriers" to women's advancement in the profession and encouraged all its members to embrace "the principle that discrimination is incompatible with standards of professionalism."[67] Yet calling for an end to discrimination left law firms' punitive culture unacknowledged—especially their expectation that attorneys prioritize their careers ahead of everything else in their lives.[68]

In 1989, a high-profile activist set off a national controversy by suggesting that such high-pressure workplaces create separate, family-friendly career options for women. In the *Harvard Business Review*, the founder of the workplace advocacy group Catalyst, Felice N. Schwartz, outlined what she called "the new facts of life": women's typical domestic responsibilities made them more expensive to employ and more difficult to retain. As a result, women who sought to progress alongside of men found that supervisors were reluctant to invest in and mentor them, while women who sought to balance work and primary caregiving were unable to meet their employers' expectations of a worker whose job came first. Schwartz wrote, "Women are different from men, but what increases their cost to the corporation is principally the clash of their perceptions, attitudes, and behavior with those of men, which is to say, with the policies and practices of male-led corporations." But rather than push for more systemic changes to professional jobs, Schwartz suggested that employers should offer women new choices in the form of two job tracks. "Career-primary" women would be mentored and progress alongside of men; they would not have children or would receive significant help with childcare, while "career-and-family" women would trade less prestigious assignments for more flexibility and less pressure.[69] This arrangement would benefit everyone involved, Schwartz claimed, by clarifying expectations and boosting efficiency. "Companies are looking for solutions, not excuses," Schwartz explained, and women should work with businesses toward these solutions rather than striking an adversarial position and waging dramatic demands.[70]

Schwartz defended her proposed system as a means to maximize women's choices, but other advocates feared that framing those options by pitting careers against motherhood would inherently stigmatize all women. Feminist and *Washington Post* columnist Judy Mann argued that policies that acknowledged sex differences would automatically imply women's inferiority. "One of the things that women and minorities have in common is that when society has tried to make them separate but equal, they have historically ended up separate and unequal."[71] A 1989 article in *Ms.* accused Schwartz of peddling "ancient sexist assumptions" that cast child rearing as a uniquely female activity while overlooking the pressures facing working-class women, for whom wage earning was not optional.[72] Feminists demonstrated their concern that workplace options that acknowledged the work/family conflict many women faced could stigmatize and handicap them all—a fear that had come to outweigh their commitment to pragmatic solutions that accounted for the reproductive labors most women continued to shoulder in their own homes. This downplaying of domestic labors in women's workplace rights advocacy helped to cement the notion that they were wholly a private sphere concern that were irrelevant to employers and the state alike. The "mommy track" conflict revealed how mainstream discourse on workplace rights had narrowed over three decades, with debates over the terms of choice for individual women replacing demands for systemic change in the name of sex equality.

A version of the "mommy track" debate also played out in Congress. Starting in the late 1980s, legislators debated a law that would require employers to accommodate workers who faced acute and substantial burdens at home. State supports for child care had long been a feminist goal, advocated by labor feminists at midcentury and nearly won in the early 1970s, when funding for the Comprehensive Child Care Development Bill passed both Houses of Congress but was vetoed by President Richard Nixon.[73] Feminists kept up the pressure for a law that might help offset the challenges faced by workers who were also primary caregivers. After decades of interest group pressure and nine years of internal struggle, Congress passed the Family and Medical Leave Act (FMLA) in 1993. FMLA grants certain employees twelve weeks of unpaid leave per year in the case of one's own grave health condition, or to care for a similarly ill family member or a newborn or recently adopted child. To its advocates, family leave represented a crucial step toward workplace equality that acknowledged the caring labor women tended to perform and reflected recent shifts in American family patterns and the labor force. Yet advocates also pointed out that the FMLA fell far short of similar provisions in other Western nations. When the FMLA was passed, nine European countries provided paid parental leave to men and women, and more than seventy-five countries and all other industrialized nations provided paid maternity benefits in some form.[74]

By the time the FMLA was first introduced in 1984, conservatives were increasingly adept at deploying the language of the free market and personal choice to oppose redistributive notions of women's rights. They framed the provision as an illegitimate intrusion into the relationship between employers and their workers that would stifle economic growth and disadvantage women. Labor Secretary Elizabeth Dole spoke out against what she called the "mandated approach to employee benefits," proclaiming instead that workers and employers should negotiate leave policies on their own.[75] An editorial in the *Birmingham* (Alabama) *Post Herald* called the bill "unhealthy big-government intrusion being peddled under a pro-family label."[76] Conservatives also warned that the FMLA would raise the cost of doing business, which would ultimately result in higher prices for consumers.

The U.S. Chamber of Commerce crowed that the FMLA would cost businesses $16 billion annually.[77] A conservative South Carolina newspaper pre-
dicted that the law could end up harming those individuals it had been
intended to help by convincing employers not to hire women of childbearing age for fear that they would come to demand FMLA leaves at dispro-
portionate rates—ignoring the fact that this was precisely the type of
discrimination that existing laws had been interpreted to intercept.[78] Conservatives used the language of choice and market freedom in opposing
the FMLA, even as they sought to limit the options for workers balancing
domestic and professional commitments.

Even proponents of the law engaged narrow conceptions of the state's obligations to working women as they pursued its passage. They emphasized
that the FMLA merely guaranteed to workers the right to return to their jobs
free of retaliation for taking time off.[79] NOW president Eleanor Smeal testified before Congress that the provision would "allow women to compete
equally and fully in our paid labor force."[80] Feminists also emphasized the
probusiness aspects of FMLA. A NOW flyer explained that the FMLA would
help employers to "retain . . . a loyal, experienced and more productive
workforce and [to save] on costs for hiring and training replacement workers."[81] Publications produced by the Women's Equity Action League
(WEAL) similarly emphasized aspects of the FMLA that protected businesses: the leaves were "limited in duration;" small businesses were exempt;
and employers who voluntarily provided such leaves were at a competitive
disadvantage absent a minimum national standard.[82] WEAL also framed
the FMLA as preferable to more intensive and redistributive solutions. Patricia Blau Ruess, WEAL's legislative director, wrote that unpaid leave that
would "keep . . . families working" was far preferable to welfare payouts.[83]
Like the FMLA's opponents, its prominent supporters argued that the goals
of the corporation and the goals of workers were essentially aligned; workers
just needed a basic safety net to help them to keep their private sphere obligations private. Absent in this debate were references to the inherent social
value of care for the young and infirm, or to broader questions of how to
compensate valuable yet unwaged labor in the home beyond the ability to
resume one's waged labor once the need for care had lapsed.

Surviving nine years of congressional wrangling and two vetoes by President George H. W. Bush, the FMLA became law in 1993. Feminists proclaimed a significant victory, yet FMLA's terms were much less expansive
than similar provisions that protected workers in most other countries. But

this narrowness starts to make sense when the FMLA is placed in the context of the longer-term domestic struggles over workplace sex equality that had been unfolding since the 1960s. After three decades, the lingering questions about Title VII's promise to women had been resolved in favor of non-distinction between the sexes and the removal of formal barriers based on sex-role stereotypes. The law of workplace sex equality had come to view the state's main role as protecting women's right to be treated like breadwinning men. Thus, family leave that included generous and affirmative benefits lacked political traction by the early 1990s—even though women increasingly participated in the waged labor force throughout their childbearing years—because of a consensus definition of sex equality provisions as meant to grant women access to what men already had.

Operating on increasingly tenuous terrain, feminists doubled down on arguments for the sexes' interchangeability. They framed their arguments in terms of businesses' prerogatives and more modest gains in order to remain part of the evolving conversation. But this conversation had little to offer those working-class women with the greatest need for generous family leave policies and the least potential to have employers who provided them. Just as *Johnson Controls* ultimately positioned sex equality against workplace safety, the early-1990s debates over working women's rights that unfolded in the law and culture placed sex equality in tension with more substantive benefits while naturalizing the underlying structures of work.

*   *   *

Conceptions of sex equality as job access and opportunity, widespread by the last decade of the twentieth century, enshrined Title VII as a critical weapon in the fight against sexist workplace culture. In the early 1990s, opposing sexual harassment became the high-profile cutting edge of Title VII—a significant development for working-class and more elite women alike. The U.S. Supreme Court first defined sexual harassment as a violation of Title VII in 1986, but the 1991 showdown between Anita Hill and Clarence Thomas laid bare the potential for humiliation and abuse inherent in workplace relationships. Yet from the early years of Title VII, working women held a range of responses to state regulation of interactions between the sexes at work. Some argued that attention to sex difference did not pose a universal disadvantage to women and that a broadly framed definition of sexual harassment policed by employers and the state would cause more harm than good. African American women described the harassment they experienced as a product of intersectional racism and sexism whose effects were expressed in but extended beyond the workplace. Three decades of conflict over the meaning of Title VII's sex equality provision cemented its relationship to workplace culture by shading any attention to a worker's sex or gender as potentially illicit. The Hill-Thomas showdown represented the triumph of the ideology of women's workplace rights that saw the potential for abuse and coercion embedded in language and interactions that drew attention to women's femininity—developments that yielded important protections while helping to secure the definition of sex discrimination as an interpersonal, rather than systemic, problem whose solution was workers' increased interchange- ability and the downplaying of differences.

As the historian Julie Berebitsky has shown, before feminists coined the term "sexual harassment," the "unwanted sexual suggestions, jokes, and physical contact or sexual coercion that could be a part of women's employ- ment experience were commonly acknowledged."[84] The movement against sexual harassment was forged by two groups of activists who merged their efforts in the mid-1970s. Rape crisis activists framed the issue in terms of bodily autonomy and safety, while workplace feminists embedded it within their broader efforts to dismantle patriarchal structures and practices across the labor force.[85] Both of these groups conceptualized workplace sex dis- crimination in terms of violence, intimidation, and the implications of workplace interactions for wider societal relationships. While they believed that the causes of sexual harassment were deeply entrenched in American culture, many activists against sexual harassment saw mobilizing the law and government agencies against the problem as an important practical step.[86] Working Women United Institute (WWUI), founded in 1977, built a network of more than 150 attorneys nationwide and compiled a bank of briefs filed in sexual harassment cases. WWUI encouraged aggrieved women to file charges with government nondiscrimination agencies, collaborated with the ACLU Women's Rights Project, gathered data from state and local agen- cies to use in pressuring legislators to act against sexual harassment, and testi- fied before hearings of the New York State Assembly and the U.S. Department of Labor.[87] To these organizations, sexual harassment was a systemic prob- lem that manifested interpersonally and, absent dramatic cultural changes, could best be solved using the law and government resources.

Soon after activists named and began to fight sexual harassment, the concept entered mainstream debates about women and work. A 1976 survey of *Redbook* readers cited nine thousand responses. More than 92 percent of respondents proclaimed sexual harassment to be a problem, 88 percent of respondents had experienced sexual harassment at work, and 50 percent of respondents claimed to know someone who had left a job or been fired because of the practice.[88] A survey of women employees of the United Nations revealed that more than half of eight hundred respondents had experienced or observed "exertion of sexual pressure, overt or subtle, by persons in positions of authority."[89] A female aide to a U.S. senator declared that on the Hill, it was "an open secret . . . that some of our congressmen won't hire a woman unless they 'try her out' first."[90] A survey of employees of the Department of Housing and Urban Development revealed that women there faced widespread sexual pressures.[91] In the mid-1970s, federal courts began to accept sexual harassment as a violation of Title VII.[92]

Yet in sexual harassment's early years as a mainstream concept, women did not agree that the problem required a legal solution. They did not report these experiences to state and federal agencies at the rates feminists expected. In early 1978, the Chicago women's workplace activist group Women Employed reported having received very few complaints of sexual harassment. The Chicago Human Relations Commission had received fewer than fifty sexual harassment allegations out of more than six thousand sex discrimination allegations received in the previous four years.[93] Also in 1978, the EEOC received thirty thousand complaints of sex discrimination—nearly half the total number it received that year—and fewer than thirteen thousand complaints were categorized as "intimidations and reprisals," the category most closely related to sexual harassment.[94] Day Creamer, director of Women Employed, admitted, "We know that [sexual harassment] exists, [but] we don't know how common it is."[95]

Feminists offered several potential explanations for women's reluctance to pursue litigious remedies to the problem of sexual harassment. Lin Farley, a founder of WWU and the author of *Sexual Shakedown*, alleged that women avoided speaking out against the practice for fear of "suddenly being seen as crazy, a weirdo, or, even worse, a loose woman."[96] A representative of Chicago NOW hypothesized that many women accepted sexual harassment as "part of a male-female thing." National NOW officer Dee Estelle Alpert agreed. "By American standards, making a pass at secretaries is as American as apple pie."[97] Feminists also hypothesized that aggrieved women who

refused to speak out were either intimidated into submission or were sym-
pathizing with their oppressors. Farley declared those who perceived sexual
harassment to be "trivial" or "funny" to have "adopted male attitudes toward
it."[98] Silverman accused women who kept quiet about sexual harassment
of being "male-identified." She reasoned, "When women begin to think of
their husbands, lovers, etc. as the people doing the harassing, resistance
stiffens." To oppose this, Silverman suggested that feminists use consciousness-
raising to break down women's "tendency to view themselves and those
around them personally, outside of structural, political context."[99]

Women's fear of reprisal from unsympathetic employers certainly contributed to their relative silence.[100] Yet the discrepancy also reflected women's
uncertainty of the terms of the problem and lack of consensus on the best
course of action.[101] Working women's letters and writings from the early
years of organizing against sexual harassment indicate that women held a
variety of relationships to power in pink-collar, blue-collar, and professional
workplaces. These women sought to be in the workforce, but they worried
that the eradication of intimacy and trust would be unwanted byproducts of
redefining men's and women's proper interactions in the workplace.[102] Many
wondered whether a litigious and adversarial approach was the best way to
either end harassment or advocate for themselves. Thus, feminist definitions
of the problem of sexual harassment and its solution were neither universally
held nor universally practicable.

Women's responses to the first feature-length story in *Ms.* to examine
sexual harassment provide a window into the range of understandings working women brought to the problem of sexual harassment.[103] The first major
story about sexual harassment printed in *Ms.*, "Sexual Harassment on the
Job and How to Stop It," was the cover story in November 1977. The article
described sexual harassment as a problem that affected women from small
towns to the nation's capital. The author explained that "women have often
suffered sexual harassment in silence, assuming nothing could be done, and
that it was their personal dilemma, that they were at fault for not being able to
avoid it, or even that it was somehow an inevitable part of 'women's lot.' "[104]
The article suggested that victims of sexual harassment avoid blaming themselves, talk with the offender and their supervisor, keep a written record of
all conduct, and eventually file criminal charges.[105]

Ms. retained a cache of representative letters from readers responding to
the sexual harassment story. None of their letters implied that women should
not participate in the paid labor force or should not be independent—thus,

they shared a broadly feminist bent—and yet they held competing perspectives on sexual harassment as a problem. The women disagreed on how to define and avoid the problem and how to conduct themselves in the workplace most effectively. They offered divergent opinions on whether men were potential allies or incapable of working with women. Some of the respondents were optimistic that sexual harassment had become a legal cause of action, but many others proclaimed the benefits of other kinds of tactics or expressed regret that confrontational approaches to sexual harassment seemed to divide women and men at work.

Some respondents credited the *Ms.* piece for alerting them to or publicizing the problem of sexual harassment, and they generally had the same approach to the issue as *Ms.* A woman from Redding, California, claimed that the article "brought tears of anger and frustration to my eyes" because it "brought home to me the most painful discrimination of all—being reduced to a worthless rag."[106] A Pennsylvania woman declared sexual harassment to be "the respectable man's form of rape. It is every bit as humiliating and devastating to a woman's life. . . . It is about time we protested loudly the continuation of sexual intimidation in our offices."[107] Another correspondent expressed regret at how deeply her sex colored her interactions with others. "Just once I'd like to work as a colleague with a man or a woman who accepted me as a valid, ok person—even because I don't play the sexist games! Not religious, not humorless, not queer—just a real person with knowledge, skills and ideas."[108] They shared their stories of successfully repelling sexual harassment through the channels *Ms.* suggested. "Making complaints to men about men does little or nothing," proclaimed a woman who sued her employer and won a settlement after she was assaulted on the job.[109] A woman who worked for a construction company claimed that when she first read the article, "I felt a little snobbish, since I'd never had any such trouble." When one "old codger" had recently begun "pawing" her, she warned her boss to "do something about the SOB before I did something. I can and will deal with him physically—punch him out or kick him in the balls." Instead, she asked her union to intervene, and the problem stopped.[110]

But other women critiqued the article for implying that all women who interacted informally with men were subject to harassment, thereby depicting women as blameless and helpless victims. A letter carrier for the U.S. post office said, "I encounter hey honey types all the time on the job because I walk the streets." Because they "cover the same turf . . . the garbage men, police, UPS, delivery men and maintenance men often chat with me. We share gossip and grumble about the boss and the weather. These guys will interrupt a conversation with me to hassle another woman walking by. Guess I'm one of the boys. It's ok by me. I see that as a way of showing me respect."[111] A woman from Fort Wayne, Indiana, was "truly upset" by the article for its implication that "all men are getting their jollies these days by exploiting women."[112] A Chicago woman argued that men and women could interact informally without the woman being stigmatized or disempowered. She was affectionate with coworkers she trusted. "With verbal remarks, I usually do not react at all, but sometimes with benign tolerance. Once in awhile, the remarks are really funny, and we all enjoy a joke."[113] A Canadian woman suggested that women should take a more direct approach. She accused the article of being too "civilized, lady-like and 'nice.' . . . If any man, boss or otherwise asked me for a blow job I'd kill the bastard—or at the very least make him a tenor."[114] These letters to *Ms.* are not a representative sample of women's approaches to the problem of sexual harassment. But they do suggest that women held a range of opinions on how to solve the problem of unwanted sexual attention at work that varied according to their jobs, coworkers, and personal experiences.

As workers, courts, and activists debated the definition of sexual harassment and how best to address it, feminists and their allies increasingly rose to positions of prominence in government. They brought with them a legally oriented understanding of sexual harassment as a form of sex discrimination, and they worked to expand Title VII to include it. A pivotal figure in this movement was Eleanor Holmes Norton, the first female chairperson of the EEOC and a prominent advocate of comparable worth, as seen in Chapter 4. Norton's vision involved changing the ways men and women interacted at work—both empowering women and adjusting men's behavior. She claimed that men and women must work together to eradicate sexism "instead of seeing that scourge as a trap that ensnares women alone." She asked, "Are we changing the fundamental personal relationship between man and woman, or do we conceive our mission in disastrously narrow terms? . . . Just as women have spent the last few years raising their own consciousnesses, it is time that such sessions were now conducted with men, not in recrimination as with traditional 'enemies' but in the spirit of honest searching that should be associated with love in its purest form."[115] Norton viewed strengthening sexual harassment education and provisions as key to remaking these relationships (Figure 10).

Figure 10. Eleanor Holmes Norton, a progressive attorney and the chairperson of the Equal Employment Opportunity Commission from 1977 to 1981, fought to stretch Title VII's coverage to include comparable worth and sexual harassment. Her efforts for the latter met far more success than those for the former. Photograph by Michael J. Zaremba. Courtesy of the *Cleveland Plain-Dealer.*

Yet Norton also believed in expanding sexual harassment law and deploying it against harassers. In her leadership roles, Norton shepherded passage of stronger provisions against sexual harassment in New York City and nationwide. In 1980, the EEOC issued strict and explicit guidelines outlawing sexual harassment, defined as sexual advances, intimidation, or hostile behavior that interferes with a worker's job. The new guidelines assigned to employers an "affirmative duty" to prevent or eliminate sexual harassment and empowered the EEOC to seek back pay, reinstatement, or promotion for aggrieved workers.[116] After her term as EEOC chair, Norton testified in support of robust sexual harassment laws and enforcement before the Senate Committee on Labor and Human Resources in 1981.[117]

Throughout the 1980s, feminist organizations pursued legal strategies to oppose sexual harassment. At the local, state, and federal level, they sought stronger laws, court decisions, and grievance procedures that gave victims meaningful remedies and absolved them from retaliation.[118] As the historian Serena Mayeri has shown, many of the earliest sexual harassment plaintiffs were African American women, and their advocates deliberately analogized sex- and race-based harassment, even as their particular experiences of racialized sexual harassment came to be obscured.[119] Largely because of feminist efforts and test cases, the U.S. Supreme Court weighed in on their side in the 1986 case *Vinson v. Meritor Savings Bank*. That case established sexual harassment as a violation of Title VII and defined its two forms: "hostile environment," wherein workplace conditions interfere with a worker's ability to perform her or his duties, and "quid pro quo," employer behaviors that related conditions of employment to sexual favors.[120]

Several years later, the abstract terms of this newly affirmed legal doctrine were concretized on national television. Anita Hill was a graduate of Yale Law School and an upwardly mobile civil servant. She accused her former supervisor, Clarence Thomas, of sexually harassing her after he was nominated for the U.S. Supreme Court. Thomas was also highly accomplished. He had served as assistant secretary of education, chairman of the Equal Employment Opportunity Commission, and a federal judge. The public showdown between Hill and Thomas hinged on whether Thomas had sought to date Hill, punished her when she rejected his advances, offered unsolicited comments on her appearance, and "use[d] work situations to discuss sex." Hill sought to make the relationship "a proper, cordial, and professional one." She wanted no special attention paid to the fact that she was female, that Thomas was male, or that she was sexually attractive to Thomas.[121] Thomas denied the harassment, refuting the allegation that their relationship had ever had a sexual element. "Throughout the time that Anita Hill worked with me I treated her as I treated my other special assistants. I tried to treat them all cordially, professionally, and respectfully."[122] Both Hill and Thomas described the agony of discussing such private matters and the enormous personal and professional strain the ordeal caused. Hill recalled having been hospitalized for a stress-induced gastric disorder, while Thomas declared that his mother was bedridden with despair. Thomas was confirmed by a narrow margin, and both parties maintained the truthfulness of their testimony.

The Hill-Thomas showdown provoked a cultural broadening. When Thomas was confirmed over significant feminist protest, women celebrated Hill for her dignity and strength of purpose.[123] Gloria Steinem thanked Hill for "corralling our anger." At a 1992 conference about sexual harassment, Hill was likened to Susan B. Anthony and Rosa Parks. Irene Natividad, chairwoman of the National Commission of Working Women, claimed, "What she's done is to make sexual harassment the great connector among working women. This is one of those awakenings. It's like before, and we feel powerful again, and she did this." A Pennsylvania candidate for the Democratic U.S. Senate nomination featured commercials showing Arlen Specter questioning Hill during the hearings. She asks, "Did this make you as angry as it made me?"[124] *New York Times* columnist Maureen Dowd observed that the hearings were conducted by an "old boy's network," and Congresswoman Nancy Pelosi hypothesized that Thomas triumphed because men could not understand Hill's perspective.[125] A group of sixteen thousand African American women, "in defense of ourselves," signed a public letter in the *New York Times* condemning Thomas and the system that promoted him. The letter read, "We are particularly outraged by the racist and sexist treatment of Professor Anita Hill, an African American woman who was maligned and castigated for daring to speak publicly of her own experience of sexual abuse. The malicious defamation of Professor Hill insulted all women of African descent and sent a dangerous message to any woman who might contemplate a sexual harassment complaint."[126]

The 1991 Hill-Thomas hearings thus brought the problem of sexual harassment into new focus and gave it new urgency. A year after the Hill-Thomas hearings, sexual harassment allegations derailed the New York City deputy mayoral appointment of Randy Daniels. He declined the appointment after a former assistant accused him of sexually harassing her years earlier. Daniels denied guilt but did not accept the post for fear of causing pain to his family. The case dramatized the continuing mistrust between men and women, for men feared that women's ability to allege harassment would ruin careers unjustly, while women feared that men still did not take harassment seriously enough. Presidential candidate Bill Clinton faced multiple accusations of sexual harassment and misconduct that threatened to derail his political career.[127] The Hill-Thomas hearings cemented sexual harassment as a serious political issue and spurred women's activism. Fifty percent more sexual harassment charges were filed with the EEOC in the second half of 1992 than in the same period the previous year. More women ran for public offices at all levels, and female political donors saw increasing women's representation in governmental bodies as a way to build their power.[128] But while women still report sexual harassment to the EEOC in high numbers, racialized sexual harassment remains difficult for the law to perceive and punish.[129] The "good old boys" network still exists, and men's fears of accusations of sexual harassment can lead them to exclude women from the informal sociability at the heart of many business transactions.

*   *   *

By the early 1990s, the lingering questions about the nature of state-enforced sex equality were answered in favor of nondistinction between men and women and the removal of formal barriers based on sex-role stereotypes. Women overwhelmingly rejected the "mommy track," fearful that the existence of a separate feminized path would handicap all women's efforts to be treated as men's equals. Instead, advocates developed—and courts accepted—the concept of "family responsibilities discrimination," protection for workers from differential treatment on account of their actual or perceived caretaking responsibilities. Workers also won passage of the FMLA, which granted some workers up to twelve weeks of leave. However, because the leave was unpaid, FMLA forced working-class women to choose between time for caretaking and the wages their families needed. Courts also pitted sex equality claims against workers' safety. In *United Auto Workers v. Johnson Controls*, the U.S. Supreme Court held that employers must address workplace hazards in a sex-blind fashion—at once removing barriers to dangerous jobs and leaving to women the decision whether to risk bearing lead-exposed children.

The issue of sex equality as it related to workplace culture was resolved in the early 1990s with the enshrinement of sexual harassment as the cutting edge of sex discrimination law and policy. The Hill-Thomas ordeal fed into growing employer concerns about liability and cemented the definition of sexual harassment as any unwanted attention to a worker's sex or gender. Stronger and less flexible sexual harassment laws provided women with a critical defense against unwanted sexual attention on the job, but those provisions also made it more difficult to identify and redress some of the subtle disadvantages that remained.[130] Fearful of losing access to the long closed off male world of work, women's workplace advocates had adopted the market-based language that assumed that the needs of women and the needs of business were essentially aligned. They sought to retain the gains women had made in the decades since Title VII's passage.

Since the 1990s, in light of the diminished version of the FMLA that was established, advocates have had more success in convincing courts to ban employers from treating workers differently on account of assumptions about domestic responsibilities than in forcing employers to accommodate those roles. Some have argued that women have not voluntarily "opted out" of high-pressure jobs, but instead employers pushed them out through inflexible policies.[131] Legal scholars coined the concepts of the "maternal wall"—which they defined as the combination of formal and informal limitations on mothers' pay and career advancement rooted in employers' assumptions about mothers as undedicated workers. They also framed discrimination against male and female workers as motivated by assumptions about caregiving responsibilities as illegal sex-role stereotyping.[132] Federal courts have agreed, ruling that treating pregnant workers and parents differently on account of stereotypes about their condition was illegal sex discrimination. While legal scholars like Joan Williams have advocated equal treatment for parents in concert with more flexible policies, many advocates have agreed that in the absence of such accommodations, the state should at least protect women's right to be treated like breadwinning men. Other legal scholars have cast doubt on the merits of policies designed to balance home and work—part-time work, shorter hours, and more flexibility—for working-class parents for whom the ability to work more and earn higher wages is paramount.[133] And as legal scholar Martha Chamallas has argued, banning disparate treatment of working mothers does not benefit women whose domestic obligations prevent them from fulfilling core workplace responsibilities on their employers' terms.[134] When faced with the rising demands of time-intensive careers, many women have self-adjusted, choosing lower-pressure options within elite professions. By resegregating areas of the labor force, these women are effectively creating the female-dominated "mommy tracks" condemned by feminists decades ago. Absent earlier decades' robust debates about state and employer obligations to adjust the terms of work in the name of sex equality, such women are exercising what limited choice has remained for them.

The simultaneous rejection of the mommy track, erosion of sex-specific workplace protections, and flowering of high-stakes struggles over sexual harassment reveal how sharply the terms of debate on state-enforced sex equality has narrowed. In Title VII's early years, many women had hoped that the new law of sex equality would both boost women's access to good jobs and make all jobs better. By the early 1990s, they had been forced to sacrifice the latter vision in pursuit of the former, even as the range of jobs that afforded good wages, benefits, and autonomy was diminished by the pressures of neoliberalism. This limited advocates to framing women's workplace problems and their solutions by affirming market-based answers, minimizing costs to employers, and working to create a "sanitized" workforce where references to sex were minimized.[135] Redistributive solutions such as the mommy track and an expansive FMLA seemed to endanger women's quest for parity, just as their reproductive potential seemed to stand in contrast to their potential as workers. Employees won protections against differential treatment for workers who were also mothers, but their efforts to use Title VII to force employers to help offset some of working moms' challenges met resistance or outright defeat.[136] Legal scholars have further refined their critique of the choice framework that underpins reproductive rights, pointing out that it affirms broad societal inequalities and the gutting of the social safety net.[137]

In the end, the terms of work did not change much to accommodate women's rights claims where they diverged from men's. To the extent that women downplayed the behaviors that marked them as female, Title VII might lift them in their climb. This limited help elevated more women into positions of workplace authority, but those women risked their newfound status by bringing attention to the inequities that remained. By the end of the twentieth century, women's access to power at work was contingent on their tacit agreement not to try to use that power to change the system itself.

Conclusion: Illusions of Sex Equality

The American workplace has changed quite a bit—in both structure and culture—from the mid-twentieth century gendered world of work. In particular, sex equality law and a transformative feminist movement have remade bedrock assumptions about the relationship between work and identity and the meaning of gender in American life. Millions of women now have access to professional careers in their own right. The glass ceiling persists in the form of barriers to upward mobility, sexist workplace culture, and disparate treatment, but Title VII has been women's most powerful weapon in their efforts to erode the stigmas that once represented common-sense logic about them as a group. Title VII has also weakened the division of labor between the sexes within the working class, boosting men's access to some feminized jobs, and to a lesser extent, opening blue-collar work to women.[1]

But these gains have come at great cost. In its current form, sex equality law protects the white, male, breadwinner standard, mainly assisting workers in their efforts to conform to that model. The consensus interpretation of Title VII, forged over the decades, permitted employers to rebrand the long-standing gendered division of labor as a class divide. Conservative forces in politics and business have since widened that divide, creating a low-paid, contingent, and international workforce of women and men while undermining workers' efforts to gain protected accommodations for childbearing or childcare. Increasingly, the relationship between the male boss and female support staff has been replaced by a depersonalized corporation whose power is buttressed by our legal system. Title VII was the cornerstone of efforts to realize a new regime of sex equality, but this reworking did not fundamentally displace the socioeconomic order on which it was grounded—leaving

Figure 11. When Betty Dukes sought promotion and higher pay at Walmart, she was punished with a demotion and a pay cut. Dukes agreed to serve as the lead plaintiff of a class action lawsuit filed in 2000 that accused Walmart of discriminating against more than one million current and former female employees. Thus far, federal courts have refused to certify their class, interpreting the sexism the women encountered more as the result of individual employment decisions than a systemic and collective problem. Photograph by Ben Margot. Courtesy of the Associated Press.

privileges for white, professional, masculine, and heterosexual workers firmly in tact while naturalizing the inequalities that remain.

∗   ∗   ∗

Brief profiles of two recent standard-bearers of workplace feminism illustrate the legacy of the struggles to fix the meaning of sex equality this book has examined. Betty Dukes is an African American woman who was born in 1950 in rural Tallulah, Louisiana (Figure 11). A self-described "low-income worker for [her entire] working career," Dukes hoped that the entry-level customer service job she entered at a northern California Wal-Mart in the mid-1990s would be the first rung on a career ladder there. But when managers consistently blocked all routes to upward mobility, she complained and was punished with a demotion and 5 percent pay cut. Dukes described the indignity of being unable to put money away or financially support her mother despite many years of full-time work. "When you subtract my living [expenses]," Dukes explained, "I'm not living—I'm existing."[2] In 2000, Dukes and a group of women filed suit against their employer, Wal-Mart Corporation, for workplace sex discrimination under Title VII. They alleged that their class consisted of nearly 1.5 million current and former female employees of the corporation who had been systematically subjected to lower pay, diminished opportunities for promotion, and sexist workplace culture.[3]

The law's tightening focus on discrimination as an interpersonal problem has foreclosed collective rights campaigns like the Walmart women's. Theirs was stymied in 2011, when the U.S. Supreme Court ruled that they did not share enough commonalities to constitute a single class. In the majority opinion, Justice Antonin Scalia rejected the notion that the sex discrimination they described constituted adequate "glue holding . . . together" the "literally millions of employment decisions" the women experienced as individuals. Two years later, a smaller class of West Coast Walmart women met a similar fate in U.S. District Court. Judge Charles Breyer wrote that the plaintiffs had illuminated "attitudes of gender bias held by managers," but they had not proven that "intentional discrimination was a general policy affecting the entire class." Breyer indicated that the women could sue Walmart as individuals, but not collectively, undermining their hopes that federal courts would perceive sex discrimination as a systemic phenomenon.[4]

While working-class women have continued to forge collective labor rights claims, courts have tended to interpret sex discrimination as a matter of personal sexist intent, overlooking the institutional sexism embedded within workplace systems. In 2007, for example, the U.S. Supreme Court ruled that home health care workers could be denied the labor protections provided by the Fair Labor Standards Act on account of the "companionship exemption" applied to laborers in several feminized caregiving fields. But even the equal treatment to men pursued by the Walmart plaintiffs would not put an end to the employer-driven deskilling and outsourcing that continue to chip away at the dignity and autonomy of the most vulnerable American workers.[5]

By contrast to working-class women's collective campaigns, white-collar feminists have advocated more individualistic responses to the pressures that shape their lives. Debora L. Spar is a former professor at Harvard Business School and the current president of Barnard College. Born in 1963, Spar described her privileged position as a beneficiary of many of the changes workplace feminism won during her childhood. As Spar mentioned in a 2013 interview, "I made it all the way through college and graduate school and the early years of my professional life without thinking that being a woman was anything but an advantage to me." But starting her own family compounded the challenges of her job and refracted Spar's perspective, and she began to notice that many of the talented women around her were retreating from positions of power.[6] Spar's 2013 book, *Wonder Women: Sex, Power, and the Quest for Perfection,* is part of a new cottage industry of memoirs and self-help books that capture the challenges—and even the collective misery—endured by the women who broke the glass ceiling. These books' titles describe these professionals as "overwhelmed," "maxed out," and even "on the brink." Despite some variation, these works offer personal solutions, admonishing women to "lean in" to corporate jobs, adopt new "confidence" and "self-assurance," and stop making "unconscious mistakes" that "sabotage their careers."[7] By urging women to adjust to the world of work as it is, these authors tend to avoid engaging the basic structures of work that reproduce gendered inequalities across the labor force.[8]

This rhetoric of corporate feminism demonstrates how the patriarchal aspects of work have been renaturalized since Title VII's passage. White-collar women have found that the freedom to enter formerly male-dominated spheres leaves unspoken, and often unaddressed, the challenges that remain for workers who do not fit a white, male, heterosexual, able-bodied model. Most employers have not changed their work patterns or expectations since the days when each male professional could be expected to count on a full-time housewife to manage his life at home. Employer-provided on-call child care services and on-site breastfeeding rooms help women to hide such responsibilities while perpetuating the expectation that they will remain equally productive workers. The rising presumption of a "round-the-clock" professional workforce places a special burden on women balancing children and career.[9] Many have had to downplay their reproductive and domestic obligations in order to be regarded as committed to their jobs, and the need to be both acceptably feminine and sufficiently authoritative remains a difficult balancing act.[10] Women have been welcomed into male-typed employment where they have sacrificed or concealed the same domestic commitments that make men appear as devoted breadwinners. Some corporate employers have couched ongoing sex and race discrimination by emphasizing the importance of workplace "culture" and "fit."[11]

The class-specific workplace feminist politics produced in the age of Title VII have sundered the coalition of diverse professional and pink-collar women which once sought to identify shared problems and solutions. But the fates of these women have remained intertwined. The issues of balancing home and work, maternity leave, workplace safety, and fair pay—concerns that had always preoccupied working-class women—became increasingly important to their more elite sisters once they secured a seat at the table. And white-collar women have had to employ other women to take care of feminized domestic tasks for which their high-pressure jobs leave them no time. As long as workers are pitted against each other in the name of equality and encouraged to advocate for themselves as sexless individuals, fundamental change will remain evasive. This system has offered little to working-class women. But elite women who have pursued the tokens of success as men have defined them should be encouraged to demand more systemic changes that would benefit workers of both sexes and all classes.

The long history of Title VII should encourage us to seek a strong and flexible employment rights policy as an essential aspect of sex equality. As we have seen, the conception of employment rights that primarily protects workers' freedom from unequal treatment due to stereotypes about their sex roles cannot counterbalance employers' ability to assume that truly dedicated workers, male and female, have access to the unlimited domestic labor of paid help or stay-at-home spouses. At the same time, we must also work to end occupational sex-typing. Assumptions about what men and women are like and should do at work have consistently degraded jobs associated with women while presenting obstacles to women seeking male-typed employment.

While the past few decades have seen several bright spots in the law—notably the Lilly Ledbetter Fair Pay Act and the expansion of workplace protections for sexual minorities—aggrieved workers and activists must not focus solely on legal solutions.[12] The past half-century has seen hard-fought civil rights advances threatened by a legal narrowing on many fronts, as other provisions designed to boost social equality have been stunted or gutted.[13] Strategies must therefore be mixed, engaging organized labor, politics, and broader culture. The Fight for Fifteen worker rights movement and recent corporate accommodations for queer civil rights suggest that corporations can be pressured to accommodate workplace justice demands absent direct legal pressure. For example, one day after the *New York Times* spot-lighted Starbucks barista Jannette Navarro's struggles to make ends meet and care for her son amid the company's inflexible scheduling system, the company issued a public promise to adjust that system to workers' benefit. Scholars can contribute to these efforts as well. Rather than rehashing nostalgic postmortems of the New Deal order, they should seek lessons from its strengths as well as its considerable limits in imagining policy solutions from diverse workers' perspectives, especially working-class women and women of color.[14]

Above all, we should strive to become a society that sees all laboring people as complex human beings. That will mean no longer funneling the most pay and respect toward those who fit a white, heterosexual, male paradigm while dividing the rest according to how closely others can meet that standard. We must insist on a broader definition of workplace equality that compensates work fairly, affords greater control over its structure and rhythm, and protects every worker's right to cultivate a fulfilling life once the workday is done.

Abbreviations

ACLU	American Civil Liberties Union Archives, 1950–1990, Series 3
ACLU-GRC	American Civil Liberties Union of Southern California Lesbian and Gay Rights Chapter Records
AFSCME-Program	American Federation of State, County and Municipal Employees Program Development Department Records
AFSCME-Lucy	AFSCME Office of the Secretary-Treasurer: William Lucy Records
AFSCME-Wurf	AFSCME Office of the President: Jerry Wurf Records
BWF	Betsy Wade Files on the Newspaper Guild of New York
CEP-SL	Catherine East Papers
CLUW	Coalition of Labor Union Women Records
CNOW	National Organization for Women, Chicago Chapter Records
CTP	Charles Thorpe Papers
DCEDW-NARA	U.S. District Court for Eastern District of Wisconsin
DOL-Wirtz	General Records of the Department of Labor, Office of the Secretary of Labor, Records of Secretary of Labor W. Willard Wirtz, 1962–1969
EEOC-CCF	Office of the EEOC Chairman Chronological Files, 1969–1979
EEOC-CD	Records of EEOC Compliance Division, 1965–1966

EEOC-FDR	Records of EEOC Chairman Franklin Delano Roosevelt Jr., 1965–1966
EEOC-RP	Records of the Equal Employment Opportunity Commission, Reports and Publicity, 1966–1967
EEOC-Shulman	Records of EEOC Chairman Stephen Shulman, 1966–1968
HM-SS	Harvey Milk Archives–Scott Smith Collection
Holleran	Susan Holleran Papers
HTC-Bobst	New York Hotel and Motel Trades Council Records
JKP	Jenny Knauss Papers
LAGLC	Los Angeles Gay and Lesbian Center Records
LCC	Luther Christman Collection
MLC	*Ms.* Letters Collection
MOEP	Mary O. Eastwood Papers
Newman-LOC	Winn Newman Papers
NGNY	Newspaper Guild of New York Records
NOW	National Organization for Women Records, 1959–2002
NOW-Collins	Mary Jean Collins National Organization for Women Officer Papers
NOW-LDEF	National Organization for Women Legal Defense and Education Fund Records
NYTMCA	New York Times Minority Class Action Lawsuit Records
NYTWC	New York Times Women's Caucus Records
ONE	ONE National Gay and Lesbian Archives
PCS	Records of the Pacific Counseling Service and Military Records
PMP	Pauli Murray Papers
PRM	Papers of Robin Morgan
RCP	Rob Cole Papers
RDP	Robert DeSantis Papers
SPF-SL	Papers of Sonia Pressman Fuentes
WB-DLS	General Records of the Women's Bureau Division of Legislation and Standards 1920–1966
WB-DRM	Women's Bureau Division of Research and Manpower Program Development, 1940–1945

WB-GCII	Women's Bureau General Correspondence 1948–1963
WB-SFD	Records of the Women's Bureau of the Department of Labor Subject Files of the Director, 1964–1970
WEAL	Women's Equity Action League Records
WER	Women Employed Records
WREI	Papers of the Women's Research and Education Institute

Notes

Introduction

1. "Pre-1965: Events Leading to the Creation of EEOC," EEOC Main Site, http://eeoc.gov/eeoc/history/35th/pre1965/index.html, accessed April 15, 2012.

2. Thelma Pilch, Methuen, Mass., to FDR Jr., March 10, 1966, Compliance-Ex Sec Controlled folder, box 2, Records of the Compliance Division, 1965–66, Equal Employment Opportunity Commission, Record Group 403 (National Archives and Records Administration, College Park, Maryland; hereafter "EEOC-CD.")

3. United States Department of Labor, "Women in the Civilian Labor Force, 1890–1971," *Women's Bureau Bulletin #294: 1969 Handbook on Women Workers*, 10.

4. Alice Kessler-Harris, *In Pursuit of Equity: Women, Men, and the Quest for Economic Citizenship in Twentieth-Century America* (Oxford: Oxford University Press, 2003), 5–6. On how gendered assumptions have shaped labor practices and economic citizenship, see Kessler-Harris's vast body of scholarship, especially *Out to Work: A History of Wage-Earning Women in the United States, Twentieth Anniversary Edition* (New York: Oxford University Press, 2003), *A Woman's Wage: Historical Meanings and Social Consequences* (Lexington: University Press of Kentucky, 1991), and *Gendering Labor History* (Urbana: University of Illinois Press, 2006). On how gender was infused into federal policy, see also Linda Gordon, *Pitied but Not Entitled: Single Mothers and the History of Welfare, 1890–1935* (Cambridge, Mass.: Harvard University Press, 1998), and Suzanne Mettler, *Dividing Citizens: Gender and Federalism in New Deal Public Policy* (Ithaca, N.Y.: Cornell University Press, 1998). On sites of labor as gendered and racialized work systems, see Kathleen Barry, *Femininity in Flight: A History of Flight Attendants* (Durham, N.C.: Duke University Press, 2007); Julie Berebitsky, *Sex and the Office: A History of Gender, Power and Desire* (New Haven: Yale University Press, 2012); Eileen Boris and Jennifer Klein, *Caring for America: Home Health Care Workers in the Shadow of the Welfare State* (New York: Oxford University Press, 2012); and Venus Green, *Race on the Line: Gender, Labor and Technology in the Bell System, 1880–1980* (Durham, N.C.: Duke University Press, 2001).

5. Title VII of the Civil Rights Act of 1964 (Pub. L. 88-352, 78 Stat. 241, enacted July 2, 1964); see also the Equal Pay Act of 1963 (Pub. L. No. 88-38, 77 Stat. 56, enacted June 10, 1963); and Executive Order 11246 (30 F.R. 12319, 12935, 3 CFR, 1964–65 Comp., p. 399, signed by President Lyndon B. Johnson on September 24, 1965). Ruth Rosen, *The World Split Open: How the Modern Women's Movement Changed America*, rev. ed. (New York: Penguin, 2006); Sara M. Evans, *Tidal Wave: How Women Changed America at Century's End* (New York: Free Press, 2004).

6. Nancy MacLean, *Freedom Is Not Enough: The Opening of the American Workplace* (New York: Russell Sage Foundation and Cambridge, Mass.: Harvard University Press, 2006), esp. chs. 1–3; Risa Goluboff, *The Lost Promise of Civil Rights* (Cambridge, Mass.: Harvard University Press, 2007); John D. Skrentny, *The Minority Rights Revolution* (Cambridge, Mass.: Belknap Press of Harvard University Press, 2002); Anthony S. Chen, *The Fifth Freedom: Jobs, Politics, and Civil Rights in the United States, 1941–1972* (Princeton: Princeton University Press, 2009); Dennis DeSlippe, *Protesting Affirmative Action: The Struggle over Equality After the Civil Rights Revolution* (Baltimore: Johns Hopkins University Press, 2012); Paul D. Moreno, *From Direct Action to Affirmative Action: Fair Employment Law and Policy in America, 1933–1972* (Baton Rouge: Louisiana State University Press, 1997).

7. Serena Mayeri, *Reasoning from Race: Feminism, Law, and the Civil Rights Revolution* (Cambridge, Mass.: Harvard University Press, 2011).

8. See especially Dorothy Sue Cobble, *The Other Women's Movement: Workplace Justice and Social Rights in Modern America* (Princeton: Princeton University Press, 2004); Eileen Boris, "Fair Employment and the Origins of Affirmative Action in the 1940s," *NWSA Journal* 10 (1998): 142–51; Kessler-Harris, *Out to Work*, 180–214; and Kessler-Harris, *In Pursuit of Equity*. On protective labor legislation and labor feminism, see Eileen Boris, *Home to Work: Motherhood and the Politics of Industrial Homework in the United States* (Cambridge, U.K.: Cambridge University Press, 1994); Cynthia Harrison, *On Account of Sex: The Politics of Women's Issues, 1945–1968* (Berkeley: University of California Press, 1988); Mark Hendrickson, "Gender Research as Labor Activism: The Women's Bureau in the New Era," *Journal of Policy History* 20 (2008): 482–515; Sibyl Lipschultz, "Hours and Wages: The Gendering of Labor Standards in America," *Journal of Women's History* 8 (Spring 1996): 114–36; John Thomas McGuire, "Making the Case for Night Work Legislation in Progressive Era New York, 1911–1915," *Journal of the Gilded Age and Progressive Era* 5 (January 2006): 47–70; John Thomas McGuire, "Gender and the Personal Shaping of Public Administration in the United States: Mary Anderson and the Women's Bureau, 1920–1930," *Public Administration Review* 72 (March–April 2012): 265–71; Julie Novkov, *Constituting Workers, Protecting Women: Gender, Law, and Labor in the Progressive Era* (Ann Arbor: University of Michigan Press, 2001); Kathryn Kish Sklar, "Two Political Cultures in the Progressive Era: The National Consumers' League and the American Association for Labor Legislation," in *U.S. History as Women's History: New Feminist Essays*, ed. Linda K. Kerber, Alice Kessler-Harris, and Kathryn Kish Sklar (Chapel Hill: University of North Carolina Press, 1995), 36–62; and Landon R. Y. Storrs, *Civilizing Capitalism: The National Consumers' League, Women's Activism, and Labor Standards in the New Deal Era* (Chapel Hill: University of North Carolina Press, 2000).

9. On how popular rights claims and pressure "from below" have reshaped citizenship rights, see Ellen Carol DuBois, *Harriot Stanton Blatch and the Winning of Woman Suffrage* (New Haven: Yale University Press, 1999); Laura F. Edwards, *The People and their Peace: Legal Culture and the Transformation of Inequality in the Post-Revolutionary South* (Chapel Hill: University of North Carolina Press, 2009); Felicia Kornbluh, *The Battle for Welfare Rights: Politics and Poverty in Modern America* (Philadelphia: University of Pennsylvania Press, 2007); Larry D. Kramer, *The People Themselves: Popular Constitutionalism and Judicial Review* (Oxford: Oxford University Press, 2005); Tomiko Brown-Nagin, *Courage to Dissent: Atlanta and the Long History of the Civil Rights Movement* (Oxford: Oxford University Press, 2011); Goluboff, *The Lost Promise of Civil Rights*; Felicia Kornbluh and Karen Tani, "Below, Above, Amidst: The Legal History of Poverty," in *A Companion to American Legal History*, ed. Alfred Brophy and Sally E. Hadden (Malden, Mass., John Wiley & Sons, 2013), 329–48; and Daniel Winunwe Rivers, *Radical Relations: Lesbian*

Mothers, Gay Fathers, and Their Children in the United States Since World War II (Chapel Hill: University of North Carolina Press, 2013).

10. Thelma Pilch's letter, which demanded substantive fairness in the name of equal rights, echoed arguments raised in the years after the Civil War, when constituent political groups debated whether merely integrating freedpeople into preexisting patterns of work and life could deliver them the social equality intended by the Thirteenth, Fourteenth, and Fifteenth Amendments. Decades later, the devastation of the Great Depression sparked novel types of grassroots rights claims and legal strategies calling for economic justice in the name of equality. More recently, the disability rights movement has emphasized the distinction between formal and material equality. The former prioritizes the process of equal treatment, while the latter asks whether such treatment can yield equal membership in society. Chen, *Fifth Freedom*; Michele Landis Dauber, *The Sympathetic State: Disaster Relief and the Origins of the American Welfare State* (Chicago: University of Chicago Press, 2012); George I. Lovell, *This Is Not Civil Rights: Discovering Rights Talk in 1939 America* (Chicago: University of Chicago Press, 2012); Goluboff, *Lost Promise of Civil Rights*; Eileen Boris, "Ledbetter's Continuum: Race, Gender, and Pay Discrimination," in *Feminist Legal History: Essays on Women and Law*, eds. Tracy Thomas and Tracey Boisseau (New York: New York University Press, 2011), 240–55; Megan Taylor Shockley, *"We, Too, Are Americans": African American Women in Detroit and Richmond, 1940–54* (Urbana: University of Illinois Press, 2003); Boris and Klein, *Caring for America*, esp. 123–48; Zaragosa Vargas, *Labor Rights Are Civil Rights: Mexican American Workers in Twentieth-Century America* (Princeton: Princeton University Press, 2007); Arlene B. Mayerson and Silvia Yee, "Symposium: Facing the Challenges of the ADA: The First Ten Years and Beyond," *Ohio State Law Journal* 62 (2001): 535–54; Felicia Kornbluh, "Disability, Antiprofessionalism, and Civil Rights: The National Federation of the Blind and the 'Right to Organize' in the 1950s," *Journal of American History* 97 (March 2011): 1023–47.

11. Carl M. Brauer, "Women Activists, Southern Conservatives, and the Prohibition of Sex Discrimination in Title VII of the Civil Rights Act of 1964," *Journal of Southern History* 49 (February 1983): 37–56; Jo Freeman, "How 'Sex' Got into Title VII: Persistent Opportunism as a Maker of Public Policy," *Journal of Law and Inequality* 9 (1991): 163–84; Cindy Deitch, "Gender, Race, and Class Politics and the Inclusion of Women in Title VII of the Civil Rights Act of 1964," *Gender and Society* 7 (1993): 183–203; Hugh Davis Graham, *The Civil Rights Era: Origins and Development of National Policy, 1960–1972* (New York: Oxford University Press, 1990); Cynthia Harrison, *On Account of Sex*; Phil Tiemeyer, *Plane Queer: Labor, Sexuality, and AIDS in the History of Male Flight Attendants* (Berkeley: University of California Press, 2013), 80–107.

12. Most prominent is the path-breaking and synthetic study by Nancy MacLean, *Freedom Is Not Enough*; see also Barry, *Femininity in Flight*, 144–73, esp. 172; MacLean, "The Difference a Law Can Make," *Labor: Studies in Working-Class History of the Americas* 11 (2014): 19–24; and Tiemeyer, *Plane Queer*, 80–108. On Title VII's interpretation and related activism, see also Kenneth Mack, "Bringing the Law Back into the History of the Civil Rights Movement," *Law and History Review* 27 (Fall 2009): 657–69 and Nancy MacLean, "Response to Ken Mack—and New Questions for the History of African American Legal Liberalism in the Age of Obama," *Law and History Review* 27 (Fall 2009): 671–79.

13. Chen, *Fifth Freedom*, 170–229; Frank Dobbin, *Inventing Equal Opportunity* (Princeton, N.J.: Princeton University Press, 2009); Nelson Lichtenstein, *State of the Union: A Century of American Labor* (Princeton: Princeton University Press, 2002), esp. 192–95; and Judith Stein, *Running Steel, Running America: Race, Economic Policy and the Decline of Liberalism* (Chapel

Hill: University of North Carolina Press, 1998), 69–120, esp. 87–88. On Title VII's limits for working-class women, see Eileen Boris, "Where's the Care?" *Labor: Studies in Working-Class History of the Americas* 11 (March 2014): 43–47.

14. On state building as meaning making, see Margot Canaday, *The Straight State: Sexuality and Citizenship in Twentieth-Century America* (Princeton: Princeton University Press, 2011). Corporate personnel departments also shaped the meaning and reach of EEO laws. See Frank Dobbin, *Inventing Equal Opportunity* (Princeton, N.J.: Princeton University Press, 2009).

15. Kessler-Harris, *In Pursuit of Equity*, 239–90. Most recent scholarship suggests that mid-century feminism's central focus on achieving social justice through workplace transformation was expanded and ultimately displaced by less labor centric concerns in the 1960s and 1970s. These works foreground feminist coalition building, local politics, campaigns for reproductive rights and bodily autonomy, the coexistence of multiple feminisms, racial and other identity politics, and efforts to boost women's access to welfare, civic participation, and public spaces. Where historians have analyzed women's workplace rights activism in those years, they tend to portray it as a relatively moderate push for equal treatment, locating the radical edge of feminist efforts elsewhere. See, for example, Stephanie Gilmore, *Groundswell: Feminist Activism in Postwar America* (New York: Routledge, 2013); Stephanie Gilmore et al., *Feminist Coalitions: Historical Perspectives on Second-Wave Feminism in the Postwar United States* (Urbana: University of Illinois Press, 2008); Kornbluh, *Battle for Welfare Rights*; Nancy A. Hewitt, *No Permanent Waves: Recasting Histories of U.S. Feminism* (New Brunswick: Rutgers University Press, 2010); Danielle L. McGuire, *At the Dark End of the Street: Black Women, Rape, and Resistance—A New History of the Civil Rights Movement from Rosa Parks to the Rise of Black Power* (Alfred A. Knopf, 2010); Annelise Orleck, *Rethinking Women's Activism* (New York: Routledge, 2014); Anne M. Valk, *Radical Sisters: Second-Wave Feminism and Black Liberation in Washington, D.C.* (Urbana: University of Illinois Press, 2010); Anne Enke, *Finding the Movement: Sexuality, Contested Space, and Feminist Activism* (Durham, N.C.: Duke University Press, 2007); Tamar Carroll, *Mobilizing New York: AIDS, Antipoverty, and Feminist Activism* (Chapel Hill: University of North Carolina Press, 2015); Melissa Estes Blair, *Revolutionizing Expectations: Women's Organizations, Feminism, and American Politics, 1965–1980* (Athens, Ga.: University of Georgia Press, 2014); Dorothy Sue Cobble, Linda Gordon, and Astrid Henry, *Feminism Unfinished: A Short, Surprising History of American Women's Movements* (New York: Liveright, 2014); Jennifer Brier, *Infectious Ideas: U.S. Political Responses to the AIDS Crisis* (Chapel Hill: University of North Carolina Press, 2011); Christine Stansell, *The Feminist Promise, 1792 to the Present* (New York: Modern Library, 2010); Judy Wu, *Radicals on the Road: Internationalism, Orientalism and Feminism During the Vietnam Era* (Ithaca, N.Y.: Cornell University Press, 2013); Winifred Breines, *The Trouble Between Us: An Uneasy History of White and Black Women in the Feminist Movement* (Oxford: Oxford University Press, 2006); Benita Roth, *Separate Roads to Feminism: Black, Chicana, and White Feminist Movements in America's Second Wave* (Cambridge, U.K.: Cambridge University Press, 2004). A few notable exceptions are Barry, *Femininity in Flight*; Boris and Klein, *Caring for America*; Lisa Levenstein, "'Don't Agonize, Organize!' The Displaced Homemakers Campaign and the Contested Goals of 1970s Feminism," *Journal of American History* 100 (March 2014): 144–68; Nancy MacLean, "The Hidden History of Affirmative Action: Working Women's Struggles in the 1970s and the Gender of Class," Feminist Studies 25 (Spring 1999): 43–78; and Dorothy Sue Cobble, "'A Spontaneous Loss of Enthusiasm': Workplace Feminism and the Transformation of Women's Service Jobs in the 1970s," *International Labor and Working-Class History* 56 (October 1999): 23–44.

16. Cobble, *Other Women's Movement*; MacLean, *Freedom Is Not Enough*, ch. 4; Nancy Cott, *The Grounding of Modern Feminism* (New Haven, Conn.: Yale University Press, 1989).

17. Mayeri, *Reasoning from Race*.

18. See especially Daniel T. Rodgers, *Age of Fracture* (Cambridge, Mass.: Belknap Press of Harvard University Press, 2011) and Robert O. Self, *All in the Family: The Realignment of American Democracy Since the 1960s* (New York: Hill and Wang, 2012).

19. Despite a few notable exceptions, class has been a neglected category in women's and gender history. See Gerda Lerner, "U.S. Women's History: Past, Present and Future," *Journal of Women's History* 16 (Winter 2004): 10–27. This is starting to change. See Eileen Boris, "Class Returns," *Journal of Women's History* 25 (2013): 74–87; Boris and Klein, *Caring for America*; Carroll, *Mobilizing New York*; Nancy Fraser, "Feminism, Capitalism, and the Cunning of History," in *Fortunes of Feminism: From State-Managed Capitalism to Neoliberal Crisis* (London: Verso, 2013), 209–25; Kornbluh, *Battle for Welfare Rights*; Lisa Levenstein, *A Movement Without Marches: African American Women and the Politics of Poverty in Postwar Philadelphia* (Chapel Hill: University of North Carolina Press, 2009); Annelise Orleck, *Storming Caesar's Palace: How Black Mothers Fought Their Own War on Poverty* (Boston: Beacon, 2005); Orleck, *Rethinking American Women's Activism*.

20. Stein, *Running Steel, Running America*, 195.

21. Jefferson Cowie, *Stayin' Alive: The 1970s and the Last Days of the Working Class* (New York: New Press, 2010), 200; Judith Stein, *Pivotal Decade: How the United States Traded Factories for Finance in the Seventies* (New Haven, Conn.: Yale University Press, 2010). For a notable critique of this argument, see Jennifer Klein, "Apocalypse Then, and Now," *Democracy: A Journal of Ideas* 19 (Winter 2011), http://www.democracyjournal.org/19/6794.php?page=all.

22. This metaphor is a twist on David Roediger's conception of the wages of whiteness. Roediger, *The Wages of Whiteness: Race and the Making of the American Working Class* (London: Verso, 2007). Dorothy Sue Cobble, "Introduction," *The Sex of Class: Women Transforming American Labor* (Ithaca, N.Y.: Cornell University Press, 2007), esp. 3. On how gendered, racialized assumptions shaped Great Society programs in these years, see Marisa Chappell, *The War on Welfare: Family, Poverty, and Politics in Modern America* (Philadelphia: University of Pennsylvania Press, 2010). On postwar political economy and its implications for work, culture, and society, see, for example, Jefferson Cowie, *Capital Moves: RCA's Seventy-Year Quest for Cheap Labor* (Ithaca, N.Y.: Cornell University Press, 1999); Leon Fink, *The Maya of Morganton: Work and Community in the Nuevo New South* (Chapel Hill: University of North Carolina Press, 2007); Erin Hatton, *The Temp Economy: From Kelly Girls to Permatemps in Postwar America* (Philadelphia: Temple University Press, 2011); Nelson Lichtenstein, *The Retail Revolution: How Wal-Mart Created a Brave New World of Business* (New York: Metropolitan Books, 2009); Ruth Milkman, *Farewell to the Factory: Auto Workers in the Late Twentieth Century* (Berkeley: University of California Press, 1997); Bethany Moreton, *To Serve God and Wal-Mart: The Making of Christian Free Enterprise* (Cambridge, Mass.: Harvard University Press, 2010).

23. MacLean, *Freedom Is Not Enough*, 225–61.

24. A wave of recent historical scholarship has examined how business and political conservatism have gone hand-in-hand and shaped the past century. See, for example, Sophia Z. Lee, *The Workplace Constitution from the New Deal to the New Right* (Cambridge, U.K.: Cambridge University Press, 2015); Nelson Lichtenstein and Elizabeth Tandy Shermer, eds., *The Right and Labor: Politics, Ideology, and Imagination* (Philadelphia: University of Pennsylvania Press, 2012); Kim Phillips-Fein, *Invisible Hands: The Businessmen's Crusade Against the New Deal*

(New York: Norton, 2010); Kim Phillips-Fein and Julian E. Zelizer, eds., *What's Good for Business: Business and American Politics Since World War II* (Oxford: Oxford University Press, 2012); Schulman and Julian E. Zelizer, eds., *Rightward Bound: Making America Conservative in the 1970s* (Cambridge, Mass.: Harvard University Press, 2008); and Ben Waterhouse, *Lobbying America: The Politics of Business from Nixon to NAFTA* (Princeton: Princeton University Press, 2014).

Chapter 1. Defining Sex Discrimination

1. Frank Cantwell, Department of Labor Women's Bureau Legislative Liaison, to Senator Robert F. Kennedy, April 7, 1965, Women's Employment, 3–4 folder, box 51, Records of the Women's Bureau of the Department of Labor Subject Files of the Director, 1964–1970, Record Group 86, National Archives and Records Administration, College Park, Md. (hereafter "WB-SFD").

2. Cantwell to Kennedy, April 7, 1965, Women's Employment, 3–4 folder, box 51, WB-SFD.

3. Richard Graham to Franklin Delano Roosevelt Jr., November 9, 1965, Graham, Richard: Commissioner folder, box 2, Records of EEOC Chairman Franklin Delano Roosevelt Junior, 1965–66, Record Group 403, National Archives and Records Administration, College Park, Md. (hereafter "EEOC-FDR").

4. Vera Glaser, "U.S. Job Bias Agency Is Hit in Resignation," *Detroit News*, November 13, 1966, Commissioner Hernandez folder, box 6, Records of EEOC Chairman Stephen Shulman, 1966–67, Equal Employment Opportunity Commission, Record Group 403, National Archives and Records Administration, College Park, Md. (hereafter "EEOC-Shulman").

5. James P. Gannon, "Uphill Bias Fight," *Wall Street Journal*, April 12, 1967, 1.

6. Robert B. Semple Jr., "Bigger U.S. Fight on Job Bias Seen," *New York Times*, March 5, 1967, 35.

7. Risa Goluboff details the process, occurring in the 1930s and 1940s, by which civil rights for African Americans, including employment rights, became cemented as formal and procedural. Alternative notions of substantive and redistributive civil rights were abandoned as elites' priorities and organizational politics shaped the process. See Goluboff, *The Lost Promise of Civil Rights*.

8. President's Commission on the Status of Women, *American Women: The Report of the President's Commission on the Status of Women* (Washington, D.C.: U.S. Government Printing Office, 1963), 240–41.

9. Carl M. Brauer, "Women Activists, Southern Conservatives, and the Prohibition of Sex Discrimination in Title VII of the Civil Rights Act of 1964," *Journal of Southern History* 49 (February 1983): 37.

10. In this chapter, I have retained these letters' original phrasing and spelling. Dorothy Sue Cobble, *The Other Women's Movement*.

11. See, for example, Harrison, *On Account of Sex*, 182–209; Kessler-Harris, *In Pursuit of Equity*, 246–67; MacLean, *Freedom Is Not Enough*, 117–54, esp. 127–33; Orleck, *Rethinking Women's Activism*, 84–87; Self, *All in the Family*, 114–19; and Stansell, *Feminist Promise*, 208–17. John D. Skrentny has written on the Commission's internal struggles over Title VII's sex clause. Skrentny, *Minority Rights Revolution*, 111–16.

12. *Reed v. Reed*, 404 U.S. 71 (1971); *Frontiero v. Richardson*, 441 U.S. 667 (1973); *Craig v. Boren*, 429 U.S. 190 (1976).

13. Margery Davies, *Woman's Place Is at the Typewriter: Office Work and Office Workers, 1870–1930* (Philadelphia: Temple University Press, 1984); Kessler-Harris, *Out to Work*, 3–44;

Susan Lehrer, *Origins of Protective Labor Legislation for Women, 1905–1925* (Albany: SUNY Press, 1987), 18–19; Annelise Orleck, *Common Sense and a Little Fire: Women and Working-Class Politics in the United States, 1900–1965* (Chapel Hill: University of North Carolina Press, 1995).

14. *Lochner v. New York*, 198 U.S. 45 (1905); *Muller v. Oregon*, 208 U.S. 412 (1908); Kessler-Harris, *Out to Work*, 180–216; Kathryn Kish Sklar, "Two Political Cultures in the Progressive Era: The National Consumers' League and the American Association for Labor Legislation," in *U.S. History as Women's History: New Feminist Essays*, ed. Linda K. Kerber, Alice Kessler-Harris, and Kathryn Kish Sklar (Chapel Hill: University of North Carolina Press,1995), 36–62; Storrs, *Civilizing Capitalism.*

15. Eileen Boris, "'You Wouldn't Want One of 'Em Dancing with Your Wife': Racialized Bodies on the Job in World War II," *American Quarterly* 50 (March 1998): 77–80; Boris, "Fair Employment and the Origins of Affirmative Action"; Ruth Milkman, *Gender at Work: The Dynamics of Job Segregation During World War II* (Urbana: University of Illinois Press, 1987); Michael Sovern, *Legal Restraints on Racial Discrimination in Employment* (New York: Twentieth Century Fund, 1966), 9–10.

16. Alice Leopold to Millard Cass, Deputy Undersecretary of Labor, re: New Proposals for 1961 Legislative Program, September 20, 1960, Legislation folder, box 133, Women's Bureau General Correspondence 1948–1963, Record Group 86, National Archives and Records Administration, College Park, Md. (hereafter "WB-GCII"); Notes on Meeting of Committee to Consider Possible Equalization of Special and Prohibitory Labor Laws for Women, August 3, 1944, State Labor Officials Conference, August 16–17, 1944 folder, box 175, Women's Bureau Division of Research and Manpower Program Development, 1940–45, Record Group 86, National Archives and Records Administration, College Park, Md. (hereafter "WB-DRM"); Laughlin, *Women's Work and Public Policy*, 69–92.

17. Boris, "Fair Employment and the Origins of Affirmative Action in the 1940s," 143; Cobble, *Other Women's Movement*, 5, 28, 98–99, 163–67; Nancy Gabin, *Feminism in the Labor Movement: Women and the United Auto Workers, 1935–75* (Ithaca, N.Y.: Cornell University Press, 1990), 157. See also "Wartime Status of State Laws for Women," January 1944, Conference on Postwar Adjustments of Women Workers folder, box 175, WB-DRM; "Exemptions from State Hour Laws for Women and Minors, September 1, 1942," Labor Laws and Legislation, 1942 (11–17) folder, box 186, WB-DRM; "Exemptions from State Hour Laws for Women and Minors, September 1, 1942," Labor Laws and Legislation, 1942 (11–17) folder, box 186, WB-DRM; Alice Leopold to Millard Cass, Deputy Undersecretary of Labor, re: New Proposals for 1961 Legislative Program, September 20, 1960, Legislation folder, box 133, WB-GCII.

18. "1959 Summary of State Labor Laws for Women," PCSW folder, box 38, General Records of the Women's Bureau Division of Legislation and Standards 1920–1966, Record Group 86, National Archives and Records Administration, College Park, Md. (hereafter "WB-DLS"). WB-DLS; "State Labor Legislation Affecting the Employment of Women, 1959," Laws Affecting Women folder, box 15, WB-DLS; Jane Walstedt, "State Labor Laws in Transition: From Protection to Equal Status for Women," U.S. Department of Labor, Pamphlet 15, 1976, 3.

19. Chen, *Fifth Freedom*, 32–87; Andrew Kersten, *Race, Jobs, and the War: The FEPC in the Midwest, 1941–46* (Urbana: University of Illinois Press, 2000); MacLean, *Freedom Is Not Enough*, 22–23.

20. George Reedy, Press Release, "From the Office of Vice President Lyndon Johnson," February 5, 1962, folder 7, box 8, Office Files of White House Aides, LBJ Library, Austin, Tx.; Press

Release, President's Committee on EEO, January 23, 1963, General Records of the Department of Labor, Office of the Secretary of Labor, Records of Secretary of Labor W. Willard Wirtz, 1962–69, Record Group 174, National Archives and Records Administration, College Park, Md. (hereafter "DOL-Wirtz"); Secretary's Working Papers, Meeting, August 20, 1963, 1963-—Committee—President's Committee on Equal Employment Opportunity folder, box 64, DOL-Wirtz.

21. 110 Cong. Rec., June 10, 1964, 13319; EEOC Press Release, October 8, 1965, folder: "EEOC Press Releases," box 1, EEOC-FDR; "'Liberated Negro,' FDR Jr. Pleads Here," *Boston Globe*, October 30, 1965, 19; EEOC Press Release, October 6, 1965, EEOC Press Releases folder, box 1, Records of EEOC Chairman Franklin Delano Roosevelt Jr., 1965–66, Equal Employment Opportunity Commission, Record Group 403, National Archives and Records Administration, College Park, Md. On early EEOC efforts to interpret Title VII and combat race discrimination, see Chen, *Fifth Freedom*, 170–229; David Hamilton Golland, *Constructing Affirmative Action: The Struggle for Equal Employment Opportunity* (Lexington: University Press of Kentucky, 2011); Paul D. Moreno, *From Direct Action to Affirmative Action: Fair Employment Law and Policy in America, 1933–1972* (Baton Rouge: Louisiana State University Press, 1999), 199–266; Skrentny, *The Minority Rights Revolution*, 85–129.

22. From the text of Title VII; see http://www.eeoc.gov/policy/vii.html; Richard K. Berg, "Title VII: A Three-Years' View," *Notre Dame Law Review* 44 (February 1969): 312.

23. John T. McQuiston, "Franklin Roosevelt Jr., 74, Ex-Congressman, Dies," *New York Times*, August 18, 1988, D22; "Franklin Delano Roosevelt, Jr.," Biographical Dictionary of the United States Congress, http://bioguide.congress.gov/scripts/biodisplay.pl?index=r000425, accessed September 19, 2009.

24. Julius Duscha, "Son of FDR Chosen for Rights Job," *Washington Post*, May 11, 1965, A1.

25. Roosevelt lost the race for governor of New York to incumbent Nelson Rockefeller in 1966. Cynthia Harrison Interview with Richard Graham, July 31, 1985, 4, folder 44, box 26, Catherine East Papers, Schlesinger Library, Radcliffe Institute, Harvard University, Cambridge, Mass. (hereafter "CEP-SL").

26. "Profile," *EEOC Newsletter* 1 (February–March 1966): 4, folder 1, box 3, Papers of Sonia Pressman Fuentes, Schlesinger Library, Radcliffe Institute, Harvard University, Cambridge, Mass. ("hereafter SPF-SL"); EEOC Press Release, "EEOC Discovers Dividends as It Solves 20 Cases," September 10, 1965, EEOC Press Releases folder, box 1, EEOC-FDR.

27. "Old Stereotypes Are Her Target," *Washington Post*, May 25, 1965, D1; Cynthia Harrison Interview with Richard Graham, July 31, 1985, 1–2, folder 44, box 26, CEP-SL.

28. Cynthia Harrison Interview with Richard Graham, July 31, 1985, 2–4, folder 44, box 26, CEP-SL.

29. EEOC Press Release, September 10, 1965, EEOC Press Releases folder, box 1, EEOC-FDR; "Aileen Hernandez Biographical Data," folder 43, box 1, National Organization for Women Records, 1959–2002, Schlesinger Library, Radcliffe Institute, Harvard University, Cambridge, Mass. (hereafter "NOW"); Valena M. Williams, "Women's Lib," undated, 32, folder 43, box 1, NOW.

30. "Old Stereotypes Are Her Target," *Washington Post*, May 25, 1965, D1.

31. Vera Glaser, "Mrs. Hernandez Works with FDR Jr.," *Washington Star*, August 1, 1965, Aileen Hernandez folder, box 2, EEOC-FDR; Elizabeth Shelton, "Is the Computer Responsible?" *Washington Post*, July 1, 1965, Aileen Hernandez folder, box 2, EEOC-FDR.

32. Lyndon Johnson Remarks Before White House Conference on Equal Employment Opportunity, August 20, 1965, White House Conference on EEO folder, box 1, EEOC-FDR.

33. EEOC Press Release, July 20, 1965, EEOC Press Releases folder, box 1, EEOC-FDR; Ken Millstone, "Journey from Berlin to Potomac," folder 7, box 1, SPF-SL; Marlena Thompson, "Local Woman Is a Leader in Feminist Fight," December 16, 1999, folder 5, box 1, SPF-SL; Sonia Pressman, "Segregation, Never," undated (ca. 1956), *Miami Hurricane*, folder 6, box 1, SPF-SL; "Beauty Out-Talks 15 Men," *Miami Herald*, April 29, 1956, folder 6, box 1, SPF-SL; Louise Goodson, "Confidentially," October 24, 1957, folder 6, box 1, SPF-SL; "Office of Sonia Pressman: Major Ongoing Operations," May 1970, folder 2, box 3, SPF-SL; "Jobs Rights Post Goes to C. T. Duncan," *Washington Post*, July 21, 1965, C3.

34. "65 Investigators Will Support Equal-Hiring Policies," *Washington Post*, July 6, 1965, A6; "1965–1971: A 'Toothless Tiger' Helps Shape the Law and Educate the Public," http://eeoc.gov/abouteeoc/35th/1965-71/index.html, accessed September 15, 2009; Equal Employment Opportunity Commission, *Making a Right a Reality: An Oral History of the Early Years of the EEOC, 1965–1972* (Washington, D.C.: The Commission, 1990), 11.

35. Equal Employment Opportunity Commission, "1965–1971: A 'Toothless Tiger' Helps Shape the Law and Educate the Public," http://eeoc.gov/abouteeoc/35th/1965-71/index.html, accessed September 15, 2009.

36. *Making a Right a Reality*, 11.

37. Samuel C. Jackson to EEOC Commissioners, September 13, 1965, re: Public Image of the Commission, "Is the Computer Responsible?" *Washington Post*, July 1, 1965, Jackson, Samuel C. folder, box 2, EEOC-FDR.

38. Berg, "Title VII," 312–13; Skrentny, *Minority Rights Revolution*, 88.

39. Franklin Delano Roosevelt Jr., "EEOC Team Tours South," *EEOC Newsletter* 1 (February–March 1966): 1, folder 1, box 3, SPF-SL; Jim Wood, "'Long, Hard Pull' Is Seen for Civil Rights Movement," *Corpus Christi Call*, May 20, 1967, B1; "Negroes Call for Teeth in Fair Employment Bill,' *Washington Evening Star*, May 5, 1967.

40. MacLean, *Freedom Is Not Enough*, 78–82.

41. Statement by Franklin Delano Roosevelt Jr. Before General Subcommittee on Labor, House of Representatives, July 21, 1965, Mr. Roosevelt's Testimony folder, box 1, EEOC-FDR.

42. Cynthia Harrison Interview with Richard Graham, July 31, 1985, folder 44, box 26, CEP-SL.

43. Title VII contained other omissions. Commissioners were uncertain of whether Title VII could sustain a class action and how the commission should coexist with state administrative agencies. Further, the law required the commission to conduct an investigation, then attempt to obtain voluntary compliance within sixty days. If the commission was unable to obtain voluntary compliance in that window, the charging party had thirty days to bring suit. Yet, the law did not specify what should happen if the commission did not find reasonable cause, so did not pursue voluntary compliance; or what should happen if the EEOC was unable to obtain compliance within sixty days. Berg, "Title VII," 313–14, 325; Charles T. Duncan and Sonia Pressman to Aileen Hernandez, November 15, 1965, re: Response to Inquiry of October 21, 1965 re: Waiver by Charging Party in State Proceeding of His Federal Rights, General Counsel: Inter-Office Memos folder, box 2, EEOC-Shulman.

44. Berg, "Title VII," 326–27.

45. "EEOC's Position on the Hawkins Bill as Indicated by Chairman FDR Jr. in his Testimony on July 21, 1965," Title VII folder, box 8, EEOC-Shulman; "Update About First Three Months of EEOC," October 29, 1965, Roosevelt to President Johnson folder, box 1, EEOC-FDR.

46. Memo to Commissioner Graham, Mr. Blumrosen, Mr. Berg, Mr. Reeves, Mr. Rayburn, from N. Thompson Powers, Executive Director of EEOC, July 22, 1965, Compliance: Policy Recommendations (Powell) folder, box 2, EEOC-CD.

47. Remarks by FDR Jr., prepared for delivery before the National Council of Women's Conference on Women at Work, Hotel Biltmore, New York, October 12, 1965, Mr. Roosevelt's Speeches folder, box 1, EEOC-FDR.

48. Charles Duncan to Commissioners re: Legal Opinions-Issued and Proposed, October 6, 1965, Duncan, Charles folder, box 1, EEOC-FDR.

49. Margie Fisher, "Women Still Face Discrimination in Jobs, Female Lawyer Believes," folder 13, box 2, SPF-SL.

50. Aileen Hernandez, "The Women's Movement: 1965–1975," Symposium on the Tenth Anniversary of the EEOC, November 2–29, 1975, 9, folder 1704, Pauli Murray Papers, Schlesinger Library, Radcliffe Institute, Harvard University, Cambridge, Mass. (hereafter "PMP").

51. Memo to Executive Director from Director of Complaints, November 20, 1965, re: State Protective Laws for Women and Exemptions and Exceptions Thereto, Compliance: Inter-Office Memos folder, box 1, EEOC-CD.

52. Advisory Council to the Interdepartmental Committee on the Status of Women, "A Memorandum on Policy for the EEOC," October 1, 1965, folder 11, box 2, Mary O. Eastwood Papers, Schlesinger Library, Radcliffe Institute, Harvard University, Cambridge, Mass. (hereafter "MOEP"); Catherine East to Olya Margolin, July 27, 1965, folder 49, box 8, CEP-SL; "Workshop Report: Panel 3, Discrimination Because of Sex," White House Conference on EEO folder, box 1, EEOC-FDR; Catherine East et al. to Franklin Delano Roosevelt Jr., undated, folder 49, box 8, CEP-SL.

53. *American Women*, 132–34. See also Harrison, *On Account of Sex*, 151–54.

54. Esther Peterson Address to Training Seminar on the Equal Employment Opportunity Commission, July 8 1965, folder 2672, box 126, Esther Peterson Papers, 1884–1998, Schlesinger Library, Radcliffe Institute, Harvard University, Cambridge, Mass.

55. Memo to Executive Director from Director of Complaints, re: State Protective Laws for Women and Exemptions and Exceptions Thereto, November 20, 1965, Compliance: Inter-Office Memos folder, box 1, EEOC-CD.

56. Aileen Hernandez to EEOC General Counsel and Other Commissioners, October 10, 1966, re: Sex Discrimination and State Laws," Commissioner Hernandez folder, box 6, EEOC-Shulman.

57. Remarks by FDR Jr., prepared for delivery before the National Council of Women's Conference on Women at Work, Hotel Biltmore, New York, October 12, 1965, Mr. Roosevelt's Speeches folder, box 1, EEOC-FDR.

58. Orleck, *Rethinking American Women's Activism*, 81.

59. "EEOC Urges Legal Test of State Laws Protecting Women," *Labor Law Reports*, September 9, 1966, 1, folder 925, PMP; Richard K. Berg to Sonia Pressman, January 23, 1967, re: Cases Involving State Protective Laws, State Protective Laws folder, box 1, EEOC-Shulman; Pauli Murray to Stephen Shulman, January 24, 1967, re: Cases Involving State Protective Laws, State Protective Laws folder, box 1, EEOC-Shulman; "Statement Adopted by the EEOC," August 19, 1966, folder 11, box 2, MOEP; 29 C.F.R. 1601.1(c), 1967; Berg, "Title VII," 334–35; CCH Empl. Prac. Guide 16,900.001 n. 2 (1968); Wayne E. Green, "Sex and Civil Rights: Women's Groups Fight Last Vestiges of Bias on Job, Before the Law," *Wall Street Journal*, May 22, 1967, 1; EEOC News Re-

lease, "Release for A.M. Newspapers Tuesday September 26," September 26, 1967, folder 5, box 1, Reports and Publicity Records, 1966–67, Equal Employment Opportunity Commission, Record Group 403, National Archives and Records Administration, College Park, Md (hereafter "EEOC-RP").

60. Mary Merrifield, "Work Rights Stir a Battle of the Sexes," *Chicago Tribune*, October 20, 1966, D12.

61. *Miss Jennie Fry v. Maurer-Neuer Division, J. J. Morrell and Company*, Arkansas City, Kansas, filed September 27, 1965, Compliance: Summary of Investigative Reports folder, box 1, EEOC-CD.

62. Margaret Brooks, Ottumwa, Iowa, to FDR Jr., undated, Compliance: Execs Controlled folder, box 2, EEOC-CD.

63. Josephine Flores, St. Paul, Minn., to FDR Jr., April 23, 1966, ibid.

64. Memo to EEOC Commissioners from Richard K. Berg, Acting General Counsel, re: Swift Meatpacking Agreements, December 15, 1966, General Counsel folder, box 8, EEOC-Shulman.

65. Richard K. Berg, Acting General Counsel, to EEOC Commissioners, re: Swift Meatpacking Agreements, December 15, 1966, ibid.

66. Sonia Pressman to Stephen Shulman, re: Current Issues Under Title VII Relating to Sex Discrimination, February 3, 1967, General Counsel folder, box 8, EEOC-Shulman.

67. Sonia Pressman to United Auto Workers Women's Department, "Detroit Speech," 3, April 11, 1967, folder 1305, PMP.

68. Cobble, *Other Women's Movement*, 187.

69. Stephen Shulman to Robert C. Wahlert, Executive Vice President, Dubuque Packing Company, May 31, 1966, March 1967 folder, box 7, EEOC-Shulman.

70. Ibid.; EEOC Press Release, February 17, 1967, folder 11, box 2, MOEP; "Meat-Packing Women Alleging Discrimination Win New Work Rules," *Wall Street Journal*, February 17, 1967, 13.

71. Aileen Hernandez, "The Women's Movement: 1965–1975," 10, Symposium on the Tenth Anniversary of the EEOC, November 2–29, 1975, folder 1704, PMP.

72. On rights claims, see Michele Landis Dauber, *Sympathetic State: Disaster Relief and the Origins of the American Welfare State* (Chicago: University of Chicago Press, 2012), 185–223; Lovell, *This Is Not Civil Rights*; Shockley, *"We, Too, Are Americans,"* esp. 63–101; and Katherine Turk, "'A Fair Chance to Do My Part of Work': African American Women, War Work and Rights Claims at the Kingsbury Ordnance Plant," *Indiana Magazine of History* 108 (September 2012): 209–44.

73. Mildred Fischer to FDR Jr., October 20, 1965, General Counsel: Legal Opinions folder, box 2, EEOC-Shulman.

74. Mildred French, Gallatin, Tenn., to President Lyndon Johnson, June 30, 1967, Employment folder, box 67, WB-SFD.

75. Mrs. E. L. Greathouse to Lyndon Johnson, August 4, 1965, Women's Employment, 3–4 folder, box 51, WB-SFD.

76. Frances B. Huber to FDR Jr., May 2, 1966, Compliance-Ex Sec Controlled folder, box 2, EEOC-CD.

77. Evelyn Clesson, Decatur, Ill., to Women's Bureau, U.S. Department of Labor, October 18, 1965, Women's Employment 3–4 folder, box 51, WB-SFD.

78. Mrs. Frances Glade, Hoboken, N.J., to U.S. Department of Labor, May 12, 1966, Women 4–6 folder, box 55, WB-SFD.

79. Grace M. Ivey to Lyndon Johnson, December 16, 1965, General Counsel: Legal Opinions folder, box 2, EEOC-Shulman.

80. Marguerite Losicki, South Bend, Ind., to FDR, n.d., Compliance: Ex Sec Controlled folder, box 2, EEOC-CD.

81. Mrs. Clarence Brigham, Walpole, Mass., to Willard Wirtz, October 1965, Women's Employment, 3–4 folder, box 51, WB-SFD.

82. Imogene Philp to Lyndon Johnson, n.d., General Counsel: Legal Opinions folder, box 2, EEOC-Shulman.

83. Mrs. Antoinette Mascia, Detroit, Mich., to Director of Women's Bureau, July 2, 1965, Women's Employment, 3–4 folder, box 51, WB-SFD.

84. Mrs. Evelyn Fennell to FDR Jr., November 8, 1965, Controlled Actions folder, box 1, EEOC-CD.

85. Ruth Page to FDR Jr., November 21, 1965, Controlled Actions folder, box 1, EEOC-CD.

86. *Mrs. Meridian Miller v. Chatman Electronics Division*, Tung Sol, May 11, 1966, Compliance—Cases Pending—Processing folder, box 2, EEOC-CD.

87. Ella B. Payton to Franklin Delano Roosevelt Jr., May 11, 1966, Compliance: Ex Sec Controlled folder, box 2, EEOC-CD.

88. George L. Holland to Ella B. Payton, June 1, 1966, Compliance: Ex Sec Controlled folder, box 2, EEOC-CD.

89. Adah Payne to FDR Jr., January 25, 1966, General Counsel: Legal Opinions folder, box 2, EEOC-Shulman; Helen McCauley, Oglesby, Ill., to FDR Jr., May 18, 1966, Compliance: Ex Sec Controlled folder, box 2, EEOC-CD; Mrs. Jean Horton to FDR Jr., April 25, 1966, Compliance: Ex Sec Controlled folder, box 2, EEOC-CD.

90. Mrs. Lawrence Fiegl to FDR Jr., Filmore, N.Y., February 28, 1966, Compliance: Ex Sec Controlled folder, box 2, EEOC-CD.

91. Miss Wilma Asbury, Charleston, W.Va., to FDR Jr., March 29, 1966, Compliance: Ex Sec Controlled folder, box 2, EEOC-CD.

92. Virgie Spradling to Lyndon Johnson, December 1965, General Counsel: Legal Opinions folder, box 2, EEOC-Shulman.

93. Grace M. Ivey to Lyndon Johnson, December 16, 1965, General Counsel: Legal Opinions folder, box 2, EEOC-Shulman.

94. Jane Martin to Stephen Shulman, undated, General Counsel: Legal Opinions folder, box 2, EEOC-Shulman.

95. Ibid.

96. Antonia Groitia to FDR Jr., March 30, 1966, General Counsel: Legal Opinions folder, box 2, EEOC-Shulman.

97. Kenneth F. Holbert to Stephen Shulman, December 12, 1966, Inter-Office Memos folder, box 1, EEOC-CD.

98. Compliance Report filed by George L. Holland, Director of Compliance, re: *Myrtle Moore v. Kroger Baking Company*, March 2, 1966, Compliance: Summary of Investigative Reports folder, box 1, EEOC-CD. Memo to Executive Director from Richard Graham, June 8, 1966, re: Sex Violations Discovered During the Processing of a Race Complaint, Graham, Richard folder, box 2, EEOC-FDR.

99. *Elvera Martin v. Maison Blanche Department Store*, September 14, 1965, Compliance—Policy Recommendations folder, box 2, EEOC-CD.

100. "65 Investigators Will Support Equal-Hiring Policies," *Washington Post*, July 6, 1965, A6; "1965–1971: A 'Toothless Tiger' Helps Shape the Law and Educate the Public," http://eeoc.gov /abouteeoc/35th/1965-71/index.html, accessed September 15, 2009; Making a Right a Reality," 8, 11; "The Lost Agency," *Nation*, December 19, 1966, 73; Vera Glaser, "U.S. Job Bias Agency Is Hit in Resignation," *Detroit News*, November 13, 1966, Commissioner Hernandez folder, box 6, EEOC-Shulman.

101. Kenneth Holbert to Stephen Shulman, re: Summary of Meeting of September 6, 1966, Admin—Backlog folder, box 1, EEOC-Shulman; Gordon Chase to Richard Lewis re: Flow of Decisions from Summer Interns and Permanent Staff, June 4, 1967, Filing folder, box 2, EEOC-FDR.

102. Samuel C. Jackson to Stephen Shulman, October 14, 1966, re: Cases Involving U.S. Steel and/or the Steelworkers Union, Commissioner Jackson folder, box 6, EEOC-Shulman.

103. Richard Graham to EEOC Commissioners, May 13, 1966, re: Proposed Commissioner's Charge Against Carolina Telephone and Telegraph Company, Graham, Richard: Commissioner folder, box 2, EEOC-FDR.

104. EEOC News Release, "Coverage of Equal Employment Law Expanded," July 1, 1967, folder 5, box 1, EEOC-RP.

105. Aileen Hernandez and Samuel Jackson to Stephen Shulman and Luther Holcomb, October 25, 1966, re: Commission's Backlog and Use of Other Federal Agencies to Assist in Eliminating Same, Commissioner Hernandez folder, box 6, EEOC-Shulman.

106. Sonia Pressman Fuentes to Aileen Hernandez, July 26, 1967, folder 2, box 2, SPF-SL.

107. Kenneth F. Holbert to EEOC Commissioners, January 10, 1967 re: Recommended Policy Change Regarding Deferrals of Commissioner Charges to Illinois State Commission, Memo-Compliance folder, box 1, EEOC-Shulman; Chief of Analysis and Advice to Acting Director of Compliance, January 4, 1967 re: Recommended Policy Change Regarding Deferrals of Commissioner Charges to Illinois State Commission, Memo—Compliance folder, box 1, EEOC-Shulman; "EEOC Moves into the Field," *EEOC Newsletter* 1, no. 5 (July–August 1966), Office of Compliance Statistics folder, box 8, EEOC-Shulman; Statement of Stephen Shulman to Senate Labor and Public Welfare Subcommittee on Employment, Manpower and Poverty, May 4, 1967, Senate Labor Subcommittee Hearing on S. 130 folder, box 5, EEOC-Shulman; Richard Graham to Charles Duncan, April 27, 1966, re: Establishment of Commission Policy Through Commissioner Decisions, Graham, Richard: Commissioner folder, box 2, EEOC-FDR; N. Thompson Powers to EEOC Staff, October 18, 1965, Powers, N. Thompson, Executive Director folder, box 1, EEOC-FDR; Peter Robertson to Stephen Shulman, re: Program Recommendations on Compliance Activities, May 12, 1967, Program Planning and Review folder, box 3, EEOC-Shulman. "From the Office of Lyndon Johnson," Press Release, February 5, 1962, folder 7, box 8, Office Files of White House Aides: George Reedy, LBJ Library, Austin, Tx.

108. Vera Glaser, "U.S. Job Bias Agency Is Hit in Resignation," *Detroit News*, November 13, 1966, Commissioner Hernandez folder, box 6, EEOC-Shulman.

109. "Lost Agency," 73.

110. Cynthia Harrison Interview with Richard Graham, July 31, 1985, folder 44, box 26, CEP-SL.

111. Gannon, "Uphill Bias Fight," 1.

112. Sonia Pressman to Pauli Murray, October 24, 1967, folder 1682, PMP.

113. "March 6, 1967 Progress Report," Task Force in Strengthening Staff Relations, Efficiency, and Morale in EEOC folder, box 6, EEOC-Shulman.

114. Gannon, "Uphill Bias Fight," 1.

115. Ibid.

116. Richard Graham to EEOC Commissioners and Jack Royer, March 17, 1966, Graham, Richard: Commissioner folder, box 2, EEOC-FDR.

117. Timothy Jenkins to Stephen Shulman, re: A Rationale and Framework for Commission Planning and Program, Development and Review, October 5, 1966, Timothy Jenkins folder, box 6, EEOC-Shulman.

118. Aileen Hernandez, "The Women's Movement: 1965–1975," Symposium on the Tenth Anniversary of the EEOC, November 2–29, 1975, folder 1704, PMP.

119. Martha W. Griffiths, "Women Are Being Deprived of Legal Rights by the EEOC," June 20, 1966, folder 11, box 2, MOEP.

120. NOW Statement of Purpose, http://now.org/about/history/statement-of-purpose/, accessed August 20, 2015.

121. Sonia Pressman Fuentes, "Solving the Child Care Nightmare," undated, folder 1, box 1, SPF-SL; Marlena Thompson, "Local Woman Is a Leader in Feminist Fight," December 16, 1999, folder 5, box 1, SPF-SL; Ken Millstone, "Journey from Berlin to Potomac," folder 7, box 1, SPF-SL.

122. Barbara Ruben, "Sonia Pressman Fuentes," *Washington Senior Beacon*, October 12, 2000, 1, folder 1, box 2, SPF-SL.

123. Barry, *Femininity in Flight*, 152–61; Evans, *Tidal Wave*, 24–25; Self, *All in the Family*, 114–19; Tiemeyer, *Plane Queer*, 89–91.

124. Gannon, "Uphill Bias Fight," 1.

125. Robert E. Baker, "Equal Jobs Unit Plans Industry-Wide Program," *Washington Post*, November 18, 1966, A26.

126. Gannon, "Uphill Bias Fight," 1.

127. Charles Duncan to Roger F. Lewis, October 18, 1966, Admin—Backlog folder, box 1, EEOC-Shulman.

128. Alfred Blumrosen, Chief of Conciliations, to Gordon Chase, Staff Director, March 1967, re: Planning for the Future of the Commission, Inter-Office Memos folder, box 1, EEOC-CD.

129. FDR Jr. Statement, December 16, 1965, Public Hearing on Employer Reporting System folder, box 1, EEOC-FDR; EEOC Standard Form 100, January 1966, EEO-1 Report Forms folder, box 1, EEOC-Shulman.

130. "EEOC Press Release, June 8, 1967," Speeches-SNS folder, box 10, EEOC-Shulman.

131. Supporting Statement by the EEOC with Submission to the Budget Bureau of Standard Form 83 for Renewal and Revision of Standard Form 100 (EEO-1), 1967, Research-EE01 folder, box 10, EEOC-Shulman. On the EEO-1's origins, see also Skrentny, *Minority Rights Revolution*, 101–10.

132. Memo to Shulman from the White House, April 10, 1967, Equal Employment Opportunity Commission folder, box 39, FG 655, LBJ Library, Austin, Tx.

133. Alfred Blumrosen to Stephen Shulman, January 26, 1967, Office of Compliance—Conciliations folder, box 8, EEOC-Shulman.

134. *Samuel Jackson v. Graniteville Company*, February 1, 1967, Commissioner Charges folder, box 6, EEOC-Shulman.

135. Press Release for A.M. Newspapers, "EEOC Analysis Shows Few Women in Top Jobs," October 19, 1967, Public Affairs News Releases folder, box 1, EEOC-RP.

136. Memo to the White House from Shulman, December 30, 1966, folder 1, box 122, Administrative Histories Collection: EEOC, LBJ Library, Austin, Tx.

137. Shulman to Charles C. Diggs Jr., June 23, 1967, folder 1, box 122, Administrative Histories Collection—EEOC, LBJ Library, Austin, Tx.

138. Gannon, "Uphill Bias Fight," 1.

139. EEOC News Release, "EEOC Reports Gain in Compliance Area and Emphasis on Broader Programs in 1968," January 10, 1968, folder 5, box 1, EEOC-RP.

140. Jonathan Evan Maslow, "Is Title VII Sinking?" *Juris Doctor*, September 1974, 28–36.

141. Because the EEOC could not sue AT&T directly, commissioners sought an administrative remedy through a different federal agency. The EEOC filed a report with the Federal Communications Commission documenting sex discrimination at AT&T and requesting that the FCC oppose the company's proposed long distance rate increase until the discrimination was remedied. The FCC's 1972 investigation of AT&T yielded the first public hearing by a federal regulatory agency on the EEO record of a regulated company. Abbott Combes, "EEOC Bias Report Calls AT&T 'Largest Oppressor of Women,'" *Washington Post*, December 2, 1971, A1; Lois Kathryn Herr, *Women, Power and AT&T: Winning Rights in the Workplace* (Boston: Northeastern University Press, 2002); Marjorie A. Stockford, *The Bellwomen: The Story of the Landmark AT&T Sex Discrimination Case* (New Brunswick, N.J.:Rutgers University Press, 2004).

142. Equal Employment Opportunity Act of 1972, Pub. L. No. 92-261, March 24, 1972, 86 Stat. 103; "The 1970s: The 'Toothless Tiger' Gets its Teeth—A New Era of Enforcement," http://www .eeoc.gov/eeoc/history/35th/1970s/index.html, accessed August 20, 2015; Dobbin, *Inventing Equal Opportunity*, 166.

143. Maslow, "Is Title VII Sinking?" 29.

144. Philip Shabecoff, "Steel and Union to Adopt a Plan on Job Equality," *New York Times*, April 14, 1974, 1, 21.

145. Decision of More Than Routine Interest: ABC System Repudiated," Case No. YKC-112: *Sophie Gaughan and Julia Borovac v. Armour and Company and Local 8 of Amalgamated Meatcutters and Butcher Workmen of North America*, January 6, 1972, January 1972 folder, box 1, Office of the EEOC Chairman Chronological Files, 1969–79, Equal Employment Opportunity Commission, Record Group 403, National Archives and Records Administration, College Park, Md. (hereafter "EEOC-CCF"); M. Lee Bishop to William Brown III re: *Gaughan and Borovac v. Armour and Company and Local 8, Meat Cutters and Butcher Workmen of North America*, EEOC Decision 72-814, March 7, 1972, March 1972 folder, box 1, EEOC-CCF; William Brown III to M. Lee Bishop, re: *Gaughan and Borovac v. Armour and Company and Local 8, Meat Cutters and Butcher Workmen of North America*, EEOC Decision 72-814, March 30, 1972, March 1972 folder, box 1, EEOC-CCF; 29 C.F.R. 1604. 2.

146. *Frontiero v. Richardson*, 441 U.S. 667 (1973). Three years later, the U.S. Supreme Court instead established "intermediate scrutiny," in which the state cannot discriminate based on sex absent specific important governmental objectives. *Craig v. Boren*, 429 U.S. 190 (1976).

147. *Bowe v. Colgate Palmolive*, 272 F.Supp. 332 (S.D. Ind. 1967); *Diaz v. Pan American Airlines, Inc.* 442 F.2d 385 (5th Cir. 1971); *Weeks v. Southern Bell Telephone and Telegraph, Inc.*, 467 F.2d 95 (5th Cir. 1972); *Teamsters v. United States*, 431 U.S. 324 (1977).

148. *Griggs v. Duke Power Co.*, 401 U.S. 424 (1971).

149. *Teamsters v. United States*, 431 U.S. 324 (1977), footnote 20.

Chapter 2. Class and Class Action

1. Lois Kathryn Herr, *Women, Power and AT&T: Winning Rights in the Workplace*; Alice Kessler-Harris, *In Pursuit of Equity*, 250; Joyce L. Kornbluh and Brigid O'Farrell, *Rocking the Boat: Union Women's Voices, 1915-1975* (New Brunswick, N.J.: Rutgers University Press, 1996), 274; MacLean, *Freedom Is Not Enough*, 130-47; Marjorie Stockford, *The Bellwomen: The Story of the Landmark AT&T Sex Discrimination Case* (New Brunswick, N.J.: Rutgers University Press, 2004).

2. "Women Journalists Face Discrimination," August 19, 1972, box 1, *New York Times* Minority Class Action Lawsuit records, Robert F. Wagner Labor Archives, New York University (hereafter "NYTMCA").

3. Interview with Betsy Wade by Mary Marshall Clark, *Women in Journalism Oral History Project of the Washington Press Club Foundation*, Schlesinger Library, Radcliffe Institute, Harvard University, Cambridge, Mass., 257.

4. For general histories of the *New York Times*, see Edwin Diamond, *Behind the Times: Inside the New New York Times* (Chicago: University of Chicago Press, 1995); Seth Mnookin, *Hard News: The Scandals at the New York Times and Their Meaning for American Media* (New York: Random House, 2004); Susan E. Tifft and Alex S. Jones, *The Trust: The Private and Powerful Family Behind the New York Times* (Boston: Back Bay Books, 2000); Gay Talese, *The Kingdom and the Power: Behind the Scenes at the New York Times; The Institution that Influences the World* (New York: Random House Trade Paperbacks, 2007).

5. For a first-person account of the Timeswomen's campaign, see Nan Robertson, *The Girls in the Balcony*. For a similar account of women journalists' campaign against *Newseek*, see Lynn Povich, *The Good Girls Revolt: How the Women of Newsweek Sued Their Bosses and Changed the Workplace* (New York: PublicAffairs, 2012).

6. See, for example, Barry, *Femininity in Flight*, esp. 60-94 and 174-209; Cobble, *The Other Women's Movement*, 180-222; Evans, *Tidal Wave*, esp. 85-91; and MacLean, *Freedom Is Not Enough*, esp. 117-53.

7. Betsy Wade to Yetta Riesel, May 30, 1974, box 2, folder 24, New York Times Women's Caucus Records, Schlesinger Library, Radcliffe Institute, Harvard University, Cambridge, Mass (hereafter "NYTWC").

8. Alice Fahs, *Out on Assignment: Newspaper Women and the Making of Modern Public Space* (Chapel Hill: University of North Carolina Press, 2011); Jean Marie Lutes, *Front-Page Girls: Women Journalists in American Culture and Fiction, 1880-1930* (Ithaca, N.Y.: Cornell University Press, 2007); Jan Whitt, *Women in American Journalism: A New History* (Urbana: University of Illinois Press, 2008), 6, 38; "Shopping, School Subjects of Two New Columns," *Editor and Publisher*, January 25, 1964, 26. For general histories of journalism, see David Paul Nord, *Communities of Journalism: A History of American Newspapers and Their Readers* (Urbana: University of Illinois Press, 2006); Martin Conboy, *Journalism: A Critical History* (New York: Sage, 2004).

9. "Reader Requests Keep Women's Pages Timely," *Editor and Publisher*, February 15, 1969, 30.

10. Whitt, *Women in American Journalism*, 5.

11. Davies, *Woman's Place Is at the Typewriter*.

12. Whitt, *Women in American Journalism*, 5.

13. Robertson, *Girls in the Balcony*, 7-8; Whitt, *Women in American Journalism*, 5; Times Women to Arthur O. Sulzberger, Iphigene Sulzberger, Richard Cohen, Marian Heiskell, A. M. Rosenthal, Daniel Schwartz, and John Oakes, undated, folder 4, box 1, NYTWC.

14. Diamond, *Behind the Times*, 38, 51; Mnookin, *Hard News*; Tifft and Jones, *Trust*; Talese, *Kingdom and the Power*; "Too Many is Not Enough," *Time* (July 14, 1961), 54.

15. "Grace Glueck," folder 2, box 1, NYTWC; Joanna Foley, "The Times—Are They A-Changing? Media Women Want Better Jobs and More Money," *Seven Days*, October 13, 1978, 6–7, folder 26, box 2, NYTWC; Robertson, *Girls in the Balcony*, 137–40.

16. Wade interview, 228.

17. Robertson, *Girls in the Balcony*, 176.

18. Wade interview, 53.

19. "Betsy Wade Deposition, October 1978," folder 20, box 2, NYTWC.

20. Robertson, *Girls in the Balcony*, 84–85.

21. "Eileen Shanahan," folder 2, box 1, NYTWC; Robertson, *Girls in the Balcony*, 107–13.

22. Eileen Shanahan interviewed by Mary Marshall Clark, *Women in Journalism Oral History Project of the Washington Press Club Foundation*, Schlesinger Library, Radcliffe Institute, Harvard University, Cambridge, Mass., 141.

23. Robertson, *Girls in the Balcony*, 105; Shanahan interview, 141.

24. Shanahan interview, 129.

25. Wade interview, 142.

26. Robertson, *Girls in the Balcony*, 140, 175.

27. Glueck quoted in Robertson, *Girls in the Balcony*, 142; Wade interview, 190.

28. "Betsy Wade Deposition, October 1978," folder 20, box 2, NYTWC.

29. Wade interview, 190.

30. "Times Caucus," undated, ca. February 1972, folder 4, box 1, NYTWC.

31. Undated letter to Times Women, folder 4, box 1, NYTWC.

32. "Report to the Women of the *New York Times*," March 14, 1972, folder 4, box 1, NYTWC.

33. Wade interview, 204–6, 209.

34. Ibid., 204–5.

35. "Report to the Women of the *New York Times*," March 14, 1973, folder 5, carton 1, NYTWC.

36. Grace Glueck statement, undated, folder 1, carton 1, NYTWC.

37. Elizabeth Moody to Women's Caucus, undated, folder 11, box 1, NYTWC.

38. Laurie Johnston to the Negotiating Committee, undated, folder 18, carton 1, NYTWC; Betsy Wade to Harriet Rabb, July 22, 1973, folder 24, carton 2, NYTWC.

39. "Louise A. McKellip, WXQR Department, Extension 1152," folder 11, box 1, NYTWC.

40. Louise McKellip to Women's Caucus, undated, ca. 1973, folder 9, carton 1, NYTWC.

41. Grace Glueck Notecards for Caucus Meeting, undated, ca. Fall 1972, folder 11, carton 1, NYTWC.

42. "Report to the Women of the *New York Times*," March 14, 1973, folder 5, carton 1, NYTWC.

43. Rita to Betsy, May 8, 1973, folder 9, box 1, NYTWC; Rita to Betsy, n.d., folder 9, box 1, NYTWC.

44. Grace L. to Grace G., undated, folder 14, box 1, NYTWC; see also Belva Davis, *Never in My Wildest Dreams: A Black Woman's Life in Journalism* (Sausalito, Calif.: Polipoint Press, 2010).

45. "The Other Side of It," undated, Ca. July 1975, box 1, folder 4, NYTWC.

46. Betsy Wade to Yetta Riesel, May 30, 1974, box 2, folder 24, NYTWC; Linda Greenhouse to Betsy Wade, box 1, folder 11, NYTWC.

47. Ursula Mahoney to Betsy Wade, January 27, 1973, folder 24, box 2, NYTWC.

48. "Breakthroughs at NYT-Mabel Phelan," *Other Side of It*, Spring 1977, folder 4, box 1, NYTWC.

49. Memo to Timeswomen, signed by Timeswomen, September 28, 1973, folder 1, carton 1, NYTWC.

50. Grace Glueck, Grace Lichtenstein, and Betsy Wade, "*New York Times* Women Give Tips to Other Women," *Media Report to Women* 2 (December 1, 1974): 5, folder 3, carton 1, NYTWC.

51. Wade interview, 198.

52. Ibid., 212.

53. Betsy Wade to Grace and Joan, August 12, 1974, folder 14, box 1, NYTWC.

54. "Rights of Women," June 27, 1975, *New York Times*, 34.

55. Women's Caucus Response to "Rights of Women," undated, folder 4, box 1, NYTWC.

56. Mary Dresser, "newsroom bias: Establishment style," *off our backs* 1 (April 25, 1970): 4.

57. Patricia Bradley, *Mass Media and the Shaping of American Feminism, 1963-1975* (Jackson, Miss.: University Press of Mississippi, 2004).

58. Margaret Cronin Fisk, "Steinem Knocks Newspaper Coverage of Women's Issues," *Editor and Publisher*, May 5, 1973, 11.

59. On *Ms.'* history, see Amy Erdman Farrell, *Yours in Sisterhood: Ms. Magazine and the Promise of Popular Feminism* (Chapel Hill: University of North Carolina Press, 1998); Stansell, *Feminist Promise*, 216; Mashinka Good, "Feminists Urge Liberation of News Media from Sexism," *Editor and Publisher*, June 1, 1974, 29.

60. Daniel J. Leab, *A Union of Individuals: The Formation of the American Newspaper Guild, 1933-1936* (New York: Columbia University Press, 1970); Luther A. Huston, "'Professional' Idea Lost Out in Guild," *Editor and Publisher*, January 3, 1959, folder 3, box 123, Newspaper Guild of New York Records (hereafter "NGNY"); "Women and the Guild," November 1970, folder 22, box 75, NGNY; "The Newspaper Guild," ca. 1972, 22, folder 3, box 123, NGNY; "ANG [American Newspaper Guild] Report to the Conference on Minority Recruitment and Training," April 2-4, 1971, folder 5, box 74, NGNY; Charles A. Perlik, "Official Call to the ANG Conference on Recruitment and Training of Minority Group Employees," April 2, 1971, folder 5, box 74, NGNY; Mabel Pollock to Guild and Auxiliary Delegates, June 26, 1944, folder 30, box 2, NGNY; "Welcome Address," May 25, 1944, folder 30, box 2, NGNY; Peg Frank to International Executive Board, American Newspaper Guild, May 25, 1944, folder 30, box 2, NGNY.

61. Resolution, April 18, 1955, folder 3, box 89, NGNY; Margin Berger to Thomas J. Murphy, April 28, 1955, folder 3, box 89, NGNY.

62. "American Newspaper Guild Conference on Sex Discrimination and Women's Rights in the Industry: Report of the Professional Interest Group," November 21, 1970, folder 22, box 75, NGNY; "Conference on Sex Discrimination and Women's Rights in the Industry Preamble to Interest Group Reports," folder 23, box 75, NGNY. Charles A. Perlik Jr., "Equality-Now!" November 1970, folder 22, box 75, NGNY.

63. Betsy Wade to Yetta Riesel, December 13, 1974, folder 37, box 2, Betsy Wade Files on the Newspaper Guild of New York, Robert F. Wagner Labor Archives, New York University (hereafter "BWF"); Betsy Wade to Yetta Riesel, January 23, 1975, folder 37, box 2, BWF; Betsy Wade to Ellis Baker, November 5, 1975, folder 37, box 2, BWF.

64. Betsy Wade to Yetta Riesel, May 30, 1974, box 2, folder 24, NYTWC.

65. Wade interview, 226.

66. Betsy Wade to Gertrude Samuels, *Times* Sunday Department, June 11,1973, box 1, folder 11, NYTWC.

67. Betsy Wade to Editor of *Village Voice*, May 20, 1979, folder 38, box 1, BWF.

68. Armistead S. Pride and Clint C. Wilson, *A History of the Black Press* (Washington, D.C.: Howard University Press, 1987), 128–30; Tifft and Jones, *Trust*, 277. See also Gwyneth Mellinger, *Chasing Newsroom Diversity: From Jim Crow to Affirmative Action* (Urbana, Ill.: University of Illinois Press, 2013).

69. Morgan Jin Resume, undated, box 1, NYTMCA; "Morgan Jin Discusses Historic *New York Times* Affirmative Action Lawsuit," *East-West: The Chinese American Journal*, May 27, 1981, box 1, NYTMCA; Morgan Jin Comments Delivered at Annual *New York Times* Stockholder Meeting, April 18, 1973, 74–75, box 1, NYTMCA.

70. "Morgan Jin Discusses Historic *New York Times* Affirmative Action Lawsuit."

71. NYT Minority Caucus Press Release, n.d., box 1, NYTMCA; "Morgan Jin Discusses Historic *New York Times* Affirmative Action Lawsuit," Lee Lescaze, "Minorities Set to Testify Against *Times*," *Washington Post*, May 29, 1979, 1; *Rosario, Jones et al. v. New York Times*, Civil Action File No. 74-4457, October 10, 1974, 3, box 1, NYTMCA.

72. Times Women to Arthur O. Sulzberger, Iphigene Sulzberger, Richard Cohen, Marian Heiskell, A. M. Rosenthal, Daniel Schwartz, and John Oakes, undated, folder 4, box 1, NYTWC.

73. Ibid.

74. Transcript of Meeting Between Women's Caucus and *Times* Management, May 31, 1972, folder 8, box 1, NYTWC.

75. Ibid.

76. Shanahan interview, 165.

77. Grace Glueck Introduction for Harriet Rabb at Thursday Caucus of National Women's Political Caucus, October 26, 1978, folder 2, box 1, NYTWC.

78. Women in *New York Times Magazine*, Book Review and Entertainment Sections to Max Frankel, January 2, 1973, folder 14, box 1, NYTWC.

79. Ibid.

80. Sulzberger memo to staff, quoted in Robertson, *Girls in the Balcony*, 157.

81. "Woman Sues Yale for Press Pass," *Editor and Publisher*, August 2, 1969, 14.

82. 34 F.R.D. 325; 37 F.R.D. 520; and 383 U.S. 1030. See also *McLaughlin on Class Actions* §1:1 (8th ed.); "Developments in the Law: Class Actions," *Harvard Law Review* 89 (May 1976); and Stephen C. Yeazell, "Group Litigation and Social Context: Toward a History of the Class Action," *Columbia Law Review*, October 1977, 866–96.

83. Rhoda Weiss, "Women Journalists Face Discrimination," *Journal-News* (Rockland County, N.Y.), August 19, 1972, 6a, box 1, NYTMCA.

84. "*Newsday* Women Charge Sex Bias," *Editor and Publisher*, January 5, 1964, 12.

85. Adrian Peracchio, "*Newsday*, Female Employees Settle Suit," folder 7, box 89, NGNY.

86. Ibid.; "Guild Settles 10-Year-Old Sex and Race Discrimination Case Against the Associated Press," June 15, 1983, folder 11, box 89, NGNY; "The President's Quarterly Report: The Guild and Human Rights," October 1978, folder 16, box 116; "Newspaper Guild Discrimination Caselog," October 1978, folder 16, box 116, NGNY.

87. "Women Journalists Stage 'Counter Gridiron,'" *Editor and Publisher*, April 27, 1974, 40.

88. Jane Levere, "Newswomen Urged to Press on for Women's Rights," *Editor and Publisher*, April 6, 1974, 14.

89. "14 Women Win $10,000 Prize Money," *Editor and Publisher*, January 2, 1965, 34.

90. "Writers Look in the Mirror at Changing Image of Women," *Editor and Publisher*, April 4, 1970, 9.

91. "Times Caucus," undated, folder 4, box 1, NYTWC.

92. "Women vs. the *New York Times*," *Ms.*, September 1978, folder 4, box 1, NYTWC; "Foremother Rabb," *More*, October 1977, 37.

93. Grace Glueck Introduction for Harriet Rabb at Thursday Caucus of National Women's Political Caucus, October 26, 1978, folder 2, box 1, NYTWC.

94. Betsy to Grace, May 14, 1973, folder 11, box 1, NYTWC.

95. Ibid.

96. Charges of Discrimination, 1973, box 2, folder 24, NYTWC.

97. Wade interview, 211.

98. Shanahan interview, 124–25.

99. Robertson, *Girls in the Balcony*, 163.

100. Wade interview, 256.

101. Ibid., 243–44.

102. Shanahan interview, 167.

103. "Times Caucus," undated, folder 4, box 1, NYTWC.

104. Women's Caucus to Times Women, September 28, 1973, folder 4, box 1, NYTWC.

105. "To Times Women's Caucus," February 1974, folder 4, box 1, NYTWC.

106. Women's Caucus to Times Women, December 1974, folder 2, box 1, NYTWC.

107. "To Times Women's Caucus," September 1974, folder 4, box 1, NYTWC.

108. Betsy to Grace and Joan, August 15, 1974, folder 14, box 1, NYTWC.

109. Betsy Wade to Harriet Rabb and Howard Rubin, September 30, 1974, folder 14, box 1, NYTWC.

110. Wade interview, 228.

111. Betsy to Grace and Joan, August 15, 1974, folder 14, box 1, NYTWC.

112. Wade interview, 228.

113. Shanahan interview, 166.

114. Wade interview, 235.

115. Ibid., 197.

116. Shanahan interview, 175.

117. Ibid. interview, 172.

118. Grace Glueck Introduction for Harriet Rabb at Thursday Caucus of National Women's Political Caucus, October 26, 1978, box 1, folder 2, NYTWC.

119. Robertson, *Girls in the Balcony*, 184, 187.

120. Terry Zintl, "Double Victory in a Bias Case?" October 16, 1978, folder 8, box 1, NYTWC.

121. Shanahan interview, 170.

122. Ibid., 171.

123. "Women vs. the *New York Times*," *Ms.*, September 1978, 66–67, box 1, folder 4, NYTWC.

124. Wade interview, 190.

125. Negotiating Committee to Times Women, May 23, 1973, folder 26, box 2, NYTWC.

126. Wade interview, 228–29.

127. Ibid., 228.

128. Davis quoted in Robertson, *Girls in the Balcony*, 176–77.

129. Amended Complaint, Class Action 74 Civ. 4891, folder 20, box 2, NYTWC.

130. Plaintiffs' Answers to Defense Interrogatories, 13, folder 2, box 1, NYTWC.

131. Fact Sheet: *Boylan v. New York Times*, folder 2, box 1, NYTWC.

132. Wade to Rabb and Rubin, August 1974, folder 14, box 1, NYTWC; Affidavit of Joel C. Balsam, attorney for *New York Times*, folder 20, box 2, NYTWC.

133. Amended Complaint, Class Action 74 Civ. 4891, folder 20, box 2, NYTWC.

134. Affidavit of Joel C. Balsam, Attorney for *New York Times*, 27, folder 20, box 2, NYTWC.

135. "Nancy Davis," folder 2, box 1, NYTWC.

136. Affidavit of Mabel Phelan, 2, folder 20, box 2, NYTWC.

137. *New York Times* Response to Class Action Complaint, folder 1, box 1, NYTWC.

138. Settlement Press Release, October 6, 1978, folder 2, box 1, NYTWC; Notice to Class of Proposed Final Consent Decree, 5, ibid.

139. *New York Times* Consent Decree, folder 20, box 2, NYTWC.

140. Employment Rights Project Press Release, October 6, 1978, 1, folder 20, box 2, NYTWC.

141. "Women Sports Reporters Win Access Ruling," *Editor and Publisher*, September 30, 1978, 22; "Guild Settles 10-Year-Old Sex and Race Discrimination Case Against the Associated Press," June 15, 1983, folder 11, box 89, NGNY; "*N.Y. Times* Bias Case Pact Is Unprecedented," *New York Newspaper Guild Reporter*, September 26, 1980, NYTMCA; "*Times* and Minority Employees Reach Accord on Suit," *New York Times*, September 18, 1980, 1; Herb Denton, "*New York Times* Agrees to Pay $685,000 to End Bias Suit," *New York Times*, September 18, 1980, B1.

142. Grace Glueck Introduction for Harriet Rabb at Thursday Caucus of National Women's Political Caucus, October 26, 1978, box 1, folder 2, NYTWC.

143. Marion Knox, "Women and the *Times*: Why They Settled," *Nation*, December 9, 1978, 637.

144. "*Times* Settles, AP Charged on Bias," *Guild Reporter*, October 13, 1978, 1, folder 3, carton 1, NYTWC.

145. Settlement Press Release, October 6, 1978, folder 2, box 1, NYTWC.

146. Ibid.

147. "Eileen Shanahan," box 1, folder 2, NYTWC.

148. Terry Zintl, "Double Victory in a Bias Case?" October 16, 1978, folder 8, box 1, NYTWC.

149. *Media Report to Women* 2, n. 12, box 1, folder 4, NYTWC.

150. The previous year, the Eighth Circuit Court of Appeals ruled in *DeGraffenreid v. General Motors* that Title VII did not apply when workers experienced discrimination on account of both their race and their sex. *DeGraffenreid v. General Motors Company,* 558 F.2d 480 (8th Cir. 1977). See also Kimberle Crenshaw, "Demarginalizing the Intersection of Race and Sex: A Black Feminist Critique of Antidiscrimination Doctrine, Feminist Theory, and Antiracist Politics," *University of Chicago Legal Forum*, 1989, 139–67.

151. Robertson, *Girls in the Balcony*, 233–34, 238.

Chapter 3. Feminism and Workplace Fairness

1. On such early and mid-twentieth-century women's reform campaigns, see Cobble, *The Other Women's Movement*; Orleck, *Common Sense and a Little Fire*; and Landon R. Y. Storrs,

Civilizing Capitalism: The National Consumers' League, Women's Activism, and Labor Standards in the New Deal Era (Chapel Hill: University of North Carolina Press, 2000).

2. "NOW Statement of Purpose," http://www.now.org/history/purpos66.html, accessed November 24, 2013; "Honoring NOW's Founders and Pioneers," http://www.now.org/history/founders.html, accessed November 24, 2013.

3. Barry, *Femininity in Flight*, 144–173; Kessler-Harris, *In Pursuit of Equity*, 258–59; MacLean, *Freedom Is Not Enough*, 127–29; Self, *All in the Family*, 116–17. On NOW's national leadership, see Barakso, *Governing NOW* and Wandersee, *On the Move*, 36–54. On NOW chapters, see Gilmore, *Groundswell*, and "Dynamics of Second-Wave Feminist Activism in Memphis"; Reger, "Organizational Dynamics and Constructions of Multiple Feminist Identities in the National Organization for Women"; Reger and Staggenborg, "Patterns of Mobilization in Local Movement Organizations; and Gilmore and Kaminski, "A Part and Apart." Studies of specific NOW campaigns include Lisa Levenstein, "Don't Agonize, Organize."

4. Katherine Turk, "Out of the Revolution, into the Mainstream: Employment Activism in the NOW Sears Campaign and the Growing Pains of Liberal Feminism," *Journal of American History* 97 (September 2010): 399–423.

5. Mayeri, *Reasoning from Race.*

6. Evans, *Tidal Wave*, 176–78; Self, *All in the Family*, 276–305; Marjorie Spruill, "Gender and America's Right Turn," in *Rightward Bound: Making America Conservative in the 1970s*, ed. Bruce J. Shulman and Julian E. Zelizer (Cambridge, Mass.: Harvard University Press, 2008), 71–89; *Act NOW* 7 (March 1974): 1, folder 115, box 14, acc. no. 81-18, National Organization for Women, Chicago Chapter Records, Richard J. Daley Library, University of Illinois at Chicago (hereafter "CNOW").

7. On similar developments in movements for African Americans' rights, see Lani Guinier, "From Racial Liberalism to Racial Literacy: *Brown v. Board of Education* and the Interest-Divergence Dilemma," *Journal of American History* 91 (June 2004): 92–118; and Goluboff, *The Lost Promise of Civil Rights.*

8. Letter to Congresswoman Edith Green from Heide, January 3, 1973, folder 16, box 18, Wilma Scott Heide National Organization for Women Officer Papers, Schlesinger Library, Radcliffe Institute, Harvard University, Cambridge, Mass.; "Chapter Structural Plan, 1970–1975," folder 35, box 9, NOW. On the diverse tactics NOW members and leadership developed in these years, see Barakso, *Governing NOW*, 42–50.

9. Barakso, *Governing NOW*, 40; Carol Kleiman, "NOW's Baby Grows Up," *Chicago Tribune*, May 9, 1974, B6; Wandersee, *On the Move*, 47.

10. "How to Retain and Attract Members by Promoting Various Action Projects," folder 30, box 9, NOW; Reger, "Organizational Dynamics."

11. "Who Are We? Results of Survey of NOW's Membership," *Do It NOW* 7 (July 1974): 1, folder 31, box 9, acc. no. 81-18, CNOW.

12. Kornbluh and O'Farrell, *Rocking the Boat*, 247.

13. "Results of 1973 Survey of Chicago NOW Members," folder 4, box 3, acc. no. 83-27, CNOW.

14. Evans, *Tidal Wave*, 85–87; Laura Kaplan, *The Story of Jane: The Legendary Underground Feminist Abortion Service* (Chicago: University of Chicago Press, 1995), xviii.

15. Lynne Van Matre, "A Step Toward 'True Liberation'? Women's Study Courses: Meeting a Need," *Chicago Tribune*, December 27, 1970, G10. University of Chicago conference participants included the University of Illinois at Chicago, DePaul University, Mundelein College, and Northeastern Illinois University. "Women at U of C Schedule Confab," *Chicago Daily Defender*, October

4, 1969, 13; Terri Schultz, "Women's Lib: Bra-Burner Tactics Out as Lawsuits Gain Ground," *Chicago Tribune*, June 28, 1971, 1.

16. Fredi A. Smith, "First Black YWCA Executive Director Feels Organization Is Women's Movement," *Chicago Daily Defender*, February 24, 1970, 19; Carol Kleiman, "Why the 'Y' is Fem-Land," *Chicago Tribune*, January 1, 1974, B1.

17. In archival sources, Mary Jean Collins is sometimes referred to as Mary Jean Collins-Robson. Mary Jean Collins interview by Jennifer Frost, February 11–13, 1992, audiotape, side a, tape 127, *Documenting the Midwestern Origins of the Twentieth-Century Women's Movement* (State Historical Society of Wisconsin, Madison); Mary-Ann Lupa interview by Katherine Turk, March 13, 2004, transcript (in Katherine Turk's possession), 1.

18. On the connections between feminism and the New Left, see Sara Evans, *Personal Politics: The Roots of Women's Liberation in the Civil Rights Movement and the New Left* (New York: Vintage, 1979); McGuire, *At the Dark End of the Street*; and Doug Rossinow, *The Politics of Authenticity: Liberalism, Christianity, and the New Left in America* (New York: Columbia University Press, 1998), 297–334.

19. Evans, *Tidal Wave*, 90–91; Anne Ladky interview by Turk, February 25, 2004, transcript (in Turk's possession), 1; Lupa interview, 1.

20. Ladky interview, 3; Collins interview, side b, tape 127; Suzanne Staggenborg, *The Pro-Choice Movement: Organization and Activism in the Abortion Conflict* (New York: Oxford University Press, 1991), 174–75.

21. "Results of the 1973 Chicago NOW Member Survey"; "New Members of the Chicago Chapter of NOW, 8-9-74," folder 8, box 2, acc. no. 81-18, CNOW; "Membership Questionnaire," n.d., ibid; "A Decade of Feminism: Chicago NOW Highlights from the 1970s," n.d., folder 18, box 39, ibid.; Collins interview, side a, tape 128; Lupa interview, 1, 3; Ladky interview, 3.

22. Collins interview, side b, tape 127; Madeline Schwenk quoted in Staggenborg, *Pro-Choice Movement*, 39; "Results of the 1973 Chicago NOW Member Survey"; "New Members of the Chicago Chapter of NOW, 8-9-74," folder 8, box 2, acc. no. 81-18, CNOW.

23. Wandersee, *On the Move*, 43–44; Patricia Koval, "Some Find the Lib Rally Here a Bed of Thorny Roses," *Chicago Sun-Times*, August 27, 1970, 47.

24. "Decade of Feminism."

25. "Checklist of Questions for Potential Witnesses in *NOW v. City of Chicago*," n.d., folder 190, box 23, acc. no. 81-18, CNOW; "In Chicago, Every Day Is Ladies' Day . . . or Is It?" n.d., folder 115, box 14, acc. no. 81-18, ibid.; *Act NOW* 7 (April 1975): 1, folder 115, box 14, acc. no. 81-18, ibid.

26. Collins interview, side a, tape 127.

27. *NOW Compliance Newsletter* 8 (March 1973): 1, folder 8, box 2, acc. no. 78-34, CNOW; "EEOC on the Track System," *NOW Compliance Newsletter* 10 (September 1973): 8, folder 8, box 2, acc. no. 78-34, CNOW.

28. *Sears Action Bulletin*, no. 1 (July 1974): 3, folder 4, box 15, Papers of NOW Officer Mary Jean Collins, Schlesinger Library, Radcliffe Institute, Cambridge, Mass. (hereafter "NOW-Collins"); Herr, *Women, Power, and AT&T*, xiv, 5, 17. On the AT&T campaign, see also Stockford, *Bellwomen*.

29. Herr, *Women, Power, and AT&T*, 152–53; Kornbluh and O'Farrell, *Rocking the Boat*, 251.

30. Testimony of Anne Ladky, *Hearing Before the United States Commission on Civil Rights: Hearing held in Chicago, Ill.*, 2 vols. (Washington, D.C.: The Commission, 1974), 2: 48.

31. Tell, "Disparity or Discrimination?" *Society* 24 (September–October 1987): 4; Gordon L. Weil, *Sears, Roebuck, USA: The Great American Catalog Store and How It Grew* (Briarcliff Manor, N.Y.: Stein and Day, 1977), 2; Lupa interview, 7.

32. Collins interview, side a, tape 128; Ladky interview, 4–5.

33. "Sex Discrimination Cases Filed," n.d., folder 16, box 1, Lynne Darcy National Organization for Women Officer Papers, Schlesinger Library, Radcliffe Institute, Harvard University, Cambridge, Mass.; "Mailing to NOW Chapter Presidents from Mary Jean Collins," November 9, 1974, folder 5, box 15, NOW-Collins.

34. "Decade of Feminism"; Kay Rutherford, "Personnel List Trade Secret, Sears Tells Rights Panel," *Chicago Sun-Times*, August 23, 1974, 88; "Dear Media Representative," n.d., folder 320, box 39, acc. no. 81-18, CNOW.

35. Ladky interview, 7; "Decade of Feminism."

36. Ladky interview, 5; Sanford Jacoby, *Modern Manors: Welfare Capitalism Since the New Deal* (Princeton, N.J.; Princeton University Press, 1997), 95–108, esp. 106.

37. Moreton, *To Serve God and Wal-Mart*, 49–66; "Another Look at the Annual Report," n.d., folder 5, box 15, NOW-Collins; Collins interview, side a, tape 128.

38. "Letters to NOW and a Progress Report," *Tower Tattler* no. 7 (March 14, 1975): 2, folder 4, box 15, NOW-Collins.

39. *Tower Tattler*, n.d., folder 8, box 2, acc. no. 78-34, CNOW; "Letters to NOW and a Progress Report, September 19, 1974, folder 5, box 15, NOW-Collins; *Tower Tattler*, n.d., folder 5, box 15, ibid.; Ladky interview, 7; Testimony of Anne Ladky, *Hearing Before the United States Commission on Civil Rights: Hearing held in Chicago, Ill.*, 2 vols. (Washington, D.C.: The Commission, 1974), 2: 49. On sex discrimination and credit, see also Louis Hyman, "Ending Discrimination, Legitimating Debt: The Political Economy of Race, Gender and Credit Access in the 1960s and 1970s," *Enterprise and Society* 12 (2011): 200–232.

40. "Who Are We? Results of Survey of NOW's Membership"; "1973 Chicago NOW Member Survey," folder 4, box 3, acc. no. 83-27, CNOW; "New Members of the Chicago Chapter of NOW, 8-9-74," folder 8, box 2, acc. no. 81-18, ibid.; "Membership Questionnaire"; Collins interview, side a, tape 127.

41. *Hearing Before the United States Commission on Civil Rights: Hearing held in Chicago, Ill.*, 2 vols. (Washington, D.C.: The Commission, 1974), 2: 1.

42. Darlene Stille Testimony, *Hearing Before the United States Commission on Civil Rights: Hearing held in Chicago, Ill.*, 2 vols. (Washington, D.C.: The Commission, 1974), 1: 255, 45.

43. Ibid., 2: 45–46.

44. *Hearing Before the United States Commission on Civil Rights: Hearing held in Chicago, Ill.*, 2 vols. (Washington, D.C.: The Commission, 1974), 2: 50. On Sears' profit-sharing plan, see Jacoby, *Modern Manors*, 108–9.

45. *Hearing Before the United States Commission on Civil Rights: Hearing held in Chicago, Ill.*, 2 vols. (Washington, D.C.: The Commission, 1974), 2: 50.

46. *Tower Tattler*, n.d., folder 8, box 2, acc. no. 78-34, CNOW; "Letters to NOW and a Progress Report, September 19, 1974, folder 5, box 15, NOW-Collins; *Tower Tattler*, n.d., folder 5, box 15, ibid.; Ladky interview, 7.

47. Testimony of Judy Krusinger, *Hearing Before the United States Commission on Civil Rights: Hearing held in Chicago, Ill.*, 2 vols. (Washington, D.C.: The Commission, 1974), 2: 29, 35–39.

48. Ibid., 2: 29.

49. Testimony of Geraldine Holder, *Hearing Before the United States Commission on Civil Rights: Hearing held in Chicago, Ill.*, 2 vols. (Washington, D.C.: The Commission, 1974), 2: 36.

50. Testimony of Toby Atherton, *Hearing Before the United States Commission on Civil Rights: Hearing held in Chicago, Ill.*, 2 vols. (Washington, D.C.: The Commission, 1974), 2: 36–38.

51. Testimony of Deborah Easley, *Hearing Before the United States Commission on Civil Rights: Hearing held in Chicago, Ill.*, 2 vols. (Washington, D.C.: The Commission, 1974), 2: 58.

52. Testimony of Danoe Raggs and Deborah Easley, *Hearing Before the United States Commission on Civil Rights: Hearing held in Chicago, Ill.*, 2 vols. (Washington, D.C.: The Commission, 1974), 2: 58–59.

53. Testimony of Charles F. Bacon, *Hearing Before the United States Commission on Civil Rights: Hearing held in Chicago, Ill.*, 2 vols. (Washington, D.C.: The Commission, 1974), 2: 100.

54. Ibid., 111.

55. Ibid., 2: 77.

56. Ibid., 2: 74.

57. Ladky interview, 5.

58. Jacoby, *Modern Manors*, 95–142.

59. *Sears Action Bulletin,* no. 1 (July 1974): 1–2, folder 4, box 15, NOW-Collins; *Sears Action Bulletin* 4 (October 1974): 1, ibid.; *Sears Action Bulletin,* no. 6 (November 1974): 1, ibid.

60. *Sears Action Bulletin*, no. 1 (July 1974): 3, folder 4, box 15, NOW-Collins.

61. Mary Jean Collins-Robson and Anne Ladky, Memo to NOW Chapter Presidents, Sears Subcommittee, Board of Directors and Task Force Coordinators, November 9, 1974, folder 4, box 15, NOW-Collins.

62. Ibid.

63. *Sears Action Bulletin*, no. 2 (July 1974): 1, folder 4, box 15, NOW-Collins.

64. *Sears Action Bulletin,* no. 2 (August 1974): 4, folder 4, box 15, NOW-Collins.

65. Atlanta NOW Research Report, 4–5, November 1974, folder 18, box 44, NOW.

66. *Sears Action Bulletin*, no. 2 (July 1974): 4, folder 4, box 15, NOW-Collins.

67. Judy Lightfoot to Employment Committee, "Sears Ponce de Leon Store," August 20, 1974, folder 12, box 3, Judith Lightfoot NOW Officer Papers, Schlesinger Library, Radcliffe Institute, Harvard University, Cambridge, Mass.

68. "*NOW v. Sears Roebuck* March 1975 Update," NOW-Collins, folder 4, box 15; *Sears Action Bulletin* 2 (August 1974), folder 4, box 15, NOW-Collins.

69. Statement by Cynthia Hlass, President of Atlanta NOW, November 19, 1974, folder 19, box 44, NOW.

70. *Sears Action Bulletin,* no. 3 (September 1974): 3, folder 4, box 15, NOW-Collins.

71. NOW Sears Sample Press Release, May 1975, folder 4, box 15, NOW-Collins.

72. *Sears Action Bulletin,* no. 6 (December 1974): 1–3, folder 4, box 15, NOW-Collins.

73. *Act NOW* 8 (December 1975): 1, folder 115, box 14, acc. no. 81-18, CNOW.

74. "NOW Meets with EEOC Chairman Powell," NOW Compliance Newsletter 15 (June 1975): 5, folder 4, box 15, NOW-Collins.

75. "National Conference Resolutions," 1973, folder 30, box 23, NOW.

76. Ibid.

77. For information on increased membership between 1971 and 1973, see "Statement of Dorothy Haener Before General Labor Subcommittee of the House Education and Labor Committee on H.R. 475746.17," undated, folder 17, box 46, NOW; "National Conference Campaigns and

Elections, 1972–3," folder 27, box 23, ibid. For additional election materials, see "National Conference Campaign Material, 1975," folder 74, box 23, ibid.

78. Lupa interview, 6; Conroy quoted in Kornbluh and O'Farrell, *Rocking the Boat, 247.*

79. "Karen DeCrow," *Tully-Crenshaw Feminist Oral History Project*, 4–5, Schlesinger Library, Radcliffe Institute, Harvard University, Cambridge, Mass.; Collins interview, side b, tape 126. On how Karen DeCrow and Collins encouraged their respective chapters, see "Karen DeCrow," *Tully-Crenshaw Feminist Oral History Project*, 6. Collins interview, side b, tape 127; "NOW Chapter Newsletters," New York–Syracuse folder, box 19, NOW. For more information on DeCrow, see Karen DeCrow, *Sexist Justice* (New York: Random House, 1974), 73.

80. Collins to NOW Membership, 1974 Sears Action Kit, folder 2, box 1, acc. no. 83-27, CNOW.

81. Kleiman, "NOW's Baby Grows Up." On Mary Jean Collins's Career in NOW, see *Do It NOW* 5 (May 1972), folder 31, box 9, acc. no. 81-18, CNOW; Collins interview, side a, tape 128.

82. DeCrow, *Sexist Justice*, 3; "Karen DeCrow," *Tully-Crenshaw Feminist Oral History Project*, 5, 7, 8, 10. Karen DeCrow speech, 1974, folder 56, box 23, NOW.

83. Evans, *Tidal Wave*, 109–11; Barbara Ryan, *Feminism and the Women's Movement: Dynamics of Change in Social Movement Ideology and Activism* (New York: Routledge, 1992), 71–73; Wandersee, *On the Move*, 49–52.

84. Wandersee, *On the Move*, 51.

85. Evans, *Tidal Wave*, 110; "Karen DeCrow (KDC) to National Task Force Coordinators re: Reorganization of Substantive Feminist Issues Within NOW," November 9, 1975, folder 1, box 6, acc. no. 78-34, CNOW.

86. Barakso, *Governing NOW*, 61.

87. Kleiman, "NOW's Baby Grows Up"; Majority Caucus Publication, n.d., folder 5, box 24, NOW.

88. On the postsuffrage politics of the ERA, see Cott, *The Grounding of Modern Feminism.* On women's grassroots conservatism, see Donald Critchlow, *Phyllis Schlafly and Grassroots Conservatism: A Woman's Crusade*; Michelle Nickerson, *Mothers of Conservatism*; Stacie Taranto, "Defending 'Family Values': Women's Grassroots Politics and the Republican Right, 1970–1980" (Ph.D. diss., Brown University, 2010). On the politics of the ERA in the 1970s and early 1980s, see Mary Frances Berry, *Why ERA Failed: Politics, Women's Rights, and the Amending Process of the Constitution* (Bloomington: Indiana University Press, 1986); Janet Boles, *The Politics of the Equal Rights Amendment: Conflict and the Decision Process* (New York: Longman, 1979); Jane Mansbridge, *Why We Lost the ERA* (Chicago: University of Chicago Press, 1984); Donald G. Matthews and Jane Sherron De Hart, *Sex, Gender and the Politics of ERA: A State and the Nation* (New York: Oxford University Press, 1990); Erin Kempker, "Coalition and Control: Hoosier Feminists and the Equal Rights Amendment," *Frontiers: A Journal of Women Studies* 34, no. 2 (Fall 2013): 52–81; Alison Lefkovitz, "The Problem of Marriage in the Era of Women's Liberation" (Ph.D. diss., University of Chicago, 2010).

89. Phyllis Schlafly, "A Short History of ERA," 1986, http://www.eagleforum.org/psr/1986/sept86/psrsep86.html.

90. Kleiman, "NOW's Baby Grows Up."

91. Collins interview, side a, tape 128; Judy Goldsmith to Wisconsin State Members of NOW, memo, 1975, folder 3, box 24, NOW.

92. Ladky interview, 8. On the absence of Chicagoans from the national stage, see Collins interview, side a, tape 128. Barakso, *Governing NOW*, 56.

93. "Should You Go to Kansas in October?" folder 12, box 24, NOW. Staggenborg, *Pro-Choice Movement*, 165.

94. DeCrow, *Sexist Justice*, 45, 264–65.

95. Cynthia Harrison to NOW Credit Committee, undated, folder 21, box 43, NOW; De-Crow to NOW National Board, memo, January 8, 1976, folder 10, box 24, NOW.

96. Eleanor Smeal Acceptance Speech, 1977, folder 25, box 24, NOW. On critics' fears that NOW's agenda had become too narrow, see Kay Whitlock, "Moving Towards Autocracy: Power Brokerage and Single-Issue Politics in NOW," *Quest* 5 (Spring 1979): 36–55.

97. Emily Zuckerman, "The Cooperative Origins of *EEOC v. Sears*," in *Feminist Coalitions*, ed. Gilmore, 225–51; *Equal Employment Opportunity Commission v. Sears, Roebuck, and Company*, 628 F. Supp. 1264 (N.D. Ill. 1986); Sandi E. Cooper and Jacqueline Dowd Hall, "Women's History Goes to Trial: *EEOC v. Sears, Roebuck and Company*," *Signs* 11 (Summer 1986): 751–79; Katherine Jellison, "History in the Courtroom: The Sears Case in Perspective," *Public Historian* 9 (Autumn 1987): 9–19; Alice Kessler-Harris, "*Equal Employment Opportunity Commission v. Sears, Roebuck and Company*: A Personal Account," *Feminist Review* 25 (Spring 1987): 46–69; Ruth Milkman, "Women's History and the Sears Case," *Feminist Studies* 12 (Summer 1986): 375–400; and Joan Scott, "The Sears Case," in *Gender and the Politics of History* (New York: Columbia University Press, 1988).

Chapter 4. Reevaluating Women's Work

1. "Sharon Isker Makes the Case for Pay Equity," *AFSCME Public Employee*, 1980, folder 12, box 4, Susan Holleran Collection, Walter P. Reuther Library of Labor and Urban Affairs, Detroit, Mich. (hereafter "Holleran").

2. On how gendered ideologies have legitimated women's low wages, see Alice Kessler-Harris, *A Woman's Wage* and Kessler-Harris, *In Pursuit of Equity*.

3. Tamar Lewin, "Pay Equity for Women's Jobs Finds Success Outside Courts," *New York Times*, October 7, 1989, A1.

4. Henry J. Aaron, *The Comparable Worth Controversy* (Washington, D.C.: Brookings Institution Press, 1986); Joan Acker, *Doing Comparable Worth: Gender, Class, and Pay Equity* (Philadelphia: Temple University Press, 1989); Linda M. Blum, *Between Feminism and Labor: The Significance of the Comparable Worth Movement* (Berkeley: University of California Press, 1991); Paula England, *Comparable Worth: Theories and Evidence* (Piscataway, N.J.: Aldine Transaction, 1992); Sara M. Evans and Barbara J. Nelson, *Wage Justice: Comparable Worth and the Paradox of Technocratic Reform* (Chicago: University of Chicago Press, 1989); and Norma Riccucci, *Women, Minorities and Unions in the Public Sector* (Westport, Conn.: Greenwood, 1990).

5. Cobble, *The Other Women's Movement*, 98–99, 163–67; Heidi Hartmann and Stephanie Aaronson, "Pay Equity and Women's Wage Increases: Success in the States, a Model for the Nation," *Duke Journal of Gender Law and Policy* 69, no. 1 (1994): 72.

6. Blum, *Between Feminism and Labor*, esp. 4, 20–53, 129; McCann, *Rights at Work*, 103–4.

7. Eleanor Holmes Norton, quoted in Lorraine Sorrel, "Comparable Worth," *off our backs* 13 (July 31, 1983): 1.

8. Marjorie Hunter, "Candidates' Relatives Testify for Equitable Pay Proposal," *New York Times*, April 4, 1984, A18.

9. Works that have emphasized the 1970s as the decade that laid the groundwork for various forms of conservatism to sweep the nation in the 1980s include Cowie, *Stayin' Alive*; Bruce J. Schulman and Julian E. Zelizer, eds., *Rightward Bound: Making America Conservative in the*

1970s (Cambridge, Mass.: Harvard University Press, 2008); Self, *All in the Family*, 309–98, esp. 309–11; Stansell, *The Feminist Promise*, esp. 355–56; Stein, *Pivotal Decade*. On public sector workers' failure in the mid-1970s to win their version of the broad labor protections granted to some private sector workers by the Wagner Act, see Joseph McCartin, "A Wagner Act for Public Employees: Labor's Deferred Dream and the Rise of Conservatism, 1970–1976," *Journal of American History* 95 (June 2008): 123–48.

10. Nelson Lichtenstein, *State of the Union: A Century of American Labor*, 213.

11. The sociologist Michael W. McCann offers a more optimistic interpretation, suggesting that despite federal courts' failure to affirm comparable worth, the labor-led litigation heightened workers' expectations and sense of collective identity. Michael W. McCann, *Rights at Work: Pay Equity Reform and the Politics of Legal Mobilization* (Chicago: University of Chicago Press, 1994).

12. Quoted in Ruth Milkman, *Gender at Work*, 81.

13. Chapter 5 of this study examines the widespread practice of sex segregation and unequal wages in the hotel industry.

14. S. 1178, 79th Congress, 1st Session, 1945; Cobble, *Other Women's Movement*, 105–6.

15. National Committee on Pay Equity, "Closing the Wage Gap: An International Perspective," p. 2, October 1988, folder 22, box 4, Holleran.

16. Cobble, *Other Women's Movement*, 105–6; Boris, "Ledbetter's Continuum."

17. President's Commission on the Status of Women, *American Woman*, 7.

18. 108 Cong. Rec. 9225, Daily Edition, June 14, 1962.

19. Michael C. McGoings, United States Commission on Civil Rights Assistant General Counsel, "Background Paper on Legal Aspects of Comparable Worth," March 27, 1984, 4, folder 10, box 398, Winn Newman Papers, Manuscript Division, Library of Congress, Washington, D.C. (hereafter "Newman-LOC"); "Equal Pay for Comparable Work," undated, ca. 1980, 11, 15, folder 40, box 94, NOW.

20. Equal Pay Act of 1963 (77 Stat. 56).

21. Cobble, *Other Women's Movement*, 98–99, 107, 163–67.

22. Joseph Slater, *Public Workers: Government Employee Unions, the Law, and the State, 1900–1962* (Ithaca, N.Y.: ILR, 2004).

23. On Taft-Hartley, see Elizabeth Fones-Wolf, *Selling Free Enterprise: The Business Assault on Labor and Liberalism* (Urbana: University of Illinois Press, 1994), esp. 42–48.

24. William Brown III, Chairman, Equal Employment Opportunity Commission, to Robert J. Brown, Special Assistant to President Nixon, July 1, 1971, Chron. July 1971 folder, box 1, EEOC-CCF.

25. Ronnie Steinberg and Lois Haignere, "Separate but Equivalent: Equal Pay for Work of Comparable Worth," in *Gender at Work: Perspectives on Occupational Segregation and Comparable Worth*, a publication of Women's Research and Education Institute of the Congressional Caucus for Women's Issues, 1984, p. 14, folder 7, box 43, Papers of the Women's Research and Education Institute, Schlesinger Library, Radcliffe Institute, Cambridge, Mass. (hereafter "WREI").

26. Joan S. Lublin, "Getting Organized: More Women Enroll in Unions, Win Office and Push for Changes," *Wall Street Journal*, January 15, 1979, 1.

27. "AFSCME Hails Supreme Court Decision as It Plans Future Legal Action," June 9, 1981, folder 1, box 121, Newman-LOC; Wurf 1966 Keynote Speech, folder 11, box 49, AFSCME Office of the President: Jerry Wurf Records, Walter P. Reuther Library of Labor and Urban Affairs, Wayne State University, Detroit, Mich. (hereafter "AFSCME-Wurf").

28. Joseph McCartin, "Bringing the State's Workers In: Time to Rectify an Imbalanced US Labor Historiography," *Labor History* 47 (February 2006): 73–94. On AFSCME's relationship to labor law and internal changes in the 1960s, see also Joseph E. Hower, "Big Brother Unionism? The Landrum-Griffin Act and the Fight for AFSCME's Future, 1961–1964," *Labor: Studies in Working-Class History of the Americas* 11 (2014): 61–84.

29. On these general trends, see Julia Kirk Blackwelder, *Now Hiring: The Feminization of Work in the United States* (College Station: Texas A&M University Press, 1997), esp. 177–221.

30. Blum, *Between Feminism and Labor*, 9, 25–26.

31. Resolution on Sex Discrimination Adopted by the Nineteenth Annual International Convention, May 29–June 2, 1972, folder 1, box 63, AFSCME Office of the Secretary-Treasurer: William Lucy Records, Walter P. Reuther Library of Labor and Urban Affairs, Wayne State University, Detroit, Mich. (hereafter "AFSCME-Lucy").

32. National Commission on the Observance of International Women's Year, *Employment: A Workshop Guide* (Washington, D.C.: U.S. Government Printing Office, 1977), 53.

33. *AFSCME Leadership Letter*, March 1974, folder 9, box 5, American Federation of State, County and Municipal Employees Program Development Department Records, Walter P. Reuther Library on Labor and Urban Affairs, Wayne State University, Detroit, Mich. (hereafter "AFSCME-Program").

34. "Update," folder 17, box 22, AFSCME-Wurf; *AFSCME Public Employee* (February 1980).

35. Janet Kohn and Wendy Kahn to Jerry Wurf, re: "Discrimination on the Basis of Sex: The Law," November 10, 1973, folder 3, box 5, AFSCME-Program; "Interim Committee on Sex Discrimination Meeting Minutes," Washington, D.C., November 9–10, 1973, folder 3, box 5, AFSCME-Program; AFSCME International Executive Board Sex Discrimination Memo, October 1973, AFSCME-Program; First Meeting of the Interim Committee on Sex Discrimination Proposed Agenda, September 8, 1972, folder 1, box 63, AFSCME-Lucy; AFSCME Interim Committee on Sex Discrimination Report to International Executive Board, October 1972, folder 1, box 5, AFSCME-Program; William Lucy Memo, July 26, 1972, folder 1, box 63, AFSCME-Lucy; List of Interim Committee on Sex Discrimination Members, ca. July 1972 folder 1, box 63, AFSCME-Lucy; Mary Lou Hennessey to Jerry Wurf and Bill Lucy re: Meeting of the Interim Committee on Sex Discrimination, August 28, 1972 folder 1, box 63, AFSCME-Lucy.

36. Gerald W. McEntee, Statement Before U.S. House of Representatives Subcommittee on Civil Rights, Subcommittee on Human Resources, Subcommittee on Compensation and Employee Benefits, September 21, 1982, p. 1, folder 20, box 4, Holleran.

37. Gerald McEntee to AFSCME Women's Regional Conference, Milwaukee, Wisconsin, September 7, 1985, p. 17, folder 11, box 2, Holleran.

38. Norm Schut, Executive Director, Washington Federation of State Employees, to Daniel J. Evans, Governor of Washington, November 20, 1973, folder 2, box 1, AFSCME-Program.

39. Joan Acker, *Doing Comparable Worth*, 9.

40. Daniel J. Evans to Douglas E. Sayan and Leonard Nord, November 28, 1973, folder 2, box 1, AFSCME-Program.

41. Douglas E. Sayan and Leonard Nord to Daniel J. Evans, folder 3, box 1, AFSCME-Program; Gerald W. McEntee, Statement Before U.S. House of Representatives Subcommittee on Civil Rights, Subcommittee on Human Resources, Subcommittee on Compensation and Employee Benefits, September 21, 1982, p. 1, folder 20, box 4, Holleran.

42. "Affirmative Action in Washington State," July 1974, p. 2, folder 9, box 5, AFSCME-Program.

43. Larry Goodman to Winn Newman, August 8, 1983, re: Basic History of Salary Setting in Washington State, folder 3, box 1, AFSCME-Program; "... It All Began with Council 28," *AFSCME Public Employee*, September 1981, folder 12, box 4, Holleran.

44. George T. Floros, "The Comparable Worth Theory of Title VII Sex Discrimination in Compensation," *Missouri Law Review* 47 (Summer 1982): 499–500.

45. For the text of the Bennett amendment, see 110 Cong. Rec. 13.647 (1964); for the text of the amended Fair Labor Standards Act cited by the Bennett amendment, see 29 U.S.C. 206(d). See also Michael Evan Gold, "A Tale of Two Amendments: The Reasons Congress Added Sex to Title VII and Their Implication for the Issue of Comparable Worth," Faculty Publications— Collective Bargaining, Labor Law, and Labor History, Paper 11 (1981), http://digitalcommons.ilr .cornell.edu/cbpubs/11.

46. *Schultz v. Wheaton Glass* 421 F.2d 259 (3d Cir. 1970); *Corning Glass Works v. Brennan*, 417 U.S. 188 (1974); *IUE v. Westinghouse*, 631 F.2d 1094 (3d Cir. 1980); *Lemons v. City and County of Denver*, 620 F.2d 228 (10th Cir. 1980); *Christensen v. Iowa*, 563 F.2d 353 (8th Cir. 1977); Stephen Wermiel, "High Court Looks at Women's Pay in Dispute on 'Comparable Worth,'" *Wall Street Journal*, May 14, 1981, 29.

47. See Julie A. Saltoun, "*County of Washington v. Gunther*: Sex-Based Wage Discrimination Extends Beyond the Equal Pay Act," *Loyola of Los Angeles Law Review* 16 (1983): 151–71.

48. Louise Ott, "Equal Pay for Work of Comparable Value: A Story of Dollars and Sense," *Matrix*, Spring 1980, 23, folder 19, box 52, Papers of Toni Carabillo and Judith Meuli, Schlesinger Library, Radcliffe Institute, Harvard University, Cambridge, Mass.

49. McCann, *Rights at Work*, 61–62; Winn Newman Statement Before U.S. House of Representatives Subcommittee on Civil Rights, Subcommittee on Human Resources, Subcommittee on Compensation and Employee Benefits, p. 22, September 16, 1982, Holleran. See also Winn Newman, "Presentation III," *Signs* 1 (Spring 1976): 265–72.

50. McCann, *Rights at Work*, 61–62; "A New Step Toward Equal Pay for Women," *McCall's*, November 1981, 64.

51. Winn Newman Statement Before U.S. House of Representatives Subcommittee on Civil Rights, Subcommittee on Human Resources, Subcommittee on Compensation and Employee Benefits, pp. 4–5, 8, 12, September 16, 1982, folder 26, box 4, Holleran.

52. "Surrounding Info from the Case *AFSCME v. Washington*, Appeal No. 84-3569, Excerpt of Record v. 1," folder 1, box 28, Newman-LOC.

53. "Plaintiffs' Answers to Defendants' Interrogatories," folder 3, box 52, Newman-LOC.

54. *AFSCME v. Washington* Trial Transcript, folder 4, box 28, Newman-LOC.

55. Newman was also a member of the legal team representing the Hotel Trades Council in its struggle over the wages of maids and housemen. See Chapter 6 of this study and "Winn Newman, 70: Fought Salary Bias," *New York Times*, June 28, 1994, A15.

56. Ray Marshall Testimony, folder 4, box 51, Newman-LOC.

57. *AFSCME v. Washington* Trial Transcript, 15, folder 4, box 51, Newman-LOC.

58. Affidavit of Roger Sanford, taken August 1983, folder 4, box 34, Newman-LOC.

59. Testimony of June O'Neill: Exhibit TTT, box 34, folder 12, Newman-LOC.

60. "Outline of Statement by Winn Newman on Behalf of AFSCME Before Joint Economic Committee of U.S. Congress," April 10, 1984, folder 3, box 383, Newman-LOC.

61. *Detroit Free Press*, Morning Edition, December 12, 1983, folder 1, box 58, Newman-LOC.

62. "Fair-Pay Group Hails Ruling," *Detroit Free Press*, December 21, 1983, 13A.

63. "Washington State Told to Pay Women in Sex-Bias Lawsuit,' *Wall Street Journal*, December 5, 1983, 47.

64. Jim Drinkhall, "Washington State Fears Sex Bias Award to Have 'Devastating' Effect on Economy," *Wall Street Journal*, December 6, 1983, 10.

65. "A 16% Hike in San Jose—and Maybe Much More on the Way," *AFSCME Public Employee*, 1980, folder 12, box 4, Holleran; "San Jose Strike Gains," *Comparable Worth Project Newsletter*, December 1981, folder 2, box 382, Newman-LOC.

66. Judy Baston, "L.A. Clericals: 'We're Not Just Coffeemakers Anymore,'" AFSCME Public Employee, 1980, folder 12, box 4, Holleran.

67. "List of Wage Discrimination Charges Pending at EEOC Filed by Winn Newman," ca. 1983, folder 3, box 383, Newman-LOC. For more detail on AFSCME's litigation strategy in these years, see McCann, *Rights at Work*, 48–91.

68. Winn Newman Statement Before U.S. House of Representatives Subcommittee on Civil Rights, Subcommittee on Human Resources, Subcommittee on Compensation and Employee Benefits, p. 14, September 16, 1982, folder 26, box 4, Holleran.

69. Joy Simard, "How We Did the Job Evaluation," folder 1, box 382, Newman-LOC; "Supervisors' Job Analysis Questionnaire, 1984," State of Wisconsin Task Force on Comparable Worth, folder 14, box 2, Holleran.

70. "State Proposals, 1974–1986: Hawaii," folder 1, box 1, Holleran.

71. Gerald W. McEntee, Statement Before U.S. House of Representatives Subcommittee on Civil Rights, Subcommittee on Human Resources, Subcommittee on Compensation and Employee Benefits, September 21, 1982, 1, folder 20, box 4, Holleran.

72. Ibid., 2–3.

73. "New Panel Spurs Drive to Upgrade Wages," *AFSCME Public Employee*, 1980, folder 12, box 4, Holleran.

74. National Committee on Pay Equity Statement of Principles, undated, ca. 1980, folder 29, box 94, NOW.

75. "NCPE Information Update: 1981–2 Program Summary," p. 1, folder 1, box 25, Coalition of Labor Union Women Records, Walter P. Reuther Library of Labor and Urban Affairs, Wayne State University, Detroit, Mich. (hereafter "CLUW").

76. Ronnie Steinberg and Lois Haignere, "Separate but Equivalent: Equal Pay for Work of Comparable Worth," in *Gender at Work: Perspectives on Occupational Segregation and Comparable Worth*, a publication of Women's Research and Education Institute of the Congressional Caucus for Women's Issues, 1984, pp. 13–26, folder 7, box 43, WREI.

77. "Call to the First National Conference of the Coalition of Labor Union Women," ca. Winter 1974, folder 15, box 1, CLUW.

78. "CLUW Statement of Purpose, Structure and Guidelines, Adopted by the Coalition of Labor Union Women Founding Conference, March 23–24, 1974, folder 17, box 1, p. 5, CLUW.

79. Lublin, "Getting Organized."

80. "McNorriell, Mozell M," *Who's Who Among African Americans*, ed. Katherine H. Nemeh, 18th ed. (Detroit: Gale, 2005), 855.

81. Mary Jean Collins, "Issue: Pay Equity," December 8, 1984, folder 30, box 94, NOW.

82. Judy Goldsmith to Ronald Reagan, September 14, 1984, folder 31, box 94, NOW.

83. "A Business Group Fights 'Comparable Worth,'" *Businessweek*, November 10, 1980, 100.

84. "A Fair Payday Is All They Ask," *San Diego Union*, December 3, 1982, D1.

85. Blum, *Between Feminism and Labor*, 24.

86. Ibid., 49–50.

87. Louise Ott, "Equal Pay for Work of Comparable Value: A Story of Dollars and Sense," *Matrix*, Spring 1980, 23, folder 19, box 52, Papers of Toni Carabillo and Judith Meuli, Schlesinger Library, Radcliffe Institute, Harvard University, Cambridge, Mass.

88. Ronnie Steinberg and Lois Haignere, "Separate but Equivalent: Equal Pay for Work of Comparable Worth," in *Gender at Work: Perspectives on Occupational Segregation and Comparable Worth*, a publication of Women's Research and Education Institute of the Congressional Caucus for Women's Issues, 1984, p. 15, folder 7, box 43, WREI.

89. Floros, "Comparable Worth Theory of Title VII," 499; Ronnie Steinberg and Lois Haignere, "Separate but Equivalent: Equal Pay for Work of Comparable Worth," in *Gender at Work: Perspectives on Occupational Segregation and Comparable Worth*, a publication of Women's Research and Education Institute of the Congressional Caucus for Women's Issues, 1984, pp. 13–26, folder 7, box 43, WREI.

90. "EEOC Opens Hearings on Comparable Worth," *BNA Daily Labor Report* 83 (April 28, 1980): 1.

91. Ibid., A-14.

92. Loren Chumley to Liz Nicholson, "EEOC Amicus Brief to Gunther/1981 Guidelines to Process Pay Equity Charges," June 19, 1985, folder 7, box 90, NOW.

93. Ibid.; "Notice Adopted by EEOC to Provide Interim Guidance to Field Offices on Identifying and Processing Sex-Based Wage Discrimination Charges Under Title VII and the Equal Pay Act," issued August 25, 1981, reprinted in *The Comparable Worth Issue: A BNA Special Report* (Washington, D.C.: Bureau of National Affairs, 1981), 79–83; Winn Newman Statement Before U.S. House of Representatives Subcommittee on Civil Rights, Subcommittee on Human Resources, Subcommittee on Compensation and Employee Benefits, pp. 14–18, September 16, 1982, folder 26, box 4, Holleran.

94. Joan Acker, *Doing Comparable Worth*, 9.

95. See, for example, Rodgers, *Age of Fracture*; Mark A. Smith, *The Right Talk: How Conservatives Transformed the Great Society into the Economic Society* (Princeton, N.J.: Princeton University Press, 2007); Schulman and Zelizer, *Rightward Bound*; Stein, *Pivotal Decade*; and Waterhouse, *Lobbying America*.

96. Editorial, "Liberty or License? EEOC Evidently Opts for the Latter," *Barron's National Business and Financial Weekly*, May 31, 1976, 7; Steven V. Roberts, "White Males Challenge Affirmative Action Programs," *New York Times*, November 24, 1977, 1; Morton Mintz, "Religious Freedom vs. Work Rules: Court Rules Employers Aren't Required to Grant a Specific Sabbath Day," *Washington Post*, June 17, 1977, A2; "Business Group Fights 'Comparable Worth,'" 100; Wermiel, "High Court Looks at Women's Pay in Dispute on 'Comparable Worth,'" 29; Equal Employment Advisory Council, *Comparable Worth: Issues and Alternatives* (Washington, D.C.: Equal Employment Advisory Council, 1980).

97. Donna Blanton, "Business Lobby Successfully Stalls Comparable-Worth Bill," *Ft. Lauderdale News*, April 4, 1985, folder 1, box 5, Holleran.

98. Robert Pear, "U.S. Report Assails Idea of Job Worth: Study Calls Requirements on Wages 'Profoundly Flawed,'" *New York Times*, March 28, 1985, A29.

99. Robert Pear, "U.S. Report Assails Idea of Job Worth Idea," *New York Times*, March 28, 1985, A29.

100. *Daily Herald* (Arlington Heights, Ill.), April 5, 1985, folder 2, box 5, Holleran.

101. "Comparable Worth Idea Rejected," *Dallas Morning News*, H2. Undated clipping, folder 30, box 94, NOW.

102. William E. Clayton, "Texans on Rights Panel Differ over 'Comparable Worth' Issue," *Houston Chronicle*, March 29, 1985, sec. 1, p. 3.

103. *Chicago Daily Law Bulletin*, April 11, 1985, folder 3, box 5, Holleran.

104. Beth Kivel, "Pay Equity Advocates Fight Back," *off our backs* 15 (January 31, 1985): 4; *Daily Herald* (Arlington Heights, Ill.), April 5, 1985, folder 2, box 5, Holleran.

105. *Chicago Daily Law Bulletin*, April 11, 1985, folder 3, box 5, Holleran.

106. "Statement of Judy Goldsmith, National NOW President, in Response to U.S. Civil Rights Commission's Adoption of Anti-Comparable Worth Report," April 11, 1985, folder 32, box 94, NOW.

107. Eileen Stein, "Draft Testimony Before Civil Rights Commission," April 16, 1985, p. 2–3, folder 10, box 80, CLUW.

108. Winn Newman Statement Before U.S. House of Representatives Subcommittee on Civil Rights, Subcommittee on Human Resources, Subcommittee on Compensation and Employee Benefits, p. 16–17, September 16, 1982, folder 26, box 4, Holleran.

109. Statement by EEOC Chairman Clarence Thomas, June 17, 1985, folder 5, box 382, Newman-LOC.

110. Statement by Clarence Thomas on First EEOC Comparable Worth Decision, June 17, 1985, p. 2, folder 32, box 94, NOW.

111. Blum, *Between Feminism and Labor*, 24–25.

112. *AFSCME v. Washington*, 770 F.2d 1401 (9th Cir. 1985). See also R. J. Arnold, "*AFSCME v. Washington*: The Death of Comparable Worth?" *University of Miami Law Review* 40 (1986): 1039; and Rhonda Y. Cline, "A Rejection of Comparable Worth: *AFSCME v. Washington*," *University of Cincinnati Law Review* 55 (1986): 275; "Pay Equity—State Updates," *National Now Times*, undated, ca. 1984, 5–6, folder 30, box 94, NOW; *ANA v. Illinois*, 783 F.2d 716, 40 FEP Cases 244 (7th Cir. 1986).

113. *Watson v. Fort Worth Bank and Trust*, 487 U.S. 977 (1988).

114. Tamar Lewin, "Pay Equity for Women's Jobs Finds Success Outside Courts," *New York Times*, October 7, 1989, A1.

115. National Committee on Pay Equity, "Closing the Wage Gap: An International Perspective," October 1988, folder 22, box 4, Holleran; "NCPE Record of Goals and 1985 Accomplishments," ca. January 1986, folder 6, box 25, CLUW.

116. National Committee on Pay Equity, "Survey of State Government-Level Pay Equity Activity," 1988, p. 2, folder 22, box 4, Holleran.

117. Lewin, "Pay Equity," A8.

Chapter 5. Sex Equality and the Service Sector

1. Nancy Smith Barrett, "Women in the Job Market: Occupations, Earnings, and Career Opportunities," *The Subtle Revolution: Women at Work*, ed. Ralph E. Smith (Washington, D.C.: Urban Institute, 1979), 31, 47; Reagan, "De Facto Job Segregation," *Women in the U.S. Labor Force*, ed. Ann Foote Cahn (New York: Praeger, 1979), 90, 94–95; *Schultz v. Wheaton Glass Co.*, 421 F.2d 259 (1970); *Corning Glass Works v. Brennan*, 417 U.S. 188 (1974).

2. "Equal Pay Act Signed Fifty Years Ago Today," EEOC Press Release, June 10, 2013, http://www.eeoc.gov/eeoc/newsroom/release/6-10-13.cfm; "Maids, Janitors Must Be Paid Equal Wages, Federal Appeals Court Affirms," folder 2, box 2, Women Employed Records, Richard J. Daley Library Special Collections and University Archives, University of Illinois at Chicago (hereafter

"WER"); *Brennan v. Houston Endowment Company*, 511 F. 2d 1190 (5th Cir. 1975); "Union Hits Hotel Association Stalling; Asks Sheraton to Meet for Pay Equalization Talks," *Hotel Voice* 26, March 6, 1978, folder 4, box 140, Newman-LOC; Albert A. Formicola to Jay Rubin, August, 2, 1977, folder 5, box 136, Newman-LOC; Formicola to Vito Pitta and Vangel M. Kamaras, December 15, 1977, folder 5, box 136, Newman-LOC.

3. Deposition of Lucy Osorio, 7, May 21, 1986, folder 9, box 166, Newman-LOC.

4. On tensions between and among claimants and their advocates in other contexts, see Brown-Nagin, *Courage to Dissent*, 307–56; and Goluboff, *The Lost Promise of Civil Rights*, esp. 217–37. On workers' rights struggles' diminished potential in the 1980s, see also Lee, *Workplace Constitution*, 238-55; MacLean, *Freedom is Not Enough*, 300–332; and Mayeri, *Reasoning from Race*, 186–224.

5. See, for example, Thomas Jessen Adams, "The Servicing of America: Political Economy and Service Work in Postwar Southern California," (Ph.D. diss., University of Chicago, UMI Publishing, 2009); Blackwelder, *Now Hiring*; Boris and Klein, *Caring for America*; Braverman, *Labor and Monopoly Capital*, esp. 203–59; Carla Freeman, *High Tech and High Heels in the Global Economy: Women, Work, and Pink-Collar Identities in the Caribbean* (Durham, N.C.: Duke University Press, 2000); Green, *Race on the Line*; Jacoby, *Modern Manors*, 95–142; and Moreton, *To Serve God and Wal-Mart*.

6. Dorothy Sue Cobble and Michael Merrill, "Collective Bargaining in the Hospitality Industry in the 1980s," in *Contemporary Collective Bargaining in the Private Sector*, ed. Paula Voos (Industrial Relations Research Association, Madison, 1994), 467; "Hotel Trades Council History," MN#5469, #-R-7448, box 1, New York Hotel and Motel Trades Council Records, Robert F. Wagner Labor Archive, Bobst Library, New York University (hereafter "HTC-Bobst").

7. "Hotel Trades Council History," MN#5469, #-R-7448, box 1, HTC-Bobst.

8. Matthew Josephson, *Union House, Union Bar: The History of the Hotel and Restaurant Employees and Bartenders International Union AFL-CIO* (New York: Random House, 1956), xii, 15.

9. Ibid., 67–68.

10. Ibid., 40.

11. Ibid., 40–41.

12. Louis Ferrand's Notes About Interview with Betty Benz Ruben, August 4, 1988, folder 7, box 186, Newman-LOC.

13. Morris Horowitz, *The New York Hotel Industry: A Labor Relations Study* (Cambridge, Mass.: Harvard University Press, 1960), 1, 18, 103.

14. Josephson, *Union House, Union Bar*, 281. On the creation of joint trades councils in the hospitality industry, and especially their benefits for women, see Cobble, *Dishing It Out*.

15. Horowitz, *New York Hotel Industry*, 80, 89.

16. "Hotel Trades Council History," MN#5469, #-R-7448, Box 1, HTC-Bobst; Josephson, *Union House, Union Bar*, 279-81; Horowitz, *New York Hotel Industry*, 69–70.

17. Joshua Freeman, *Working Class New York*, 44.

18. Horowitz, *New York Hotel Industry*, 151.

19. Richard A. Greenwald, *The Triangle Fire, the Protocols of Peace, and Industrial Democracy in Progressive Era New York* (Philadelphia: Temple University Press, 2005), 189–205.

20. Job Descriptions for Hotels and Restaurants, April 1938, 229, folder 2, box 144, Newman-LOC.

21. Ibid.

22. "Union Job Classification Committee," folder 5, box 133, Newman-LOC.

23. Job Descriptions for Hotels and Restaurants, April 1938, 325, 327, folder 2, box 144, Newman-LOC.

24. "Industry-Wide Collective Bargaining Agreement Between Hotel Association and New York Hotel Trades Council," Hotel Trades Council—Minutes—1/6/1955–12/1/1955 folder, Reel 1, HTC-Bobst; Horowitz, *New York Hotel Industry,* 170.

25. Cobble Notes, April 16, 1989, folder 6, box 135, Newman-LOC.

26. Edward Corsi, Industrial Commissioner, New York State Department of Labor, "Wages and Hours in the Hotel Industry in New York State, 1950," folder 4, box 134, Newman-LOC.

27. Cobble Notes, April 16, 1989, folder 6, box 135, Newman-LOC.

28. "Housekeeping Department," *Hotel and Club Voice,* April 1956, 15, folder 9, box 144, Newman-LOC.

29. "Times Square Story—31 Maids Led the Struggle," *Hotel Voice,* March 15, 1976, 3, folder 1, box 140, Newman-LOC.

30. "Begin Survey of Housekeeping Departments in the Hotels," *Hotel Voice,* April 10, 1948, folder 3, box 139, Newman-LOC.

31. "Maid Upheld in Spurning Porter Work," *Hotel Voice,* November 18, 1950, folder 14, box 139, Newman-LOC.

32. Ibid.

33. "Big Load Off Marcy Maids as Linen Lifting Ends," *Hotel Voice,* October 20, 1945, folder 14, box 139, Newman-LOC.

34. "Edison Maids Oppose Vacuum Cleaner Chore," *Hotel Voice,* May 15, 1948, folder 14, box 139, Newman-LOC.

35. "Hotel: Weekly Newspaper of the Hotel and Motel Workers of New York," April 20, 1964, HTC-Bobst.

36. Minutes of the Meeting of the Executive Board of the New York Hotel Trades Council, May 7, 1964, folder 13, box 1, HTC-Bobst.

37. Minutes of Meeting of the Executive Board, November 5, 1964, folder 13, box 1, HTC-Bobst.

38. "1966 Contract," Agreements: Hotel Assignments folder, box 6, HTC-Bobst.

39. *Brennan v. Wheaton Glass; Kouba v. Allstate Insurance Company,* 691 F.2d 873 (9th Cir. 1982). Catharine A. MacKinnon, *Sex Equality* (New York: Foundation Press, 2001), 178.

40. *Brennan v. Houston Endowment, Inc.,* 7 E.P.D. Sec. 9204 (S.D. Tex. 1974), aff'd per curiam, 511 F.2d 1190 (5th Cir. 1975); Equal Pay Act of 1963, 29 U.S. Code Chapter 8 Section 206(d); "Domestic Equality," *New York Amsterdam News,* July 9, 1975, C1. See also "About Wage-Hour" and "Opinion Letters," Wages and Hours Division, United States Department of Labor, http://www.dol.gov/whd/opinion/opinion.htm, accessed December 16, 2009.

41. Minutes of the Meeting of the Executive Board, September 1, 1977, Minutes Ex Board, 1977 folder, box 2, HTC-Bobst.

42. Ibid.

43. Minutes of the Meeting of the Executive Board, January 26, 1978, Minutes Ex Board, 1978 folder, box 2, HTC-Bobst; Joseph Formicola to Vangel Maranas, President, and Vito Pitta, Secretary-Treasurer, Local 6, Hotel, Motel and Club Employees Union, December 15, 1977, Lynch, Louis: Daily File folder, box 4, HTC-Bobst.

44. Formicola, Executive Vice President, Hotel Association, to Vangel M. Kamaras, President, and Vito Pitta, Secretary-Treasurer, Local #6, Hotel, Motel and Club Employees Union, December 15, 1977, folder 5, box 136, Newman-LOC.

45. Jay Rubin to Joseph Formicola, February 9, 1978, folder 5, box 136, Newman-LOC.

46. Minutes of the Meeting of the Executive Board, September 1, 1978, Minutes Ex Board, 1978 folder, box 2, HTC-Bobst; Jay Rubin, President, HTC, to Klaus R. Ottoman, General Manager, New York Sheraton Hotel, February 9, 1978, folder 5, box 136, Newman-LOC.

47. Arbiter's Final Conclusion, January 14, 1985, folder 1, box 136, Newman-LOC; "Memo re: Further Clarification of Decisions #85-10; 85-22; 85-42; 85-56," undated, folder 5, box 136, Newman-LOC.

48. Newman to John Turchiano, lawyer on the case at Shea and Gould, December 24, 1987, folder 2, box 155, Newman-LOC; "Memo re: Further Clarification of Decisions #85-10; 85-22; 85-42; 85-56," undated, folder 5, box 136, Newman-LOC; Cass statement, undated, folder 5, box 136, Newman-LOC.

49. Newman to Pitta, December 6, 1985, folder 5, box 136, Newman-LOC.

50. Ibid.

51. "Job Description—Houseman," folder 5, box 136, Newman-LOC.

52. "Job Description—Room Attendant," ibid.

53. "Memo," folder 4, box 137, Newman-LOC.

54. Local 6 to Room Attendants and Housekeeping Attendants at the Essex House Hotel re: Upcoming Tours of Essex House, 1985, folder 5, box 153, Newman-LOC.

55. Interview of Norman Willis, Job Evaluator, July 1988, folder 7, box 146, Newman-LOC.

56. Ibid.

57. "Proof—Hotel Case—August 1 1988 Draft," folder 3, box 137, Newman-LOC; Newman Comments on Ferrand Memo, September 6, 1989, folder 3, box 199, Newman-LOC.

58. Cobble, *Other Women's Movement*.

59. Marie Adamson Deposition, January 9, 1986, 16, folder 1, box 160, Newman, LOC.

60. Ibid., 116–17.

61. Deposition of Elise Andre, 114, folder 4, box 160, Newman-LOC.

62. Deposition of Jacqueline Larry, 88–99, June 24, 1988, folder 1, box 164, Newman-LOC.

63. Deposition of Jeanine Jolibois, 200, July 27, 1988, folder 4, box 164, Newman-LOC.

64. Deposition of Mildred Prince, 133–34, folder 6, box 169, Newman-LOC.

65. "Room Attendants Paid from Defense Fund for Illegal Dockings," *Hotel Voice*, April 29, 1985, 3, folder 5, box 136, Newman-LOC; *Hotel Voice*, June 10, 1985, folder 1, box 137, Newman-LOC.

66. Deposition of Mildred Prince, 132, folder 6, box 169, Newman-LOC.

67. Ibid., 133–34.

68. Deposition of Jacqueline Larry, 69–70, June 24, 1988, folder 1, box 164, Newman-LOC.

69. Deposition of Maria Rubinos, 141, folder 3, box 170, Newman-LOC.

70. Deposition of Marie Adamson, 151, January 9, 1986, folder 1, box 160, Newman, LOC.

71. Deposition of Yvonne Simon, 75–78, folder 8, box 172, Newman-LOC.

72. Christine Owens to Raymond Hart, Assistant to the President of the Union, March 21, 1985, folder 18, box 153, Newman-LOC.

73. Louis Lynch to Christine Owens, January 30, 1985, folder 18, box 153, Newman. LOC.

74. Mercado to Hendriksen, May 26, 1987, folder 2, box 155, Newman-LOC.

75. Jim Hendriksen to Newman and Sobol re: Zelidea Rovera, One of Two Plaintiffs at the St. Moritz, January 7, 1986, folder 6, box 137, Newman-LOC.

76. Christine Owens to Lou Lynch, December 20, 1984, folder 18, box 153, Newman-LOC.

77. Owens to Mary Moriarty, Shea and Gould, November 15, 1984, folder 3, box 186, Newman-LOC.

78. Mary Moriarty to Christine Owens, March 15, 1985, folder 1, box 154, Newman-LOC.

79. Memo to File from JAH [Jim A. Hendriksen], October 31, 1986, re: Summary of October 31 Meeting with Housemen, folder 7, box 137, Newman-LOC.

80. Ibid.

81. "Answers to Norm Willis' Questions," February 22, 1989, folder 2, box 157, Newman-LOC.

82. Jim Hendrickson to Newman and Sobol, June 10, 1986, folder 1, box 137, Newman-LOC.

83. Joshua Freeman, *Working Class New York*, 293.

84. William Serrin, "Hotel Talks: An Era of Peace Ends," *New York Times*, May 31, 1985, B1.

85. Grievance at Berkshire Place, #79-94, re: Maids' Refusal to Make Beds with New Spreads, May 2, 1979, folder 3, box 186, Newman-LOC.

86. Arbitration Decision, Beverly Hotel, Decision #78-901, Issued December 7, 1978, re: Insistence of Management on Having Maids Wash Dishes, Clean Stoves and Refrigerators, folder 3, box 186, Newman-LOC.

87. Louis G. Ferrand to Hotel Case File, July 14, 1988, re: Interview with Day Room Attendants at the Essex House, folder 6, box 186, Newman-LOC.

88. Grievance at Drake Hotel, Decision #82-28, Issued February 18, 1982, re: Floor Housekeepers Complaint That Doors to Guest Rooms Are Too Heavy, folder 3, box 186, Newman-LOC.

89. Hearing #82-164, Decision Issued August 26, 1982, Office of Impartial Chairman, Plaza Hotel, Hearings at Office of Impartial Chairman, folder 3, box 186, Newman-LOC.

90. Hilton Hotels Inter-Office Correspondence from Jorge Portero to Thomas Nemeth, January 27, 1980, folder 3, box 177, Newman-LOC.

91. Arbitration Decision, Waldorf-Astoria Hotel, #81-61, re: Non-Compliance with Paragraph 32(c) of the Industry-Wide Collective Bargaining Agreement Pertaining to Automation of the Telephone Department, Issued April 30, 1981, folder 3, box 186, Newman-LOC.

92. Ronald Smothers, "3 Hotels Reach Pacts, but Strike Nears," *New York Times*, May 31, 1985, B1, B6.

93. Ibid.

94. Ronald Smothers, "Unions Threaten Hotel Strike If No Pact by Friday," *New York Times*, May 28, 1985, B3; William Serrin, "Hotel Talks: An Era of Peace Ends," *New York Times*, May 31, 1985, B1.

95. Ronald Smothers, "Union Group Head Says He Focuses on 'Bottom Line,'" *New York Times*, June 10, 1985, B2.

96. Joseph Berger, "Tentative Pact Set in Walkout at City's Hotels," *New York Times*, June 27, 1985, A1.

97. "Three Hotels in New York Reach Accord with Union," *Wall Street Journal*, May 31, 1985, 6; Deposition of Gladys Morris, 83–88, folder 1, box 166, Newman-LOC; "Three Hotels in New York Reach Accord with Union," *Wall Street Journal*, May 31, 1985, 6; Berger, "Tentative Pact," A1.

98. Cobble and Merrill, "Collective Bargaining in the Hospitality Industry in the 1980s," 449.

99. William Serrin, "Hotel Talks," B1.

100. Minutes of Meeting of Executive Board, October 13, 1965, folder 13, box 1, HTC-Bobst.

101. Minutes of the Special Meeting of the Executive Board, June 17, 1976, Minutes Ex Board, 1976 folder, box 2, HTC-Bobst.

102. Willis to Sobol, September 30, 1985, folder 5, box 153, Newman-LOC.

103. Minutes of the Meeting of the Executive Board, 7, December 5, 1984, Minutes Ex Board, 1984 folder, box 2, HTC-Bobst.

104. Newman to Pitta, March 14, 1986, folder 5, box 153, Newman-LOC.

105. Jim Hendriksen to Vito Pitta, n.d., folder 6, box 137, Newman-LOC.

106. Richard Sobol to Winn Newman, June 16, 1986, folder 6, box 3, Newman-LOC.

107. Jim Hendrickson to Newman and Sobol, June 10, 1986, folder 8, box 137, Newman-LOC.

108. Winn Newman to Art Schiller and Laura Einstein, May 7, 1988, folder 8, box 137, Newman-LOC.

109. Newman to Pitta, December 19, 1989, folder 7, box 158, Newman-LOC.

110. Kenneth C. Crowe, "Hotel Agreement Reached," *New York Newsday*, February 8, 1990, folder 7, box 158, Newman-LOC.

111. "Delegates Accept Hotel Association's Contract Offer," *Hotel Voice*, February 5, 1990, folder 7, box 158, Newman-LOC; "Memorandum of Understanding Between Hotel Association and Trades Council," accepted January 30, 1990, folder 2, box 187, Newman-LOC.

112. Defense Response, folder 2, box 186, Newman-LOC; "Plaintiff's and Defendant's Joint Memorandum in Support of Motion for Approval of Stipulation of Settlement of Class Action," undated, Doc #255, folder 2, box 186, Newman-LOC.

113. *Hotel Voice*, August 10, 1992, folder 5, box 197, Newman-LOC.

114. Joanne L. Goodwin, *Changing the Game*, esp. 116; Greenhouse, *Big Squeeze*, 176–82; Milkman introduction in Milkman and Ott, *New Labor in New York*, 10.

115. AFL-CIO Working for America Institute, "US Hotels and Their Workers: Room for Improvement," September 2002, http://www.hotel-online.com/News/PR2002_3rd/Aug02_HotelJobs .html, accessed December 16, 2009; Frank Bruni, "A Better Wage Becomes a Luxury," *New York Times*, October 23, 1995, B1.

116. Bruce Weber, "Hotel Workers Agree to Keep on Negotiating," *New York Times*, July 1, 1995, 23; *Hotel Voice*, August 10, 1992, folder 5, box 197, Newman-LOC.

117. Annette Bernhardt, Laura Dresser, and Erin Hatton, "The Coffee Pot Wars: Unions and Firm Restructuring in the Hotel Industry," in *Low Wage America: How Employers are Reshaping Opportunity in the Workplace*, eds. Eileen Appelbaum, Annette Bernhardt, and Richard J. Murnane (New York: Russell Sage Foundation, 2003): 39–44; "Hilton Times Square," http:// www1.hilton.com/en_US/hi/hotel/NYCTSHF-Hilton-Times-Square-New-York/index.do ?brand_id=HI&brand_directory=/en/hi/&xch=535554162,Q0CRK1HTGJNWKCSGBJC4D4Q, accessed December 15, 2009; UNITE HERE, "Creating Luxury, Enduring Pain: How Hotel Work Is Hurting Housekeepers," http://www.hotelworkersrising.org/pdf/Injury_Paper.pdf, 2006, accessed December 16, 2009; "Hilton to Home: Serenity Mattress and Box Spring," http://www .hiltontohome.com/productGroup.aspx?category1=Bedding&category1Name=Bedding &categoryLevel=0&itemID=HIL-124, accessed December 15, 2009; Bernhardt, Dresser, and Hatton, "The Coffee Pot Wars," 43; UNITE HERE Hope for Housekeepers, "Housekeeping Fact Sheet 2," http://www.hotelworkersrising.org/media/HousekeepingFactSheet2.pdf, accessed October 31, 2009; UNITE HERE, "Creating Luxury, Enduring Pain"; see AFL-CIO Working for America Institute, "U.S. Hotels and Their Workers: Room for Improvement," September 2002. Bureau of Labor Statistics Occupational Employment and Wages, Maids and Housekeeping Cleaners (37-2012), May 2008, http://www.bls.gov/oes/current/oes372012.htm, accessed December 5, 2009; and Charles V. Bagley, "With More Rooms Empty, Hotels Seek to Cut Worker Pay," *NYT*, April 9, 2009, A17; Eric Frumin et al., "Workload-Related Musculoskeletal Disorders Among Hotel

Housekeepers: Employer Records Reveal a Growing National Problem," April 19, 2006, http://www.hotelworkersrising.org/pdf/hskpr_analysis0406.pdf, accessed December 5, 2009; UNITE HERE, "Creating Luxury, Enduring Pain"; Wage and Hour Division, Department of Labor, "11240 Maid or Houseman," Service Contract Act Directory of Occupations, http://www.dol.gov/whd /regs/compliance/wage/pl1240.htm (December 16, 2009); "Career Guide to Industries: Hotels and Other Accommodations Bureau of Labor Statistics," March 12, 2008, http://www.bls.gov/oco/cg /cgs036.htm#earnings, accessed December 5, 2009; Susan Buchanan et al., "Occupational Injury Disparities in the US Hotel Industry," *American Journal of Industrial Medicine* (2009): 1–10.

Chapter 6. A Man's World, but Only for Some

1. Francisco Valdes, "Queers, Sissies, Dykes, and Tomboys: Deconstructing the Conflation of 'Sex,' 'Gender,' and 'Sexual Orientation' in Euro-American Law and Society," *California Law Review* (1995): 155.

2. "EEOC Rejects Charges Filed by Gays," *Sexual Law Reporter* 2 (March–April 1976): 21; "EEOC Ruling: Commission Refuses to Protect Gays," *It's Time: Newsletter of the National Gay Task Force*, March 1976, folder 12, box 1, Los Angeles Gay and Lesbian Center Records, ONE National Gay and Lesbian Archives, Los Angeles, Calif. (hereafter "LAGLC"); William Parker, "Homosexuals and Employment," 1970, folder 39, box 1, Charles Thorpe Papers, James C. Hormel Gay and Lesbian Center, San Francisco Public Library, San Francisco, Calif. (hereafter "CTP"); and "Employment Commission Disclaims Jurisdiction for Gays," *Sexual Law Reporter* 2 (November–December 1976): 65.

3. *DeSantis v. Pacific Telephone and Telegraph*, 608 F.2d. 327 (9th Cir. 1979). In its rejection of effeminate men's Title VII claims, the court cited the previous year's similar ruling by the 5th Circuit Court of Appeals in *Smith v. Liberty Mutual Insurance Co.*, 569 F.2d 325 (5th Cir. 1978). Legal scholars have shown how judges have melded aspects of sex, gender, and sexual orientation in limiting the scope of sex equality laws. See especially Mary Ann Case, "Disaggregating Gender from Sex and Sexual Orientation: The Effeminate Man in the Law and Feminist Jurisprudence," *Yale Law Journal* 105 vol. 1 (1995): 1–105; Zachary A. Kramer, "The Ultimate Gender Stereotype: Equalizing Gender-Conforming and Gender-Nonconforming Homosexuals Under Title VII," *University of Illinois Law Review*, 2004, no. 2, 47; Zachary A. Kramer, "Heterosexuality and Title VII," *Northwestern University Law Review* 103 (Winter 2009): 205–47; Christine A. Littleton, "Double and Nothing: Lesbianism as a Category," *UCLA Women's Law Journal* 7 (1996): 14–16; Olivia Szwalbnest, "Discriminating Because of 'Pizzazz': Why Discrimination Based on Sexual Orientation Evidences Sexual Discrimination Under the Sex-Stereotyping Doctrine of Title VII," *Texas Journal of Women and the Law* 20 (Fall 2010): 75–94; and Valdes, "Queers, Sissies, Dykes, and Tomboys," esp. 154–57.

4. Allan Berube, " 'Queer Work' and Labor History," in *My Desire for History: Essays in Gay, Community, and Labor History* (Chapel Hill: University of North Carolina Press, 2011), 261–63.

5. On men's legal campaigns for flight attendant jobs, as well as a fuller discussion of "queer work," see Tiemeyer, *Plane Queer*. Cary Franklin, "The Anti-Stereotyping Principle in Constitutional Sex Discrimination Law," *New York University Law Review* 85, no. 1 (2010): 83–173; Mayeri, *Reasoning from Race*. See also Berube, " 'Queer Work' and Labor History"; Adams, "The Servicing of America," 168–75.

6. On how gender shaped medical care in the twentieth century United States, see Judith Walzer Leavitt, *Make Room for Daddy: The Journey from Waiting Room to Birthing Room* (Chapel

Hill: University of North Carolina Press, 2009); Carolyn Herbst Lewis, *Prescription for Heterosexuality: Sexual Citizenship in Cold War America* (Chapel Hill: University of North Carolina Press, 2010); and Leslie Reagan, *When Abortion Was a Crime: Women, Medicine, and Law in the United States, 1867–1973* (Berkeley: University of California Press, 1997). Some men in nursing argue that being labeled "male nurses" implies that they care only for male patients. In this chapter, I employ the terms "male nurses" and "men in nursing" interchangeably and to refer to men who perform the labor of nursing, regardless of the sex of their patients.

7. *Celio Diaz, Jr. v. Pan American World Airways, Inc.*, 442 F. 2d 385 (5th Cir. 1971); and *Wilson v. Southwest Airlines Co.*, 517 F. Supp. 292, 301 (N.D. Tex. 1981). Tiemeyer, *Plane Queer*, 80–107. On flight attendants and the BFOQ, see also Barry, *Femininity in Flight*, 155–71. On sex equality, privacy, and the BFOQ, see George J. Annas, "Law and the Life Sciences: Male Nurses in the Delivery Room," *Hastings Center Report* 11 (December 1981): 20–21; Katharine T. Bartlett, "Only Girls Wear Barrettes: Dress and Appearance Standards, Community Norms, and Workplace Equality," *Michigan Law Review* 92 (August 1994): 25–42; Jillian B. Berman, "Defining the 'Essence of the Business': An Analysis of Title VII's Privacy BFOQ After Johnson Controls," *University of Chicago Law Review* 67 (Summer 2000): 749–75; Deborah A. Calloway, "Equal Employment and Third Party Privacy Interests: An Analytical Framework for Reconciling Competing Rights," *Fordham Law Review* 54: 327–75; Mary Anne Case, "Why Not Abolish the 'Laws of Urinary Segregation'?" in *Toilet: Public Restrooms and the Politics of Sharing*, ed. Harvey Molotch (New York: New York University Press, 2010), 211–24; Amy Kapczynski, "Same-Sex Privacy and the Limits of Antidiscrimination Law," *Yale Law Journal* 112 (2003): 1257–93; Kenneth W. Kingma, "Sex Discrimination Justified Under Title VII: Privacy Rights in Nursing Homes," *Valparaiso University Law Review* 14 (Spring 1980): 577–600; Kate Manley, "The BFOQ Defense: Title VII's Concession to Gender Discrimination," *Duke Journal of Gender Law and Policy* 16 (2009): 169–210; Sharon M. McGown, "The Bona Fide Body: Title VII's Last Bastion of Intentional Sex Discrimination," *Columbia Journal of Gender and Law* 77 (January 2003): 77–127; Suzanne Wilhelm, "Perpetuating Stereotypical Views of Women: The BFOQ Defense in Gender Discrimination Under Title VII," *Women's Rights Law Reporter* 28 (2007): 73–91; Elsa M. Shartsis, "Privacy as Rationale for the Sex-Based BFOQ," *Detroit College Law Review* 1985 (Fall 1985): 865–902; Emily Gold Waldman, "The Case of the Male OB-GYN: A Proposal for the Expansion of the Privacy BFOQ in the Healthcare Context," *University of Pennsylvania Journal of Labor and Employment Law* 6 (2004): 357–93; and Kim Yuracko, "Private Nurses and Playboy Bunnies: Explaining Permissible Sex Discrimination," *California Law Review* 92 (January 2004): 147–213.

8. N. R. Kelly, M. Shoemaker, and T. Steele, "The Experience of Being a Male Student Nurse," *Journal of Nursing Education* 35 (1996): 171; Roxanne Nelson, "Men in Nursing: Still Too Few," *American Journal of Nursing* 106 (February 2006): 25–26; J. Poliafico, "Nursing's Gender Gap," *RN* 61 (October 1998): 39–42; Stephen Rallis, "I Want to Be a Nurse, Not a Stereotype," *RN* 53 (April 1990): 160; Christine L. Williams, *Still a Man's World: Men Who Do Women's Work* (Berkeley: University of California Press, 1995), 81–108; Christine L. Williams, *Gender Differences at Work: Women and Men in Nontraditional Occupations* (Berkeley: University of California Press, 1989); Adia Harvey Wingfield, "Racializing the Glass Escalator: Reconsidering Men's Experiences with Women's Work," *Gender and Society* 23 (February 2009): 5–26.

9. Mayeri, *Reasoning from Race*. On gay workers' efforts to extend their rights through the labor movement, see Miriam Frank, *Out in the Union: A Labor History of Queer America* (Philadelphia: Temple University Press, 2014).

10. 608 F.2d 327 (9th Cir. 1979) and, 24 Cal. 3d 458 (1979). On gay rights activism in California, see Elizabeth Armstrong, *Forging Gay Identities: Organizing Sexuality in San Francisco, 1950–1994* (Chicago: University of Chicago Press, 2002); Jonathan Bell, *California Crucible: The Forging of Modern American Liberalism* (Philadelphia: University of Pennsylvania Press, 2012); Jonathan Bell, "'To Strive for Economic and Social Justice': Welfare, Sexuality, and Liberal Politics in San Francisco in the 1960s," *Journal of Policy History* 22 (April 2010): 193–225; Nan Alamilla Boyd, *Wide Open Town: A History of Queer San Francisco to 1965* (Berkeley: University of California Press, 2003); Betty Luther Hillman, "'The Most Profoundly Revolutionary Act a Homosexual Can Engage In': Drag and the Politics of Gender Presentation in the San Francisco Gay Liberation Movement, 1964–1972," *Journal of the History of Sexuality* 20 (2011): 153–81; Justin David Suran, "Coming Out Against the War: Antimilitarism and the Politicization of Homosexuality in the Era of Vietnam," *American Quarterly* 53 (September 2001): 452–88.

11. As queer legal historians have argued, sexual minorities were frequently shut out of the expansion of rights other groups experienced in the 1960s and 1970s. See Margot Canaday, "Heterosexuality as a Legal Regime," in *Cambridge History of Law in America*, vol. 3, ed. Michael Grossberg and Christopher Tomlins (Cambridge, U.K.: Cambridge University Press, 2008), 442–71; Felicia Kornbluh, "Queer Legal History: A Field Grows Up and Comes Out," *Law and Social Inquiry* 36 (Spring 2011): 537–59; Jeffrey A. Mello, *AIDS and the Law of Workplace Discrimination* (Boulder, Colo.: Westview, 1995); Kevin J. Mumford, "The Trouble with Gay Rights: Race and the Politics of Sexual Orientation in Philadelphia, 1969–1982," *Journal of American History* 98 (June 2011): 49–72; Craig Rimmerman, *From Identity to Politics: The Lesbian and Gay Movements in the United States* (Philadelphia: Temple University Press, 2001); Marc Stein, *Sexual Injustice: Supreme Court Decisions from Griswold to Roe* (Chapel Hill: University of North Carolina Press, 2010); and Urvashi Vaid, *Virtual Equality: The Mainstreaming of Gay and Lesbian Liberation* (New York: Anchor Books, 1995).

12. Alice Kessler-Harris, "In the Nation's Image: The Gendered Limits of Social Citizenship in the Depression Era," *Journal of American History* 86 (December 1999): 1251–79; and Kessler-Harris, *In Pursuit of Equity*, 5–6.

13. Berube, "'Queer Work' and Labor History," 263–64.

14. Adams, "Servicing of America," 174; Berube, "'Queer Work' and Labor History," 261–63; Tiemeyer, *Plane Queer*, 2, 7.

15. For general histories of nursing in the United States, see Patricia D'Antonio, *American Nursing: A History of Knowledge, Authority and the Meaning of Work* (Baltimore: Johns Hopkins University Press, 2010); M. Patricia Donahue, *Nursing: The Finest Art*, 2nd ed. (St. Louis: Mosby,1996); Gayle Roux and Judith A. Halstead, *Issues and Trends in Nursing: Essential Knowledge for Today and Tomorrow* (Sudbury, Mass.: Jones and Bartlett, 2009); Karen Buhler-Wilkerson, *No Place Like Home: A History of Nursing and Home Care in the US* (Baltimore: Johns Hopkins University Press, 2003); Deborah Judd, Kathleen Sitzman, and G. Megan Davis, *A History of American Nursing: Trends and Eras* (New York: Jones and Bartlett, 2009); Josephine A. Dolan, M. Louise Fitzpatrick, and Eleanor Krohn Herrmann, *Nursing in Society: A Historical Perspective*, 15th ed. (Philadelphia: W. B. Saunders, 1983).

16. Cherry and Jacob, *Contemporary Nursing*, 13; Gomez, "Men in Nursing: An Historical Perspective," 13; Judd, et al., *History of American Nursing*, 4–9; O'Lynn, "History of Men in Nursing: A Review," 9–11, 22; Pokorny, "An Historical Perspective of Confederate Nursing," 28–32; Reverby, *Ordered to Care*, 2.

17. Baer et al., *Enduring Issues in American Nursing*, 12–14; Cherry and Jacob, *Contemporary Nursing*, 13; Joan Evans, "Men Nurses: A Historical and Feminist Perspective," *Journal of Advanced Nursing* 47 (July 2004): 321–28; D'Antonio, *American Nursing*, 160; Judd et al., *History of American Nursing*, 34, 45, 67, 139; O'Lynn, "History of Men in Nursing," 24; Reverby, *Ordered to Care*, 2, 9; Williams, *Still a Man's World*, 23, 30–31; Russell E. Tranbarger, "American Schools of Nursing for Men," in O'Lynn and Tranbarger, *Men in Nursing*, 46.

18. Williams, *Still a Man's World*, 35–36. Leslie Reagan notes a similar contraction of opportunities for midwives at the turn of the century, as a handful of female physicians sought to gain a foothold in obstetrics by distancing themselves from midwives. Reagan, *When Abortion Was a Crime*, 15, 93.

19. "Men Make Good Nurses," *New York Times*, February 17, 1896, 7.

20. Gail Bederman, *Manliness and Civilization*; Barbara Brooks Tomblin, *G.I. Nightingales: The Army Nurse Corps in World War II* (Lexington: University Press of Kentucky, 1996), 2.

21. Ruth Nathan Anderson, "The Image of Males in the Nursing Field Needs Intensive Care," *Chicago Tribune*, July 27, 1982, B1.

22. Noreen M. Wielgus, "Insight into a Leader: Luther P. Christman," 11, ca. 1994, "Biographical Allusions to Christman" folder, box 14, Luther Christman Collection, Division of Special Collections, Boston University, Boston, Mass. (hereafter "LCC"); Elizabeth Pittman, *Luther Christman: A Maverick Nurse—a Nursing Legend* (Victoria, British Columbia: Trafford, 2005), 39, 41.

23. Carol Kleiman, "Luther Christman, R.N.: Call This Doctor a Nurse," *Chicago Tribune*, November 26, 1978, M1.

24. O'Lynn, "History of Men in Nursing," 29; Williams, *Gender Differences at Work*, 91; Joan Evans, "Men Nurses: A Historical and Feminist Perspective," *Journal of Advanced Nursing* 47 (July 2004): 321–28.

25. William H. Beha, "What the Man Nurse Contributes," *American Journal of Nursing* 41 (December 1941): 1380.

26. Emma Harrison, "Need Is Stressed for Male Nurses," *New York Times*, October 4, 1955, 19; "U.S. Needs Male Nurses for Prisons," *Pittsburgh Courier*, May 8, 1965, 12.

27. "A Brief Chronology of the History of Men in Nursing," *Interaction: Newsletter of the American Assembly for Men in Nursing* 14 (Spring 1996): 10; "American Assembly for Men in Nursing" folder, box 16, LCC; O'Lynn, "History of Men in Nursing," 29.

28. "The Services Need More Nurses," *Saturday Evening Post*, August 7, 1943, 104; Pete Martin, "Angels in Long Underwear," *Saturday Evening Post*, July 31, 1943, 9.

29. O'Lynn, "History of Men in Nursing," 27.

30. Tomblin, *G.I. Nightingales*, 211; O'Lynn, "History of Men in Nursing," 27.

31. Tomblin, *G.I. Nightingales*, 204.

32. O'Lynn, "History of Men in Nursing," 27; Tomblin, *G.I. Nightingales*, 11; Williams, *Gender Differences at Work*, 42; Tranbarger, "American Schools of Nursing for Men," 47.

33. Luther Christman to Lois Heckman, October 27, 1975, folder 1, box 1, LCC. As the Army Nurse Corps was desegregated, the proportion of male nurses rose much higher than the general field of nursing. The ANC was 13.1 percent male in 1964 and 20.2 percent male in 1966. Kara Dixon Vuic, *Officer, Nurse, Woman: The Army Nurse Corps in the Vietnam War* (Baltimore: Johns Hopkins Press, 2010), 17.

34. "Male Student Nurse Finds Advantages at School, Job," *Chicago Daily Defender*, May 10, 1958, 15; Marilyn Marshall, "Nursing: Not Just for Women Anymore," *Ebony*, December 1981,

folder 12, box 2, LCC; "Husband Decides to Become a Nurse," *Chicago Daily Defender*, June 4, 1974, 19; Adrian Schoenmaker and David M. Radosevich, "Men Nursing Students: How They Perceive Their Situation . . . Conflict Between Expectation and Reality," *Nursing Outlook* 24 (May 1976): 298–305; Reg Arthur Williams, "Characteristics of Male Baccalaureate Students Who Selected Nursing as a Career," *Nursing Research* 22 (November–December 1973): 520–25; Bernard E. Segal, "Male Nurses: A Case Study in Status Contradiction and Prestige Loss," *Social Forces* 41 (October 1962): 31–38. Gary D. Okrainec, "Perceptions of Nursing Education Held by Male Nursing Students," *Western Journal of Nursing Research* 16 (February 1994): 94–107.

35. Marilyn Marshall, "Nursing: Not Just for Women Anymore," *Ebony*, December 1981, folder 12, box 2, LCC; "Male Student Nurse Finds Advantages at School, Job," *Chicago Daily Defender*, May 10, 1958, 15.

36. "Husband Decides to Become a Nurse," 19.

37. On men and nurses' wages, see Lorraine D. Marsh, "Men Wanted," *American Journal of Nursing* 65 (February 1965): 59; Paul Mulkins, "Man's Eye View," *American Journal of Nursing* 65 (April 1965): 53; and John W. Robinson, "Nursing Is for Men," *American Journal of Nursing* 65 (October 1965): 56.

38. O'Lynn, "History of Men in Nursing," 31. The percentage of American doctors who were women increased from 7.6 percent in 1970 to 25.8 percent in 2003. Roxanne Nelson, "Men in Nursing: Still Too Few," *American Journal of Nursing* 106 (February 2006): 25–26.

39. 110 Cong. Rec. 2718 (1964).

40. The U.S. Supreme Court has addressed the BFOQ in two cases: *Dothard v. Rawlinson*, 433 U.S. 321 (1977) and *Automobile Workers v. Johnson Controls, Inc.*, 499 U.S. 187 (1991).

41. *York v. Story*, 324 F.2d 450, 455 (9th Cir. 1963); *Dothard v. Rawlinson*, 433 U.S. 321 (1977); Elsa M. Shartsis, "Privacy as Rationale for the Sex-Based BFOQ," *Detroit College Law Review* 1985 (Fall 1985): 865–902; *Brooks v. ACF Industries*, 537 F. Supp. 1122, (S.D. W.Va. 1982); *Norwood v. Dale Maintenance Systems, Inc.*, 590 F. Supp. 1410, 1418 (N.D. Ill. 1984); *Owens v. Rush*, 654 F.2d 1370 (10th Cir. 1981); *Gunther v. Iowa State Men's Reformatory*, 612 F.2d 1079, 1087 (8th Cir. 1980); *Bagley v. Watson*, 579 F. Supp. 1099, 1103–4 (D. Or. 1983); *Michenfelder v. Sumner*, 860 F.2d 328, 333 (9th Cir. 1988); *Torres v. Wisconsin Department of Health and Social Services*, 838 F.2d 944, 953 (7th Cir. 1988); *Robino v. Iranon*, 145 F.3d 1109, 1111 (9th Cir. 1998).

42. Sonia Pressman Fuentes, "Detroit Speech," presented to United Auto Workers Women's Department, p. 3, April 11, 1967, folder 1305, PMP.

43. Prior to Wilson's case, in the 1967 dispute *Kaiser Foundation Hospital and Medical Centers*, a labor arbitrator found that female status was a BFOQ for nurses performing "sensitive personal care" for female patients. *Kaiser Foundation Hospital and Medical Centers* 67-2 Lab. Arb. Awards (CCH) (1967).

44. 488 F.2d 1338 (1973); Elsa M. Shartsis, "Privacy as Rationale for the Sex-Based BFOQ," *Detroit College Law Review* 1985 (Fall 1985): 865–902.

45. Annas, "Law and the Life Sciences"; Bartlett, "Only Girls Wear Barrettes"; Berman, "Defining the 'Essence of the Business'"; Calloway, "Equal Employment"; Kapczynski, "Same-Sex"; Manley, "BFOQ Defense"; McGown, "The Bona Fide Body"; Wilhelm, "Perpetuating Stereotypical Views of Women"; Yuracko, "Private Nurses and Playboy Bunnies."

46. *Fesel v. Masonic Home of Delaware, Inc.*, 477 F. Supp. 1346 (D. Del. 1978), aff'd mem., 591 F.2d 1334 (3rd Cir. 1979).

47. *Backus v. Baptist Medical Center*, 510 F. Supp. 1191, 1194–95 (E.D. Ark. 1981, vacated on other grounds, 8th Cir. 1982); "Labor Letter: A Special News Report on People and their Jobs in

Offices, Fields and Factories," *Wall Street Journal*, February 16, 1982, 1. See also *EEOC v. Mercy Health Center*, 29 FEP (BNA) 159 (W.D. Okla. 1982); *Jones v. Hinds General Hospital*, 666 F. Supp. 933, 44 FEP 1076 (S.D. Miss. 1987); *Jennings v. New York State Office of Mental Health*, 786 F. Supp. 376 (S.D. N.Y.), affirmed 977 F.2d 731 (2d Cir. 1992); *Healey v. Southwood Psychiatric Hospital*, 78 F.3d 128, 133 (3d Cir. 1996); *Olsen v. Marriott International*, 75 F. Supp. 2d 1052 (D. Ariz. 1999); *EEOC v. Hi 40 Corp.*, 953 F. Supp. 301, 303–4 (W.D. Mo. 1996); *Dale Spragg v. Shore Care and Shore Memorial Hospital*, 293 N.J. Super. 33, 679 A.2d 685; N.J. Super. LEXIS 302 (1996).

48. *Mississippi University for Women v. Hogan*, 458 U.S. 718 (1982).

49. *William Rolison v. Bozeman Deaconess Health Services Inc.*, 2005 MT 95; 326 Mont. 491; 111 P.3d 202; 2005 Mont. LEXIS 171, April 19, 2005.

50. *Gary Hamner v. St. Vincent Hospital and Health Care Center* (7th Cir. 2000), 224 F.3d 701; 83 FEP (BNA) 1265; 78 Empl. Prac. Dec. (CCH) P40, 170, 2000. See also *Charles Billings, Appellant, v. Jesse Brown, Secretary, Department of Veterans Affairs, Agency*, Appeal No. 01944295, 1994 EEOPUB LEXIS 1875, Nov. 4, 1994; *Charles Copkney, Complainant, v. Anthony J. Principi, Secretary, Department of Veterans Affairs, Agency*, Appeal No. 01A22074 Agency No. 200L-1995, 2003 EEOPUB LEXIS 2411, Apr. 30, 2003; *William Gillespie, Complainant, v. R. James Nicholson, Secretary, Department of Veterans Affairs, Agency*, Hearing No. 140-2004-00112X Appeal No. 01A51179 Agency No. 2004-0659-2003102927, 2005 EEOPUB LEXIS 1111, Mar. 14, 2005; and *Kenneth Stohlman, Complainant, v. Anthony J. Principi, Secretary, Department of Veterans Affairs, Agency*, Appeal No. 01A10309 Agency No. 993209, 2002 EEOPUB LEXIS 4813, July 29, 2002.

51. Myron D. Fottler, "Attitudes of Female Nurses Toward the Male Nurse: A Study of Occupational Segregation," *Journal of Health and Social Behavior* 17 (June 1976): 99–111; E. Joel Heikes, "When Men Are the Minority: The Case of Men in Nursing," *Sociological Quarterly* 32 (Autumn 1991): 389–401; Gregory A. Johnson, "Obstetric Nursing Is for Men, Too," *American Journal of Nursing* 66 (December 1966): 2714–15; "Male Nurses: What They Think About Themselves—and Others," *RN* 46 (October 1983): 61–64; Hal Rogness, "Men Nursing Students: How They Perceive Their Situation . . . a Student Surveys His Classmates," *Nursing Outlook* 24 (May 1976): 298–305; and Henry K. Silver and Patricia A. McAtee, "Health Care Practice: An Expanded Profession of Nursing for Men and Women," *American Journal of Nursing* 72 (January 1972): 78–80.

52. Carol Kleiman, "Nurses Are Getting Out of the Woodwork," *Chicago Tribune*, November 26, 1978, M1. On Christman's career, see, for example, Virginia Baird, "Luther Christman Goes to Bat for Male Nurses," *State Journal* (Lansing, Mich.), September 2, 1962, D3, folder 12, box 2, LCC; Cynthia Derr, "Profiles in Nursing: Rush University's Luther Christman," *Nursing Jobs News*, December 1982, 12, "Nursing Jobs News" folder, box 8, LCC; Michele Horaney, "Homewood's Luther Christman: No Reason More Men Shouldn't Be Nurses, Dean Says," *Star*, September 2, 1982, S13, folder 13, box 3, LCC.

53. Barbara Ehrenreich and Deirdre English, *Witches, Midwives and Nurses: A History of Women Healers* (Brooklyn, N.Y.: Faculty, 1973), 40; "Women in Our Health Care System, or Caution: Health Care May Be Dangerous to Your Health," "Healthcare—Position Papers" folder, Women's Ephemera Collection, Charles Deering Library, Northwestern University, Evanston, Ill.; "CWLU Health Project 1972," undated, folder 5, box 1, Jenny Knauss Papers, series 93, Charles Deering Library, Northwestern University, Evanston, Ill. (hereafter "JKP"); Esther Moscow, "Dear Sister," May 28, 1972, series 93, folder 5, box 1, JKP; "Report of a Workshop: Women in Medicine-Action Planning for the 1970s," "Medical College of Pennsylvania Center for Women

in Medicine" folder, Women's Ephemera Collection, Charles Deering Library, Northwestern University, Evanston, Ill.; "Nurses NOW Accomplishments," undated, folder 2, box 48, NOW.

54. Jerome P. Lyslaught, "A Luther Christman Anthology," *Nurses Digest* 6 (Summer 1978): 15, folder 9, box 1, LCC; WLS TV Chicago, "Times Changing Regarding Work," November 23, 1980, folder 14, box 3, LCC; Jack Mabley, "Male Nurse Target of Bias in Reverse," *Chicago Tribune,* February 23, 1979, 4; Pittman, *Luther Christman,* 122–24; Christman to Heckman, February 3, 1976, 2–3, folder 1, box 1, LCC; Russell E. Tranbarger, "The American Assembly for Men in Nursing: The First 30 Years as Reported in *Interaction*," in O'Lynn and Tranbarger, eds., *Men in Nursing,* 68.

55. Katrina Burtt, "Issues Update: Male Nurses Still Face Bias," *American Journal of Nursing* 98 (September 1998): 64–65; "Male Nurse Not Out of Obstetrics Just 'Cause He's a Man, High Court Says," *West Virginia Nurse,* April 1, 2004, 2; Rebecca Porter, "Hospital Fails to Justify Refusal to Hire Male Obstetrical Nurses," *Trial* 40 (May 2004): 104; Tim Porter-O'Grady, "Reverse Discrimination in Nursing: Hitting the Concrete Ceiling," in O'Lynn and Tranbarger, eds., *Men in Nursing,* ch. 7; Williams, *Gender Differences at Work,* 7, 81–108; Warren Richey, "Nurse Sues Broward County Hospital: Man Says He Was Fired from Maternity Ward Because of His Gender," *South Florida Sun-Sentinel* (Fort Lauderdale), September 17, 1994, 3B.

56. Berube, "'Queer Work' and Labor History"; Adams, " Servicing of America."

57. On the homophile movement, see, for example, John D'Emilio, *Sexual Politics, Sexual Communities,* 57–219; Faderman, *Odd Girls and Twilight Lovers,* 190–94; Gallo, *Different Daughters*; Marotta, *The Politics of Homosexuality,* esp. 42–43; Martin Meeker, *Contacts Desired: Gay and Lesbian Communications and Community, 1940s-1970s* (Chicago: University of Chicago Press, 2006): 31–108.

58. E. Carrington Boggan, Marilyn G. Haft, Charles Lister, and John P. Rupp, *The Rights of Gay People: The Basic ACLU Guide to a Gay Person's Rights* (New York: Discus, 1975), 24.

59. D'Emilio, *Sexual Politics, Sexual Communities,* 42–43; David K. Johnson, *The Lavender Scare: The Cold War Persecution of Gays and Lesbians in the Federal Government* (Chicago: University of Chicago Press, 2005), esp. 9.

60. Boggan, Haft, Lister, and Rupp, *Rights of Gay People,* 25.

61. William Parker, "Homosexuals and Employment," 1970, folder 39, box 1, CTP.

62. For more such anecdotes, see "Hearings of the Police, Fire and Safety Committee of San Francisco Board of Supervisors," March 9, 1978, "Gay Rights Ordinance" folder, box 8, Harvey Milk Archives–Scott Smith Collection, James C. Hormel Gay and Lesbian Center, San Francisco Public Library (hereafter "HM-SS").

63. Adams, "Servicing of America"; Berube, "'Queer Work' and Labor History"; Tiemeyer, *Plane Queer.*

64. *Skinner v. Oklahoma ex. Rel. Williamson,* 316 U.S. 535 (1942); *Poe v. Ullman,* 367 U.S. 497 (1961); *Griswold v. Connecticut,* 381 U.S. 479 (1965); *Stanley v. Georgia,* 394 U.S. 557 (1969); *Eisenstadt v. Baird,* 405 U.S. 438 (1972); and *Roe v. Wade,* 410 U.S. 113 (1973). "ACLU Official Hails Gays," *Advocate,* March 31–April 13, 1971, 14; "ACLU Position on Homosexuality," January 7, 1967, folder 7, box 1127, American Civil Liberties Union Archives, 1950–90, Series 3 (hereafter "ACLU"); Judy Kutulas, *The American Civil Liberties Union and the Making of Modern Liberalism, 1930–1960* (Chapel Hill: University of North Carolina Press, 2005); and Leigh Ann Wheeler, *How Sex Became a Civil Liberty* (New York: Oxford University Press, 2013), 93–119; 153–77.

65. "ACLU Position on Homosexuality."

66. *Scott v. Macy*, 121 U.S. App. D.C. 205, 349 F.2d 182 (1965); *Ward v. Firestone*, 260 F. Supp. 579 (W.D. Tenn. 1966); *Norton v. Macy*, 135 U.S. App. D.C. 214, 417 F.2d 1161 (1969). 5 C.F.R. 731.202(b). See also Patricia A. Cain, "Litigating for Lesbian and Gay Rights: A Legal History," *Virginia Law Review* 79 (October 1993): 1576–78; D'Emilio, *Sexual Politics, Sexual Communities*, 150–57; and David K. Johnson, "Homosexual Citizens: Washington's Gay Community Confronts the Civil Service," *Washington History* (Fall–Winter 1994–95): 44–63. *Singer v. U.S. Civil Service Commission*, 530 F.2d 247 (9th Cir. 1977), 429 U.S. 1034 (1977).

67. See Tommi Avicolli Mecca, "Introduction," *Smash the Church! Smash the State!* ed. Mecca (San Francisco: City Light Books, 2009), ix–xvi; Suran, "Coming Out Against the War."

68. Virginia Brooks, *Minority Stress and Lesbian Women* (Lexington, Mass.: Lexington Books, 1981); Janet S. Chafetz et al., "A Study of Homosexual Women," *Social Work* 19 (November 1974): 714–23; and Martin P. Levine and Robin Leonard, "Discrimination Against Lesbians in the Work Force," *Signs* 9 (Summer 1984): 700–710.

69. See, for example, Enke, *Finding the Movement*; Gallo, *Different Daughters*, 154–56; Daniel Winunwe Rivers, *Radical Relations*; Marc Stein, *City of Sisterly and Brotherly Loves: Lesbian and Gay Philadelphia, 1945-1972* (Philadelphia: Temple University Press, 2004); and Valk, *Radical Sisters*.

70. Gilmore and Kaminski, "A Part and Apart," 103; Faderman, *Odd Girls and Twilight Lovers*, 198, 211–20; Gallo, *Different Daughters*, 186.

71. *In Re Kreps*, N-14221, Civil Service Commission, Contra Costa County, California, March 3, 1980. See also Rivera, "Queer Law," 459–540; and Ann Rostow, "NCLR Earns Its Stripes," *Advocate*, June 7, 2005, 33.

72. Jonathan Bell, "To Strive for Economic and Social Justice," 193–94; and Bell, *California Crucible*. For more detail on gay workplace rights organizing, see Katherine Turk, " 'Our Militancy Is in Our Openness': Gay Employment Rights Activism in California and the Question of Sexual Orientation Under Title VII," *Law and History Review* 31 (May 2013): 423–69; John D'Emilio, *Sexual Politics, Sexual Communities*, esp. 117; Robert O. Self, "Sex in the City: The Politics of Sexual Liberalism in Los Angeles, 1963–79," *Gender and History* 20 (August 2008): 288–311; Tom Ammiano, "My Adventures as a Gay Teacher," in *Smash the Church, Smash the State!* 40–42; Gallo, *Different Daughters*; Randy Schilts, *The Mayor of Castro Street: The Life and Times of Harvey Milk* (New York: St. Martin's Press, 2008); and White, *Pre-Gay LA*.

73. Jay Murley to Gay Rights Committee, May–June 1973, folder 1, box 5, Rob Cole Papers, ONE National Gay and Lesbian Archives, Los Angeles, Calif. (hereafter "RCP"); "A History: The Los Angeles Gay Rights Movement," ACLU Human Rights Award Dinner, June 1, 1979, folder 11, box 2, RCP; Undated memo re: Chapter History, folder 1, box 1, American Civil Liberties Union of Southern California Lesbian and Gay Rights Chapter Records, ONE National Gay and Lesbian Archives, Los Angeles, Calif. (hereafter "ACLU-GRC"); "Gay Community Services Center Acquires Site," 1971 Press Release, Gay Community Services Center, folder 5, box 4, LAGLC; Press Release, March 15, 1978, folder 10, box 4, LAGLC; Helen McElroy to Jerry Gold, July 5, 1974, folder 59, box 7, LAGLC; Joan Johnson, Employment Counselor at Metropolitan Community Church of Los Angeles, to Jerry Gold, undated, folder 59, box 7, LAGLC.

74. Boyd, *Wide Open Town*, 5, 7; D'Emilio, *Sexual Politics, Sexual Communities*, 117; Schilts, *Mayor of Castro Street.*

75. Alice Echols, *Hot Stuff: Disco and the Remaking of American Culture* (New York: Norton, 2010), 121–28; Suran, "Coming Out Against the War"; Leo Laurence, "Glide Boycotts SF Firms That Won't Hire Homosexuals," *Advocate*, November 1967, 2; "A Guide to Revolutionary

Homosexual Draft Resistance," folder 1, box 9, Records of the Pacific Counseling Service and Military Records, Bancroft Library, University of California at Berkeley, Berkeley (hereafter "PCS"). "Homo Revolt: Don't Hide It," *Berkeley Barb*, March 28–April 3, 1969, 5, folder 1, box 1, CTP; *ACLU of Southern California Gay Rights Newsletter*, February 1978, folder 2, box 17, ACLU-GRC; "Gay, Straight Leaders Push SF Hiring Law," *Advocate*, September 15–28, 1971, 14; California State Senator Art Agnos, Sixteenth District Assemblyman, May 5, 1977, folder 2, box 7, ACLU-GRC; Paul D. Hardman, California Committee for Equal Rights, to John Monzakis, ACLU Legislative Committee, May 5, 1977, folder 2, box 7, ACLU-GRC; "It's Your Job That's on the Line!" folder 10, box 20, ACLU-GRC; "News Flash," folder 5, box 4, ACLU-GRC; Suran, "Coming Out Against the War," 455.

76. Richard Gayer, Employment Rights Committee, ACLU of Northern California, to Roger Taylor, Assistant to the Chief, Fair Employment Practices Commission, July 25, 1973, re: Appearance Before Commission, August 2, 1973, "Fair Employment Practices Commission (California)" subject file, ONE National Gay and Lesbian Archives, University of Southern California Libraries, Los Angeles, Calif. (hereafter "ONE"); and PT&T Anti-Gay Policy, "Fair Employment Practices Commission (California)" subject file, ONE.

77. Mendenhall, "Ma Bell Clings to Anti-Gay Policy in Liberated SF"; "State Agency Upholds Pacific Telephone's Rejection of SIR Ad," *Advocate*, January 6–19, 1971, 1; "Ma Bell Gives In to SIR—but Gays Want It to Be Legal," *Advocate*, September 1–14, 1971, 6.

78. Herr, *Women, Power, and AT&T*; Shapiro, "Women on the Line, Men at the Switchboard"; John Brooks, *Telephone: The First Hundred Years* (New York: Harper and Row, 1975), 10; "Openly Gay at AT&T?" *Advocate*, October 20, 1976, 9; "Northwestern Settles Past Bias as Ma Bell Decrees: No More!" *Advocate*, August 28, 1974, 2; George Mendenhall, "Ma Bell Clings to Anti-Gay Policy in Liberated SF," *Advocate*, January 3, 1973, 6.

79. "Won't Hire Gay, Says Ma Bell, But . . . ," *Advocate*, November 10, 1971, 5; Mendenhall, "Ma Bell Clings to Anti-Gay Policy in Liberated SF."

80. Letter from Don to Rob Coleman, July 31, 1972, "Telephone-Gay Issues" subject file, ONE; Mark Vandervelden, "Pacific Bell to Pay $3 Million to Gays: Company Settles Out of Court in Antigay Discrimination Suit," *Advocate*, January 6, 1987, 13; "Won't Hire Gay, Says Ma Bell, But . . ."; "Ma Bell Clings to Anti-Gay Policy in Liberated SF."

81. "PT&T Eyes Hiring Policy," *Advocate*, July 5, 1972, 13. On post-World War II military discharges and future employment, see Margot Canaday, *Straight State*, 137-72.

82. George Mendenhall, "S.F. Rights Commission Takes on Ma Bell," *Advocate*, July 30, 1975, 4.

83. "Pacific Telephone Challenged," *Advocate*, March 13, 1974, 5; "Equal Opportunity Breakthroughs and Setbacks," *Advocate*, March 9, 1977, 17.

84. Human Rights Commission of the City and County of San Francisco, 12th Annual Report, January 1976–January 1977, Human Rights Commission 12th Annual Report folder, box 8, HM-SS.

85. Richard Gayer, Employment Rights Committee, ACLU of Northern California, to Roger Taylor, Assistant to the Chief, Fair Employment Practices Commission, July 25, 1973, re: Appearance Before Commission, August 2, 1973, re: PT&T Anti-Gay Policy, "Fair Employment Practices Commission (California)" subject file, ONE; "Utility Officials Agree: Employment Equality 'Just Goal,'" *Advocate*, August 15, 1973, 5.

86. "Dear Friend," Hastings College of Law Gay Law Students Association, January 26, 1976, "Attorneys" subject file, ONE. Several months later, the ACLU filed similar charges against

Northwestern Bell, headquartered in Minnesota. In 1974, Northwestern Bell promised to comply with the Minneapolis city ban against homosexual discrimination. "Battle of Ma Bell Spreads to Minnesota," *Advocate*, August 29, 1973, 13; "Ma Bell Will Switch, Not Fight Law," *Advocate*, May 8, 1974, 12.

87. Don to Rob Coleman, July 31, 1972, "Telephone-Gay Issues" subject file, ONE.

88. "Minister's Personal Data Sheet," August 7, 1974, Personal and MCC Professional Correspondence folder, box 1, Robert DeSantis Papers, Gay, Lesbian, Bisexual, Transgender Historical Society, San Francisco, California (hereafter "RDP"); "Second Application to Become a Licensed Minister," June 23, 1974, Personal and MCC Professional Correspondence folder, box 1, RDP.

89. Robert DeSantis, "With Unity," *MCC Newsletter*, April 16, 1972, Personal and MCC Professional Correspondence folder, box 1, RDP.

90. "Class Action Suit Filed Against Ma Bell," *Advocate*, November 1975, 15; Wayne Chew, "Title VII Rights of Homosexuals," *Golden Gate Law Review* 10 (1980): 53; Arthur S. Leonard, *Sexuality and the Law: An Encyclopedia of Major Legal Cases* (New York: Garland, 1993), 406–9.

91. *Phillips v. Martin Marietta Corporation*, 400 U.S. 542 (1971); *Griggs v. Duke Power Co.*, 424.

92. *DeSantis v. Pacific Telephone and Telegraph*, 330. See also *Holloway v. Arthur Andersen & Co.*, 566 F.3d 659, 662–63 (9th Cir. 1977). The "traditional notions of sex" interpretation was upheld in the 2002 case *Rene v. MGM Grand Hotel*, 305 F.3d 1061 (9th Cir. 2002), in which the 9th Circuit held that "sex" and "gender" may be interchangeable, but that neither encompassed sexual orientation. See "Employment Law. Title VII. Sex Discrimination. Ninth Circuit Extends Title VII Protection to Employee Alleging Discrimination Based on Sexual Orientation. *Rene v. MGM Grand Hotel, Inc.*, 305 F.3d 1061 (9th Cir. 2002) (en banc), Petition for Cert. Filed, 71 U. S. L. W. 3444 (U. S. December 23, 2002) (No. 02-970)," *Harvard Law Review* 116 (April 2003): 1889–96.

93. EEOC Decision No. 76-75, 1976 Empl. Prac. Guide CCH EEOC Decisions (1983), 6495; EEOC Decision No. 76-67; 1976 Empl. Prac. Guide CCH EEOC Decisions (1983), 6493.

94. *DeSantis v. Pacific Telephone and Telegraph*, 331.

95. *DeSantis* followed a line of decisions permitting sanctions against workers who revealed their homosexuality on the job. See *Gaylord v. Tacoma School District No. 10*, 88 Wash. 2d (1977); *Safransky v. State Personnel Board*, 62 Wisc. 2d 464 215 N.W. 2d 379 (1979); and *McConnell v. Anderson*, 451 F.2d 193 (8th Cir. 1971).

96. Iver Peterson, "Homosexuals Gain Support on Campus," *New York Times*, June 5, 1974, 1.

97. *Gay Law Students Assn. v. Pacific Telephone and Telegraph Company*, 24 Cal. 3d 458; Gay Law Students Association, UC-Hastings College of Law, "Dear Friend," January 26, 1976, "Attorneys" subject file, ONE; "Landmark California Court Ruling," *Advocate*, July 12, 1979, 7; Leonard, *Sexuality and the Law*, 410–17; Douglas Warner, "Homophobia, Manifest Homosexuals and Political Activity," *Golden Gate Law Review* 11 (1981): 641.

98. *Gay Law Students Assn. v. Pacific Telephone and Telegraph*, 488.

99. Eugene Robinson, "Gays Win in High Court on Job Bias," *San Francisco Chronicle*, June 1, 1979; Don Knutson, "Landmark Rights Case for Gays: An Analysis," *Advocate*, July 12, 1979, 9.

100. Vandervelden, "Pacific Bell to Pay $3 Million to Gays," 13; and Leonard, *Sexuality and the Law*, 410, 417. In 1992, the California legislature amended its state labor code to include an explicit ban on employment discrimination against homosexuals in all public and private employment, except nonprofit organizations. See Cal. Lab. Code 1102.1.

101. *Parfitt v. D. L. Auld Co.*, No. 74-437 (S.D. Ohio 1975); *Blum v. Gulf Oil Co.*, 597 F.2d 936 (5th Cir. 1979); *Smith v. Liberty Mutual Insurance Co.*, 569 F.2d 325 (5th Cir. 1978); *Holloway v. Arthur Andersen & Co.*, 566 F.2d 659 (9th Cir. 1977); *Ulane v. Eastern Air Lines Inc.*, 742 F.2d 1081 (7th Cir. 1984).

102. Rivera, "Queer Law," 471.

103. Knutson, "Landmark Rights Case for Gays." Some legal scholars in the 1990s saw the potential for more expansive protections for gays under the "conduct as speech" framework. See William N. Eskridge Jr. and David D. Cole, "From Handholding to Sodomy: The First Amendment and the Regulation of Homosexual Conduct," *Harvard Civil Rights–Civil Liberties Law Review* 29 (1994): 320.

104. *In Re Kreps; County of Orange v. Orange County Employees Association*, No. 72-30-0201-81, July 27, 1981; Rivera, "Queer Law," 508–14; National Center for Lesbian Rights, "NCLR: Celebrating 35 Years of Making History," *On the Docket*, Fall 2011, 1,http://www.nclrights.org/site /DocServer/NCLR_Newsletter_Fall2011.pdf?docID=9101, accessed February 2, 2012.

105. Mumford, "Trouble with Gay Rights"; Gillian Frank, "'The Civil Rights of Parents': Race and Conservative Politics in Anita Bryant's Campaign Against Gay Rights in 1970s Florida," *Journal of the History of Sexuality* 22 (January 2013): 126–60; "ACLU–Southern California Gay Rights Guardian," July 1979, folder 3, box 17, ACLU-GRC; "Employment Rights Round-Up— Where We Are, Where We're Going," *Advocate*, January 29, 1975, 9. "Sexual Orientation and Employment Discrimination," ca. 1980, folder 12, box 3, Jim Long Papers, LAGLC; Philip Hager, "SF Police Going After Gays . . . to Join the Force," *Los Angeles Times*, April 1, 1979, 1; "New Protections for Homosexuals," *Los Angeles Times*, June 21, 1983, C4; "ACLU–Southern California Gay Rights Guardian," August 1979, folder 3, box 17, ACLU-GRC; Nickerson, *Mothers of Conservatism*.

106. Jackie M. Blount, *Fit to Teach: Same-Sex Desire, Gender and School Work in the Twentieth Century* (Albany: State University of New York Press, 2006), 135–55; cad, "gays battle briggotry," *off our backs* 8 (August–September 1978): 7; Margaret Cruikshank, "Reflection," *Radical Teacher* 7 (Spring 2003): 15; Al Martinez, "Snubs, Name-Calling Greet Gay Working to Defeat Prop. 6," *Los Angeles Times*, October 9, 1978, A3; "Battle over Gay Rights," *Newsweek*, June 6, 1977, 16–20; "A Self-Serving Politician Has Dreamed Up a Moral Crusade. And He Wants You to Pay for It," box 6, HM-SS. Ammiano, "My Adventures as a Gay Teacher"; William Endicott, "Gay Teacher and Antismoking Initiatives Lose," *Los Angeles Times*, November 8, 1978, A6.

107. Tiemeyer, *Plane Queer*, 194–219; Nicole Raeburn, *Changing Corporate America From Inside Out: Lesbian and Gay Workplace Rights* (Minneapolis: University of Minnesota Press, 2004); Gaines Hollingsworth, "Corporate Gay Bashing: Which Companies Discriminate Against Gays and Lesbians, and How to Fight Back," *Advocate*, September 11, 1990, 28; "Corporate Policies on Gay Rights," *Advocate*, May 31, 1978, 12; Human Rights Campaign, "Corporate Equality Index," http://www.hrc.org/issues/workplace/cei.htm, accessed March 31, 2010; John Gallagher, "American Airlines Says It Wants to Repair Its Contentious Relationship with Gays and Lesbians, but Is It Sincere?" *Advocate*, September 6, 1994, 29; "Gay Activists Launch TV Ad Campaign Boycotting United Airlines," *Business Wire*, March 31, 1999, http://www.allbusiness.com /marketing-advertising/marketing-advertising-overview/6776468-1.html, accessed May 14, 2010; and Michael Arndt, "United Tries for Gay-Friendly Skies," *Business Week*, May 24, 2000, http:// www.businessweek.com/bwdaily/dnflash/may2000/nf00524b.htm, accessed May 14, 2010.

108. Vicki L. Eaklor, *Queer America: A People's GLBT History of the 20th Century*, 216.

109. See, for example, MacLean, *Freedom is Not Enough*; and Skrentny, *The Minority Rights Revolution*.

110. Mary Ann Case argues that discrimination against effeminacy is a bellwether for the rights of working women. Case, "Disaggregating Gender from Sex and Sexual Orientation."

Chapter 7. Opting Out or Buying In

1. Gwen Ifill, "The 1992 Campaign: Hillary Clinton Defends Her Conduct in Law Firm," *New York Times*, March 17, 1992, A20.

2. Karen Lehman, "Beware the Cookie Monster," *New York Times*, July 18, 1992, 23; Marian Burros, "Now Is the Time to Come to the Aid of Your Favorite Cookies," *New York Times*, July 15, 1992, C6.

3. Bureau of the Census, Economics and Statistics Administration, United States Department of Commerce, "We the American . . . Women," 4, 7, September 1993, http://www.census.gov /apsd/wepeople/we-8.pdf, accessed May 17, 2012.

4. Susan Chira, "A Day Daughters Skip School and Go to Work: Girls Are Given a Special Day," *New York Times*, April 29, 1994, A1; "Labor Letter: Girls Get Their Turn," *Wall Street Journal*, April 20, 1993, A1; Martha Sherrill, "No Boys Allowed: At the White House Staff Gets a Workout During Daughters to Work Day," *Washington Post*, April 29, 1994, C1.

5. Bill Carter, "Back Talk from 'Murphy Brown' to Dan Quayle," *New York Times*, July 20, 1992, C14; "Murphy Brown's Baby," *Wall Street Journal*, September 21, 1992, A12.

6. Pub. L. 102–66.

7. *Testimony of Anita F. Hill, Hearings Before the Committee on the Judiciary, United States Senate, October 11, 1991, One Hundred Second Congress, First Session, on the Nomination of Clarence Thomas to be Associate Justice of the Supreme Court of the United States* (Washington, D.C.: U.S. Government Printing Office, 1991); *Testimony of Clarence Thomas, Hearings Before the Committee on the Judiciary, United States Senate, October 13, 1991, One Hundred Second Congress, First Session, on the Nomination of Clarence Thomas to be Associate Justice of the Supreme Court of the United States* (Washington, D.C.: U.S. Government Printing Office, 1991); Toni Morrison, ed., *Race-ing Justice, En-Gendering Power: Essays on Anita Hill, Clarence Thomas, and the Construction of Social Reality* (New York: Pantheon, 1992); Robert Chrisman and Robert L. Allen, eds., *Court of Appeal: The Black Community Speaks Out on the Racial and Sexual Politics of Clarence Thomas vs. Anita Hill* (New York: Ballantine, 1992); Jane Flax, *The American Dream in Black and White: The Clarence Thomas Hearings* (Ithaca, N.Y.: Cornell University Press, 1998); Timothy M. Phelps and Helen Winternitz, *Capitol Games: Clarence Thomas, Anita Hill, and the Story of a Supreme Court Nomination* (New York: Hyperion, 1992); Anita Hill, *Speaking Truth to Power* (New York: Doubleday, 1997); and David Brock, *The Real Anita Hill: The Untold Story* (New York: Free Press, 1993).

8. "'Year of the Woman,' as Predicted," *New York Times*, November 4, 1992, A1.

9. Susan Faludi, *Backlash: The Undeclared War Against American Women* (New York: Crown, 1991), 2.

10. Bureau of the Census, Economics and Statistics Administration, United States Department of Commerce, "We the American . . . Women," 8, September 1993, http://www.census.gov /apsd/wepeople/we-8.pdf, accessed May 17, 2012; Susan Douglas, "The Year of What Woman?" *Progressive* 56 (September 1992): 11.

11. Harrell R. Rodgers, *Poor Women, Poor Children: American Poverty in the 1990s*, 3rd Edition (Armonk, N.Y.: M. E. Sharpe: 1996), 4.

12. Felice N. Schwartz, "Management Women and the New Facts of Life," *Harvard Business Review*, January 1989, 65–76.

13. Juliet Schor, *The Overworked American: The Unexpected Decline of Leisure* (New York: Basic Books, 1992); Arlie Hochschild with Anne Machung, *The Second Shift: Working Parents and the Revolution at Home* (New York: Viking, 1989).

14. "Johnson Controls Inc.: Our History," http://www.johnsoncontrols.com/publish/us/en /about/our_history.html, accessed December 6, 2010.

15. Affidavit of Jean Beaudoin, August 12, 1986, *International Union, United Auto., etc. v. Johnson Controls*, 84-C-472, United States District Court for the Eastern District of Wisconsin, National Archives and Records Administration, Great Lakes Division, Chicago, Ill. (hereafter "DCEDW-NARA").

16. United States Department of Labor Occupational Safety and Health Administration, OSHA Regulations (Standards-29 CFR), "Occupational Safety and Health Standards: Toxic and Hazardous Substances: 1910.1025: Lead," http://63.234.227.130/SLTC/lead/Health Effects (April 1, 2011).

17. Memo to Battery Plant and Personnel Managers from Robert W. Schildner, Corporate Health and Safety Officer, Globe-Union Inc., re: Women in Lead Exposure, June 9, 1977, *International Union, United Auto., etc. v. Johnson Controls*, 84-C-472, DCEDW-NARA.

18. Affidavit of Jean Beaudoin, Exhibit J, Memo to Battery Plant and Personnel Managers from Robert W. Schildner, Corporate Health and Safety Officer, Globe-Union Inc., re: Women in Lead Exposure, June 9, 1977, *International Union, United Auto., etc. v. Johnson Controls*, 84-C-472, DCEDW-NARA.

19. Affidavit of Jean Beaudoin, Exhibit J, "Recital of Risks," *International Union, United Auto., etc. v. Johnson Controls*, 84-C-472, DCEDW-NARA.

20. Sara Dubow, *Ourselves Unborn: A History of the Fetus in Modern America* (Oxford, U.K. and New York: Oxford University Press, 2011), 113, 120–35.

21. Jean Beaudoin, Testimony Before the California Fair Employment and Housing Department, July 15, 1985, re: "In the Matter of the Accusation of: The Department of Fair Employment and Housing vs. Globe Battery, a Division of Johnson Controls, Respondent; Queen Elizabeth Foster, Complainant," *International Union, United Auto., etc. v. Johnson Controls*, 84-C-472, DCEDW-NARA, 153.

22. Mary E. Becker, "From *Muller v. Oregon* to Fetal Vulnerability Policies," *University of Chicago Law Review* 53 (Autumn 1986): 1226; Robert Blank, "Fetal Protection Policies in the Workplace: Continuing Controversy in Light of Johnson Controls," *Politics and the Life Sciences* (August 1992): 215–29; and Joan I. Samuelson, "Employment Rights of Women in the Toxic Workplace," *California Law Review* 65 (September 1977): 1120–21.

23. Affidavit of Jean Beaudoin, August 12, 1986, *International Union, United Auto., etc. v. Johnson Controls*, 84-C-472, DCEDW-NARA. Peter T. Kilborn, "Who Decides Who Works at Jobs Imperiling Fetuses?" *New York Times*, September 2, 1990, 1.

24. Jean Beaudoin, Testimony Before the California Fair Employment and Housing Department, July 15, 1985, 117–18.

25. Ibid., 118.

26. Jean Beaudoin Affidavit Exhibit A: M. C. Zilis, Johnson Controls Fetal Protection Policy, August 9, 1982, *International Union, United Auto., etc. v. Johnson Controls*, 84-C-472, DCEDW-NARA, 151.

27. Larry Thompson, "Pinpointing the Risk from Lead," *Washington Post*, October 16, 1990, 8.

28. *International Union, United Auto., etc. v. Johnson Controls*, 84-C-472, DCEDW-NARA; Cynthia R. Daniels, *At Women's Expense: State Power and the Politics of Fetal Rights* (Cambridge, Mass.: Harvard University Press, 1993), 63; Carin Ann Clauss, Marsha Berzon, and Joan Bertin, "Litigating Reproductive and Developmental Health in the Aftermath of UAW versus Johnson Controls," *Environmental Health Perspective Supplements* 101 (1993): 206; Evelyn Gilbert, "Women Sue to Challenge Fetal Protection Policies," *National Underwriter*, January 28, 1991, 4, folder 12, box 535, Records of the NOW Legal Defense and Education Fund, 1968-2008, Schlesinger Library, Radcliffe Institute, Harvard University, Cambridge, Mass. (hereafter "NOW LDEF").

29. Ruth Marcus, "'Fetal Protection' Policies: Prudence or Bias?" *Washington Post*, October 8, 1990, A1; Tamar Lewin, "Protecting the Baby: Work in Pregnancy Poses Legal Frontier," *New York Times*, August 2, 1988, A1.

30. Kilborn, "Who Decides Who Works at Jobs Imperiling Fetuses?" 1; Johnson Controls Battery Division Announcement re: Fetal Protection Program Implementation Procedure, February 18, 1986, *International Union, United Auto., etc. v. Johnson Controls*, 84-C-472, DCEDW-NARA.

31. Marcus, "'Fetal Protection' Policies: Prudence or Bias?" A1.

32. Kilborn, "Who Decides Who Works at Jobs Imperiling Fetuses?"

33. Lois A. Sweetman EEOC Charge, April 27, 1983, *International Union, United Auto., etc. v. Johnson Controls*, 84-C-472, DCEDW-NARA; Tamar Lewin, "Battery Producer Loses a Bias Case," *New York Times*, March 3, 1990, 10.

34. Shirley Jean Mackey EEOC Charge, October 10 1983, *International Union, United Auto., etc. v. Johnson Controls*, 84-C-472, DCEDW-NARA.

35. Mary Craig EEOC Charge, January 23, 1984, *International Union, United Auto., etc. v. Johnson Controls*, 84-C-472, DCEDW-NARA.

36. Linda Burdick, Elsie Nason, and Mary Estelle Schmitt EEOC Charge, August 8, 1983, *International Union, United Auto., etc. v. Johnson Controls*, 84-C-472, DCEDW-NARA.

37. Anna May Penney EEOC Charge, February 2, 1984, *International Union, United Auto., etc. v. Johnson Controls*, 84-C-472, DCEDW-NARA; Donald Penney EEOC Charge, January 3, 1984, *International Union, United Auto., etc. v. Johnson Controls*, 84-C-472, DCEDW-NARA; Affidavit of Donald Penney, November 30, 1984, *International Union, United Auto., etc. v. Johnson Controls*, 84-C-472, DCEDW-NARA.

38. Kilborn, "Who Decides Who Works at Jobs Imperiling Fetuses?"

39. Larry Thompson, "Pinpointing the Risk from Lead," *Washington Post*, October 16, 1990, 8.

40. Ibid.

41. Kilborn, "Who Decides Who Works at Jobs Imperiling Fetuses?"

42. Wendy Kaminer, "The Charade of Fetal Protection," *New York Times*, April 29, 1990, E21; "Reproductive Rights Amendments: NOW Legislative Proposals," September 14, 1979, folder 49, box 87, NOW; Lewin, "Protecting the Baby," A1.

43. William E. Schmidt, "Risk to Fetus Ruled as Barring Women from Jobs," *New York Times*, October 3, 1989, A16.

44. Ruth Marcus, "'Fetal Protection' Policies: Prudence or Bias?" A1.

45. Jeanne Mager Stellman and Mary Sue Henifen, "No Fertile Women Need Apply," in *Biological Woman: The Convenient Myth*, ed. Ruth Hubbard (Cambridge: Schenkman, 1982), 120; Teresa Brady, "The Legal Status of Sex-Specific Fetal Protection Policies," *NWSA Journal* 6 (Autumn 1994): 472; Mary E. Becker, "From *Muller v. Oregon* to Fetal Vulnerability Policies," *University of Chicago Law Review* 53 (Autumn 1986): 1240.

46. Kilborn, "Who Decides Who Works at Jobs Imperiling Fetuses?"

47. Ellen Goodman, "Again, a Woman's Choice," *Washington Post*, March 31, 1990, A27.

48. *International Union, United Auto., etc. v. Johnson Controls*, 84-C-472, DCEDW-NARA.

49. Amicus Brief, NOW LDEF, ACLU, et al., *Intl. Union v. Johnson Controls*: Press, 1990–91, folder 11, box 535, NOW LDEF.

50. Steve Lash, "*UAAAIWA v. Johnson Controls, Inc.*: Fighting for Women's Rights in the Workplace," in *A Good Quarrel: America's Top Legal Reporters Share Stories from Inside the Supreme Court*, ed. Timothy R. Johnson and Jerry Goldman (Ann Arbor: University of Michigan Press, 2009), 158–60.

51. Lash, "*UAAAIWA v. Johnson Controls, Inc.*," 162.

52. *Harris v. McRae*, 448 U.S. 297 (1980); Ziegler, *After Roe*, ch. 4.

53. Catharine A. MacKinnon, "Privacy v. Equality: Beyond *Roe v. Wade*," in *Applications of Feminist Legal Theory to Women's Lives*, ed. D. Kelly Weisberg and Ronnie J. Steinberg (Philadelphia: Temple University Press, 1983).

54. Catharine A. MacKinnon, *Feminism Unmodified: Discourses on Life and Law* (Cambridge, Mass.: Harvard University Press, 1988), 95–102. Other critiques of the choice framework include Rickie Solinger, *Beggars and Choosers: How the Politics of Choice Shapes Adoption, Abortion, and Welfare in the United States* (New York: Hill and Wang, 2001), and Robin West, "From Choice to Reproductive Justice: De-Constitutionalizing Abortion Rights," in *In Search of Common Ground on Abortion*, ed. Robin West, Justin Murray and Meredith Esser, (Burlington, Vt.: Ashgate, 2014).

55. "Congress Has Left This Choice to the Woman as Hers to Make," *Washington Post*, March 21, 1991, A15.

56. Consent Decree, October 1, 1993, *International Union, United Auto., etc. v. Johnson Controls*, 84-C-472, DCEDW-NARA; Brief of Defendant Johnson Controls in Support of Proposed Consent Decree, January 14, 1994, *International Union, United Auto., etc. v. Johnson Controls*, 84-C-472, DCEDW-NARA.

57. United States Department of Labor Occupational Safety and Health Administration, OSHA Regulations (Standards-29 CFR), "Occupational Safety and Health Standards: Toxic and Hazardous Substances: 1910.1025: Lead," http://63.234.227.130/SLTC/lead/Health Effects, accessed April 1, 2011.

58. United States Department of Labor Occupational Safety and Health Administration, OSHA Regulations (Standards-29 CFR), "Occupational Safety and Health Standards: Toxic and Hazardous Substances: 1910.1025: Lead," http://63.234.227.130/SLTC/lead/Health Effects, 1910.1025(j)(1)(i)-1910.1025(j)(3)(I)(F),   1910.1025(k)(1)(I)-1910.1025(k)(1)(III)(A)(2),   accessed April 1, 2011.

59. Dubow, *Ourselves Unborn*, 134.

60. Victoria Houston, *Making It Work: Finding the Time and Energy for Your Career, Marriage, Children, and Self* (New York: Simon and Schuster, 1991); Trudi Ferguson and Joan S. Dunphy, *Answers to the Mommy Track: How Wives and Mothers in Business Reach the Top and Balance Their Lives* (Farr Hills, N.J.: New Horizon Press, 1991).

61. Sally Helgesen, *The Female Advantage: Women's Ways of Leadership* (New York: Doubleday, 1990).

62. Terri Apter, *Working Women Don't Have Wives: Professional Success in the 1990s* (New York: St. Martin's, 1993); Susan Faludi, *Backlash: The Undeclared War Against American Women* (New York: Crown, 1991); Deborah J. Swiss and Judith P. Walker, *Women and the Work/Family*

Dilemma: How Today's Professional Women Are Confronting the Maternal Wall (New York: John Wiley and Sons, 1993), 1.

63. P. Elmer-DeWitt and D. E. Brown, "The Great Experiment," *Time*, Fall 1990 (Special Edition), 72; Cherlyn Skromme Granrose and Eileen E. Kaplan, *Work-Family Role Choices for Women in their 20s and 30s* (Westport, Conn.: Praeger, 1996), 13; Juliet B. Schor, *The Overworked American: The Unexpected Decline of Leisure* (New York: Basic Books, 1991), 2, 22.

64. American Bar Association Commission on Women in the Profession, "Report to the House of Delegates," 1988, 6, http://www.americanbar.org/content/dam/aba/migrated/women/womenstatistics/1988ReportToHouseOfDelegates.authcheckdam.pdf, accessed May 21, 2012.

65. Jennifer A. Kingston, "Women in the Law Say Path Is Limited by 'Mommy Track,' " *New York Times*, August 8, 1988, A1; "Attorneys Explore Part-Time Work Opportunities," *Labor Relations Reporter* 146 (August 22, 1994): 513; Cynthia F. Epstein, Robert Saute, Bonnie Oglensky, and Martha Gever, "Glass Ceilings and Open Doors: Women's Advancement in the Legal Profession," *Fordham Law Review* 64 (1995): 291.

66. Kingston, "Women in the Law Say Path Is Limited," A1.

67. American Bar Association Commission on Women in the Profession, "Report to the House of Delegates," 1988, 1, http://www.americanbar.org/content/dam/aba/migrated/women/womenstatistics/1988ReportToHouseOfDelegates.authcheckdam.pdf, accessed May 21, 2012; Kingston, "Women in the Law Say Path Is Limited," A1.

68. "Why Law Firms Cannot Afford to Maintain the Mommy Track," *Harvard Law Review* 109 (April 1996): 1376–78.

69. Felice N. Schwartz, "Management Women and the New Facts of Life," *Harvard Business Review*, January 1989, 66.

70. Felice N. Schwartz, "The Mommy Track Isn't Anti-Woman," *New York Times*, March 22, 1989, A27.

71. Judy Mann, "The Demeaning 'Mommy Track': Separate and Unequal," *Washington Post*, March 15, 1989, C3.

72. Barbara Ehrenreich and Deirdre English, "Blowing the Whistle on the 'Mommy Track," *Ms.*, July 1989, 56.

73. Deborah Dinner, "The Universal Childcare Debate: Rights Mobilization, Social Policy, and the Dynamics of Feminist Activism, 1966–1974," *Law and History Review* 28 (August 2010): 577–628.

74. "Family and Medical Leave: An Overview," undated, ca. 1988, 2, January 1988, folder 1, box 353, NOW LDEF.

75. Jeanne Saddler, "Small Business Sees Few Threats in Distracted Congress," *Wall Street Journal*, May 31, 1989, B2.

76. "Misguided Parental Leave Bill," *Birmingham* (Ala.) *Post Herald*, November 25, 1987, folder 40, box 52, Records of the Women's Equity Action League, Schlesinger Library, Radcliffe Institute, Harvard University, Cambridge, Mass. (hereafter "WEAL").

77. "Parental Leave: Some Issues Are Better Left to Collective Bargaining," *Cincinnati* (Ohio) *Enquirer*, August 15, 1987, folder 40, box 52, WEAL.

78. "Medical Leave: Mandated Benefit Not Needed," *Columbia* (S.C.) *Record*, November 20, 1987, folder 40, box 52, WEAL.

79. Wider Opportunities for Women Public Policy Associate Janet Koppelman, "The Family and Medical Leave Act of 1896," folder 39, box 52, WEAL.

80. "Testimony of NOW President Eleanor Smeal," February 25, 1987, folder 8, box 23, Papers of Patricia Ireland, Schlesinger Library, Radcliffe Institute, Harvard University, Cambridge, Mass.

81. "NOW Reports on Parental Leave," undated, ca. 1990, folder 8, box 23, Papers of Patricia Ireland, Schlesinger Library, Radcliffe Institute, Harvard University, Cambridge, Mass.

82. Letter to Member of House of Representatives, July 10, 1986, 2, folder 39, box 52, WEAL; Women's Equity Action League, undated, "The Family and Medical Leave Act Is Consistent with a Long Tradition of Labor Standards," ca. 1987, folder 41, box 52, WEAL.

83. Patricia Blau Ruess, WEAL Legislative Director, "Dear Representative," September 30, 1988, folder 1, box 53, WEAL.

84. Berebitsky, *Sex and the Office*, 3.

85. Carrie N. Baker, *The Women's Movement Against Sexual Harassment* (New York: Cambridge University Press, 2008), 27–48; Enid Nemy, "Women Begin to Speak Out Against Sexual Harassment at Work," *New York Times*, August 19, 1975, 38.

86. Alliance Against Sexual Coercion, "Sexual Harassment at the Workplace," 1977, Alliance Against Sexual Coercion Ephemeral Materials, 1976–67, Wilcox Collection of Contemporary Political Movements, Schlesinger Library, Radcliffe Institute, Harvard University, Cambridge, Mass.; Freada Klein to Sisters, August 7, 1976, Alliance Against Sexual Coercion Ephemeral Materials, 1976–77, Wilcox Collection of Contemporary Political Movements, Schlesinger Library, Radcliffe Institute, Harvard University, Cambridge, Mass.; Baker, *Women's Movement Against Sexual Harassment*, 45–46, 49–64; Rochelle Lefkovitz, "Help for the Sexually Harassed: A Grass Roots Model," *Ms.*, November 1977, 49; Catharine A. MacKinnon, *Sexual Harassment of Working Women* (New Haven, Conn.: Yale University Press, 1979), 1; Nemy, "Women Begin to Speak Out Against Sexual Harassment at Work," 38; "Violence Against Women," *Sister Courage*, June 1977, 1, Alliance Against Sexual Coercion Ephemeral Materials, 1976–77, Wilcox Collection of Contemporary Political Movements, Schlesinger Library, Radcliffe Institute, Harvard University, Cambridge, Mass.; Working Women United Institute, "Program Description and Request for Funds," March 1978, folder 5, box 26, Papers of Robin Morgan, 1929–91, Schlesinger Library, Radcliffe Institute, Harvard University, Cambridge, Mass. (hereafter "PRM"); Deirdre Silverman, "Sexual Harassment: Working Women's Dilemma," *Quest* 3 (Winter 1976/1977): 15–16, folder 5, box 26, PRM.

87. Working Women United Institute, "Program Description and Request for Funds," March 1978, folder 5, box 26, PRM.

88. "A Redbook Questionnaire: How Do You Handle Sex on the Job?" *Redbook* 146 (January 1976): 74–75.

89. Samuel Feinberg, "Office Passes: Women Are Drawing the Line," *Chicago Tribune*, April 24, 1977, D3.

90. Myra MacPherson, "Occupational Sexism Found Alive, Rampant on Capitol Hill," *Washington Post*, August 1, 1976, 4; Karen Lindsey, "Sexual Harassment on the Job and How to Stop It," *Ms.*, November 1977, 49; Mary Bralove, "Women Give Gate to Career 'Advances' by Wolves," *Chicago Tribune*, February 4, 1976, B1.

91. "Survey of Women HUD Employees Finds Widespread Sexual Harassment on Job," *Los Angeles Times*, July 27, 1979, A1.

92. *Williams v. Saxbe*, 413 F. Supp. 654 (1976); Jane Albert, "Tyranny of Sex in the Office," *Equal Times*, August 7, 1977, 6, Alliance Against Sexual Coercion Ephemeral Materials, 1976–77, Wilcox

Collection of Contemporary Political Movements, Schlesinger Library, Radcliffe Institute, Harvard University, Cambridge, Mass.; *Corne v. Bausch and Lomb*, 562 F.2d 55 (1975), *Barnes v. Costle*, 561 F.2d 983 (1977), *Miller v. Bank of America*, 600 F.2d 211 (1979), and *Tomkins v. Public Service Electric and Gas*, 568 F.2d 1044 (1977).

93. Elaine Markoutsas, "A Strategy for Self-Protection," *Chicago Tribune*, January 22, 1978, D4.

94. Cynthia Lee, "Office Romeos Are Feeling the Pinch—Legally," *Detroit News*, November 11, 1979, folder 842, box 78, WER.

95. Elizabeth Brenner, "Sexual Harassment: Hard to Define, Harder to Fight," *Chicago Tribune*, May 30, 1979, sec. 3, p. 1.

96. Lin Farley, *Sexual Shakedown: The Sexual Harassment of Women on the Job* (New York: McGraw-Hill, 1978); Enid Nemy, "Sexual Abuse on the Job," *Chicago Tribune*, August 28, 1975, B4; Anne LaRiviere, "Sexual Harassment of Women," *Los Angeles Times*, March 13, 1979, C1. Valerie Miner, "Sex: They Gave at the Office," *Los Angeles Times*, November 19, 1978, M25.

97. Markoutsas, "Sexual Harassment," sec. 5, p. 1.

98. Constance Rosenblum, "When Glances Turn To Glares . . . ," *Chicago Tribune*, February 19, 1978, sec. 5, p. 6.

99. Silverman, "Sexual Harassment: Working Women's Dilemma," 21, folder 5, box 26, PRM.

100. Feinberg, "Office Passes," D3.

101. Baker, *Women's Movement Against Sexual Harassment*, 6.

102. "Virtuous Lasses Avoid Passes, Says Schlafly," *Chicago Sun-Times*, April 22, 1981, 1.

103. According to Amy Erdman Farrell, *Ms.* was read by a wide audience. See Farrell, *Yours in Sisterhood: Ms. Magazine and the Promise of Popular Feminism* (Chapel Hill: University of North Carolina Press, 1998), esp. 44–45.

104. Karen Lindsey, "Sexual Harassment on the Job and How to Stop It," *Ms.*, November 1977, 49.

105. Ibid., 47–50.

106. Correspondent from Redding, Calif., to *Ms.*, undated, folder 148, box 5, Ms. Letters, 1972-1980, Schlesinger Library, Radcliffe Institute, Harvard University (hereafter "MLC").

107. Correspondent from King of Prussia, Pa., to *Ms.*, October 28, 1977, folder 148, box 5, MLC.

108. Correspondent from San Carlos, Calif., to *Ms.*, undated, folder 148, box 5, MLC.

109. Correspondent from Santa Monica, Calif., to *Ms.*, November 20, 1977, folder 148, box 5, MLC.

110. Correspondent to *Ms.*, November 17, 1977, folder 148, box 5, MLC.

111. Correspondent from Greenbelt, Md., to *Ms.*, October 22, 1977, folder 148, box 5, MLC.

112. Correspondent from Ft. Wayne, Ind., to *Ms.*, October 15, 1977, folder 148, box 5, MLC.

113. Correspondent from Chicago, Ill., to *Ms.*, undated, folder 148, box 5, MLC.

114. Correspondent from Hamilton, Ontario, Canada, to *Ms.*, November 26, 1977, folder 148, box 5, MLC.

115. "'New Women' Honored in NY," *Washington Post*, January 23, 1972, F14.

116. City of New York Human Resources Administration Policy Statement on Sexual Harassment, 1981, folder 15, box 27, Papers of Florynce Kennedy, 1915–2004; EEOC, "EEOC Issues Interim Guidelines on Sexual Harassment in the Office," March 11, 1980, folder 34, box 96, NOW; Robert Pear, "Sexual Harassment at Work Outlawed," *New York Times*, April 12, 1980, 1; Owen Ullmann, "Employers Held Responsible in Sex Harassment," *Washington Post*, March 12, 1980, C4; "The Legal Picture," *On the Job: Newsletter of the Working Women's Institute*, Summer 1982, 2, folder 15, box 27, Papers of Florynce Kennedy, 1915–2004, Schlesinger library, Radcliffe Institute.

117. Eleanor Holmes Norton, Testimony on Behalf of Forty-Eight Women's Organizations Before the Senate Committee on Labor and Human Resources Hearings on Sexual Harassment, April 21, 1981, folder 428, box 40, WER.

118. "The Legal Picture"; Baker, *Women's Movement Against Sexual Harassment*.

119. Mayeri, *Reasoning from Race*, 144–85.

120. For a detailed history of sexual harassment case law, see MacKinnon, *Sex Equality*, esp. 908–1056.

121. *Testimony of Anita F. Hill, Hearings Before the Committee on the Judiciary, United States Senate, October 11, 1991, One Hundred Second Congress, First Session, on the Nomination of Clarence Thomas to Be Associate Justice of the Supreme Court of the United States* (Washington, D.C.: U.S. Government Printing Office, 1991), 37.

122. *Testimony of Clarence Thomas, Hearings Before the Committee on the Judiciary, United States Senate, October 13, 1991, One Hundred Second Congress, First Session, on the Nomination of Clarence Thomas to Be Associate Justice of the Supreme Court of the United States* (Washington, D.C.: U.S. Government Printing Office, 1991), 7.

123. "African American Women in Defense of Ourselves," *New York Times*, November 17, 1991, 53; Rebecca Walker, "Becoming the Third Wave," *Ms.*, January 1992, 39.

124. Deborah Sontag, "Anita Hill and Revitalizing Feminism," *New York Times*, April 26, 1992, 31.

125. Maureen Dowd, "The Thomas Nomination: The Senate and Sexism; Panels Handling of Harassment Allegation Renews Questions About an All-Male Club," *New York Times*, October 8, 1992, 1.

126. "African American Women in Defense of Ourselves," 53; Walker, "Becoming the Third Wave," 39.

127. Michael Isikoff, Charles E. Shepard, and Sharon LaFraniere, "Clinton Hires Lawyer as Sexual Harassment Suit Is Threatened," *Washington Post*, May 4, 1994, A1; Maureen Dowd, "The Price of His Pleasure," *New York Times*, February 8, 1991, WK15; Deborah Sontag, "The Changing Face of Harassment: Volatile Issue Is Still a Murky One, New York City Case Shows," *New York Times*, November 2, 1992, B3.

128. Jill Abramson, "Image of Anita Hill Brighter in Hindsight, Galvanizes Campaigns," *Wall Street Journal*, October 5, 1992, 1.

129. Berebitsky, *Sex and the Office*, 5; Sumi K. Cho, "Converging Stereotypes in Racialized Sexual Harassment: Where Model Minority Meets Suzie Wong," *Journal of Gender, Race, and Justice*, vol. 1 (1997): 177-212; Bernadette Marie Calafell, "'Did It Happen Because of Your Race or Sex?': University Sexual Harassment Policies and the Move Against Intersectionality," *Frontiers: A Journal of Women Studies* 35, no. 3 (2014): 75–95.

130. Yoshino, *Covering*.

131. Joan C. Williams, "The Opt-Out Revolution Revisited," *American Prospect* 18 (March 2007): A12–A15.

132. Swiss and Walker, *Women and the Work/Family Dilemma*, 5; Joan Williams, *Unbending Gender: Why Work and Family Conflict and What to Do About It* (Oxford, U.K. and New York: Oxford University Press, 2001), 4–5. Between 1986 and 1995, courts heard ninety-seven family responsibilities discrimination cases; and between 1996 and 2005, they heard 481 such cases. Mary C. Still, "Litigating the Maternal Wall: U.S. Lawsuits Charging Discrimination Against Workers with Family Responsibilities," 7, July 2006, http://www.law.yale.edu/documents/pdf/FRD_report_FINAL1.pdf, accessed May 15, 2012; C. W. VonBergen, William T. Mawer, and

Robert Howard, "Family Responsibilities Discrimination: The EEOC Guidance," *Employee Relations Law Journal* 34 (Summer 2008): 14–34.

133. Michael Selmi and Naomi R. Cahn, "Women in the Workplace: Which Women, Which Agenda?" *Duke Journal of Gender Law and Policy* 13 (2006): 7–8.

134. Martha Chamallas, "Mothers and Disparate Treatment: The Ghost of Martin Marietta," *Villanova Law Review* 44 (1999): 337.

135. Hester Eisenstein, *Feminism Seduced: How Global Elites Use Women's Labor and Ideas to Exploit the World* (Boulder, Colo.: Paradigm, 2009); Fraser, "Capitalism and the Cunning of History"; Vicki Schultz, "The Sanitized Workplace," *Yale Law Journal* 112, no. 8 (2003): 2061–2193.

136. Still, "Litigating the Maternal Wall."

137. West, "From Choice to Reproductive Justice," 19–52.

Conclusion

1. Leslie McCall, "Increasing Class Disparities Among Women and the Politics of Gender Equity," in *The Sex of Class: Women Transforming American Labor*, ed. Dorothy Sue Cobble (Ithaca, N.Y.: Cornell University Press, 2007), 31; MacLean, *Freedom Is Not Enough*, 265–99; Tiemeyer, *Plane Queer*.

2. Wal-Mart Corporation changed its name to Walmart Corporation in 2009. Some publications and legal documents have continued to refer to the corporation as "Wal-Mart." Monee Fields-White, "Meet Betty Dukes, the Black Woman Who's Taking On Walmart," *New America Media*, December 13, 2010, http://newamericamedia.org/2010/12/meet-betty-dukes-the-black-woman-whos-taking-on-walmart.php; Dave Jamieson, "Betty Dukes, Renowned *Dukes v. Walmart* Plaintiff, Takes Her Fight Back to Capitol Hill," *Huffington Post*, June 20, 2012, http://www.huffingtonpost.com/2012/06/20/betty-dukes-walmart-supreme-court_n_1613305.html.

3. On the sex discrimination lawsuit, and on Walmart's business practices more generally, see "A Million Women vs. Wal-Mart," *New York Times*, August 30, 2010, A20; Anthony Bianco, *The Bully of Bentonville: How the High Cost of Wal-Mart's Everyday Low Prices Is Hurting America* (New York: Doubleday, 2006); Stanley D. Brunn, *Wal-Mart World: The World's Biggest Corporation in the Global Economy* (New York: Routledge, 2006); Liza Featherstone, *Selling Women Short: The Landmark Battle for Workers' Rights at Wal-Mart* (New York: Basic Books, 2004); Charles Fishman, *The Wal-Mart Effect: How the World's Most Powerful Company Really Works—and How It's Transforming the American Economy* (New York: Penguin, 2006); Lichtenstein, *The Retail Revolution*; Lichtenstein, ed., *Wal-Mart: The Face of Twenty-First-Century Capitalism* (New York: New Press, 2006); Bethany Moreton, *To Serve God and Wal-Mart: The Making of Christian Free Enterprise* (Cambridge, Mass.: Harvard University Press, 2009); Bill Quinn, *How Wal-Mart Is Destroying America and What You Can Do About It* (Berkeley, Ca.: Ten Speed Press, 1998); "Declaration of Betty Dukes in Support of Plaintiffs' Motion for Class Certification," *Dukes v. Wal-Mart Stores*, Case No. C-01-2252 MJJ; "Declaration of Gretchen Adams in Support of Plaintiffs' Motion for Class Certification," *Dukes v. Wal-Mart Stores*, Case No. C-01-2252 MJJ, http://www.walmartclass.com/public_declarations.html, accessed June 20, 2010. More depositions are available on the plaintiffs' website, http://www.walmartclass.com/public_declarations.html, accessed June 20, 2010.

4. *Dukes v. Wal-Mart*, 10 U.S. 227 (2011); Adam Liptak, "Supreme Court Tightens Rules in Class Actions," *New York Times*, June 20, 2011, A1; Andrew Martin, "Female Wal-Mart Employees File New Bias Case," *New York Times*, October 27, 2011, B3; Casey Sullivan and Dan Levine, "U.S.

Judge Denies Class Certification Sought by Women Suing Wal-Mart," *Reuters*, August 3, 2013, http://www.reuters.com/article/2013/08/03/us-walmart-women-idUSBRE97203320130803.

5. *Long Island Care at Home v. Evelyn Coke*, 127 U.S. 2339 (2007). Barbara Ehrenreich, *Nickel and Dimed: On (Not) Getting By in America* (New York: Metropolitan Books, 2004); Arlie Russell Hochschild and Barbara Ehrenreich, eds., *Global Woman: Nannies, Maids, and Sex Workers in the New Economy* (New York: Metropolitan Books, 2003); Steven Greenhouse, *The Big Squeeze*; Hatton, *The Temp Economy*; Pierrette Hondagneu-Sotelo, *Domestica: Immigrant Workers Cleaning and Caring in the Shadows of Affluence* (Berkeley: University of California Press, 2001); Beth Shulman, *The Betrayal of Work: How Low-Wage Jobs Fail 30 Million Americans and Their Families* (New York: New Press, 2003); Michael Selmi, "Sex Discrimination in the Nineties, Seventies Style: Case Studies in the Preservation of Male Workplace Norms," *Employment Rights and Employment Policy Journal* 9 (2005): 46; and Selmi, "The Price of Discrimination," *Texas Law Review* 81 (April 2003): 1249–336. Women in female-dominated trade unions advocate a robust and intersectional version of workplace justice. See Boris and Klein, *Caring for America*; Cobble, *Sex of Class*, 5; Boris, "Where's the Care?" 43–44.

6. Debora L. Spar, *Wonder Women: Sex, Power, and the Quest for Perfection* (New York: Sarah Crichton Books, Farrar, Straus and Giroux, 2013); Spar interview, *Fresh Air with Terry Gross*, September 16, 2013, http://www.npr.org/2013/09/16/223041014/barnard-president-todays -wonder-women-must-reframe-feminism.

7. Katrina Alcorn, *Maxed Out: American Moms on the Brink* (Berkeley, Ca.: Seal, 2013); Brigid Schulte, *Overwhelmed: How to Work, Love and Play When No One Has the Time* (New York: Picador, 2015); Sandberg, *Lean In*; Barbara Annis and Keith Merron, *Gender Intelligence: Breakthrough Strategies for Increasing Diversity and Improving Your Bottom Line* (New York: HarperCollins, 2014); Katty Kay and Claire Shipman, *The Confidence Code: The Science and Art of Self-Assurance: What Women Should Know* (New York: HarperCollins, 2014); Lois P. Frankel, *Nice Girls Don't Get the Corner Office: Unconscious Mistakes Women Make that Sabotage Their Careers* (New York: Business Plus, 2014).

8. Anne-Marie Slaughter notes this pattern of thought among professional women's advocates in "Why Women Still Can't Have it All," *Atlantic* (July 2012), 84–102.

9. Ann Crittenden, *The Price of Motherhood: Why the Most Important Job in the World Is Still the Least Valued* (New York: Metropolitan Books, 2001); Arlie Hochschild, *The Time Bind: When Work Becomes Home and Home Becomes Work* (New York: Metropolitan Books, 1997); Joan Williams, *Unbending Gender: Why Family and Work Conflict and What to Do About It* (Oxford: Oxford University Press, 2000); Claire Cain Miller, "The 24/7 Work Culture's Toll on Families and Gender Equality," *New York Times*, May 28, 2015, BU4.

10. Legal scholar Kenji Yoshino has argued that workers who do not face the white, straight, able-bodied male stereotype are forced to downplay their disfavored traits. Kenji Yoshino, *Covering: The Hidden Assault on Our Civil Rights* (New York: Random House, 2007). Deborah Rhode reveals the persistence of appearance-related discrimination and the particular challenges appearance, dress, and self-presentation pose to working women. Rhode, *The Beauty Bias: The Injustice of Appearance of Life and Law* (Oxford: Oxford University Press, 2010).

11. Douglas M. Branson, *No Seat at the Table: How Corporate Governance and Law Keep Women Out of the Boardroom* (New York: New York University Press, 2007); Lauren A. Rivera, "Guess Who Doesn't Fit In at Work," *New York Times*, May 30, 2015, SR5.

12. These legal advances include the Lilly Ledbetter Fair Pay Act of 2009 (Pub. L. 111–12, 181), which has extended women's ability to win back pay. See Boris, "Ledbetter's Continuum." While

the Employment Non-Discrimination Act has not yet passed, workplace rights for gay, lesbian and transgender people have been strengthened through other legal channels. For example, in July 2014, President Barack Obama signed an executive order that outlawed discrimination against LGBT workers employed by federal agencies and federal contractors. Jennifer Bendery, "Obama Signs Executive Order on LGBT Job Discrimination," Huffington Post, July 21, 2014, http://www.huffingtonpost.com/2014/07/21/obama-gay-rights_n_5605482.html, accessed August 17, 2015.

13. *Brown v. Board of Education*, the Pregnancy Discrimination Act, the Voting Rights Act, and *Roe v. Wade* are just a few.

14. Leslie McCall, "Increasing Class Disparities Among Women and the Politics of Gender Equity," in Cobble, *Sex of Class*, 15–33; Boris, "Ledbetter's Continuum"; Boris and Klein, *Caring for America*; Steven Greenhouse, "Fast Food Workers Intensify Fight for $15 an Hour," *New York Times*, July 27, 2014, B1; Jodi Kantor, "Working Anything but 9 to 5," *New York Times*, August 13, 2014, http://www.nytimes.com/interactive/2014/08/13/us/starbucks-workers-scheduling-hours.html, accessed August 13, 2014; Jodi Kantor, "Starbucks to Revise Policies to End Irregular Schedules for Its 130,000 Baristas," *New York Times*, August 14, 2014, A11; Tiemeyer, *Plane Queer*, esp. 194–218.

Index

Acknowledgments

I am delighted to be able to thank the people and institutions whose generosity made this book possible. But doing justice to this task requires reaching considerably back in time, for my earliest influences started me on my career path when I was too young to realize it. From my first memories, my maternal grandparents, Polly Jontz Lennon and Leland Jontz, impressed on me the value of knowing "who your people are." They viewed our shared Hoosier heritage as a precious commodity, and their stories of growing up in Silver Lake, Versailles, and Indianapolis made early twentieth-century Indiana seem at once exotic and deeply familiar. Our many trips to the Indianapolis Children's Museum and the living history museum Conner Prairie instilled in me a lasting desire to travel through time and place to encounter and seek to understand different people.

Since then, many excellent teachers and mentors have supported and challenged me. As a teacher at Lyons Township High School in La Grange, Illinois, the exacting and formidable Ken Price set the highest standards, but he also gave us the tools by which to meet them. To my great fortune, Peter Hayes directed the undergraduate honors seminar in history during my senior year at Northwestern University. I often think of his lessons in historical research and writing, and I hope this book reflects his influence. Simply put, this book would not exist without Nancy MacLean. A peerless undergraduate thesis advisor, she introduced me to many of the people and ideas in this book. I thank her for her encouragement and continued support over the years.

At the University of Chicago, thanks to Mary Ann Case, George Chauncey, Jane Dailey, Adam Green, Jim Grossman, Ramon Gutierrez, Thomas Holt, Rachel Jean-Baptiste, Deborah Nelson, Moishe Postone, and Kristin Schilt. This book has benefitted from Christine Stansell's attention to detail and argument. James Sparrow has been a tireless advocate and guide to the academic world, and his meticulous feedback strengthened this project considerably. Amy Dru Stanley has expertly shepherded my intellectual growth and modeled rigorous and resonant scholarship. I thank her for her generous support, exacting standards, and steadfast commitment to my development. Thanks also to Thomas Jessen Adams, C. J. Alvarez, Jacob Betz, Chris Dingwall, Susannah Engstrom, Darryl Heller, Patrick Kelly, Sam Lebovic, Alison Lefkovitz, Sarah Levine-Gronningsater, Jonathan Levy, Monica Mercado, Sarah Miller-Davenport, Celeste Moore, Kathryn Schumaker, Dwaipayan Sen, Peter Simons, Susan Gaunt Stearns, Anthony Todd, Christopher Todd, and Sarah Jones Weicksel, as well as the university's Social History, Political History, Human Rights, and Center for Gender Studies workshops.

Many other people and institutions have supported this book as it moved toward completion. Thanks especially to Jayanth Krishnan, Ajay Mehrotra, Ethan Michelson, Lauren Robel, Deborah Widiss, and Susan Williams for helping to make my year at Indiana University Maurer School of Law rewarding and productive. Ajay has remained a trusted ally, and I thank him for his counsel and support along the way. At the University of Texas at Dallas, I benefitted from the fellowship of wonderful colleagues in the School of Arts and Humanities: Matt Brown, Mike Farmer, Shari Goldberg, Kim Knight, Jessica Murphy, Cihan Muslu, Peter Park, Steve Rabe, Monica Rankin, Natalie Ring, Mark Rosen, Eric Schlereth, Sabrina Starnaman, Charissa Terranova, Shilyh Warren, Daniel Wickburg, Michael Wilson, and others. At UT-Dallas, I received generous financial support arranged by Dean Dennis Kratz and Provost Hobson Wildenthal.

I am delighted to have such warm and brilliant colleagues in my new intellectual home in the Department of History at the University of North Carolina at Chapel Hill. Thanks to Karen Auerbach, Fitz Brundage, Chad Bryant, Kathryn Burns, Emily Burrill, Flora Cassen, Kathleen DuVal, William Ferris, Joe Glatthaar, Karen Hagemann, Tobias Hof, Jerma Jackson, Konrad Jarausch, Lauren Jarvis, John Kasson, Michelle King, Lisa Lindsay, Louise McReynolds, Michael Morgan, Susan Dabney Pennybacker, Don Raleigh, Sarah Shields, William Sturkey, John Wood Sweet, Zaragosa Vargas, Benjamin Waterhouse, Brett Whalen, and Molly Worthen for making the Triangle such a friendly and stimulating place. For their generosity and expertise, I also want thank the archivists at the libraries listed in these pages—especially Ellen Shea, who expertly oversees the Schlesinger Library's many treasures.

Laura Mills of Roosevelt University, Kathy Pilat, and Mike Ensdorf assisted with the book's images. Thanks also to the activists whose stories are told here—especially Mary Jean Collins, Anne Ladky, Mary-Ann Lupa, and the Veteran Feminists of America—for their commitment to intergenerational feminist conversation.

Portions of this book have appeared elsewhere in earlier form. A section of Chapter 3 was published in "Out of the Revolution, into the Mainstream: Employment Activism in the NOW Sears Campaign and the Growing Pains of Liberal Feminism," *Journal of American History* 97 (September 2010), 399–423. A section of Chapter 6 was published in "'Our Militancy Is in Our Openness': Gay Employment Rights Activism in California and the Question of Sexual Orientation in Sex Equality Law," *Law and History Review* 31 (May 2013): 423–69. I thank the journals for allowing me to include that material here.

Friends, colleagues, and working groups have provided essential feedback on the manuscript, in whole and in part. I thank the Newberry Library Labor History Seminar, the Re-Reading the Feminist Sixties Conference at the University of California–Santa Barbara, the Dallas Area Social History Workshop, the Research Triangle Working Group on Feminism and History, and Gillian Frank and the Zwickler Workshop on the History of Sexuality. Conference panels and conversations with Heather Berg, Anne Blaschke, Margot Canaday, Tamar Carroll, Deborah Dinner, Allison Elias, Alice Kessler-Harris, Serena Mayeri, Betsy More, Phil Tiemeyer, and Marcia Walker helped me to hone my thoughts. Betty Luther Hillman, Emily Remus, and Leandra Zarnow responded thoughtfully with feedback on chapter drafts, and on short notice. Emily Heist Moss provided a careful eleventh-hour review. Dorothy Sue Cobble and Barbara Welke gave detailed and generous comments on the entire manuscript, and I thank them for the care they took to help me make this book much stronger. I would need to write a separate book, or at least a few long chapters, in order to convey just how much Eileen Boris has meant to this project and to my development. I thank her for her mentorship and camaraderie.

Other friends near and far have hosted me for research trips, lifted my spirits, and talked with me about the ideas in these pages. Thanks to Anne Blaschke, Susannah Chen, Jaime Huling Delaye, Deborah Dinner, Kimberly Gelbwasser, Kelly Guzman, Kate Kokontis, and Betsy More. I can scarcely remember a time when I was not fortified by Anthony Cotton's invaluable friendship—but why would I want to? Betty Luther Hillman has been a dear friend and essential fellow traveler since the beginning, and I harbor no illusions that I would be where I am without her. It's difficult to put into words just how much Emily Remus has meant to me as a close confidante and intellectual ally, and I'm delighted that we will remain in this academic world together.

There could be no better home for this book than the University of Pennsylvania Press. Robert Lockhart has been a steadfast advocate for this project, and it has greatly benefitted from his wise counsel and editorial skill. Margot Canaday is an incredible editor and a brilliant historian. I admire her ability to blend kind support with challenging feedback, and I hope these pages convey how much her mentorship and her own ideas have influenced my development. Thank you, Bob and Margot, for the guidance and support that allowed me to make this a much better book. Thanks also to Noreen O'Connor-Abel and Penn Press' production team for guiding me through the home stretch.

My deepest debts are to the members of my family. My uncle, Jim Jontz, did not live to see this book in print, but many of the ideas and people described on these pages would look familiar to him. I hope it captures even a small piece of his populist vision. My parents, Mary Lee Jontz Turk and Charles Turk, have never wavered in their belief that I would accomplish what I set out to do, from finding a foothold in academia to shepherding this book into print. I thank them for all their support, advice, and good humor over the years. But they would agree that the most precious gifts they have ever given to me are my sisters, Beth Turk and Emily Turk. They are remarkable women and my best friends.

We historians are supposed to reject notions of fate and inevitability as explanations for past events. But the stars aligned when I met Erik Gellman after so many years on close but not-yet-intersecting paths. Since then, he has lived this project with me, helping me to think through its broadest arguments and finest points alike. Erik's commitment to understanding working people on their own terms makes me proud, and fortunate, to know him. And his belief that history can help us see the outlines of a better world has kept me mindful of why I wanted to tell this story. For all this, and for much more, this book is for him.